The Enforcement of Regulatory Offences

AUSTRALIA
Law Book Company
Sydney

CANADA
Carswell
Toronto • Ontario

NEW ZEALAND
Brooker's
Auckland

SINGAPORE and MALAYSIA
Thomson Information (S.E. Asia)
Singapore

The Enforcement of Regulatory Offences

by

Claire Andrews
Barrister

LONDON
SWEET & MAXWELL
1998

Published in 1998 by
Sweet & Maxwell Limited of
100 Avenue Road, Swiss Cottage,
London NW3 3PF
(http://www.smlawpub.co.uk)

Typeset by Dataword Services Limited of Chilcompton
Printed by Butler & Tanner, Frome and London

*No natural forests were destroyed to make this product:
only farmed timber was used and replanted*

ISBN 0421 527 803

A catalogue record for this book is
available from the British Library

Preface

While the book was in production many changes in domestic legislation have been made, government has changed, and with it, policies which affect the activities of traders and consumers. The continued European programme of harmonisation of consumer policy has resulted in very many new legislative provisions. But against the shifting political backdrop, there are very many issues affecting the enforcement of offences under legislation which arise again and again. These have traditionally been considered in connection with a specialist topic, such as "weights and measures" or "food safety" or "consumer protection" but in fact they are relevant to much regulatory legislation. The cachet "regulatory offence" which has gained increasing currency both in the courts and amongst practitioners, is itself a recognition of the commonality of legislation which performs a regulatory function, and recognises too that the concept of regulation is not confined to the City and to those performing functions in relation to privatised utilities.

This book is intended to play a part in the evolution of this process of recognition as well as to assist local authorities and practitioners and others interested in this field to understand the enforcement and interpretation of legislation on issues central to the process of regulation. It is intended to give practical assistance as well as to describe the unifying characteristics of the material. It is not about any substantive offences, although some are touched upon. But in drawing together the common threads from so many different areas in order to describe this new topic, it has, of course been necessary to be selective. In relation to any area, some considerations have been judged to be within the area of interest for a regulatory practitioner, and some have been omitted. No doubt readers with particular interests will be able to say that the parameters have been too widely or narrowly drawn, that there has been too little detail or too much. Broadly, however, I entertain the hope that this work will cause the reader to reflect that regulation is not just another aspect of our criminal law, but is intimately tied up with both the challenge to and the proper exercise of executive power.

Claire Andrews
September 1998

Acknowledgements

I would like to record my thanks to the members of Gough Square Chambers who have contributed both wittingly and unwittingly to the content of this book, and to my clerks who have shown great patience and restraint during the period when I was determined to write it. I have been grateful for the patience and assistance of those at Sweet & Maxwell who have had the responsibility for ensuring that these pages reach print. Particularly, my thanks are to Fred Philpott, who has not only given me help and encouragement over nearly 20 years in practice at the Bar, but who also can justify be said to be a pioneer in the field of the enforcement of regulatory offences.

Contents

Chapter 1

Chapter 2

Chapter 3

Chapter 4

Chapter 5

Chapter 6

Chapter 7

Chapter 8

Chapter 9

Chapter 10

Chapter 11

Chapter 12

Chapter 13

Table of Cases

Table of Statutes

Table of Statutory Instruments

Rules of the Supreme Court

Table of European Cases
(Alphabetical)

Table of European Cases
(Numerical)

Table of European Legislation

CHAPTER 1

Regulatory Offences: Meaning and Scope

INTRODUCTION

1.1 The network of regulation. Regulatory matters affect all our lives. They govern the markings on and the quality of the food we buy, the safety of our children's toys, our protection from injury in our place of work, the steps taken to prevent fire in the hotels we stay in, the quality of our drinking water and the upkeep of aspects of our environment. They may regulate what we are told about transactions we might wish to enter with credit brokers and lenders, travel agents, estate agents or some private clinics. These are but a few of the many aspects of a vast net of legislation, primary and secondary, which control the operation of industry and commerce for the benefit of the public.

1.2 Regulation and government. Over the last 25 years, there has been an increasing control of the conduct of business by regulation. This has been not only a national trend, but has been strongly influenced both directly and indirectly by membership of the European Union. Only in the last few of those years has there been a political will to try to limit the degree of regulation to which business has become subject. Under the Conservative administration until 1997, the advent of the Deregulation Initiative was followed by the Deregulation and Contracting Out Act 1994 and its subordinate legislation. The concern about over-burdening business with detailed requirements for compliance has also continued to play its part in the new Labour administration. Although clearly committed to promoting consumer rights and protections, the "Enforcement Concordat" signed on behalf of central and local government in early March 1998, has continued the theoretical work started by the Conservatives to turn enforcers into advisers and consultants, with enforcement by prosecution as a remedy of the last resort. Similarly, work continues to be undertaken to reduce the burdens of compliance by identifying and repealing unnecessary legislation. This was a substantial commitment of the former administration, and a volume of legislation was reviewed and repealed or replaced pursuant to the Deregulation and Contracting Out Act 1994. The category of regulatory offences is not closed nonetheless, and despite the deregulation initiative, in each year more regulatory offences are created or existing offences extended, often led by European directives and given effect by subordinate legislation. (In many of these cases, the offence may be laid down by the parent Act rather than by the regulation, but the regulation specifies the required standard of conduct, noncompliance with which may constitute an offence under the parent legislation.) A tiny proportion of new regulatory measures in 1997, for example, included the Beef Bones Regulations 1997, the Wheeled Child Conveyances (Safety) Regulations 1997, the Imported Food Regulations 1997, the Food Protection (Emergency Prohibitions) (Oil and Chemical Pollution of Fish) Order 1997, Foods Intended for Use in Energy Restricted Diets for Weight Reduction Regulations 1997, the Fireworks (Safety) Regulations 1997, the Trading Schemes (Exclusion) Regulations 1997 (also amended in the same year), the Fish Health Regulations 1997, the Energy Efficiency (Refrigerators and Freezers) Regulations 1997, the Novel Foods and Novel Food Ingredients Regulations 1997 and the Timeshare Regulations 1997. Regulation is here to stay and with it for the foreseeable future, regulatory offences.

1.3   Origin of regulation.   Although the amount and significance of regulation may have increased in our national efforts to bring our standards into line with those of the European Community, regulatory offences have their roots in more ancient legislative traditions. Uniformity of weights and measures for wine, ale, corn and cloth (and russets and haberjects) was prescribed by Magna Carta. Penalties for using unjust weights and balances (excluding consideration of the penalty of excommunication) were introduced in 1353: forfeiture of the value of goods bought or sold by unjust balances, provision for payment of four times its value and imprisonment for a year at the King's pleasure were early sanctions for non-compliance. Regulation of measures and markings for cheese, fish, honey, coal, wood, salt, etc., followed between the fifteenth and eighteenth centuries. In the area of food safety, the adulteration of various foods was prohibited on a piecemeal basis, then brought under one umbrella by the Adulteration of Food and Drink Act 1860. This Act gave rise to a prohibition on adulteration of food and made it an offence to sell food which was injurious or contained injurious ingredients. The Adulteration of Food and Drugs Act 1872 introduced a scheme similar to that in operation today, with the requirement for a local authority to appoint a public analyst and enforcement by weights and measures inspectors and "inspectors of nuisances" (Environmental Health Officers). Comparable steps were taken in relation to the protection of various classes of workers and in other areas, too. The notion that the public needed to be protected from harm by businesses of the sort from which an individual is not equipped to protect himself had taken shape before the commencement of the twentieth century and has developed into practical application throughout it.

1.4   What are "regulatory offences?".   Regulatory law covers those areas which are intended to regulate business activities for the direct benefit of the public, and regulatory offences are those offences which form part of the overall structure by which such regulation is achieved. In the main, these offences are not truly criminal. Andrew Ashworth ("Principles of Criminal Law" (2nd ed., 1995)) comments:

> "the only feature which distinguishes some . . . minor offences from civil wrongs, like breach of contract or liability in tort, is the decision by Parliament that they shall be criminal offences, attended by criminal procedures and triable in criminal courts".

Some are offences "for which any element of stigma is diluted almost to vanishing point", but not all regulatory offences are free of stigma and some (such as clocking cars) carry with them in the public perception a stigma of dishonesty which can be reflected in the sentencing even if the conviction is under section 1 of the Trade Descriptions Act 1968 rather than an offence under the Theft Act of obtaining by deception or other "truly criminal" offence. See paragraphs 6.21 to 6.29 for further discussion of criminal and quasi-criminal offences.

1.5 Consumer law. Many of the statutes referred to in this book are often embraced under the general heading of "Consumer Law". But regulatory law is not confined to consumer law. For example, the law governing environmental protection may be regarded as regulatory, but although benefiting the populace as a whole, is not consumer dependent. The same can be said of food safety which is by tradition not treated as a category of "consumer law" although its origins are more closely linked with consumer-referable topics, such as weights and measures. The essence of regulation is that it is intended to create a scheme by which businesses maintain standards for the benefit of the public. Minor offences under, say, Schedule 7 of the Electricity Act 1989 preventing interference with the meter or the cabling, etc., are not regulatory, because those offences protect the supplier of electricity rather than the public (although undoubtedly, the public is protected indirectly by the observance of law-abiding behaviour in respect of a universally utilised commodity).

1.6 Characteristics. The categories of regulatory offences are not closed, and regulatory offences may share some characteristics with other offences, such as Road Traffic offences and other offences which govern conduct but not business (such as the Dangerous Dogs Act 1991), which are not regulatory. Regulatory offences will enjoy the majority if not all of the following characteristics:

(i) they are exclusively statutory;

(ii) they govern by deterrence or mandatory requirement the conduct of those involved in commercial operations;

(iii) they are not genuinely criminal, but are "quasi-crime" (see paragraphs 6.21 to 6.29 below for a further discussion of this concept);

(iv) they cover a discreet area of activity, such as the Consumer Credit Act 1974, or cast a particular perspective over a wide range of dealings (such as the Trade Descriptions Act 1968 or the Fair Trading Act 1973);

(v) they are investigated and prosecuted primarily by specialists, whether these be agencies (such as the Environment Agency), employees of the Bank of England, or local government officers, and even though the Secretary of State may hold direct powers of investigation and intervention.

1.7 Criminal procedures apply. The consequence of the treatment of these regulatory offences in a criminal context rather than as contraventions to be monitored or punished in some administrative or other fashion (such as by an inspectorate or tribunal) is that the panoply of procedures and rules of evidence appropriate to "true" crimes also apply to regulatory matters. Although a significant body of opinion would argue for deregulation of regulatory offences in favour of administrative tribunals which can bring to bear upon alleged offenders a more flexible or discretionary approach, there are no published plans for so radical a change across the board. The new Food Standards Agency reflects a shift of emphasis towards licensing as a means of control and revenue raising, but enforcement by prosecution has not been displaced. Deregulation following the Deregulation and Contracting Out Act 1994 has brought some changes, however. Indeed, the Department of Trade and Industry did seek evidence on the appeal system pursuant to section 6 of the Deregulation and Contracting Out Act 1994 (which envisages challenge to the approach to enforcement: see paragraphs 1.11 below) although it seems likely now that the provisions of that Act will not be relied upon and may be repealed. Instead, under the Enforcement Concordat (for which see paragraphs 1.12 and 2.9 to 2.10), enforcement by prosecution is to be the remedy of last resort.

1.8   Magistrates' courts.   It falls mainly to the magistrates' courts rather than the Crown Court to deal with most prosecutions for regulatory offences and to interpret technical legislation, the meaning of which is not always perspicuous against a background of likely inexpertise in the field in question, but the criminal courts bring to the questions an understanding of the criminal process of which the legislation is part. Many of the decided cases on regulatory issues have been the result of the need to interpret the Trade Descriptions Act 1968 and to address the problem that so-called quasi-criminal offences present to the criminal justice system.

1.9   Scope of this book.   This book is concerned with addressing the issues that arise on the prosecution and defence of such offences rather than the specific offences themselves. This work is not concerned with those matters which arise by means of a self-regulatory scheme, although self regulation is also a means of ensuring compliance by professionals and others with objectively applied standards for the benefit of the wider public. This is intended to be a book which explains the ideas which can link the legal topics falling under the regulatory umbrella. There is much discussion of the offences provided for in the Trade Descriptions Act 1968 and the Food Safety Act 1990 although many other examples are given. Those who practice in the area of "regulatory law" will recognise as familiar principles and concepts many of the matters which are discussed. The book is intended to help them or those less familiar with this area to whom it falls to interpret, apply or resist the statutory provisions which provide the framework within which decisions as to liability have to be made.

1.10   A caveat.   A word of warning is necessary for this reason. Sometimes in this book, comparison is made between different pieces of legislation in connection with a discussion of the meaning of a particular word or phrase or notion. In the interpretation of statutes, the courts will sometimes decline to look at other statutes dealing with different legal topics as an aid to construction. Only statutory provisions which can be treated as *in pari materia* can be relied upon as an aid to construction, that is, provisions so related as to form a single system or code of legislation such that one statute ought to be interpreted in the light of the meanings of the other related statutory material. All regulatory offences cannot be treated as *in pari materia*, although undoubtedly within the category of regulatory offences there are a number of groups of provisions which can be so treated. For example, in interpreting the meaning of Part III of the Consumer Protection Act (misleading price indications) it is legitimate to look at the meanings ascribed to similar words or concepts under the Trade Descriptions Act 1968, an Act which was repealed in part to make way for the provisions of the 1987 Act. It would not be permissible to look at provisions of the Food Safety Act 1990 to assist in construing any provision of that Act. So, it would follow that if the meaning of the words "all reasonable precautions and all due diligence" were to fall for interpretation in any context, it would not be permissible to have reference to all other statutes in which those words appear but only to those instances within the same statutory scheme. That is not to say, however, that as a means of presenting argument, to contrast the ways in which a draftsman might express himself, the court cannot be asked to look at other statutory provisions, and indeed, the consideration of other statutory provisions may be a good practical guide to the meaning which the draftsman wished to convey. The words of a former legislative draftsman summarise the position:

> "Being by and large an imitative creature, and being invariably pressed for time, the draftsman is always interested in discovering a relevant legislative precedent.
>
> In the first place, the judicious use of a precedent can save a lot of time.
>
> Secondly, a precedent may constitute a source of ideas in addition to constituting a help in the actual drafting.
>
> Thirdly, the use of precedents from the same jurisdiction may contribute in a small way to consistency of approach which, in turn, will contribute to statute law becoming a coherent body rather than a patchwork quilt".
> (G. C. Thornton "Legislative Drafting" (3rd ed., 1987)).

DEREGULATION

1.11 The Act. The Deregulation and Contracting Out Act 1994, which received the Royal Assent on November 3, 1994 has been the umbrella for a vast miscellany of activities in the various areas affected by regulation of business activity. It has six central provisions which were intended to apply to all topics of regulation. The main features of the Act include:–

Removing costly regulations which confer no protection

Section 1 of the Act provides that if a Minister is of the opinion that the effect of a provision is to impose, require the imposition, or to authorise "a burden" affecting a person in the carrying on of any trade, business or profession, and that it would be possible (whether by amendment or repeal, with or without replacement) by Order in Council to remove or reduce the burden or as the case may be, the authorisation or requirement by which the burden may be imposed, he may by Order in Council amend or repeal the enactment. He may only do so however if he is of the opinion that there would be no removal of "any necessary protection". The term "necessary protection" is not defined, although a burden is described as "a restriction, requirement or condition (including one as to the payment of fees) together with any sanction for failure to comply with the restriction, requirement or condition and any procedural provisions (including provisions for appeal relevant to that sanction)": In short, many of the matters which are covered in this book.

The decision of the Minister, although expressed in subjective terms is likely to be susceptible to judicial review, not least on the ground of *Wednesbury* unreasonableness). Moreover, any regulations which replace those repealed must be within the scope of the parent Act (see paragraph 6.86 below). Where made, the Minister may by Order in Council do one or more of four things:

    (i)   impose a burden which is less onerous than that imposed under existing legislation but which relates to the same subject matter: this may be by way of amendment or otherwise;

   (ii)   make amendments to legislation which are consequential upon or incidental to the repeal or amendment of the enactment;

 (iii)   contain transitional provisions and savings;

 (iv)   make different provision for different classes of case.

The definition of "enactment" for the purposes of this Act includes an Act passed before or in the same session as the Deregulation and Contracting Out Act 1994. It accordingly means that primary legislation may be repealed or amended by Order in Council, a power which the House of Lords Delegated Powers Scrutiny Committee described as "unprecedented in time of peace". (*Hansard*, HL Vol. 60, para. 1).

  Because of the potential constitutional significance of this legislation, the parliamentary scrutiny applicable to deregulation orders is more rigorous than that applicable to other delegated legislation. The procedure is that:–

    (i)   the Minister must consult such organisations as appear to him to be representative of interests substantially affected by his proposals and other persons as he considers appropriate. Any variation following a first round of consultation must similarly be put to consultation (Deregulation and Contracting Out Act 1994, s.3(1)(2)).

   (ii)   a draft of the order is laid before each House together with a detailed explanatory note (section 3(3), (4), (5));

 (iii)   a specially constituted Deregulation Committee will examine the legislation in the House of Commons. In the House of Lords the Delegated Powers Scrutiny Committee performs the same task (section 4(1), (2), (3));

 (iv)   at least 60 days must elapse before an order to give effect to the proposal may be laid. When laying a further draft for implementation, the Minister concerned must take into account representations, resolutions and reports while under scrutiny and must also lay a statement giving details of all representations, resolutions and reports during the scrutiny stage and the changes made in consequence (section 4(5)). In both Houses the Government undertook not to move to approve the draft order in the face of an adverse report from either scrutiny committee unless the House had first rejected the Committee's report (*Hansard*, HC 404, paras 16–18, 33–34; HL Vol. 555 col. 956, Vol. 556 col. 490; Vol. 557 cols 867–862).

Section 2 of the Act limits the penalties (2 years imprisonment on indictment and unlimited fine, 6 months or a fine not exceeding level 5 of the standard scale on a summary trial) that may be imposed as part of a replacement regulation, unless the offence being replaced already had greater maximum penalties.

Improving enforcement procedures

Section 5 and Schedule 1 of the Act which were introduced at the report stage in the House of Lords provide a comparable mechanism in relation to a "restriction, requirement or condition". If a Minister is of the opinion that by exercising one or more of the powers in Schedule 1 it would be possible without "jeopardising any necessary protection" to improve procedures for enforcement so far as "fairness, transparency and consistency" are concerned, he may exercise the power by order. The powers are:–

(a) to provide that where an enforcement officer expresses an opinion as to what remedial action should be taken by that person, he should, if the person requests:

(1) give him a written notice;

(2) desist from taking enforcement action until a period provided for in the order,

The written notice should (a) state the nature of and the reason for remedial action and the period with which it should be taken, (b) explain what constitutes the failure to observe a restriction or comply with the requirement or condition, and 3) state the nature of the enforcement action which could be taken and explain whether there is a right to make representations or to appeal; Sched. 1 para. 1;

(b) to provide that where an enforcement officer takes immediate enforcement action or requires immediate remedial action he shall as soon as practicable give a written notice explaining why it appeared to him to be necessary. This should apply only where the person will be required to expend "a significant amount" in complying; Sched. 1 para. 22;

(c) to provide for written notice before taking enforcement action setting out the reasons and inviting representations within a specified period and requiring the enforcement officer to consider any representations made;

(d) to provide that a written notice informing the person of his right and grounds of appeal should be given as soon as practicable after taking enforcement action;

(e) to provide what similar information must be furnished to certain third parties who will be affected.

An order may make provision for the consequences of failure to comply, consequential and incidental amendments, action, transitional powers and make different provision for different classes of case. The Deregulation (Model Appeal Provisions) Order 1996 sets out some model provisions which can be specifically adopted into legislation in part or totally and with or without variations. The Enforcement Concordat makes it clear that these provisions, giving as they do a statutory right to consultation before prosecution, are unlikely to be invoked in future. Instead, the voluntary procedures envisaged by the Concordat will give to the prospective defendant an opportunity to discuss a problem informally before prosecution.

Appeals

Section 6 enables the Secretary of State to prescribe model provisions for incorporation in enactments which "include provision the effect of which is to impose or authorise or require the imposition of a restriction, requirement or condition affecting any person in the carrying on of any trade business or profession or otherwise". The Department of Trade and Industry has currently issued a consultation paper dealing with the conduct of appeals, but these, like the provisions of section 5, seem unlikely to find their way into future legislation.

The Enforcement Concordat

1.12   Statement of principle.   This new statement of principle available from the Better Regulation Unit of the Cabinet Office is intended to be a blueprint for a centrally approved standard of enforcement, which is to be adopted and applied locally by the enforcement authorities with responsibility for prosecution of regulatory matters. It is intended to replace the "minded to" provisions under section 5 of the Deregulation and Contracting Out Act 1994 which will be gradually phased out. The part of the Concordat dealing with procedures specifies that "before formal action will be taken, officers will provide an opportunity to discuss the circumstances of the case and, if possible, resolve points of difference" unless immediate action is required. In particular, this suggests that the practice of local authorities to move straight to an interview under caution (see paragraph 3.27 below) may be a thing of the past. It is anticipated that the Concordat will be adopted throughout England (there is to be a separate launch of its proposals in Wales and Scotland), although individual enforcement agencies cannot be compelled to adopt it if they choose not to. This must be particularly true of local authorities, whose councillors are free to select whatever policies they consider to be in the best interests of their electorate. A more detailed explanation of the content of the Concordat is set out at paragraphs 2.9 and 2.10 below.

REGULATORS AND POLICY MAKERS

1.13   The role of local authorities as enforcers is to be found at paragraphs 2.25 to 2.46 below. In relation to centralised bodies concerned with enforcement, only a selection is referred to here, and no consideration is given to the responsibilities of central government, which, of course, bears the ultimate responsibility in every field of enforcement activity. As this work has examples drawn mainly from local authority enforcement responsibilities, examples of the regulators and policy makers selected are connected with areas of local authority concern, largely, trading standards, food safety, and health and safety. There are, of course other regulators and policy makers not referred to.

The Office of Fair Trading

1.14   The OFT.   The Office of Fair Trading remains the principal regulator in the UK for consumer and competition matters. It was established by the Fair Trading Act 1973 (and has to some degree formed a comparator for many others which followed under the Conservative administration from 1979 to 1997, for telecommunications, electricity, water, gas, rail etc). Unlike its lesser rivals, the Office of Fair Trading has a function which is not limited by a permissive framework, such as a licence to operate, but has two widespread policy and supervisory functions, that of overseeing fair competition and of endeavouring to ensure appropriate conduct by suppliers to consumers. Its role in enforcing prohibitions on anti-competitive behaviour is very soon to be enlarged and strengthened when the Competition Act 1998 (currently the Competition Bill) comes into force. This Act will provide for new investigatory powers, powers to search premises, with powers to make binding decisions and impose fines. The Office is under the control of a Director General (currently John Bridgeman) who must advise the Secretary of State for Trade and Industry when required to do so, but it is otherwise an autonomous institution. Section 2 of the Fair Trading Act 1973 requires the Director General to keep under review the carrying on of commercial operations in relation to the supply of goods and services to consumers and to collect information about practices of persons by whom such activities are carried on. Section 2 also requires him to receive and collate information on practices adversely affecting consumers and not just economically. The administrative divisions of the OFT consist of the Competition Policy Division and the Consumer Affairs Division, with internal supporting branches: information, administration and legal. The staff are civil servants.

1.15 Liaison with local government.   The Consumer Affairs Division monitors the market for goods and services with a view to investigation and to identify patterns of consumer trading. It liaises closely with local authority trading standards services and financial services regulators. It is not necessary for there to be a specific referral of matters to the OFT before it may become involved in investigating although it is commonplace for trading standards departments of local authorities to compile lists of complaints and refer these to the OFT for investigation. The requirement for notice to be given by prosecutors to the Director General of Fair Trading before certain types of prosecution can be brought (see paragraph 8.41 below) assists him to compile information, as does a register kept by the OFT of convictions and cautions.

1.16 Liaison with businesses.   As part of its function, the Office of Fair Trading endeavours to establish fair practices at industry level. One means of achieving this is by encouraging trade associations to develop voluntary codes of practice, a responsibility imposed by section 124(3) of the Fair Trading Act 1973. This provision requires the Director General to encourage Trade Associations to "prepare and to disseminate to their members codes of practice for guidance in safeguarding and promoting the interest of consumers". These codes of practice are of particular importance when considering a due diligence defence. Clearly, compliance with an industry standard may be a guide to whether all reasonable precautions have been taken in any instance. On the other hand, assertion by a trader that he has complied with an industry guide when he has not may be an offence under the Trade Descriptions Act 1968. Lawson (in "The Supply of Goods and Services Act 1982", p. 131), makes reference to a conviction by the Wrekin magistrates in just such an instance. It should be noted, however, that not all industry codes of practice have been prompted by the actions of the OFT. Many industry-wide codes have been adopted without any OFT involvement. LACOTS (see paragraph 1.30 onwards below), as part of its submission to Ministers entitled "Codes of Practice – the way forward" in 1997 commented that, broadly speaking, those codes which were not backed by the OFT had been more effective in achieving compliance, partly due to fear of regulation, partly because of the wish to provide a service of a good standard with its obvious benefit to consumers and partly through the efficacy of sanctions. It recommended the repeal of section 124(3) of the Act.

1.17 Liaison with consumers.   The OFT announced recently that a new group, the National Consumer Education Partnership has been launched, with the objective of informing consumers about their rights and seeking redress when standards slip. This organisation is an alliance of consumer and trade organisations and also of educational specialists. The OFT does not deal with individual consumers in relation to individual complaints, although, no doubt, any complaint made would be recorded and kept for information purposes.

1.18   Consumer credit.   The Consumer Credit Act 1974 imposes further duties on the Director General of Fair Trading. He bears the responsibility under that legislation for licensing of lenders, hirers, those who provide debt counselling, credit broking and debt-adjusting or who run credit agencies. The Director General is empowered to revoke or to refuse to renew consumer credit licences under Part III of the Consumer Credit Act 1974 if the applicant or licensee or an appointee is not a fit and proper person to hold a licence. The Director General also has a responsibility for reviewing the operation of the Act and, in pursuit of that responsibility, recommended various reforms after consultation with the industry as part of the process of deregulation. The same Act allows the Director General to decide disputes about entries against an individual name on records held by credit reference agencies. The OFT is itself an enforcement authority under the Act, see, for example, *Jenkins v. Lombard North Central plc* [1983] C.C.L.R. 15, where the OFT prosecuted for alleged breaches of the Consumer Credit (Advertisements) Regulations 1980, although the majority of individual prosecutions are now brought by the relevant local authority.

1.19   Estate agents.   Under the Estate Agents Act 1979 the Director General is given power to ban unsuitable people from engaging in estate agency work. The Office maintains a register of those who have been banned or who have received warning orders.

1.20   Misleading advertisements.   The Control of Misleading Advertisements Regulations 1988 permits the Director General to apply to the Court to ban by injunction advertisements which are misleading. One of many examples of the exercise of this power was *Director General of Fair Trading v. Green and Varley* ("Fair Trading", published by the OFT, Autumn 1996) in which the Director successfully obtained an injunction preventing advertisements for a slimming product which were misleading and offensive. A characteristic of the advertising method to which the Director General objected was the appearance of the advertisement which looked as though a personal friend had attached a written note to the advertising material. These powers lie alongside broadcasting and other self-regulatory controls in relation to advertisements and the powers of the Advertising Standards Authority, which also exercises a voluntary control over advertisers. The Director General also has comparable powers in relation to unfair terms included in consumer contracts under the Unfair Terms in Consumer Contracts Regulations 1994.

1.21   Unfair trading.   Where traders have persisted in a course of conduct which contravenes their civil or criminal duties and that course of conduct is detrimental to the interests of consumers in the U.K., the Director General of Fair Trading has power under section 34 of the Fair Trading Act 1973 to require them to give written assurances as to their future conduct. Breach of those assurances or a refusal to give them may result in civil proceedings in the Restrictive Practices Court (or a County Court unless the trader is a company with a share capital exceeding £10,000 or the point is one of general application) for a court order. Breach of that court order is a contempt of court.

The Food Standards Agency

1.22 Objectives. In January 1998, the Government published its white paper on the proposed Food Standards Agency (called "The Food Standards Agency: a Force for Change"). The objective is to lift the uncertainty and confusion experienced by consumers about the quality and safety of the food they buy by putting many of the more difficult issues out of the hands of disparate governmental and non-governmental bodies and placing them in the hands of the new agency. The agency is to be broadly modelled on the Health and Safety Executive and Commission and will be a non-departmental public body with executive powers. Government will not dictate its work plan nor direct its activities unless it appears to be acting outside the scope of its guiding principles (see paragraph 1.24 below). There will be a governing Commission which is likely to consist of a Chairperson and no more than 12 members. The Commission will reach its decisions collectively, although individual Commissioners would take responsibility for specific areas as well. The Commission will then decide upon the delegation of responsibilities to the Chief Executive and staff. The Chief Executive should be a Crown Office Holder but not a civil servant following a civil service career path. The staff of the Commission will be civil servants and other appointees and they will be responsible to the Commission, not to Ministers.

1.23 Proposed functions of the agency. The agency will formulate policy and advise Ministers on all aspects of food safety and standards from the first link in the "food chain" – the control of a live animal or crop on the farm to its advertisement and supply to the consumer. The interests of the consumer are to predominate. The agency will also advise on some aspects of nutrition. It may publish the advice that it has furnished so that the public will know what advice Ministers have been given and can monitor any departure for that advice but it may also have the power to decide not to publish. It will provide information and educational material to the public about food. It is to take scientific advice and may commission research and surveillance. The aim is to set standards for enforcement and in this context it will monitor the consistency of enforcement throughout the U.K., working alongside government departments and other bodies which have responsibilities for food production, safety and public health. Where there are already local or specialist arrangements which could undertake the responsibilities of enforcement more readily, the agency will not take a primary role, but it will in many cases have power to take direct action if there is a failure in the primary system. This applies, in particular to enforcement by local authorities. This proposal is particularly supported by LACOTS (see below) which comments that:

> "local authorities are committed to protecting consumers, promoting best practice and effectiveness by developing multi-functional regulatory services which ensure that intelligence gathered from one regulatory function is harnessed to promote the public interest in others. Modern regulatory law is inextricably linked and to separate out food standards and food safety functions alone would not, in the opinion of LACOTS make the best use of scarce resources."

(LAC 5 98 5 "Enforcement and FSA".

The FSA will draft secondary legislation. It will negotiate in the European Community and internationally at official level, although the political functions will continue to be addressed by the Ministers for Health and MAFF. It will operate openly and transparently on established guiding principles which place the public interest unequivocally at the forefront.

1.24 Guiding principles. There are nine guiding principles that the Food Standards Agency will adopt:

   (i) the essential aim is to protect public health in relation to food;

  (ii) its assessment of food standards and safety will be unbiased and based on "the best available scientific advice", provided by experts invited in their own right to give independent advice;

 (iii) its decisions and actions will be;

      — proportionate to the risk; having regard to costs as well as benefits and avoiding over-regulation;

      — independent of specific sectoral interests;

  (iv) the Agency will strive to ensure that the public have adequate, clearly presented information so that the public can make an informed choice, without raising unjustified alarm;

   (v) the Agency' s decision making processes will be "open, transparent and consultative" so that the public and other interested parties;

      — can make their views known;

      — can see the basis on which decisions have been taken;

      — can reach an informed judgment about the quality of the Agency's processes and decisions;

  (vi) the Agency will consult widely before taking action;

 (vii) it will aim to be consistent and clear in its approach;

(viii) it will take account of obligations under European law;

  (ix) it will aim for economy and efficiency.

1.25 Financing the agency. The white paper proposal is that the Agency should be part self-financing and part sponsored by the Department of Health. The white paper also recognises that the Agency's role in the setting of standards for enforcement is likely to lead to increased enforcement costs at local level in Environmental Health and Trading Standards Departments. The proposal was that the burden of much of the costs should be borne by the food industry not the taxpayer, although it acknowledged that indirectly the cost would be passed on to the taxpayer by way of higher food prices. The Government has recently indicated that the taxpayer must bear the cost, not the food industry. The system would be in the hands of local authorities and the fees used to offset the costs of the Agency and other enforcement activities initiated by the Agency, as well, presumably, as the costs associated with implementing any new scheme of licensing or registration.

The Health and Safety Commission and Executive

1.26 The commission. The Health and Safety Commission appointed pursuant to powers under the Health and Safety at Work etc. Act 1974 consists of a chairman appointed by the Secretary of State and between six and nine other members, three of whom are appointed after consultation with employer's associations and three appointed after consultation with employee's associations. Its powers and duties are to be found in the Health and Safety at Work etc. Act 1974 and the Employment Protection Act 1975. The Commission has overall responsibility for administering and overseeing health and safety matters and has specific responsibilities for advising government of health and safety matters and submitting proposals for regulations to the Secretary of State and approval of Codes of Practice. It may delegate some of its functions to the Health and Safety Executive. In particular, this refers to the carrying out of research into health and safety, publicity and education. The Commission is directly responsible to the Secretary of State for Employment.

1.27 Following an incident. The Commission has powers to request the Health and Safety Executive to investigate and report on any accident, occurrence, situation or matter which in the Commission's opinion ought to be investigated. With the consent of the Secretary of State, the Commission may also initiate any inquiry into an incident.

1.28 The health and safety executive. This consists of three people, one (the Director) appointed by the Commission and the other two appointed by the Commission after consultation with the Director. The Executive is the enforcement arm of the Commission, and its primary responsibility is to make adequate arrangements for the carrying out of its statutory duties. It also produces a number of publications on a very wide range of health and safety topics. This it does by the appointment of inspectors to carry out the functions of the Executive.

1.29 Inspectors. In addition to Inspectors appointed directly by the Executive, the Secretary of State may by regulation enable an employee of a local authority to act as a health and safety inspector. The inspectors have powers not only to prosecute, but also to issue executive notices (see paragraph 4.1 onwards below). Improvement notices may be issued if statutory provisions are being contravened and it is likely that the contravention will continue or be repeated. Under previous guidance from the Commission, inspectors were required to give notice of intention to issue an improvement notice and to allow two weeks within which to receive representations about the requirements of the proposed notice. This procedure may be replaced by the terms of the Enforcement Concordat (see paragraphs 2.9 and 2.10 below). Prohibition notices may be issued if the inspector considers that an activity involves a risk of serious personal injury. There is an appeal within 21 days against the notices to the industrial tribunal and failure to comply with the notices constitutes an offence. (For further consideration of the use of notices, see Chapter 11 where notices are considered as a discreet topic).

LACOTS

1.30 LACOTS. The Local Authority Co-ordinating Body on Food and Trading Standards is a unique and authoritative body. The Association of County Councils and the Association of Metropolitan Authorities reached agreement in 1976 under which LACOTS was established to consult and negotiate with central government and trade and industry bodies with a view to establishing standards of quality. It is a company limited by guarantee and consists of twelve councillors appointed by the Local Government Association, the Welsh Local Government Association and its Scottish and Northern Irish counterparts with the assistance of a Chief Executive and approximately 150 chief officers and technical advisors. It is financed from the Revenue Support grant, and in 1997/8, its budget was approximately £1 million. Its terms of reference published in February 1998 are eight fold: to promote quality regulation and good practice and co-ordinate enforcement; to provide advice, guidance and codes for food safety and trading standards authorities; to advise central government and the European Union on relevant legislation; to promote the Home Authority principle as the key method of enforcement co-ordination; to administer statutory arrangements as the U.K. Single Liaison Body for trans-border food problems; to develop information and central record databases to assist enforcement practitioners; to liaise with industry, trade and consumer organisations; and to collaborate with overseas agencies. Its relationship with the local authority Associations is governed by a protocol, which recognises LACOTS' status as a service or support body rather than one responsible for the formulation of policy or principle, which function remains with the individual local authorities and the local government Associations. LACOTS publishes circulars and advice for trading standards services and also, where appropriate makes submissions to central government on the practical implementation of policy issues. Copies of this material can also be obtained by business and other interested parties. Although the future LACOTS' role in relation to food is now somewhat uncertain in the light of the impending Food Standards Agency, LACOTS have put forward in LAC 5 98 5 "Enforcement and the FSA" a strong case for the recognition of the Home Authority Principle (see paragraph 1.31 below) and, indeed, it suggests that the principle be put on a formal footing in relation to the safety of food. Moreover, in LAC 5 98 6 "LACOTS and the FSA" LACOTS has advocated that it retain its existing functions, at least at present, rather than surrender them to the FSA. The Enforcement Concordat also has recognised the important role that LACOTS continues to play in co-ordinating, monitoring and producing policy in relation to other aspects of enforcement.

1.31   **The home authority principle.**   Of great impact in recent years has been the development of the Home Authority Principle. Devised and applied to trading standards issues in 1980, its application was extended to food safety in the 1990s. The principle involves the appointment (achieved through negotiation between the business and the local authority) of a local authority to be its "home authority". This may be the local authority of the head office or principal factory or outlet. Where the business is decentralised, there may also be an "originating authority" for the area in which goods or services originate. The aim of the home authority is fourfold. It promotes emphasis by enforcement authorities on goods and services arising within their area. It assists local authorities to give advice and guidance on the procedures and standards in place within the business to try to assist it to comply (notably, the Enforcement Concordat has underlined the great importance of this role and endorses it). It encourages efficient liaison between local authorities and, fourthly, sets up a system for resolving disputes. Where the home authority is appointed, it holds itself out as providing advice and guidance on a regular basis to the trader, rendering itself a point of contact in the event of any query, maintaining records of incidents, due diligence procedures and business policies, and it undertakes to answer enquiries (including the notification of "indulgences" for subsequently corrected errors), to any local authority considering prosecution. In order to be able to provide useful advice and guidance, there has to be a great deal of co-operation between the business and the local authority, with, on the part of the business, great candour, and on behalf of the local authority, an assumption of confidentiality. LACOTS monitors and supports its operation, assists in the location of suitable home authorities, participates in the resolution of disputes on policy issues and maintains a database of home authorities. Although the appointment of the home authority is not itself protection against enforcement by another local authority, the enforcing authority should contact the home authority in advance of any decision to prosecute, thus avoiding as much as possible disparate views in different authorities.

CHAPTER 2

Executive Decisions and the Authority to Prosecute

IDENTIFYING THE AUTHORITY WITH RESPONSIBILITY FOR ENFORCEMENT

Public and private prosecutions

2.1 Specialist prosecutions. A characteristic of regulatory offences is that the primary powers of enforcement often lie, not with the police or Crown Prosecution Service, but with a branch of the executive or a self-regulator able to apply its specialist knowledge of the area covered by the statutory scheme. In relation to consumer offences, this is often a weights and measures authority or environmental health department within the umbrella of local government, but the generalisation also applies to other organisations with specific areas of specialisation, such as the Health and Safety Inspectorate, the Environment Agency, or the Bank of England.

2.2 Local authority powers. Local authorities have a responsibility in the following categories which it falls usually to their T.S.O.s (trading standards officers) or E.H.O.s (environmental health officers) to undertake on their behalf. Some of these responsibilities involve regulatory offences. The following is not an exhaustive list of local authority activities, and not all the listed topics are the sole responsibility of either trading standards or environmental health officers, but the matters listed illustrate how the local authority may be acting in the capacity of local prosecutor:

    (i) Public Health (including powers under the Public Health Act 1936, the Clean Air Act 1956, the Public Health Act 1961 and the Local Government (Miscellaneous Provisions) Act 1976, Public Health (Control of Disease) Act 1984, Building Act 1984 in so far as the above provisions have not been repealed and the Environmental Health Act 1990);

    (ii) Acupuncture, tattooing, ear-piercing and electrolysis (powers under the Local Government (Miscellaneous Provisions) Act 1982 enable local authorities to set up schemes of registration of these activities and to make bye-laws to govern cleanliness and hygiene: breaches of the provisions as to registration, or of the bye-laws, are offences);

(iii) Animals (including under the Animal Boarding Establishments Act 1963, the Breeding of Dogs Acts 1973 and 1991, the Pet Animals Act 1951, the Riding Establishments Act 1964, the Dangerous Wild Animals Act 1976, the Zoo Licensing Act 1981);

(iv) Buildings (principal powers are contained in the Building Act 1984, a consolidation Act, but the local authority also enjoys powers in relation to the safety of buildings under the Local Government (Miscellaneous Provisions) Act 1982 as well as powers which are ancillary to their statutory obligations in relation to housing);

(v) Caravan sites (Caravan Sites and Control of Development Act 1960);

(vi) Cinemas and Clubs, Music and Dancing (Cinemas Act 1985, Local Government (Miscellaneous Provisions) Act 1982);

(vii) Fire (under the Fire Services Act 1947 and the Fire Precautions Act 1971);

(viii) Food Safety (the main power is the Food Safety Act 1990 and regulations made under it, although the areas of responsibility extend to include slaughterhouses – the Slaughterhouses Act 1974, the Slaughter of Poultry Act 1967, the Animal Health and Welfare Act 1984 – and fertilisers and feedstuffs under powers contained in the Agriculture Act 1970 and associated legislation);

(ix) Health and Safety at Work (the areas of local government responsibility are now set out in the Health and Safety (Enforcing Authorities) Regulations 1977 although residual responsibilities remain through other legislation, for example, the Rag Flock and Other Filling Materials Act 1951 which is largely concerned with storage);

(x) Noise (the Environmental Protection Act 1995 and the Noise Act 1996);

(xi) Pests (the Prevention of Damage by Pests Act 1949);

(xii) Petrol (the Petroleum (Consolidation) Act 1928 contains a licensing power in respect of "petroleum spirit licences" giving rise to offences as to its quality and storage);

(xiii) Poisons (other than those held in a pharmacy: Poisons Act 1972);

(xiv) Pollution and refuse (including the Control of Pollution Act 1974);

(xv) Safety of Sports Grounds (under the 1975 Act);

(xvi) Trading Standards matters (including matters arising under the Weights and Measures Act 1985, Trade Descriptions Act 1968, Hallmarking Act 1973, Fair Trading Act 1973, Consumer Credit Act 1974, Solicitors' Act 1974 section 22 (preparation of an instrument by an unqualified person), Aerosol Dispensers (EEC Requirements) Regulations 1977, Energy Conservation Act 1981, Consumer Protection Act 1987, Property Misdescriptions Act 1991, Timeshare Act 1992, Sunday Trading Act 1994, etc.,);

(xvii) Trees (see the Local Government (Miscellaneous Provisions) Act 1976;

(xviii) Scrap metal dealers (are required by the Scrap Metal Dealers Act 1964 to be registered with the local authority).

Where there are offences, local authority officers will be empowered by resolutions of the Council and its Standing Orders to investigate and report. In some cases the power to decide whether or not to prosecute in the name of the local authority has been conferred on even junior officers if those officers are T.S.O.s or E.H.O.s (see paragraph 2.35 below).

2.3 Police powers. The above is not intended to imply that the police and Crown Prosecution Service may not prosecute these specialist offences. In many instances, such as under the Trade Descriptions Act 1968, their powers of prosecution arise, not by virtue of the Act, but by reference to their wider powers. Prosecutions following investigation by police officers are not infrequent in that area. Also, a private individual has the right to prosecute, even, seemingly, if he is a competitor, save that if the prosecutor is driven by improper motives the prosecution may be an abuse of the process of the court which the court will stay (see paragraphs 10.26 *et seq.* below). The Trade Descriptions Act 1968, however, imposes the duty of enforcement on the local weights and measures authority (section 26), and, indeed, it is the weights and measures authority which is required to give notice to the Director General of Fair Trading of an impending prosecution under section 130 of the Fair Trading Act 1973 (so providing a mechanism by which enforcement can be monitored). No such duty is imposed on other prosecutors, nor is the weights and measures authority required to notify the Director General of prosecutions of which it is aware but does not bring.

In the case of every statutory scheme it is necessary to examine the provisions empowering enforcement and to determine in relation to the power envisaged whether it is an exclusive power or one subject to wider enforcement. An example of a limited right to prosecute is found in section 83 of the Weights and Measures Act 1985 where the prosecution may only be brought by a weights and measures authority or by a chief officer of police.

2.4 Private prosecutions. For an instance of a prosecution brought by a private individual or competitor, see *Donnelly v. Rowlands* [1971] 1 All E.R. 9, where no criticism was raised of the prosecution of the case by a competitor, also *Snodgrass v. Topping* (1952) 116 J.P. 312; *Falconer v. White* (1908) S.C.(J) 40. In addition to prosecutions brought by interested individuals or competitors, there are a small number of associations which have formed to enforce standards and which bring prosecutions in trading cases. The leading example is FACT – the Federation Against Copyright Theft Ltd, which prosecutes offences associated with infringements of intellectual property rights. Note, however, that an unincorporated association cannot lay a criminal information (*Rubin v. D.P.P.* [1989] 2 All E.R. 241). In the Crown Court, a private prosecutor will usually be required to employ counsel or a solicitor, although in the magistrates court, a private prosecutor may appear. Where a prosecution is commenced by a private prosecutor, the Crown Prosecution Service has freedom to take over the prosecution and to make decisions in relation to it (and, in particular, may discontinue the prosecution) (Prosecution of Offences Act 1985, s.6). Also, some statutory provisions permit intervention by statutory enforcers. In the Food Safety Act 1990, for example, section 6 gives a power of intervention to the Secretary of State, seemingly both in respect of prosecutions commenced by food authorities and in respect of prosecutions commenced by others.

The Decision to Prosecute or take other Enforcement Action

2.5 The importance of the decision. The importance of the decision to prosecute in practice may be overlooked by prosecutors in favour of more apparently pressing but associated considerations, such as the choice of offence or the time limit within which to lay an information. This risks that the taking of the decision to enforce becomes subordinated to the mechanics of its own implementation. In some cases this error has led to ill-considered prosecutions or prosecutions both which lie outside the band of those within the local authority's policy to prosecute and where insufficient care has been taken to ensure that prosecution is in the public interest (see as an example of the latter *Mulvenna v. Snape* and *Walker v. Simon Dudley Ltd* [1997] Tr.L. 69). The sanction is in costs.

The decision to prosecute is important in its own right because it is the executive act upon which criminal proceedings hinge. It is an abuse of process to commence proceedings before the decision to prosecute has been taken (*R. v. Brentford Justices, ex p. Wong* [1981] Q.B. 451) and if the decision to prosecute is not taken lawfully, the prosecution of the offence may founder (see paragraphs 10.26 onwards below). The decision to take other enforcement action requires equal care, because it is by its nature a balancing exercise involving the curbing by executive power of private freedoms. To be weighed are various considerations, perhaps different considerations on each occasion, depending on the facts of the alleged offence. Essential to each decision, however, is a consideration of the protection of the public interest including the question whether the enforcement option envisaged is the best way of achieving this and whether there is a need to invoke those deterrent and retributive factors which are part and parcel of the criminal law. (For a more detailed consideration of the relevant factors, see paragraphs 2.11 *et seq.*, below).

Discretion not to prosecute

2.6 The exercise of a discretion. Whether the prosecutor is a Crown prosecutor or local authority or other body empowered to bring proceedings for the protection of the public, there is, even in the absence of an express provision to that effect, a discretion whether or not to commence proceedings which must be exercised in each case. In a frequently quoted speech, Lord Shawcross (*Hansard*, HC, Vol. 483, col. 681 (January 29, 1951)) described the exercise of the decision to prosecute as "the exercise of a discretion in a quasi-judicial way" and confirmed that not all suspected criminal offences must lead inevitably to prosecution. In the regulatory sphere, Viscount Dilhorne, Lord Cross of Chelsea and Lord Kilbrandon rejected the notion that the discretion not to prosecute was precluded by statute and criticised the prosecution of a company which canned peas for an offence under the Food and Drugs Act 1955 when a small, green, sterile caterpillar escaped the tests designed to detect foreign bodies and was supplied to a consumer in *Smedleys Ltd v. Breed* [1974] A.C. 839. The prosecution was said to have been not in the public interest.

2.7 Crown prosecutors. The Code for Crown Prosecutors ,1994, issued pursuant to section 10 of the Prosecution of Offences Act 1985 identifies two questions which need to be addressed:

   (i) is there enough evidence to provide a "realistic prospect of conviction" taking into account the likely defence case and the reliability and admissibility of the prosecution evidence;

   (ii) if there is enough evidence, is prosecution in the public interest? Paragraph 6.4 of the Code refers to some public interest factors in favour of prosecution. Factors which may be relevant to regulatory offences include:

     (a) the likelihood of a significant sentence;

     (b) the fact that an offence was pre-meditated;

     (c) any previous convictions or cautions;

     (d) the likelihood of continuance or repetition of an offence if a prosecution is not brought

     (e) a widespread offence.

Considerations which weigh against prosecution are:

   (i) the likelihood that a sentence will be small or nominal (in *Smedleys Ltd v. Breed* (above) Viscount Dilhorne referred to the magistrates power to give an absolute discharge);

   (ii) that the offence was committed as a result of a genuine mistake or understanding;

   (iii) that the loss or harm was minor and the result of a single incident;

   (iv) delay between the offence and the likely trial date;

   (v) that the defendant has put right the loss.

These considerations apply to the continuance of the prosecution as well as to its initiation. Moreover, in some cases, where one or other of the factors which weigh against prosecution apply, the Code may be prayed in aid as part of the mitigation for the offence (see paragraph 11.58 below).

2.8 Local authority prosecutions. Local authorities and private prosecutors (such as the National Society for the Prevention of Cruelty to Animals, or the organisation FACT (see paragraph 2.4 above) are not within the scope of the Guidelines (Prosecution of Offences Act 1985, s.6), although the Attorney General had issued guidelines addressing private prosecutors in 1983. It has been observed that "An agency responsible for the enforcement of strict liability offences is particularly vulnerable to charges of over-interference and persecution and thus the agency must choose its prosecutions with care" (Richardson: "Policing Pollution" (1983)) Where the prosecuting body is a private prosecutor, the need for care is yet so much greater.

2.9   **The partnership principle and the Concordat.**   A restrained approach to prosecution of regulatory offences achieved greater currency in latter years following the Government's "Deregulation Initiative" in the early 1990's and consequent enactment of the Deregulation and Contracting Out Act 1994, mirrored by the approach urged upon local authority prosecutors in respect of the treatment of alleged offenders. The Deregulation Minister in an address to the Conservative Party conference in 1994 described the role of enforcement officers, not without hyperbole, as "handmaidens of business – helping them to comply – rather than the local branch of the Gestapo" (*The Weekly Telegraph,* Issue no. 118, 1994). The Government Publication "Getting a Good Deal in Europe – Deregulatory Principles in Practice" (October 1994) urged a partnership between enforcement authorities and industry. Underlying this partnership was the notion that compliance with regulation is onerous, that prosecution is not necessarily the best way of achieving compliance but that co-operation and advice is, and that the public is best served by compliance. Accordingly, a greater exercise of the discretion not to prosecute was envisaged. Although this idea was frequently referred to as the basis of dealings between local authorities and the retail trade, it was a partnership the notional existence of which appeared in practice to be more clearly perceived by some local authorities than by many traders, some of the largest of whom continued to be prosecuted for strict liability offences in spite of significant safeguards approved by their Home Authorities. The Chairman of the Institute of Trading Standards Administration supporting the approach of the new Labour administration that the balance has latterly fallen too heavily on the side of business rather than consumers, has emphasised the importance of protecting consumer rights. In his address to the Institute of Trading Standards Administration in June 1997, the Chairman commented that consumer protection has been an ebbing tide since the 1970's, "marked by signposts such as BSE, mis-selling of pensions, misuse of pension funds and exploitation of children through under-age sales . . .". On March 4, 1998 the Cabinet Office issued a policy document its content agreed by the Access Business Group (officially described as a partnership between central and local government and business, established in July 1997) and signed by Central and Local Government, called "The Enforcement Concordat". This Concordat aims to facilitate local government working with industry to try to achieve higher standards, rather than pursuit of offenders with a view to prosecution. It is intended to displace the "minded to" procedures of section 5 of the Deregulation and Contracting Out Act 1994 (see paragraph 1.11 above), but on the other hand, endeavours to replace the benefits to business with an informal flexible procedure which underlines the involvement that local government is to have in achieving compliance by the trader.

2.10   **The Enforcement Concordat.**   The document begins by setting out its general objectives, commenting:

> "The effectiveness of legislation in protecting consumers or sectors in society depends crucially on the compliance of those regulated. We recognise that most businesses want to comply with the law. We will therefore take care to help business and others meet their legal obligations without unnecessary expense, while taking firm action, including prosecution where appropriate, against those who flout the law or act irresponsibly."

The policy of the Concordat is that local authorities should:

  (i) draw up clear standards identifying the level of service and performance that the public and business can expect from central and local government enforcers;

 (ii) provide and disseminate information and advice in plain language on the rules that the enforcers apply and will be open about their activities;

(iii) advise and assist business to comply, especially in relation to small and medium-sized business, with appropriate systems of expeditious and efficient response to requests;

(iv) provide well-publicised complaints procedures;

 (v) link costs of compliance to the risk. As far as the law allows, enforcers will "take account of the circumstances of the case and the attitude of the operator when considering action";

(vi) have arrangements in place for complaints;

(vii) exercise duties fairly and consistently. In particular it seems that LACOTS (the Local Authority Co-ordinating Body on Food and Trading Standards) and LANTAC (the Local Authority National Type Approval Confederation) will promote schemes and liaise to facilitate consistent action.

In addition to this, the Concordat promises to explain the need to businesses for remedial work in clear language, and to provide an opportunity to discuss any case and resolve points of difference prior to any enforcement action (except where immediate action is required, such as for health and safety, environmental protection or to prevent the destruction of evidence). Even where immediate action has been taken, an oral explanation will be given at once and a written confirmation will be tendered within 5 or 10 working days.

Enforcement policies

2.11   **Enforcement policies.**   The decision to prosecute needs in every case to be approached carefully, with a full appreciation of the relevant factors, all the more so following the adoption of the Concordat. One of those factors is the enforcement policy adopted by the local authority, which continues to remain a matter discrete from the aspirations of the Concordat, although differences in prosecution policies may be a matter for consideration as part of the drive to ensure consistency between the actions of enforcers. As matters stand, however, local authorities will continue to exercise their own judgment on matters of enforcement and to hold their own policies.

If the facts of an alleged offence take it outside the scope of the policy on prosecution, it would not inevitably be wrong to prosecute, but the local authority should be on notice that care is appropriate. If the facts of an alleged offence bring it within the policy, the discretion not to prosecute arises. The following principles apply to the use of policies affecting prosecution:

  (i) It is proper for enforcement authorities to adopt a policy on the initiation of prosecutions, and having adopted a policy, the policy must be applied, not rigidly, but flexibly and in good faith, taking into account all the circumstances (*R. v. Commissioners of Inland Revenue, ex p. Mead* [1993] 1 All E.R. 772);

(ii) A prosecutor must not fetter its discretion for the future. It is not permissible, therefore, to take a decision not to prosecute a whole class or category of offender, because that would be a fetter on the discretion of the local authority to prosecute and an abuse of power (*R. v. Chief Constable of Devon and Cornwall, ex p. Central Electricity Generating Board* [1982] Q.B. 458);

(iii) Where there is a policy, failure to apply the policy resulting in a decision not to prosecute may, as with an overly rigid adherence to the policy in favour of prosecution, be susceptible of judicial review (*R. v. Director of Public Prosecutions, ex p. Chaudhary* [1995] 1 Cr. App. R. 136). Rather than judicial review, however, an aggrieved person's first recourse may be to launch a prosecution as a private prosecutor (see, by analogy, *R. v. DPP, ex p. Camelot Group plc, The Independent,* April 22, 1997, DC).

(iv) Where the prosecutor is the Crown Prosecution Service and a decision in favour of prosecution is made, judicial review will only lie if the decision has been made regardless of, or clearly contrary to the prosecution policy or without enquiry, or if there has been some fraud or dishonesty in reaching the decision (*R. v. Chief Constable of the Kent County Constabulary, ex p. L* [1993] 1 All E.R. 756, *R. v. Metropolitan Police Commissioner, ex p. Blackburn* [1968] 1 All E.R. 763);

(v) Where a prosecutor other than the CPS is concerned with a decision in favour of prosecution, the scope of a judicial review of the decision may be wider, having regard to the powers, functions and procedures of the prosecuting body and the manner in which it has handled the matter (*R. v. General Council of the Bar, ex p. Percival* [1990] 3 All E.R. 137);

(vi) It is doubtful whether the Divisional Court would adopt a different approach in the case of local authorities from that adopted in the case of the Crown Prosecution Service, save that it may permit an investigation into the authority of the decision-maker to act. In the case of private prosecutors it seems unlikely that this issue can arise independently of questions of the abuse of the process of the court.

2.12 Prosecution policy guidelines. As part of the process of investigating areas in which deregulation could have an impact (see paragraph 2.9 above and paragraph 1.11), attention was drawn to inconsistent enforcement of regulatory offences (for example, the Department of Trade and Industry has published "Review of the Implementation and Enforcement of E.C. Law in the U.K. – An Efficiency Scrutiny Report" (July 1993) and "De-Regulation – Cutting Red Tape" (January 1994)). LACOTS (see paragraphs 1.30 and 1.31 above) undertook detailed research into enforcement policies in relation to Food Safety and produced enforcement policy guidelines in February 1994, the wisdom of which could be translated to other matters which are not covered by these guidelines ("Guidance on Food Safety Enforcement Policies"). Notably, however, LACOTS has not recommended such widespread use of its carefully formulated approach to other types of enforcement, although it is respectfully suggested that its role in monitoring the uniformity of enforcement may result in further consideration of this, particularly in the light of the Enforcement Concordat which has set out principles which are intended to supplement or replace the enforcement policies of individual councils (see paragraphs 2.9 and 2.10 above for details of the Enforcement Concordat).

2.13 Policy considerations. Some considerations from the Food Safety Guidance are set out below, not least, it is submitted, as a suggestion of "best practice" in both food and in other cases where an analogy can safely be drawn.

2.14 Food safety guidance: a documented policy. LACOTS recommended that each local authority should have a written policy document specifying the authority's objectives in relation to food law enforcement, committing support to the Codes of Practice issued under section 40 of the Food Safety Act 1990 and directing that all enforcement action be primarily based upon an assessment of risk to public health. Risk assessment has now become mandatory under the Food Safety (General Food Hygiene) Regulations 1995 and in some other areas had already become a feature of health and safety and environmental safety policy (for an example of the last mentioned, see the Environmental Protection Act 1990, s.108). Officers should be trained in the enforcement policy and any departure from the policy must be exceptional and capable of justification. It should be considered fully by local managers if there is to be a departure from the policy. LACOTS did not specify that the written policy document must be made public, although in practice a copy of an enforcement policy will usually be provided if requested. In any case of reluctance, strength might in due course be added to a prospective defendant's arm in requiring the document by Schedule 1 of the Deregulation and Contracting Out Act 1994 (see paragraph 1.11 above). Also, see *R. v. Bromley Magistrates Court, ex p. Smith and Wilkins* (1994) 159 J.P. 251 and discussion at paragraphs 10.59 and 10.60 below). LACOTS set out that the policy should make clear:

(i) who is authorised to prosecute (see paragraphs 2.31 to 2.40 below);

(ii) who has to be consulted before a decision is made;

(iii) the limits of any delegation.

LACOTS also recommended that each local authority ensures that the decision-maker is properly qualified.

2.15 Food safety guidance: choices for action. These are:

(i) to take no action;

(ii) to take informal action;

(iii) to use statutory notices (see Chapter 4 below);

(iv) to take civil proceedings (such as for an injunction, see Chapter 5 below);

(v) to use formal cautions;

(iv) to prosecute.

LACOTS stressed the importance of discussions between the local authority considering prosecution and any other authority which takes a different view, or, where there is a Home Authority which takes a different view, with the Home Authority (for the meaning and significance of the Home Authority see paragraph 1.31 above). While many companies try to ensure that their due diligence procedures are approved by the Home Authority, LACOTS made it clear that this is not justification for ignoring the enforcing authority. If enforcement action impacts upon aspects of an enterprises' policy which has been agreed by a Home Authority (see paragraph 1.31 above), however, reference to the Home Authority before taking action was described as "essential". Indeed, in some cases, defendants have called a representative of the Home Authority as a witness of fact and opinion in the course of a prosecution by another authority, and where the Home Authority has approved a trader's procedures, that fact is frequently referred to by defendants in evidence in support of a due diligence defence.

2.16   Food safety guidance: informal action.   The policy document should make clear when informal action should be taken. The circumstances may include:

   (i) where the act or omission is not sufficiently serious to justify formal action;

  (ii) where the trader's past history leads to the expectation that informal action will achieve compliance;

 (iii) where confidence in the trader's management is high;

  (iv) where the consequences of non-compliance will not pose a significant risk to public health;

   (v) where informal action is otherwise more appropriate (such as where the trader is a voluntary organisation staffed by volunteers: a W.R.V.S. refreshment stall might be a good example).

On the basis of these criteria, one might expect that the major retailers (by way of an example) would rarely be prosecuted. Not so. It may be that local authorities take the view that those best equipped to do better in terms of food safety deserve to be confronted with their failures by prosecution in circumstances where another, smaller and less influential outfit would be treated more leniently by the enforcement authority, perhaps with informal action.

Informal action may include the offering of advice, warnings, requests for action, letters or food hygiene inspection reports. LACOTS drew attention to the need to distinguish between good hygiene practice and legal requirements.

The possibility of taking informal action, of course, extends not only to the area of food safety but to other areas of regulatory enforcement.

2.17   Food safety guidance: statutory notices.   A statutory notice can only be served where the legislation to be enforced has the machinery for service and enforcement of notices. Such machinery exists not only in the case of food, but also for the control of pollution, health and safety and other areas. The power to deal with enforcement problems in this way is far from universal, however. For more detailed discussion of the law relating to notices, see Chapter 4 below. In the case of food safety:

Improvement Notices

These are notices which require improvements to food safety systems or food premises to be made within a period and are subject to appeal – see paragraphs 4.12 onwards below. LACOTS recommended that the following criteria govern a decision to serve an improvement notice:

(a) where there are significant contraventions of legislation;

(b) if there is a lack of confidence in the proprietor;

(c) if there is a history of non-compliance with informal action;

(d) where standards are generally poor with little management awareness of statutory requirements;

(e) where non-compliance could have serious implications for public health;

(f) if action needs to be taken immediately.

In the food safety sphere, the Deregulation (Improvement of Enforcement Procedures) (Food Safety Act 1990) Order 1996 has provided that written notice of consideration of an improvement notice must be given so that the food proprietor has an opportunity to make written or oral representations to the local authority. The Order provides that those representations must be considered.

Emergency Prohibition Notices

These provide for an immediate cessation of the specified activity. They should be issued:

(a) where the consequences for public health would be unacceptable were immediate and decisive action not to be taken;

(b) where an imminent risk to public health can be demonstrated;

(c) if the Guidance Criteria in the Code of Practice are fulfilled;

(d) where there is no confidence in an unprompted offer by a proprietor to close premises or stop using equipment, etc;

(e) if the proprietor is unwilling to make such an offer or will not confirm it in writing.

Special care must be taken in relation to the issue of emergency prohibition notices because of the risk that compensation may be payable in the event that the notice was not justified (Food Safety Act 1990, s.12(10)).

2.18 **Food safety guidance: cautions.** A formal caution in accordance with Home Office Circular 18/1994 can be an alternative to prosecution. Although it is not a conviction, it can be cited in court should it become relevant on a subsequent occasion – say – for the purpose of sentencing. The purpose of a caution is to deal quickly with less serious offences outside the courts and to reduce the chances of repeated offences. Before a caution is administered there must be sufficient evidence that the offence has been committed sufficient to give a realistic prospect of conviction, and the suspected offender must admit the offence. The offender must also give informed consent to being cautioned. A "cautioning officer" who is authorised to issue formal cautions must be authorised by the local authority. The policy document should set out who is to be informed of the caution (such as the Home Authority). If the accused does not admit the offence or agree to be cautioned it may be appropriate to take no action rather than immediately proceed to prosecution: prosecution is not a sanction for non-co-operation with the cautioning procedure.

2.19 Food safety guidance: injunctions. The Guidance on Food Safety Enforcement Policies did not cover the need to seek injunctions, which procedure has been adopted by local authorities to prevent future illegality, particularly in the past in the field of Sunday trading (see paragraphs 5.1 to 5.11 below).

2.20 Food safety guidance: prosecution. The circumstances in which prosecution may be pursued are:

(i)   where there has been such a flagrant breach of the law that the health, safety or well-being of consumers has been put at risk;

(ii)   where the suspected offender has failed to correct a serious identified risk, having been given a reasonable opportunity to comply with the lawful requirements of an authorised officer;

(iii)   where the offence involves a failure to comply (fully or partly) with a statutory notice;

(iv)   where there is a history of similar offences related to a risk to public health.

LACOTS, as with the Code for Crown Prosecutors, made clear that the decision-maker must be satisfied that there is relevant, admissible, substantial and reliable evidence that an offence has been committed by an identifiable person, and moreover, that the public interest provisions of the Code for Crown Prosecutors are referred to, as well, of course, as the Code of Practice under section 40 of the Food Safety Act 1990. Interestingly, LACOTS advised that suspected offenders should always be offered an opportunity to put forward an explanation before a prosecution decision is taken, a proposal adopted by the Enforcement Concordat, which envisages that the explanation may be put forward otherwise by way of interview under caution.

2.21 Prosecutions in practice. In practice, some authorities do adopt an approach to prosecution of other regulatory offences which is broadly based on these guidelines although some authorities will prosecute purely on the basis of a perceived expectation of conviction which, amongst other advantages to the local authority, gives a chance of recovery of all or part of the investigation costs (see paragraphs 13.4 to 13.6 below). It is submitted that many prosecutions are pursued which do not satisfy the seriousness of the criteria envisaged by LACOTS here.

2.22 The defendant's explanation. The opportunity to be afforded to prospective defendants to offer an explanation for an offence has until latterly usually arisen only in the interview under caution (see paragraph 3.27 onwards). Prosecuting authorities have often been reluctant to conduct "without prejudice" discussions, although this sometimes occurred. The reason for this reluctance is said to be that any information obtained otherwise than under caution may be inadmissible at trial if a satisfactory explanation is not given by the prospective defendant. It is at least possible that this line of approach increased the number of prosecutions brought for regulatory offences, because local authorities found it necessary to pursue the prosecution in the light of a denial of guilt in the interview. This is a failing, because two different functions are performed by an interview under caution and without prejudice discussions. An interview under caution is inevitably part of the process for collecting evidence for the purpose of proceedings, and both questions and answers are tailored accordingly: a "without prejudice" meeting can be used to determine an outcome other than prosecution without the need for either side to put their rival contentions to the other. The unwillingness to participate in meetings to "sort out" difficulties which have arisen probably reflects also the pressure on local authority time. Unlike traders, who, when faced with prosecution are willing to devote a significant amount of time and resources to pursuing a favourable outcome, officers of local authorities are constrained by a more limited timetable and budget, in which an individual prosecution may be one of several on-going issues. Accordingly, there has often been a reluctance to approach any individual prosecution in an unorthodox fashion. Such an approach is now de rigueur, however, for any local authority which adopts the Enforcement Concordat.

2.23 Judicial challenges to the decision. Judicial review is the only direct judicial avenue of complaint about the decision to prosecute, although it is clear that the matter might be raised as an abuse of process in the event of prosecution, such that, if the argument succeeds, the proceedings may be stayed. It might have been expected, following the decision in *Bennett* (see paragraphs 10.30 and 10.31 below) that the appropriate way of challenging this decision would be limited to applications for leave to apply for judicial review – as an abuse of power – rather than by way of raising an allegation of an abuse of process. Nevertheless, in *Bennett*, no criticism was made of the earlier case of *R. v. Croydon Justices, ex p. Dean* [1993] 3 All E.R. 129, in which the Court held that the Crown Court could investigate and stay proceedings as an abuse of process where the CPS decided to proceed with the prosecution of an individual, notwithstanding an earlier promise that he would not be prosecuted and on the basis of which promise he had altered his position. Moreover, subsequent cases have underlined the importance of the principle (see paragraph 10.37 below). In *R. v. Inland Revenue Commissioners, ex p. Mead* [1993] 1 All E.R. 772, similarly, the Divisional Court, in upholding the power to challenge a decision to prosecute by way of judicial review, also referred to the alternative remedies available in the Crown Court, such as the power to stay proceedings as an abuse of process. For further discussion of abuse of process, see paragraphs 10.26 onwards, below.

If any appeal process is to be implemented in future legislation pursuant to section 6 of the Deregulation and Contracting Out Act 1994 against enforcement action and if it should apply to the decision to prosecute, the monitoring of local authority decision-making will move into the quasi-judicial, administrative sphere. So, too, the range of matters which could be taken into account on review of the decision may be expanded (see paragraph 1.11 above).

2.24 Delegation. It is not permissible to delegate the decision to prosecute to an interested party. Not only might that be outside the powers granted to the prosecuting body, it might also be an abuse of the process of the court (see paragraph 10.36 below). It is the decision to prosecute which is important, however. The mere giving of help by an interested party in the conduct of investigations is quite lawful, and the decision to prosecute which is taken independently by the prosecuting authority on the basis of such evidence cannot be impugned. In *R. v. Milton Keynes Magistrates Court, ex p. Roberts* [1995] Crim.L.R. 224 this distinction was drawn. It was held to be no abuse of process where a manufacturer of motor spares had co-operated in the investigation of an offence involving the sale of counterfeit motor spares by providing resources and assistance. The decision to prosecute had been taken by the Trading Standards Officer independently.

LOCAL AUTHORITIES AS PROSECUTORS

2.25   **General.** The vast majority of regulatory offences are prosecuted by local authorities following investigation by trading standards officers or environmental health officers operating within their department of local government, which might be called a trading standards or consumer protection department, but equally might bear another name or be amalgamated with another responsibility. A substantial number of offences are prosecuted by the weights and measures authority which must employ at least one inspector of weights and measures (a trading standards officer: "T.S.O."). The prosecution will then be commenced, following:

(i)   a decision to prosecute (see paragraphs 2.28 to 2.35 above) taken by a person authorised by the local authority to make the decision,

(ii)   the laying of the information by a person authorised to commence proceedings on behalf of the local authority (see paragraphs 2.36 to 2.40 below).

The organisation and powers of local authorities

2.26   **Constitution.** Local authorities are corporations, although it is the council and not the corporation which is the local authority for the purposes of the Local Government Act 1972 as amended (*Hazell v. Hammersmith & Fulham London Borough* [1992] 2 A.C. 1). There are different categories of council, with differing functions. Principal councils include the metropolitan and non-metropolitan counties, metropolitan and non-metropolitan district councils and London Borough Councils in England and counties and County Boroughs in Wales (section 270) as well as (for some purposes) joint authorities, a joint board or joint committee discharging the functions of two or more councils and certain other bodies (section 101 J). In addition, the new unitary authorities have begun operation in England and Wales. In order to promote the principles of competition and publicity and to make government more effective and economical, the Local Government Act 1992 enabled structural reform of local government. This has enabled the creation of new unitary authorities in the "shire counties" (non-metropolitan counties) where they have been found by the Local Government Commission to be appropriate. The perceived benefits of such changes include greater identification with the localities served by the authorities, that responsibilities for services cannot be confused and that the overlapping of activities between tiers of local government be dispensed with. Where they have been created, the new unitary authorities are created by order following report and recommendations by the Local Government Commission. A parish or community council is not a principal authority and different rules of procedure and regulation apply to these. All councils are creatures of statute which (apart from joint authorities, committees and boards and those with special functions such as fire) consist of elected members. Committees to deal with various aspects of local authority functions are appointed. These are mandatory in respect of certain matters, such as education or social services, but are appointed as a matter of convenience in relation to other functions, such as planning and works, health, housing, etc. They need not consist wholly of members, but can include co-opted members (usually employees). Co-opted members must not exceed one third of the membership of the committee (section 102 of the 1972 Act). Answerable to committees, usually, are sub-committees, which can consist wholly or mainly of employees, and thereafter chief officers (employees), deputy chief officers, with some other tiers of employees. Parish and community councils frequently operate with only a clerk to assist the councillors.

2.27   Local authority decisions.   Section 101(1) of the Local Government Act 1972 provides that subject to express statutory provision in the 1972 Act or subsequent legislation, local authorities specified under the 1972 Act may arrange for the discharge of any of their functions by:

    (i)   a committee

   (ii)   a sub-committee

  (iii)   an officer of the authority.

Moreover, a committee to whom a function is entrusted may, unless the local authority otherwise directs, arrange for the discharge of its functions by a sub-committee or an officer and, where the functions may be exercised by a sub-committee, the sub-committee may arrange for the discharge of its functions by an officer unless the local authority or committee otherwise directs (section 101(2)). Additionally, a local authority may arrange for the discharge of its functions by another local authority or jointly with it.

These provisions have the effect of making lawful actions taken by an individual, sub-committee or committee acting on behalf of the Council, provided that their authorisation is derived properly from the council itself in accordance with the preceding sub-section. It should be noted that the delegation of decisions to sub-committees and officers is permitted unless the contrary is expressed, but this contrasts with the position affecting an individual council member who cannot lawfully act alone on behalf of the Council: delegation to an "officer" does not include delegation to a member of the Council and delegation to a committee cannot mean delegation to one person acting alone (*R. v. Secretary of State for the Environment, ex p. Hillingdon London Borough Council* [1986] 1 W.L.R. 192 and 807, CA). The powers to appoint committees are to be found at section 102 of the 1972 Act and must be exercised formally by resolution or the Council will not be bound (*Western Fish Products Ltd v. Penwith District Council* [1981] 2 All E.R. 204 at 219g).

The decision to prosecute

2.28   Ultra vires.   The local authority must act within the powers which are given expressly or impliedly by statute, both when performing its executive functions and when engaging in litigation. Acts undertaken by a local authority in excess of its powers are *ultra vires* and void. This means in general terms that a local authority:

    (i)   must not undertake activities which are beyond the scope of its proper functions including its subsidiary powers under section 111 of the Act (*R. v. Hammersmith & Fulham London Borough Council, ex p. Beddowes* [1987] Q.B. 1050; *Hazell v. Hammersmith and Fulham London Borough*

Council [1992] A.C. 1; *McCarthy & Stone (Developments) Ltd v. Richmond upon Thames* [1992] 2 A.C. 48);

(ii) must act in good faith and for the purposes for which the power was conferred (*Westminster Bank Limited v. Minister of Housing and Local Government* [1971] A.C. 508; *H. Lavender & Son v. Minister of Housing and Local Government* [1970] 1 W.L.R. 1231);

(iii) must take into account all relevant matters and not take into account irrelevant matters (*Associated Picture Houses Ltd v. Wednesbury Corporation* [1948] 1 K.B. 223; *Secretary of State for Education and Science v. Tameside Metropolitan Borough Council* [1977] A.C. 1014);

(iv) must not be so unreasonable that its decision could not be reached by any reasonable body (*Wednesbury* (above));

(v) must not act under the direction of any other body in the exercise of its functions, nor must it delegate its authority in the absence of express or implied authority to do so;

(vi) must observe the rules of natural justice and act fairly in the making of decisions. It does not follow from this that a local authority will always be required to permit an oral hearing, nor allow the making of representations, nor to give reasons for its decision (*Windsor Securities Ltd v. Liverpool City Council* (1978) 129 N.L.J. 117, CA) but where the local authority is so required, it must do so. The more akin the matter before the Council to a disciplinary decision or decision affecting a person's status, the greater the requirements imposed by questions of procedural fairness (see, for example, *R. v. Liverpool Corporation ex p. Liverpool Taxi Fleet Operators Association* [1972] 2 Q.B. 299);

(vii) must not fetter its own discretion (*R. v. Chief Constable of Devon and Cornwall, ex p. Central Electricity Generating Board* [1982] Q.B. 458).

2.29   Challenges to the exercise of powers by a local authority.   Activities of local authorities are challenged by judicial review or by statutory audit under the Local Government Finance Act 1982. If an auditor is persuaded that any item of account may be contrary to law, he may apply to the court for a declaration to that effect unless the expenditure has been sanctioned by the Secretary of State. The court's power of enquiry permits investigation of the merits of a case so that the court can reach its own conclusion (*Lloyd v. McMahon* [1987] 1 All E.R. 1118). If the court makes the declaration, it may also order repayment by the person concerned, rectification of accounts and in some cases disqualification of the persons concerned from being members of the Council. This draconian sanction is sometimes invoked or threatened as a means of discouraging or challenge to a perceived unfairness or an improperly taken decision. Also see paragraph 2.46 below.

2.30   Ultra vires as a defence to proceedings taken by a council.   As a broad proposition, if steps are taken by a Council which exceed the powers bestowed on the council, those proceedings will be *ultra vires* and void. Where proceedings are taken apparently on behalf of a local authority as a consequence of the actions of an individual within the Council, the authority of the individual to bind the Council is frequently investigated. As a simple proposition, if the individual had no authority to act, his actions will be *ultra vires* and any proceedings based upon those actions will not bind the Council. Unless the individual can take the proceedings in question in his individual capacity, the proceedings will be void. It is arguable that if the individual could have taken the same proceedings in his private capacity, this will not affect their validity, although it may have consequences as to costs (see paragraph 2.40 below).

2.31   Authority to act.   An investigation of the authority of an individual to undertake any act on behalf of the Council may focus both on the authorisation which would have been known about at the time of his action and also on any subsequent act capable of validating a previous unauthorised act retrospectively. Authorisation before the event can be determined by inspection and interpretation of relevant records and hearing evidence. Authorisation after the event is more difficult. It is sometimes said that a void act of a local authority cannot be ratified. Insofar as there can be retrospective authorisation, this is clearly relevant in the case of the taking of a decision to prosecute, and may be relevant when considering the commencement of proceedings. Clearly, if the prosecution is not authorised at the time of trial it can never be treated by the court as proceedings taken by the Council.

2.32   Ratification.   In *Warwick Rural District Council v. Miller-Mead* [1962] Ch. 441 civil action had been taken against a caravan site owner under section 100 of the Public Health Act 1936 by the solicitors to the local authority without their formal authorisation. Subsequently, the local authority recorded its opinion that action should be taken. It was argued that the proceedings were invalid, because they had not been authorised at the point of their commencement. The Court of Appeal took the view that section 100 should not be construed so strictly as to require the opinion of the authority to have been recorded prior to the issue of civil proceedings, rather than at some point before the matter came to an effective stage before the court. The same issue arose in *Poppett's (Caterers) v. Maidenhead Borough Council* [1971] 1 W.L.R. 69.

2.33   Ratification or renewal.   Although the decision in *Miller-Mead* (above) spoke of ratification of the earlier decision, it remains uncertain whether an earlier decision can be ratified, or whether the correct view is that a subsequent decision can found the jurisdiction. If the latter position is correct, there can presumably be no ratification if a critical point in time has been reached prior to that subsequent decision. *Miller-Mead* distinguished the earlier decisions of *St. Leonard's Vestry v. Holmes* (1885) 50 J.P. 132 and *Bowyer, Philpott & Payne Ltd v. Mather* [1919] 1 K.B. 149 where it had been held that prior authorisation was necessary before an officer could commence proceedings, because of the interpretation placed on section 100. *Miller-Mead* was applied in *Stoke-on-Trent City Council v. B&Q Retail Ltd* [1984] Ch. 1 where the Council issued proceedings for an injunction to stop unlawful Sunday trading. The Council relied upon section 222 of the Local Government Act 1972 (see paragraph 2.37 below) as authority for the proposition that the proceedings could be commenced directly and without the consent of the Attorney General as a relator action. The court held that the Council was entitled to rely upon this section, provided that they had complied with its statutory requirements, namely that they had to have considered whether the commencement of proceedings was expedient for the promotion or protection of the interests of inhabitants in their area. The committee of the Council which had occasioned the institution of proceedings had not addressed this consideration at all. Subsequently, the policy committee of the Council had. This was said to have been a sufficient decision on which to justify the Council's conduct. Also see *R. v. Southwark London Borough Council ex p. Bannerman* [1990] C.O.D. 115. Rose J. in *R. v. Rochester-upon-Medway County Council ex p. Hobday* (1989) 58 P. & C.R. 424, declined to regard an *ultra vires* decision as capable of ratification. Instead he interpreted a decision which upheld the earlier action of the officer as a fresh determination of the issue. This approach cannot apply, however, where the action of the officer has had immediate effect (*Webb v. Ipswich Borough Council* (1989) 21 H.L.R. 325; *Attorney General ex rel. Co-op Retail Services v. Taff-Ely Borough Council* (1982) 42 P. & C.R. 1).

2.34 Do the same considerations apply to the decision to prosecute and steps taken to commence proceedings?. In the case of a prosecution, there are three relevant stages when the authority of the individual, sub-committee or committee purporting to act on behalf of the Council may be the subject of challenge. The first is the time when the decision to prosecute is taken. The second is when the proceedings are in fact commenced. The third is at trial. At all points, action purportedly taken on behalf of the Council should be authorised. It is yet to be decided whether the unauthorised initiation of criminal proceedings can be ratified. If there is a challenge to the legitimacy of the prosecution, it appears that any decision to approve the unlawful proceedings (whether that be a ratification or otherwise: see below) must at least have been taken before the challenge to the lawfulness of the proceedings is made, and it is arguable that it must have been before the prosecution was commenced.

2.35 Delegating the decision to enforce to council employees. In the case of a regulatory offence the investigation will have been carried out by an officer of the Council. Quite how the decision as to enforcement is then to be taken varies from authority to authority. It is very common for the Council to have delegated the taking of a decision to enforce statutory provisions to a committee or sub-committee or an individual officer, either because the power has been expressly delegated by a resolution or in Standing Orders or by resolution or because section 101 operates to permit delegation where the contrary is not expressed. This can involve an investigation and interpretation of the resolutions, minutes, Standing orders and other documents of the Council to see how the authority of the decision-maker is derived. Some pertinent considerations are:

(i) Not all categories of decision are delegated in the same way. Standing orders which, say, grant the power to act and investigate do not necessarily include the power to decide to commence legal proceedings unless the Standing Orders specify such, or unless they are capable of being interpreted in that way. So, authority to delegate powers will not necessarily be interpreted as a power to delegate duties (*Mungoni v. A.G. of Northern Rhodesia* [1960] A.C. 336). On the other hand, in *James v. Stein* (1946) 110 J.P. 279, a resolution under section 223 of the Local Government Act 1972 (see paragraph 2.38 below) that an employee should be authorised to:

"act as an officer within the said county for the carrying out . . . of the Food Act . . ., or any Act extending or amending the same or incorporated therewith, or any orders made thereunder, and to prosecute before a court of summary jurisdiction or justices any information, complaint of proceedings arising under the same discharge of his duties"

also included a delegation of the exercise of a discretion as to whom he should prosecute.

(ii) It is important to be sure that a delegation has truly occurred. If a matter stands "referred" to a committee or an individual, this may be a contrary intention for the purposes of section 101 and not a delegation at all. If that expression is used, it is likely that decisions taken or recommended by the referee are not valid unless they have been approved by the referrer, whether that be the local authority, a committee or sub-committee (*Goddard v. Ministry of Housing and Local Government* [1958] 3 All E.R. 482).

(iii) It is important to consider the powers of the delegate. It sometimes occurs that the standing orders or a Council resolution purports to give authority to the delegate further to delegate the decision. This can only be lawful if it is authorised by statute. Section 101 says nothing which indicates that a power to sub-delegate may be granted. There is a strong presumption against there being a power of sub-delegation (*Ratnagopal v. Attorney General* [1970] A.C. 974 PC), particularly in respect of a decision to which the delegate should address his own mind – such as a disciplinary or judicial power. On the other hand, where it would be impracticable for all the powers and duties conferred upon a named person to be carried out by him, then it will readily be implied in the case of administrative functions that he may sub-delegate (*Provident Mutual Life Assurance Association v. Derby City Council* [1981] 1 W.L.R. 173, HL). A decision to prosecute, however, is not an administrative function but a function of a quasi-judicial character.

The question of delegation arose for consideration in *Hilliers Ltd v. Sefton Metropolitan Borough Council* (unreported, DC, November 29, 1996). The case concerned a pork pie containing a metal bolt. The decision to prosecute appeared to have been taken by a Mr Hutchings, who was a deputy chief officer. The Standing Orders delegated the decision to the chief officer of one department, but also permitted him to delegate in certain circumstances. It was argued that section 101 of the Local Government Act 1972 did not permit the sub-delegation of functions by a person to whom the function was delegated. The Divisional Court concluded that sub-delegation was permissible under the Standing Orders and observed that evidence could have been called from the Council to address the issue as to delegation of functions. The problem was identified not so much as a question of the interpretation of section 101, but as a matter of private arrangement within the respondent Council to determine whether the powers could be sub-delegated by an officer of the Council. Schiemann J. accepted that the Council could have nominated the deputy chief officer directly, and commented:

"Once one says that the Council could have decided to name everybody on its staff for the discharge of its functions it seems to me that it can say 'we leave it to the head of department to nominate whomsoever he pleases' ".

It is submitted that this is a false premise. The Council could not have nominated every member of its staff to discharge its functions – at least – not without *Wednesbury* unreasonableness (see paragraph 2.28 above). If that premise is not adopted, the asserted lawfulness of the sub-delegation is less compelling. It is difficult to see why section 101 needed expressly to address the questions of sub-delegation if the powers already exist by way of private arrangement within the council. Also on this subject is *Fitzpatrick v. Secretary of State for the Environment* (1988) unreported, in which the District Secretary had been instructed by resolution to issue enforcement notices under the Town and Country Planning Act 1971. The notices were prepared by a member of his staff who endorsed them with a facsimile of the District Secretary's signature. The Divisional Court upheld their validity.

(iv) there should be a record of the decision made. If the decision is made by a committee or sub-committee, minutes will normally have been taken. If the decision has been made by an officer, there may be a record book. In *Hilliers* (above) a further point was taken on the validity of the decision to prosecute because the record of prosecutions showed the name and address of the company secretary of the defendant, and not the defendant. Although this was an objection which was not successful, the case demonstrates the need for care by Council staff in the completion of records on this subject.

Authority to initiate proceedings

2.36 Commencing proceedings. As with an enforcement decision, the initiation of proceedings on behalf of a local authority by laying the information (see paragraph 8.4 below) must be an authorised act. To be lawful, the local authority must be empowered to prosecute and the individual must be authorised to prosecute on their behalf.

2.37 Section 222. Although certain statutory provisions make express reference to the power to commence proceedings, the general power of a local authority to prosecute is found within section 222 of the Local Government Act 1972. This provides, inter alia, that where a local authority considers it expedient for the promotion or protection of the interests of inhabitants of their area, it may prosecute or appear in legal proceedings in its own name. In *R. v. Jarrett and Steward* [1997] Crim. L.R. 517, the Court of Appeal made clear that the powers of a local authority were not limited to the regulatory powers it might possess, so that a local authority was entitled to prosecute for conspiracy to defraud. The powers under this section extend even to civil proceedings for an injunction which would, in the absence of this provision, need to be commenced in the name of the Attorney General (*Solihull Metropolitan Borough Council v. Maxfern Ltd* [1977] 2 All E.R. 177 and see Chapter 5 below).

2.38 Section 223. Section 223 of the Local Government Act 1972 provides that where a person is authorised by an authority to prosecute or defend in proceedings, he may appear in those proceedings, and conduct them, even though he is not a solicitor holding a practising certificate. This gives the right (to an officer only and not to a third party: *Oberst v. Coombs* (1955) 53 L.G.R. 316) not only to lay the information but also to appear on behalf of the local authority as a prosecutor in the same case. He does not have to do both (*R. v. Northumberland Justices, ex p. Thompson* (1923) J.P. 95). The considerations as to whether an officer is in fact authorised to commence proceedings are similar to those relating to the decision to prosecute. Where authorisation is necessary however, it must be formally proved by production of the resolution, if in issue. It is not enough merely to rely upon the officer's appointment or position (*Bob Keats Ltd v. Farrant* [1951] 1 All E.R. 899). On the other hand, production of the authorisation is not a condition precedent to the prosecution (*Campbell v. Wallsend Slipway and Engineering Co. Ltd* [1978] I.C.R. 1015).

2.39 Can the prosecution be authorised after the commencement of proceedings? In the case of the commencement of proceedings, if at the time the information was laid, the person laying the information had no authority to act, it is difficult to see how this can subsequently be validated. It is submitted that the commencement of proceedings is a matter which takes immediate effect (see paragraph 2.33 above). If the commencement of proceedings is a nullity, it cannot subsequently be cured. The relevant question is whether the commencement of proceedings by an unauthorised person is truly a nullity.

2.40 Consequences of a want of authority to commence or continue proceedings. If the officer is not authorised to commence proceedings but nevertheless does so, purportedly on behalf of the Council, the validity of the proceedings may depend upon whether the individual could have brought proceedings in his own capacity. A number of authorities have suggested that the want of entitlement to prosecute can be raised as a defence, and, if it is raised, the validity of the prosecution is a matter which the prosecution must prove (failure to do so will entitle the justices to find that there is no case to answer: *Anderton v. Frost* [1984] R.T.R. 106). On the other hand, this issue was addressed in *MFI Furniture Centre Ltd v. Hibbert* (1995) 160 J.P. 178. The Minutes of Delegation were difficult to construe, and it was far from clear that the power to prosecute an offence under section 20 of the Consumer Protection Act 1987 had been delegated to the person laying the information. The Divisional Court, construing the document in favour of the Council, also considered the possibility that they might have been wrong in that construction. Balcombe L.J. observed that Part III of the Consumer Protection Act 1987 did not limit the power of prosecution to the weights and measures authority. He said:

> "The fact that, on this hypothesis, he may have been mistaken in his belief that he had power to prosecute on behalf of the Council, cannot alter the fact that he, as an individual, did lay the informations which led to the issue of the summonses, and thereafter continued the prosecution. His authority to do so on behalf of the Council was irrelevant to the validity of the proceedings, although it might have been relevant on the question of costs, had the prosecution failed."

Collins J. added the sentiment that it was "unnecessary and undesirable for the criminal court to have to investigate whether there is proper authority to act", but distinguished the position where to act without authority might be an abuse of the process of the court, such as where a person who knew he had no authority tried to lay an information and so mislead the court. He referred to the obligation on the justices clerk to check when the information is laid that there is apparent authority to lay it (*Price v. Humphries* (1958) 122 J.P. 423 – and see paragraph 8.29 below). Presumably the same considerations apply to conducting the hearing. Also see paragraph 2.3 above for the position where the proceedings must be instituted by a specific person. Institution of proceedings by the wrong person will, in that context, be fatal to the prosecution.

Trading Standards Officers

2.41 Weights and measures. Modern trading standards officers have their origins in the inspectorate of weights and measures, although they now exercise a substantial number of other functions cast upon them both as officers of the local authority and also because the role of the weights and measures authority has been enlarged to embrace enforcement of other areas (see paragraph 2.2 above). The Director General of Fair Trading, said when announcing the winners of the Excellence in Trading Standards Award 1997:

> "Trading standards officers are responsible for enforcing 50 pieces of legislation which protect the public, yet their efforts often go unappreciated. The service is often seen as the Cinderella of local government when in fact it is the front line".

2.42 Weights and measures authorities. Section 69 of the Weights and Measures Act 1985 (the modern successor of earlier legislation) designates the local weights and measures authority in England as the Council of each non-metropolitan county, metropolitan district or London Borough, the Common Council of the City of London (which includes the Temples) and the Council of the Isles of Scilly. In Wales the local weights and measures authority is the County Council or County Borough Council. In Scotland the authority is the council constituted under section 2 of the Local Government, etc., (Scotland) Act 1994 as the council for the area. These weights and measures authorities may also have jurisdiction over inland and territorial waters if the Secretary of State has made an order to such effect (section 69(4)). As well as enforcement powers, local weights and measures authorities are empowered expressly to provide and arrange for the provision of advice for the benefit of consumers (section 69(5)).

2.43 Local government reorganisation. The Local Government Act 1992 gave to the Local Government Commission power to make recommendations as to structural changes, and section 17 of the 1992 Act provides power in the Secretary of State to implement changes, which has resulted in the introduction in some areas of new unitary authorities. Although such new authorities do not correspond with the local weights and measures authorities designated under section 69 of the Weights and Measures Act 1985, the Secretary of State has a power to make regulations and govern special functions, such as weights and measures and also to provide that joint authorities may jointly provide specified functions. This latter power supplements the powers already existing under section 101 of the Local Government Act 1972 to combine forces to carry out specific functions.

2.44 Organisation of a weights and measures authority. Although the weights and measures authority is the council of a local authority, and not its officers, the operation of a weights and measures authority is not purely a matter for the local authority to administer. The Weights and Measures Act 1985 provides both for supervision of its functions by central government and also specifies in part the organisation of the authority itself.

Report and Inspection

Each local weights and measures authority must in relation to each year report to the Secretary of State for Trade and Industry as to the arrangements for giving effect to the purposes of the 1985 Act and the other weights and measures functions which have been specified by the Secretary of State (section 70). Additionally, the Secretary of State is empowered through an appointed officer to carry out inspections from time to time of each weights and measures authority and the results are contained in a written report which is sent to the Secretary of State, the weights and measures authority and the chief inspector of weights and measures (section 71). There is no current provision for local inquiries as a result of complaints, but allegations of maladministration may be investigated by the Commissioners for Local Administration under Part III of the Local Government Act 1974.

Inspectors of Weights and Measures

(Trading Standards Officers (T.S.O.s))

Appointment

Section 72 of the Act provides that each local weights and measures authority shall appoint:

(a) a chief inspector of weights and measures and

(b) other inspectors of weights and measures as is necessary for "the efficient discharge in the authority's area of the functions conferred or imposed on the inspectors under the Act".

The Chief Inspectors are responsible to the local weights and measures authority for the custody and maintenance of local standards, testing and stamping equipment, and for the operation of the arrangements to give effect to the purposes of the Act. Both the Chief Inspector and his subordinates must be qualified. The purpose of these provisions seems to be that the lines of management within weights and measures (trading standards) departments should be clearly defined. What is less clear is whether the Chief Inspector of Weights and Measures should be a chief officer of the local authority reporting directly to the Council or to a Committee, or whether he should have a more sub-ordinate role. In many local authorities, the Chief Inspector of Weights and Measures reports to another officer who in turn reports to an established committee of the local authority. It is frequently perceived that this is unsatisfactory. The editor of O'Keefe's Weights and Measures (Butterworths) comments:

"In the context of local government the weights and measures function is unique in that it provides for an essential element in the social and commercial infrastructure of the area; it imposes statutory responsibilities directly on officers of the authority rather than the authority itself; the officers must perform their duties on pain of criminal liability and they must have a certificate of qualification".

Qualifications

Initially qualifying examinations for prospective inspectors of weights and measures were held by the Secretary of State. Since 1980 this function has been taken over by the Diploma in Trading Standards Council, which offers the qualification known as a Diploma in Trading Standards. This is now the recognised certificate of qualification as an inspector. The Diploma in Trading Standards Council which operates under the auspices of the Local Government Training Board includes members drawn from various local authority associations, the Institute of Trading Standards Administration and the Department of Trade. The Department of Trade is responsible for testing the candidates in the practical and oral test of the weights and measures sections of the examination. The enlargement of the scope of the qualification is a recognition of the very many more functions that the weights and measures inspector is required to perform than those which arise under the 1985 Act. An alternative qualification, offered by the Institute of Trading Standards Administration for local authority employees who do not wish to be weights and measures inspectors but who can carry out other trading standards functions is the Diploma in Consumer Affairs.

Offences

An inspector of weights and measures may be guilty of a criminal offence if he knowingly commits a breach of duty under the 1985 Act or otherwise misconducts himself in the execution of his office, or if he stamps weighing or measuring equipment in contravention of the Act or its regulations or if he stamps it without testing or if he derives a profit from the making, adjusting or selling of weighing or measuring equipment (section 75). There is also an offence of acting or purporting to act as an inspector of weights and measures by a person who is not an inspector (section 75(2)).

Environmental Health Officers

2.45 **Environmental Health Officers.** Environmental Health Officers are employed by local authorities to deal with a number of the aspects of the activities of a local authority. These include Food control, Health and Safety at Work, Pollution and Environmental Control – all regulatory matters – as well as public housing. Depending on the size and organisation of the local authority, they may work as generalists or in a specialist area, such as food, or pollution. Nearly all Environmental Health Officers are members of the Chartered Institute of Environmental Health. All Environmental Health Officers will have completed a qualification in Environmental Health, usually by way of a degree in Environmental Health on an accredited course. This course will cover science, technology, statistics, social science, public administration and law as well as involving a detailed study of food, occupational health, pollution and housing.

INVESTIGATION OF IMPROPER ENFORCEMENT ACTION WITHIN THE LOCAL AUTHORITY

2.46 **Remedies against improper prosecution.** Some statutes provide for an avenue of complaint to Ministers or other responsible persons. An example is section 6 of the Food Safety Act 1990 which may give an avenue of complaint to Ministers in a proper case to those persons aggrieved by the decision to prosecute with consequential powers for the Minister to intervene by relieving the authority of its responsibilities in a particular area or particular case. If this occurred, clearly it would be capable of causing political embarrassment to the prosecuting authority, but the cases in which this would be likely must be few and far between. A more common avenue of complaint is by way of reference to the public auditor of the local authority, who may, in respect of any expenditure consider whether it is in the public interest to make a special report in the course of or prior to the audit (Local Government Finance Act 1982, section 15(3)). This is then sent to the local authority in question as well as to the Local Government Commission (section 18) and see paragraph 2.29 above. Complaint to the local "Ombudsman" is less likely to be successful. The powers of the Commission for Local Administration are excluded where there is a right of complaint to the court if the person aggrieved has or had a remedy by way of proceedings in law.

CHAPTER 3

Investigating Offences

POWERS AND DUTIES OF ENFORCEMENT OFFICERS

3.1 Statutory powers and the general law. The origin of the powers of an enforcement officer is both in the general law as well as under the enactments giving rise to specific offences. In reviewing the powers of the enforcement officer regard must be had both to the legislation which donates the investigative powers, and also to the modifications or application of the wider, non-regulatory, legal framework.

3.2 PACE Codes. One such wider consideration, and the most important, is the impact of the Codes of Practice made pursuant to the Police and Criminal Evidence Act 1984. By section 67(9) of the 1984 Act it is provided that:

> "persons other than police officers who are charged with the duty of investigating offences or charging offenders shall in the discharge of that duty have regard to any relevant provision of such a code".

The expression "have regard to" has been understood to mean that, where relevant, officers who have a statutory duty to investigate must abide by the Codes of Practice in so far as they can be made to apply. Those who have duties of investigation imposed otherwise than by statute similarly are bound by the Codes. So, it is clear that local authority officials are covered by the provisions of section 67(9) (*Dudley Metropolitan Borough Council v. Debenhams plc* (1994) 159 J.P. 18). Equally it appears that an employee of the Federation against Copyright Theft Ltd may be bound by the codes, as may be a member of the RSPCA (*Joy v. F.A.C.T. Ltd* [1993] Crim.L.R. 588, *Stilgoe v. Eager, The Times,* January 27, 1994). Store detectives and security staff are bound by the code. On the other hand, a prospective private prosecutor who is seeking evidence in a manner which would not be permitted under the Codes, say, by conversation, or by hoping to trap a prospective defendant into making an admission, will not be bound by the provisions of section 67(9) unless his activities are in some way a response to a duty imposed upon him. It should be recalled, however, that even where the Codes do not apply, their provisions may well be relevant to any question of exclusion by reason of unfairness which arises under section 78 of the Police and Criminal Evidence Act 1984 (see paragraph 10.105 below).

3.3   The Codes.   There are 5 codes relating to Stop and Search (Code A), Seizure of Property (Code B), Detention, Treatment and Questioning (Code C), Identification (Code D) and Tape Recording of Interviews (Code E). Of these, Codes B, C and E most frequently have relevance to regulatory offences, although Codes A and D may also apply in respect of the investigation of some offences. Code A, in particular, may have relevance where local authority inspectors require to search a pedlar, market trader's vehicle or investigate conduct at a car boot sale where the question of entry on to premises and search is not an issue.

ENTRY, SEARCH AND SEIZURE

Powers of entry

3.4   The statutory power to enter.   The power to enter onto premises and carry out inspections will arise from the legislation which the inspector is required to enforce. By way of example, a common form is found in Section 79 of the Weights and Measures Act 1985 which provides that:

> "subject to the production if so requested of his credentials, an inspector, within the area for which he was appointed inspector, may at all reasonable times:—

> (a) inspect and test any weighing or measuring equipment which is, or which he has reasonable cause to believe to be, used for trade or in the possession of any person or upon any premises for such use,

> (b) inspect and test goods to which any of the provisions of Part 4 of this Act or any instrument made under that Part for the time being applies or which he has reasonable cause to believe to be such goods and,

> (c) enter any premises at which he has reasonable cause to believe there to be any such equipment or goods, not being premises used only as a private dwelling house."

This provision addresses itself specifically to the obligations of an inspector of weights and measures to inspect goods and instruments. In Section 28 of the Trade Descriptions Act 1968, the same format permitting entry and inspection is used to address the issues arising under that legislation as follows:-

> "a duly authorised officer of a local weights and measures authority or of a government department may, at all reasonable hours and on production, if required, of his credentials, exercise the following powers, that is to say,

> (a) he may for the purpose of ascertaining whether any offence under this Act has been committed, inspect any goods and enter any premises other than premises used only as a dwelling; . . ."

The corresponding provision in the Food Safety Act 1990 provides that:

> "an authorised officer of an enforcement authority shall, on producing, if so required, some duly authenticated document showing his authority, have a right at reasonable hours:—

(a) to enter any premises within the authority's area for the purposes of ascertaining whether there is or has been on the premises any contravention of the provisions of this Act, or of regulations or orders made under it; and

(b) to enter any business premises, whether within or outside the authority's area, for the purpose of ascertaining whether there is on the premises any evidence of any contravention within that area of any such provision; and

(c) in the case of an authorised officer of a food authority, to enter any premises for the purpose of the performance by the authority of their functions under this Act;

but admission to any premises used only as a private dwelling house shall not be demanded as of right unless 24 hours' notice of the intended entry has been given to the occupier".

It can be seen that the five material ancillary considerations which arise out of the power of entry given in each of the above examples are:

(i) the need for evidence of authorisation. Although the officer must produce his credentials if required to do so, it does not follow from this that the power of entry can only be exercised if there is someone to whom the credentials can be produced *Grove v. Eastern Gas Board* [1952] 1 K.B. 77;

(ii) the need for the entry or inspection to take place within reasonable hours. What are reasonable hours is a matter of fact. So, for example, in *Small v. Bickley* (1875) 32 L.T. 726 Sunday afternoon, when the shop was closed, was said not to be a reasonable time. Also, in *Davies v. Winstanley* (1930) 95 J.P. 21, it was not a reasonable time to inspect a dangerous drugs register when the cupboard in which it was kept was locked and the manager (who had the key) was not present;

(iii) the purpose for which the entry and inspection is to be made; and

(iv) the saving from the powers of private dwelling houses. In the case of the Food Safety Act 1990 this saving is limited only to the requirement of reasonable notice. A private dwelling house is unlikely to include a hostel, boarding house or guest house, even if it is partly occupied as a private dwelling by its owners (*Tendler v. Sproule* [1947] 1 All E.R. 193; *Stevens (G.E.) (High Wycombe) Ltd v. High Wycombe Corporation* [1962] 2 Q.B. 547).

(v) the distinction, if any, between the exercise of the powers within the area of the local authority and when outside it. As an illustration, environmental officers within their own area are entitled to enter "any premises" whereas if in another local authority area are entitled to enter only "business premises".

The main consideration in the case of each power of entry, however, is the legislative purpose of entry which may be either express or implied. This issue was taken up in *Walkers Snack Foods Ltd v. Coventry City Council (The Times*, April 9,

1998) where it was alleged that the prosecution had exceeded its statutory powers of entry and search by looking for material connected with a due diligence defence rather than with the commission of an offence. The powers in question related to evidence of a "contravention" of the provisions of the Act. The Divisional Court dismissed this argument on the grounds that if a due diligence defence could be established, there was no "contravention". This is hard to square with those authorities which make clear that an offence under the Act is quite different in quality from a defence. To apply a different significance to the word "contravention" is to create no more than a semantic distinction.

3.5 Occupier's consent. The above powers give to the officer a right to enter the premises. The mere conferral of the right to enter does not necessarily mean that the officer may enter without consent. Consent does not necessarily mean express consent. In *Robson v. Hallett* [1967] 2 Q.B. 939 the Divisional Court considered the lawfulness of three police officers on premises. Two were in the garden. The third was admitted to the house when he knocked on the door. The Divisional Court found that there was an implied consent to enter the garden and to knock on the door, and that the permission given to the officer to enter the house was only revoked after he had been given a reasonable opportunity to leave. The scope of any implied license will vary according to the circumstances. In *Brunner v. Williams* [1975] Crim.L.R. 250, the scope of the implied permission did not extend to entry into the back garden of premises, but only to the nearest or front door. So if legislation does not permit entry without consent, investigating officers may need to ask for express permission when entering a factory or warehouse, or other place which is not open to the public, but many investigating officers take the view that it is not necessary to seek consent when entering premises which are otherwise open to the public. It may be necessary for the determination of whether it is incumbent upon investigating officers to seek express permission and other questions (for example, whether Code B applies or whether, if there has been a breach of the Code, certain evidence ought to be excluded or whether the offence of obstruction has been committed) to consider whether the powers granted to the officer by the statutory provisions permit him to enter without consent. This is, perhaps, a separate question from whether there is a right to use force in the absence of consent. Where the power of entry is dependent upon the consent of the occupier, the investigating officer may not use force and enter without a warrant obtained from a Magistrates' Court if the occupier refuses to allow the investigating officer to enter the premises. On the other hand, to refuse to admit an investigating officer into premises which he is empowered to inspect may be to commit an offence of obstruction of the officer (see paragraphs 3.22 to 3.25 below).

3.6 Use of force. The clearest indication whether the statute will permit the use of force is express provision. In some cases, such as the Food and Environment Protection Act 1985, express permission is given. Schedule 2 to that Act provides at paragraph 8 that:

> "An officer may use reasonable force, if necessary, in the performance of his functions".

It is not, however, certain under every statute containing powers of entry similar to those set out above that force cannot be used if the occupier has been asked to consent to entry and has declined, or if the occupier is not present at the premises for permission to be sought. In *Grove v. Eastern Gas Board* [1952] 1 K.B. 77, for example, the Court of Appeal held that the Gas Act 1948, Sched. III contained a power to enter with force, although the empowering provisions made no express reference to force. In particular, the reasoning of the court took account of the statutory requirement that unoccupied premises should be left secure against trespassers and also that there was a provision for compensation for damage.

3.7 **Consent necessary to enter.** In contrast, although the three regulatory examples given in this chapter also contain provision for unoccupied premises to be left secure, in the absence of consent those premises should only have been entered under the aegis of a warrant obtained from the magistrates' court. This is clear because, although there is no express prohibition on the use of force, the statute provides for the issue of a warrant. The terms of section 32(2) of the Food Safety Act 1990 provide, for example, that:

"If a justice of the peace, on sworn information in writing, is satisfied that there is reasonable ground for entry into any premises for any purpose as is mentioned in subsection (1) above and either:

(a) that admission to the premises has been refused, or a refusal is apprehended, and that notice of intention to apply for a warrant has been given to the occupier; or

(b) that an application for admission, or the giving of a notice, would defeat the object of the entry, or that the case is one of urgency, or that the premises are unoccupied or the owner temporarily absent,

the justice may by warrant signed by him authorise the authorised officer to enter the premises if need be by reasonable force."

It is submitted that this material distinction renders it highly improbable that the powers of entry cited are intended to include a power to enter with force in the absence of the occupier's consent. There would be no need for a warrant to allow entry with reasonable force if the grant of the power to enter already allowed reasonable force to be used. Similarly, Section 79(3) of the Weights and Measures Act 1985 enables the issue of a warrant if there is reasonable ground to believe that instruments or goods or items which might be seized and detained are on the premises or if there is reasonable ground to believe that an offence under the Act or subordinate legislation (excepting Part 5 of the Act) has been, is being or is about to be committed on the premises. (For a discussion of the meaning of the expression "reasonable grounds to believe" see paragraph 4.12 below.) Notably, the warrants envisaged in the above legislation are for entry, not for search. Once the officer has obtained entry, he may use his general powers to inspect, seize documents, etc, but may not, seemingly, use force to do so.

Powers of search

3.8 **Code B.** This is concerned with the powers and duties of the officer when he has entered premises and does not have a search warrant. In a regulatory case, the duties of the enforcement officer when entering premises by consent may depend on whether he is investigating a suspected offence or making a routine visit in the exercise of his powers. The distinction lies in the obligation of the investigating officer under Code B (in the form enacted on April 10, 1995 by virtue of the Police and Criminal Evidence Act 1984 (Codes of Practice) (No. 3) Order 1995). Code B, namely "the code of practice for the searching of premises by police officers and the seizure of property found by police officers on persons or premises" does not, in its terms, make plain that it is to apply to the investigation of regulatory offences. However, by virtue of Section 67(9) (above) it is clear that the Code extends beyond the powers of police officers, and paragraph B:1.3 sets out that the Code applies to "searches of premises undertaken for the purposes of an investigation, with the occupier's consent . . .". A new paragraph 1.3(b) states that the Code does not apply to the exercise of a statutory power to enter premises or to inspect goods, equipment or procedures if the exercise of that power is not dependent on the existence of grounds for suspecting that an offence may have been committed *and* the person exercising the power has no reasonable grounds for such suspicion. This is the case at the commencement of most routine inspections by Trading Standards officers and other authorised inspectors, so that Code B need not be followed from the moment of entry on the premises. If, on the other hand, an offence is suspected, where, for example, officers are investigating a consumer complaint or an offence becomes suspected during the course of a routine visit, then it is necessary for the protections envisaged by Code B to be observed by the enforcement officers. It is surprising, perhaps, that in *Walkers Snack Foods Ltd v. Coventry City Council, The Times*, April 9, 1998, that the magistrates found that there was no reason for suspicion of an offence notwithstanding that Environmental Health Officers were carrying out a search while in possession of a crisp packet, thought to have come from the appellant's factory, and a piece of, plastic alleged by a perfectly respectable witness to have come from the packet! This finding was not, however, challenged in the Divisional Court either for *Wednesbury* unreasonableness or because the wrong test had been applied.

The change made in 1995 to the provisions of Code B was to reverse the effect of the decision in *Dudley Metropolitan Borough Council v. Debenhams Plc* [1994] 159 J.P. 18, DC in which it was held that a routine inspection by a Trading Standards Officer was a search, so that the provisions of Code B would apply from the outset. In that case enforcement officers had entered shop premises under the powers conferred on them by Section 29 of the Consumer Protection Act 1987. At the point of entry there were no grounds to suspect that an offence had been committed and the officers did not have powers, under that Act, to require an employee to provide a business record because (as there was no suspicion of an offence) there were no grounds upon which a search could lawfully have been carried out. Accordingly, when they asked for a computer print-out to be provided (held by the court to be a search) they were dependent upon the employee's consent being given willingly. The Court held that Code B should have been utilised to warn the employee of the powers and rights of search and to inform him that he was not obliged to consent to the investigator's request. Since the amendment to reverse the effect of the *Debenhams* decision, the anomalous position is reached that where the investigating officer has no suspicion of an offence, he may look for evidence to find one, but where the investigating officer has a reasonable suspicion that an offence has been committed he must alert the occupier to that fact, and give him the right to refuse consent before he searches for evidence.

3.9   What is a search?   In the *Debenhams* case (above) Smith J. addressed this question as follows:

"We were referred by Counsel for the Respondent to the dictionary definition of the word 'search'. He quoted the *Oxford Pocket Dictionary* in which it appears that search means to look or go over (a place or book) for what may be found. The Respondents submitted that a search takes place when a person enters premises and looks about himself. It is not necessary, submitted the respondents, in opposition to the appellants submission, that there should be any physical interference with goods such as rummaging, opening drawers or matters of that kind.

It seems to me that the nature of an official visit by a Trading Standards Officer is an inspection to see *inter alia* whether any offences have been committed. He has a duty to enforce compliance with the Consumer Protection Act, and he has in mind the intention to consider a prosecution if evidence is discovered.

For my part, I cannot accept the submission that such an activity does not amount to a search. In my judgment, the submission of the respondents in this regard is correct, that entry and looking about amounts to a search".

It would seem to follow from the above, that many regulatory powers are searches. These powers would include the following examples:

(i) An inspection of equipment or goods on the premises (*e.g.* under the Weights and Measures Act 1985);

(ii) An inspection of premises;

(iii) A power to require the production of books or documents (most regulatory legislation);

(iv) A power to require a person to break open a vending machine or container, and in default to do so himself (*e.g.* under the Trade Descriptions Act 1968);

(v) A power to require access to and check the operation of any computer (*e.g.* under the Food Safety Act 1990);

3.10 Test purchases. Many regulatory provisions governing the relationship between the consumer and the retail trade allow for the making of test purchases. Usually power to make a test purchase arises for the purposes of ascertaining whether an offence has been committed or whether any provision has been contravened. Sometimes, however, a test purchase is made by officers with the intention of providing evidence to any court which might be required to try an allegation of infringement of any provision. It is unclear whether the power to make a test purchase could fall within the provisions as to "search". Where the making of a test purchase involves the entry on premises, the selection of goods and the purchase of them at a cash register in exchange for a receipt which will be used in evidence, it is possible that that activity could be categorised as a search, at least in cases where the purchase does not form the *actus reus* of the offence charged. If a test purchase is made in circumstances where the TSO suspects an offence, it is at least arguable that the provisions of Code B should apply, so that the prospective defendant should be informed and given the opportunity to consent. A test purchase which is made without the entry on to premises, say, by mail order, however, may pose a different problem. Such a purchase is unlikely to be a search, and no warning needs to be given, even if the inspector believes that an offence may have been committed. In the main, it seems that enforcement officers tend to view that the exercise of a power to make test purchases (such as under section 28 of the Consumer Protection Act 1987) is not a search and that there needs to be no compliance with Code B. As it cannot always be said that test purchases are made in circumstances where the enforcement officer has no reasonable grounds for suspecting an offence, this issue remains to be taken and decided.

3.11 **Searches and consent.** Paragraph B:4 which deals with search with consent provides:–

> B:4.1 "Subject to paragraph 4.4 below, if it is proposed to search premises with the consent of a person entitled to grant entry to the premises the consent must, if practicable, be given in writing on the Notice of Powers and Rights before the search takes place. The officer must make enquiries to satisfy himself that the person is in a position to give such consent."

These enquiries are of particular importance, because, whereas an employee might be permitted by his employer to deal with enforcement officers in a general way at the premises which the enforcement officer wishes to inspect, his authority to represent his employer may not extend to representing the company in circumstances where an offence may have been committed, or permitting a search. Clearly, if the employee is not in a position to give consent, the search cannot be conducted without a warrant or permission from a more senior employee with the necessary authority or from an owner.

> B:4.2 "Before seeking consent the officer in charge of the search shall state the purpose of the proposed search and inform the person concerned that he is not obliged to consent and that anything seized may be produced in evidence. If at the time the person is not suspected of an offence, the officer shall tell him so when stating the purpose of the search."
> B:4.3 "An officer cannot enter and search premises or continue to search premises under 4.1 above if the consent has been given under duress or is withdrawn before the search is completed."
> B:4.4 "It is unnecessary to seek consent under paragraphs 4.1 and 4.2 above where in the circumstances this would cause disproportionate inconvenience to the person concerned."

The notice of powers and rights is referred to in paragraph B:5.7. This provides that:

> "if an officer conducts a search to which this code applies he shall, unless it is impracticable to do, provide the occupier with a copy of a notice in a standard format:
>
> (i) specifying whether the search is made under warrant, or with consent, . . . (the format of the notice shall provide for . . . consent to be indicated where appropriate);
>
> (ii) summarising the extent of the powers of search and seizure conferred in the Act; (the powers referred to here, of course, are those set out in the Police and Criminal Evidence Act. There is, however, no reason why other powers should not be referred to where the search is conducted

under the auspices of other statutory provisions and it is usual for a Notice of Powers and Duties to set out on its reverse the full panoply of enforcement powers which the enforcement officer might have);

(iii) explaining the rights of the occupier, and of the owner of property seized in accordance with the provisions of 6.1 to 6.5 below, set out in the Act and in this Code;

(iv) explaining that compensation may be payable in appropriate cases for damage caused in entering and searching premises, and giving the address to which an application for compensation should be directed; and

(v) stating that a copy of the Code is available to be consulted at any police station."

B:5.8 "If the occupier is present, copies of the notice mentioned above . . . should if practicable be given to the occupier before the search begins, unless the officer in charge of the search reasonably believes that to do so would frustrate the object of the search or endanger the officers concerned or other persons. If the occupier is not present, copies of the notice . . . should be left in a prominent place on the premises or appropriate part of the premises and endorsed with the name of the officer in charge of the search . . . [the Code provides for the name of the police station to which a police officer is attached and the date and time of the search to be included. There is no reason why the name of the officer and his local authority department should not similarly be given]."

B:5.9 "Premises may be searched only to the extent necessary to achieve the object of the search, having regard to the size and nature of what area is sought. A search under warrant may not continue under the authority of that warrant once all the things specified in it have been found, or the officer in charge of the search is satisfied that they are not on the premises."

B:5.10 "Searches must be conducted with due consideration for the property and privacy of the occupier of the premises searched, and with no more disturbance than necessary. Reasonable force may be used only where this is necessary because the cooperation of the occupier cannot be obtained or is insufficient for the purpose."

B:5.11 "If the occupier wishes a friend, neighbour or other person to witness the search then he must be allowed to do so, unless the officer in charge has reasonable grounds for believing that this would seriously hinder the investigation. A search need not be unreasonably delayed for this purpose."

B:7.1 "Where premises have been searched in circumstances to which this Code applies, other than in the circumstances covered by paragraph 4.4 above, the officer in charge of the search shall, on arrival at a police station, make or have made a record of the search. That record shall include:

(i) the address of the premises searched;

(ii) the date, time and duration of the search;

(iii) the authority under which the search was made. Where the search was made in the exercise of a statutory power to search premises without warrant, the record shall include the power under which the search was made; and where the search was made under warrant, or with written consent, a copy of the warrant or consent shall be appended to the record or kept in a place identified in the record;

    (iv) the names of all the officers who conducted the search . . .;

    (v) the names of any persons on the premises if they are known;

    (vi) either a list of any article seized or a note of where such a list is kept and, if not covered by a warrant, the reasons for their seizure;

    (vii) whether force was used, and, if so, the reason why it was used;

    (viii) details of any damage caused during the search, and the circumstances in which it was caused."

3.12 Warrants and the code. It does not appear that the Code applies to a search of premises which takes place under warrants issued pursuant to regulatory legislation. Some of the provisions of the Code may, however, remain good practice and, in particular, where premises have been searched under a warrant, the endorsement of the warrant to show:

    (i) whether any articles specified in the warrant were found;

    (ii) whether any articles were seized;

    (iii) the date and time at which it was executed;

    (iv) the names of the officers who executed it . . .;

    (v) whether a copy together with a copy of the notice of powers and rights was handed to the occupier . . ..

Seizure

3.13 Seizure. Seizure relates to the power to take material off the premises of its owner, whether that be an original or copy document or item of evidence or sample. In order for an officer to remove any such item, there must be express statutory authority. In some cases, that authority may be hedged about with ancillary requirements, such as the obligations which usually relate to the taking of samples (see paragraph 3.18 below). Code B applies to the seizure and retention of property by providing that:

B.6.1 "Subject to paragraphs 6.2 below an officer who is searching any premises under any statutory power or with the consent of the occupier may seize:

    (a) anything covered by a warrant; and

    (b) anything which he has reasonable grounds for believing is evidence of an offence or has been obtained in consequence of the commission of an offence.

Items under (b) may only be seized where this is necessary to prevent their concealment, alteration, loss, damage or destruction."
B:6.2 "No item may be seized which is subject to legal privilege (as defined in Section 10 of the Police and Criminal Evidence Act 1984)."
B:6.3 "An officer who decides that it is not appropriate to seize property because of an explanation given by the person holding it, but who has reasonable grounds for believing that it has been obtained in consequence of the commission of an offence by some person, shall inform the holder of his

suspicions and shall explain that, if he disposes of the property, he may be liable to civil or criminal proceedings."

B:6.4 "An officer may photograph or copy or have photographed or copied, any document or other article which he has power to seize in accordance with paragraph 6.1 above."

B:6.5 "Where an officer considers that a computer may contain information that could be used in evidence, he may require the information to be produced in a form that can be taken away and in which it is visible and legible."

The powers of investigation which are referred to in Code B overlap with those statutory provisions which authorise officers in many proceedings (see paragraph 3.15 below). Little may turn upon the application of this paragraph save where items are seized in a manner which is inconvenient to their owner, although whether that factor alone could be sufficient to justify the exclusion of evidence derived from it must be highly unlikely. An apparent breach of the Code, however, may be a persuasive reason for the return of the property to someone aggrieved by its removal.

3.14 Retention. Retention of the property is provided for in B:6.6 of the Code. This specifies that:

"subject to paragraph 6.7 below, anything which has been seized in accordance with the above provisions may be retained only for as long as is necessary in the circumstances. It may be retained, among other purposes:

(i) for use as evidence at a trial for an offence;

(ii) for forensic examination or for other investigation in connection with an offence; or

(iii) where there are reasonable grounds for believing that it has been . . . obtained by the commission of an offence, in order to establish its lawful owner.

"B:6.7 'Property shall not be retained in accordance with 6.6(i) and (ii) (*i.e.* for use as evidence or for the purposes of investigation) if a photograph or copy would suffice for those purposes' ".

The Code also specifies that the rights of owners of the property, namely the person who had custody or control of it immediately prior to its seizure, must, on request, be provided with a list or description of the property within a reasonable time (B:6.8). He or his representative must be allowed supervised access to the property to examine it or have it photographed or copied or must be provided with a photograph or copy, in either case within a reasonable time of any request and at his own expense, unless the officer in charge of an investigation has reasonable grounds for believing that this would prejudice the investigation of an offence or any criminal proceedings. In this case a record of the grounds must be made.

3.15 Inspection of documents. Nearly all regulatory legislation contains provisions which permit the inspection of books, records, documents and in most cases, the removal of copies is also permitted. For example, under the Trade Descriptions Act 1968 the powers which a duly authorised officer of a local weights and measures authority or government department enjoy are as follows:–

(i) to require any person carrying on a trade or business or employed in connection with a trade or business;

(a) to produce any books or documents relating to the trade or business;

(b) to take copies of any book or document or any entry in such book or document;

if he has reasonable cause to suspect that an office under the Act has been committed.

(ii) to seize and detain any goods for the purposes of ascertaining by testing or otherwise whether an offence has been committed *if* he has reasonable cause *to believe* that an offence under the Act has been committed;

(iii) to seize and detain any goods or documents if he has reason to *believe* they may be required as evidence in proceedings for an offence under the Act;

In the case of seizing goods or documents the officer is obliged to inform the person from whom they are seized. The Food Safety Act 1990 similarly provides for entry and inspection of records in whatever form they are held relating to a food business. It adds the further provision that where any records are kept by means of a computer, the authorised officer may have access to and inspect and check the operation of that computer and any associated apparatus or material which has been used in connection with the records. He may similarly require any person having charge of or otherwise concerned with the operation of the computer, apparatus or material to afford him such assistance as he may reasonably require. In addition to this, in relation to computer records he may also require the records to be produced in a form for him in which they may be taken away. Care must be taken in connection with the investigation of computer records, however. The power to require the prospective defendant's employees to take action to allow access to the computer may not be all-embracing. In *Toys 'R' Us v. Gloucestershire County Council* (1994) 159 J.P. 338, the court expressed the opinion that a requirement by a Trading Standards Officer to close down a training till and make it available for his purpose went beyond the powers contained in section 29(5)(a) of the Consumer Protection Act 1987 which require a person to produce records relating to the business.

As with the Trading Standards Officer enforcing the provisions of the Trade Descriptions Act, an Environmental Health Officer enforcing the Food Safety Act 1990 has a power to seize and detain any records which he has reason to believe may be required as evidence in proceedings under the Food Safety Act or its regulations.

By way of further illustration, a Trading Standards Officer enforcing the provisions of the Weights and Measures Act 1985 may similarly seize and detain not only any article which he has reasonable cause to *believe* is liable to be forfeited under the Act but also any document or goods which he has reason to *believe* may be required as evidence in proceedings for an offence under the Act (except under Part 5). For the distinction between "belief" and "suspicion" and the meaning of "reasonable ground to . . ." see paragraphs 4.12 below).

3.16 Computer records. Where an inspection of computer records occurs, particular care needs to be taken by investigating authorities to ensure that the evidence obtained from the computer is capable in due course of admission in evidence (should the search or seizure be for the purpose of furnishing admissible evidence). A statement in a document (which would otherwise be real evidence: that is, the entry has not involved its passing through the human mind – see *R. v. Spiby* (1990) 91 Cr.App.R. 186, *R. v. Neville* [1991] Crim.L.R. 288) is not admissible in evidence of a fact stated in it unless it can be shown that:

(i) there are no reasonable grounds for believing that the statement is inaccurate through improper use of the computer;

(ii) the computer was operating properly at all material times, or that, if it was not operating properly, that its failure was not such as to affect the production of the document or the accuracy of its contents;

(iii) that any relevant conditions in rules of court are satisfied

(Police and Criminal Evidence Act 1984, s.69).

These provisions are supplemented in Schedule 3, Part III which provides that for the purpose of deciding whether or not a statement is so admissible the court may draw any reasonable inference from the circumstances in which the statement was made or came into being or from other circumstances including the form and content of the document in which the statement is contained. The evidence as to the proper working of the computer can in some instances be given by certificate (see Schedule 3, Part II of the Act). It can also be given by any person familiar with the operation of the computer *(R. v. Shephard* [1993] A.C. 380, where evidence as to the working of a computer in use in a shop was given by the store detective). The difficulty which may present itself for investigating officers who seek to rely upon evidence from a computer contained in the premises of a suspected offender is that they may not be in a position to know whether the computer was properly operative or not, unless they can supplement the computer evidence with oral evidence about the working of the computer or in some other way. This issue has arisen particularly in relation to offences under section 20 of the Consumer Protection Act 1987 (misleading price indications) where evidence of the falsity of the price indication may in some circumstances be gleaned from the computer record of the transaction, see, for example, *Dudley Metropolitan Borough Council v. Debenhams plc* (1994) 159 J.P. 18.

3.17 Vending machines. The Trade Descriptions Act 1968 and other regulatory powers may allow the opening of vending machines and other containers for the purpose of carrying out a search or seizure. As an illustration, section 28(1) of that Act enables an enforcing officer to require any person having authority to do so to break open a container or open a vending machine only if and to the extent that it is reasonably necessary in order to secure that the provisions of the Act and any subordinate legislation are observed. If the person so required does not comply with the requirement he may do so himself. In the case of goods seized from a vending machine the investigating officer must inform the person whose name and address are stated on the machine as the proprietor. If no name and address is stated the occupier of the premises must be informed. The provisions of the Consumer Protection Act 1987 depart from the slightly curious description of the purpose of the powers in Section 28(1)(e) of the Trade Descriptions Act 1968, namely the purpose of "securing that the provisions of this Act . . . are duly observed" prior to the opening of a container or vending machine, by making it clear that an officer may require the opening of a container or vending machine to obtain goods or records "to prevent a contravention of any safety provision or of any provision made by or under Part 3 of" the Act.

3.18 Samples. In the case of the Food Safety Act 1990 there is a power both to purchase a sample of any food or substance used in the preparation of food or to take such a sample if it appears to him to have been intended for sale for human consumption or is found by him on any premises which he is authorised to enter. He may similarly take a sample from any food source or a sample of any contact material or of any other article or substance which he has reason to believe may be required as evidence in proceedings under the provisions of the Act or regulations made under it. Such a sample may be submitted for analysis by the public analyst for the area in which the sample was procured or by the public analyst for the area which consists of or includes the area of the authority. It should be added that by virtue of section 27 of the Act each food authority is required to appoint one or more public analysts for the purposes of the 1990 Act. Alternatively the officer may submit the sample for examination by a food examiner. Notably the powers to submit for analysis apply not only to an officer but also to any other person who has purchased food and who wishes it to be sampled. There are provisions in the Act for what is to happen if there is no food analyst or examiner available and the Act contains an obligation to carry out the analysis and provide a certificate specifying the result of the analysis or examination. This can then become sufficient evidence of the facts stated in it. Regulations further provide for the means by which samples may be divided or taken so that they are fair.

If there is, in relation to any statutory provision, a non-compliance, two considerations may apply. First, does the non-compliance, of itself, render the sampling process void and the results inadmissible? In some cases, the legislation makes clear that the evidence resulting from improperly taken samples is inadmissible. Section 209 of the Water Resources Act 1991 is an example. It is provided that "the result of the analysis of any sample . . . shall not be admissible in any legal proceedings unless:

(a) on taking the sample [there was notification of intention to test];

(b) "there and then" [the sample was divided into three parts]

(c) [one part was given to the defendant]".

(In *Attorney General's Reference (No. 2 of 1994)* [1995] 2 All E.R. 1000, the degree of immediacy contemplated by this section was considered as was the consequence of failure to comply.)

In other cases it is a question of construction whether the statute is intended to preclude evidence of a sampling process which has not been correctly followed. Even if the provisions are directory rather than mandatory and even if the evidence can be admitted as a matter of law, the second consideration is whether the court should exercise its discretion to exclude the evidence under section 78 of the Police and Criminal Evidence Act 1984 (for the operation of this provision see paragraph 10.105 below).

3.19 Testing. Section 30(6) of the Consumer Protection Act 1987 provides that where goods are seized and submitted to a test, the officer shall inform the persons from whom the goods are seized of the result of the test. Anybody who is a party then to subsequent proceedings who requests to have the goods tested, and it is practicable to comply with such request should be permitted to do so. Similar considerations to those applying to samples apply as to the admission of test evidence.

Consequences of illegality in entry, search and seizure

3.20 Code B. Merely because there has been a failure to comply with Code B or statutory requirements, it will not follow that the evidence which has been obtained in contravention of its provisions will become inadmissible even if the contravention adversely affects the unfairness of the proceedings *(R. v. Walsh* (1990) 91 Cr. App. R. 161). Before the evidence can be excluded under section 78 of the Police and Criminal Evidence Act 1984, it must have *such* an adverse effect on the fairness of the proceedings that the court ought not to admit it (for the full text of this provision see paragraph 10.105 below). This statutory provision follows the common law expounded in *R. v. Sang* [1980] A.C. 402 which concluded that a trial judge has no discretion to exclude evidence simply because it was obtained by improper or unfair means although there was a discretion which arose if the defendant had been induced to produce evidence voluntarily as a consequence of an unfair inducement or oppression. Each case must turn on its own facts, but it is notable that in *Dudley Metropolitan Borough Council v. Debenhams plc* (1994) 159 J.P. 18, the magistrates were willing to exclude computer evidence under section 78 of the Act where the respondents had not been warned as to the possibility of prosecution nor given notice of a search. Similarly, in *Matto v. DPP* [1987] Crim.L.R. 641 (a non-regulatory case) where two police officers had knowingly trespassed on the defendant's property and insisted that he should undergo a breath test, the evidence of the breath test was held by the Divisional Court to be inadmissible because the Crown Court had found that the officers had known that they were acting beyond their powers and this bad faith tainted all the evidence which was consequential on that bad faith. If the Crown Court had found no bad faith, however, the evidence would not have been excluded. However, bad faith does not mean that evidence will inevitably be excluded *(Sharpe v. DPP* [1993] R.T.R. 392) any more than good faith means that it will necessarily be included.

Power to require others to help

3.21 Offences. Most legislation containing powers of search, seizure, entry, detention, etc., also contains provisions which punish someone who impedes the investigation. Offences of this nature commonly address two forms of commission of an obstruction by the creation of at least two different offences: the first is often an offence of "wilful obstruction" and the second an offence (or offences) of failure to comply with a lawful requirement or provide assistance or information. An offence in the latter category does not, in the main, impose a positive obligation upon someone to assist the inspector, but punishes obstructions and failures to respond to requests for information or assistance.

3.22 Obstruction. The offence of obstruction of an inspector in its usual form requires wilful or deliberate obstruction in respect of an inspector acting in pursuance of the Act giving rise to the offence. It is not an offence if, at the time of the obstruction complained of, the inspector is not acting in pursuance of his obligations under the legislation. So in *Barge v. British Gas Corporation* (1983) 81 L.G.R. 53, a defendant was not guilty of obstruction where a Trading Standards

Officer asked for a copy of a document in purported exercise of powers under the Trade Descriptions Act 1968. The defendant did not hand over a copy, but allowed the Trading Standards Officer to take a copy. Because section 28 of the Act did not require the defendant to hand over documents, there had been no obstruction. Obstruction does not include mere passive conduct unless there is an express duty to act (*Swallow v. L.C.C.* [1916] 1 K.B. 225), however, whether there is a duty to act may be difficult to determine. It can be argued that if statutory provisions confer a right to undertake conduct, there must be a corresponding duty on another to permit that conduct. So in *Lunt v. DPP* [1993] Crim.L.R. 534, the Divisional Court had to consider whether a refusal by occupants to answer police officers shouting through the letter box in an endeavour to exercise powers of entry under section 4(7) of the Road Traffic Act 1988 could amount to obstruction. The court held that it could, because the existence of a right of entry pre-supposed the existence of a duty to admit to premises. Wilfulness can frequently be equated with "intention" rather than with hostility or malice. See, for example, *Lewis v. Cox* [1984] 3 W.L.R. 875, where Webster J. described the test for wilful obstruction as:

> "whether the defendant's conduct in fact prevented the police from carrying out their duty or made it more difficult for them to do so; and whether the defendant intended that conduct to prevent the police from carrying out their duties, or to make it more difficult for them".

Thus a person who refuses admission to premises to an inspector with a right to enter and search or inspect is likely to commit the offence of obstruction.

Moreover, where wilfulness must be shown as an element in the offence of "obstruction", it seems unlikely that a body corporate or employer can be fixed with the requisite mental state unless there has been a delegation of responsibilities or there is evidence that the defendant authorised or connived at the obstruction so as to be party to a common enterprise. In the case of a body corporate, the body corporate will be liable if the state of mind can be shown to have been that of a person who is part of the directing mind and will of the company or in relation to the statutory provisions, the rules of attribution are such that the employer is liable for the state of mind of the employee (see paragraphs 7.34 to 7.43 below).

3.23   Positive conduct.   Because obstruction is or may be so narrowly defined, it is not uncommon for statutes to impose a positive obligation which may or may not involve *mens rea* in the form of wilfulness. For example, Section 81 of the Weights and Measures Act 1985 provides that:

> "(1) Any person who—
>
> (a) wilfully fails to comply with any requirement properly made of him by an inspector under Sections 38, 39 or 40 of the Act or
>
> (b) without reasonable cause fails to give any inspector acting in pursuance of this Act any other assistance or information which the inspector may reasonably require of him for the purposes of the performance by the inspector of his functions under Parts 2, 3, 4 or 5 of this Act or under this Part shall be guilty of an offence."

In *Walkers Snack Foods Limited v. Coventry City Council, The Times,* April 9, 1998, two allegations were made of failing without reasonable cause to give assistance to Environmental Health Officers in that employees failed to give access to maintenance records and records of control procedures during an inspection and failed to give free access to their premises. Reliance was placed on what had been said by the employees in circumstances in which they had not been cautioned. It was argued that the employees had reasonable cause to fail to give assistance because there was a privilege against self-crimination (see paragraph 3.24 below) and because they had taken legal advice from a (non-lawyer) specialist in defending regulatory offences. The magistrates rejected both contentions, and their decision was upheld in the Divisional Court. Moreover in *R. v. Greater Manchester Justices ex p. Aldi GmbH* (1995) 159 J.P. 717, a "lowly" employee was prosecuted for failure to provide information to Trading Standards Officers could not rely upon the fact that her employer had told her not to answer questions as "reasonable cause" for her failure – although the Divisional Court were critical of the decision to prosecute the employee in these circumstances.

It is also an offence under Section 81(2) to give an inspector any information which he knows to be false. It seems that an offence of this nature maybe committed even during an interview under caution *(R. v. Page* [1996] Crim.L.R. 439).

3.24 Self-incrimination. It is usual for legislation to include a protection for the person asked to provide information that nothing shall be construed as requiring any person to answer any question or give information if to do so might incriminate him. It seems that the scope of this is limited, however. In *Walkers Snack Foods Ltd v. Coventry City Council* (above) the company was prosecuted for failure to provide assistance under section 33(1)(b) of the Food Safety Act 1990 by reason 9 of the conduct of their staff who were not part of the "directing mind and will" of the company. The company relied on section 33(3), which contained a protection against self-incrimination, but the decision of the Divisional Court was that the protection only availed the person answering the question rather than a third party employee. It is not clear whether this decision is intended to mean that only an individual can claim the privilege, or whether, because the individuals in question were not part of its "directing mind and will" or delegates they could not claim the privilege on behalf of another. Presumably the apparent illogicality of attributing the employee's conduct to the employer in circumstances where the same employee cannot claim the privilege is thought to be overcome by the recollection that the offence is an absolute offence for which the employer is liable for the employee.

3.25 Conduct of managers and staff during official inspections. It is clear that the position of an employee during an official inspection is of some difficulty. Failure to assist may render both an employee and employer liable for obstruction and failure to assist, and it seems that the employee only, who, following the *Aldi* decision (above) is the less likely to be prosecuted, can claim the privilege against self-incrimination.

QUESTIONING

3.26 PACE Code C. This Code governs the detention, treatment and questioning of persons. It relates principally to interviews in a police station and, as such, is difficult to transpose to the activities of enforcement officers. However, "having regard" to Code C elicits some relevant principles and these are set out here. In this work, there is no discussion of the detention of prospective offenders, nor their treatment at the police station. This part deals with the conduct of interviews by investigating officers without arrest, and the issues which arise there.

3.27   **Interview.**   Interview is a usual part of the conduct of an investigation of a regulatory offence. Code C:11.1a defines an interview as:

> "questioning of a person regarding his involvement or suspected involvement in a criminal offence or offences which, by virtue of paragraph 10.1 of Code C, is required to be under caution".

Paragraph 10.1 of Code C provides that:

> "a person whom there are grounds to suspect of an offence must be cautioned before any questions are asked about it (or further questions if it is his answers to previous questions which provide the grounds for suspicion) are put to him regarding his involvement or suspected involvement in that offence if his answers or his silence (*i.e.* failure to answer a question satisfactorily) may be given in evidence to a court in a prosecution".

Accordingly, there is no need to caution if the questions are merely to ascertain a person's address and identity, nor if the questions are in pursuance of a statutory requirement, nor if the questions are in furtherance of the proper conduct of a search (Code C 10.4). In *Walkers Snack Foods Ltd v. Coventry City Council, The Times*, April 9, 1998, questions were asked of an employee, and the answers apparently admitted as direct evidence of failure to assist the officers even though no caution had been administered, because there was a statutory duty to provide assistance. There was, accordingly, no breach of Code C. Moreover, it is notable that the caution need only to be administered to a person whom there are grounds to suspect of an offence. It is probable, however, that answers given by an employee who is not authorised to speak on behalf of the company, but is required to provide assistance to an investigating officer will be inadmissible in connection with any offence other than that of failing to assist, because the employee's answers will be hearsay against the company. Where the prospective defendant is a limited company, the person interviewed must therefore be a person who is part of the directing mind and will" of the company (see paragraphs 7.33 to 7.35 below) or some other person whose remarks can be attributed to the company. In large organisations, express authority is frequently given to an employee, such as a trading standards manager to attend interviews. Interview of an unauthorised person is likely not to constitute interview of the company.

Where the interview is under caution, its purpose is to obtain admissions which can be relied upon in court, but it is also an opportunity for the defendant to put his side of the story. Formerly, there was no obligation upon a defendant to answer questions under caution, but this is no longer the position. Section 34 of the Criminal Justice and Public Order Act 1994 provides that:

> "If a person being interviewed fails to mention any fact which is subsequently relied on in his defence, being a matter which he could reasonably have been expected to mention when so questioned, then a court may draw such inferences from the failure as appear proper".

This formulation is then repeated in the form of caution, except that the investigating officer may make minor deviations from the words of the caution if he preserves the sense of it (Code C, paragraph 10.4):

"You do not have to say anything. But it may harm your defence if you do not mention when questioned something which you later rely on in court. Anything you do say may be given in evidence".

3.28 When must the caution be administered. In addition to the requirement that a caution be administered before questions are asked of a person of whom there are grounds to suspect of an offence, the caution must also be administered where a person who has been asked questions on a previous occasion is asked further questions (Code C 10.4). It is clear that Code C will apply to situations which extend beyond interviews in police stations *(R. v. Hunt* [1992] Crim.L.R. 582, *R. v. Sparks* [1991] Crim.L.R. 128), and conversations which might occur between enforcement officers and those suspected of an offence in the context of an investigation may also require a caution to be given. Even one question may be enough *(R. v. Ward* (1994) 98 Cr. App. Rep. 337). The caution will not need to be administered, however, where there are no objective grounds for suspicion, even if the officer himself suspects that an offence has been committed *(R. v. Shah* [1994] Crim.L.R. 125), but it may be that by the time that questioning concerns inconsistencies in the answers given by a person with whom an interview is conducted, the caution ought to have been administered *(R. v. James* [1996] Crim.L.R. 650). If a suspect makes a "spontaneous remark" which is of significance to the investigation otherwise than in the context of an interview, that remark should be put to the suspect at the outset of any interview. (Code C11.2A). Where in the course of a single interview there is a break in questioning, the interviewee must be reminded that he is under caution. If there is any doubt, the caution should be given again (Code C:10.5). This principle does not apply if the break is insignificantly short, so in *R. v. Oni* [1992] Crim.L.R. 183, a break of two minutes was held not to be a breach of the Code.

3.29 Alternatives to interviewing. An interview under caution is not the only way of proceeding to investigate, however, particularly if the "partnership principle" (see paragraph 2.9 above) is observed. Many companies and businesses are willing and anxious to take part in informal (that is to say, without prejudice) fact-finding discussions which will help in the investigation of the offence, but which will not furnish evidence against the company. Attempts to conduct matters in this way, have, however, become less prevalent since investigating officers have come to expect an explanation to be given in the course of the interview pursuant to the provisions of the 1994 Act and Code mentioned above. Local Authorities who have adopted the Enforcement Concordat, however, are obliged to give an opportunity to prospective defendants to discuss the matter informally.

3.30 Interviews in regulatory cases. Where a regulatory offence is suspected, unlike a true criminal offence with a right of arrest, the opportunities for immediate interviews (that is to say, an interview when the investigating officer is first on the premises) are few and far between:

  (i) the likely defendant is frequently not on his premises or not available for immediate questioning (perhaps because the defendant is a limited company, or, even if he is an individual, it may be only his shop manager or other staff actually present at the time of the discovery of the offence);

(ii) the likely defendant may personally have had no awareness of the commission of the individual offence because the unlawful activity was carried out by a member of his staff. He may even know nothing at all about its surrounding circumstances, so that he would need to undertake an investigation before being able to comment;

(iii) the likely defendant cannot usually be taken to a place of detention and interviewed in circumstances not of his choosing. This only occurs on arrest. He has a choice whether or not to co-operate;

(iv) where the likely defendant is a corporate defendant, there is an issue as to whom should be cautioned. Only a person who is authorised to speak on behalf of the company should be cautioned and interviewed. Interview of another person may not bind the company (see paragraph 3.27 above) and so may be inadmissible in evidence;

(v) there may be no convenient recording facilities, whereas those facilities might be available at the offices of the local authority.

Accordingly, this means that an appointment for interview has usually in practice to be made and it also means that the prospective defendant has an opportunity to consider his approach to interview. It is a mistake for prospective defendants not to plan and prepare for the interview.

3.31   Preparing for interview.   Preparing for interview can involve a number of activities, depending on the circumstances. Very many regulatory defendants are convicted on the basis of admissions made in interview, often in ignorance of a defence which might have been afforded, had proper consideration been given to the facts at an early stage, rather than only after the summons is received. Staff who are to conduct interviews on behalf of companies should be trained in the relevant law and, if possible, given basic training to help them understand the interview process, well before any problem has emerged. At the very minimum, once an issue has been identified, preparation should entail a full investigation of how any alleged offence came about. Legal advice as to the offence and any potential defences which might exist and about which the prosecution should usefully be informed should be taken. The person interviewed should be fully prepared to talk about the due diligence procedures in operation, their scope, why they have been implemented in that fashion or chosen and why they have failed (if they have). The detection of offences can constitute part of due diligence procedures. It can be advantageous for the defendant in court if the interview contains, in so far as is possible, positive assertions about the trading record and compliance of the company, and not just negative acknowledgements of failure. It does not need to be said, however, that in the course of preparation for and conduct of the interview by a prospective defendant, the facts and matters in issue must not be confused with the facts and matters as they ought to have presented themselves.

3.32   Conduct of the interview.   It is not uncommon for trading standards officers to try to follow the guidance of police interviews by tape recording the interview. In particular, the whole of the interview should be recorded, with nothing said while the tape is switched off, the parties should be introduced on the tape and the defendant should also be given a copy of the tape. The practice and should follows as nearly as is reasonable the terms of PACE Code E. In any event, however, the requirements of Code C:11.5 should be followed. This provides:

"(a) An accurate record must be made of each interview with a person suspected of an offence, whether or not the interview takes place at a police station.

(b) The record must state the place of the interview, the time it begins and ends, the time the record is made (if different), any breaks in the interview and the names of all those present; and must be made on the forms provided for this purpose or in the officers pocket book or in accordance with the code of practice for the tape recording of police interviews with suspects (Code E)

(c) the record must be made in the course of the interview unless in the investigating officer's view this would not be practicable or would interfere with the conduct of the interview, and must constitute either a verbatim record of what has been said, or failing this, an account of the interview which adequately and accurately summarises it.

C:11.7 If an interview is not made during the course of the interview it must be made as soon as practicable after its completion.

C:11.8 Written interview records must be timed and signed by the maker.

C:11.9 If an interview record is not completed in the course of the interview, the reason must be recorded in the officer's pocket book.

C:11.10 Unless it is impracticable the person interviewed shall be given the opportunity to read the interview record and sign it as correct or to indicate the respects in which he considers it inaccurate. If the interview is tape recorded the arrangements set out in Code E apply . . ..

C:11.12 Any refusal by a person to sign an interview record when asked to do so in accordance with the provisions of the code must itself be recorded.

C:11.13 A written record shall also be made of any comments made by a suspected person, including unsolicited comments, which are outside the context of an interview but which might be relevant to the offence. Any such record must be times and signed by the maker. Where practicable, the person shall be given the opportunity to read that record and to sign it as correct or indicate the respects in which he considers it inaccurate. Any refusal to sign shall be recorded."

Where there has been a taped interview, instead of complete transcription a summary is sometimes produced. Defendants should check this for accuracy, ensuring that those parts upon which the defendant would wish to rely are also included.

3.33 Letters. It is very common for an interview to be followed up with correspondence on a particular point, or even, in some cases, the exchange of questions and information is conducted entirely by correspondence. The "written interview" does not figure in the PACE Codes, but it is practice for correspondence which is triggered by a letter containing a form of appropriate caution to be admitted in evidence, usually without challenge. There is no plain reason why such correspondence should not be admitted, but it has the consequence that defendants who fail to respond to an investigating officer's letter may do so at some risk that an adverse inference will subsequently be drawn from it.

3.34 Failure to administer the caution. Failure to caution before interview is usually regarded by the courts as a significant and substantial breach of the code, such that there is a strong chance that the evidence will be excluded under section 78 of the Police and Criminal Evidence Act 1984 *(R. v. Sparks* [1991] Crim.L.R. 128), although the critical issue is whether there has been *such* an adverse effect on the fairness of the proceedings that the evidence ought to be excluded. If the evidence sought to be excluded is confession evidence under section 76 of the 1984 Act, the issue is whether the failure to caution and the attendant circumstances amounted to oppression or was likely by reason of anything said or done to render the confession unreliable (see paragraph 10.104 below).

3.35 Failure to afford an opportunity for legal advice. Where a person is arrested and detained in a police station, or interviewed there, a refusal to advise the suspect of his right to legal advice or, worse, denial of a right to legal advice before interview are matters which are taken seriously by the courts in connection with the discretion to exclude evidence under section 78 (above) *(R. v. Beycan* [1990] Crim.L.R. 185). The European Court of Human Rights underlined the paramount importance of enabling legal advice before interview in the context of legislation which draws an adverse inference from failure to answer the questions of the interviewer *(Murray v. U.K.* (1996) 22 E.H.R.R. 29). A person who is to be interviewed in connection with a regulatory offence may also, it is submitted, legitimately claim the right to consult his lawyer before answering questions if sufficient time to enable this to be done has not been given. The entitlement to take legal advice does not apply, however, to the obligation to hand over documents and may not provide a defence of "reasonable cause" for a failure to give assistance or information when required nor to wilful obstruction. By analogy, in *DPP v. Billington* (1988) 87 Cr. App. R. 68, the provisions of Code C did not enable a defendant to rely on the absence of legal advice as a reasonable excuse for a failure to provide a specimen of breath, blood or urine for analysis under section 7 of the Road Traffic Act 1988.

3.36 Failure to mention material matters or refusal to answer questions. Section 34 of the Criminal Justice and Public Order Act 1994 permits an inference to be drawn from a failure to mention material facts or to answer questions. Whether an inference can properly be drawn or not is a matter of discretion, to be exercised in the light of all the circumstances. For example, it may be perfectly reasonable to fail to answer questions. The court should direct itself or the Judge should direct the jury as the case may be that failure to mention any matter cannot prove guilt, but if the failure might support the prosecution case it can be taken into account *(R. v. Condron* [1997] 1 Cr. App. R. 185). Legal advice to remain silent is a factor that the court can take into account, but the mere fact that such advice is given does not prevent an inference arising *(R. v. Argent* [1997] 2 Cr. App. R. 27, *R. v. Condron* [1997] 1 Cr. App. R. 185. Reasons for remaining silent in a regulatory case might include:

(i) ignorance of the facts surrounding the offence, because it concerned others and there has been no opportunity to investigate;

(ii) the interviewing officer had revealed insufficient facts for the suspect to know what is alleged, or for the legal adviser to know what advice to give;

(iii) the issues involved in the offence are complex, so that an immediate response would be inappropriate.

(See *R. v. Roble* [1997] Crim.L.R. 449 – not a regulatory case). It is suggested that a further consideration in a regulatory case might be that the prosecution has not given the interviewee sufficient time to consult legal advisors. Also, where the interviewee is an employee, it is almost certainly appropriate in most circumstances that the employee be allowed an opportunity to consult his employer: so that a refusal to answer questions without that opportunity in circumstances where it is the employee who is the potential object of criminal charges might be entirely justified.

CHAPTER 4

Executive Steps to Compel Compliance

NOTICES

The Principle

4.1 General. This chapter is concerned with those regulatory provisions bestowing powers by which the regulatory authority can issue notices preventing non-compliance or requiring compliance with primary and secondary legislation. These notices (described generically in this chapter as "executive notices") can operate as a sort of executive injunction which enjoins the carrying out or cessation of specified activities or the continuance of specified conditions. The executive notice is generally subject to controls which are provided for in the legislation conceding the powers. The type and extent of the controls depend upon the nature of the legislation, the type of notice and the person who is entitled to issue it.

4.2 "Minded to" provisions. Under the Conservative administration prior to May 1997, it seemed that, pursuant to the provisions of the Deregulation and Contracting Out Act 1994, enforcement action by way of executive notice would be likely in the future to come under increasing levels of scrutiny. Controls envisaged by section 5 and Schedule 1 of the Deregulation and Contracting Out Act 1994 and the Deregulation (Model Appeal Provisions) Order 1996 (see paragraph 1.11 above) were that in cases specified by order an enforcement officer should serve a notice before any enforcement steps were taken indicating that he was considering serving an executive notice and inviting representations. Such provisions are unlikely to be generally invoked in the future, however. It is clear that the present government has maintained a commitment to deregulation, although it also stresses a greater commitment also to empowerment of consumers. See, for example, the U.K. Ministerial Address of the Under Secretary of State for the D.T.I. to the Institute of Trading Standards Administration 103rd Annual Conference. The government has encouraged voluntary use of procedures which involve a similarly restrained approach to the use of enforcement action against businesses which are not "rogue traders" by its promulgation of the Enforcement Concordat (see paragraphs 1.12, 2.9 and 2.10 above). Where the enforcement authority is a local authority which has adopted the provisions of the Concordat, it can be understood to have undertaken to discuss any problem informally with the defendant before moving on to enforcement action (including the service of notices). Where this is impossible due to the need for immediate action, the Enforcement Concordat provides that an explanation of the need for immediate action shall be given at the time and subsequently confirmed in writing in most cases within 5 days and in all cases within 10 days. In Food Safety cases, however, the prosecuting authority has already become subject to a deregulatory burden additional to that imposed under the Food Safety legislation which gave rise to the power to issue an executive notice. By the Deregulation (Improvement of Enforcement Procedures) (Food Safety Act 1990) Order 1996, an authorised officer of an enforcement authority is required to give to the proprietor of a food business a written notice which states that he is considering serving an improvement notice (see paragraph 4.12 below), gives his reasons and invites the proprietor within a specified period to make written or oral representations to the officer. If the food proprietor requests an oral hearing it will be in the presence of a senior officer of the enforcement authority serving the notice. This type of procedure may have the effect of averting any abuse of power by local authority officers (see, for instance, the facts in *Weldon v. North Cornwall District Council* [1997] 1 W.L.R. 570 and below). If the procedures of the Enforcement Concordat are adopted by all local authorities and are adopted fairly, this should also provide a protection to the local authority as well as to the trader.

4.3 Notices issued by local and other authorities. Where a notice may be issued by an emanation of a local or other authority, the notice is, under many statutes, capable of appeal. If the recipient declines to appeal, it is customary for any failure to comply with the notice to constitute an offence. In the field of planning, health and safety, and housing legislation, the issue of notices to secure compliance with statutory requirements has been a familiar procedure for some time (albeit that in housing matters, appeal usually lies to the county court; in health and safety matters, to the industrial tribunal; and in planning matters, appeal on the merits may lie to planning inspectors and to the Secretary of State). The issue of notices with a right of appeal to the magistrates' court has been a feature of the powers enjoyed by the local authority to limit noise and other nuisances for a considerable time. Corresponding powers have traditionally been denied to those enforcing contraventions of the standards laid down in consumer protection and food safety legislation. Notably, as an illustration of this, the introduction of section 10 of the Food Safety Act 1990 (improvement notices: see paragraph 4.12 below) was controversial in its passage through Parliament, largely because it confers a quasi-judicial function upon an environmental health officer – an employee of the executive.

4.4 Notices issued by the Secretary of State and others. In some cases, statutory notices compelling compliance may be issued only by the Secretary of State or other more senior arm of the executive (such as the Director General of Fair Trading). In that event, there are customarily procedures for the making of representations accompanied by a right of appeal to the High Court. Some notices are not so much to compel compliance but are operative *in terrorem*. That is, they do not specify what is to be done to comply, but are intended to prevent those who have adopted unacceptable business practices from carrying on trading and by the use of such power to deter respectable traders from crossing the invisible divide between what is acceptable trading practice and what is not. An example of this category of notice is the "minded to revoke" notice issued by the Director General of Fair Trading under section 32 of the Consumer Credit Act 1974. If, after hearing representations, the Director General confirms his provisional view, an appeal lies to the Secretary of State, and (whether that right of appeal is exercised or not) to the High Court, by virtue of section 11 of the Tribunals and Inquiries Act 1992. A related *quia timet* approach is reflected in the powers given to the Minister under section 13 of the Food Safety Act 1990 to prohibit certain commercial operations in relation to food if there is an imminent risk of injury to health.

4.5   Similarities.   Although under different statutes there are different types of notice and different purposes prescribed, there are often similarities between the procedures adopted and language used which make the executive notice capable of examination as a discrete topic. The drawing of an analogy between different legislation which has comparable procedures has been further legitimised by the proposed uniform treatment of appeals against executive action in regulatory matters under The Deregulation (Model Appeal Provisions) Order 1996 – whether its powers are to be invoked or otherwise. For further consideration of the legitimacy of comparing different statutes, see paragraph 1.10 above.

The executive as advisor as well as enforcer

4.6   Dual role.   Because of the nature of the executive function, enforcement officers are frequently called upon to offer advice and assistance to those whose businesses are covered by powers of enforcement. Businesses ask informally for advice and, in some areas, the recognition of the importance of this function has become central to the way in which enforcement officers (and LACOTS) perceive their role. It underlies the Home Authority principle (see paragraph 1.31 above). Indeed, the Enforcement Concordat stresses this element of local authority functioning most forcefully. An example of difficulty commonly arises in the Food Safety field. Businesses seek advice because they wish not to be prosecuted or otherwise the subject of enforcement action and they will base their conduct on the advice received. This has, sometimes, the consequence that if enforcement action in the form of the service of notices is subsequently taken, the indignation of the recipient is great. It is clear from *Weldon v. North Cornwall* (above and below) that the recipient of a notice can in some circumstances be expected to rely upon its content (but contrast *Harris v. Evans & Anor*, April 24, 1998, CA). In a similar way, it might be thought that a trader should be able to rely upon advice proffered in the course of the enforcer's advisory role. Although as a matter of practice, a change in position by the local authority might be a matter of embarrassment to them, it is not clear that the authority can generally be bound, nor that a defence of estoppel would lie.

4.7   Estoppel.   (Where the enforcement action is prosecution, no question of estoppel arises because the criminal law does not recognise the doctrine of estoppel by representation, although in some cases prosecution following a contrary representation might amount to an abuse of the process of the court (see paragraph 10.37 below). Where the enforcement action is the service of a statutory notice, it is not clear that the same principle applies.) A hypothetical example of the emergence of the problem in the context of an improvement notice is when the design and layout of food premises are expressly approved by an Environmental

Health Officer, say, at the planning stage upon the opening of a restaurant, but subsequently an improvement notice requiring structural or plumbing changes is served (perhaps by a colleague of the first Environmental Health Officer). It will only be in the most unusual case that an estoppel will lie. Lord Widgery C.J. commented in *Brooks and Burton Ltd v. Secretary of State for the Environment* [1977] 1 W.L.R. 1294:

"... local government officers should feel free to help applicants who come and ask them questions without all the time having the shadow of estoppel hanging over them and without the possibility of their immobilising their authorities by reason of some careless remark which produces such an estoppel".

This view, expressed in the context of a planning case and approved in *Western Fish Products Ltd v. Penwith District Council* (1978) 38 P. & C.R. 7, is equally applicable to the example furnished above. An exception may arise only where there is evidence that the person affected was justified in assuming that the environmental health officer intended to and had power to bind his authority (*Lever Finance Ltd v. Westminster City Council* [1971] 1 Q.B. 222, *Bedfordia Plant Ltd v. Secretary of State for the Environment* [1981] J.P.L. 122, *Camden London Borough Council v. Secretary of State for the Environment* (1993) 67 P. & C.R. 68). Also see *Weldon v. North Cornwall District Council* [1997] 1 W.L.R. 570, where substantial damages for negligent misstatement were awarded against a local authority because an environmental health officer acting outside his powers had required excessive and inappropriate work on pain of closure of the establishment. *Weldon* must be regarded as an exceptional case in the light of *Harris v. Evans & Anor*, April 24, 1998, CA, which found that an inspector of health and safety was not similarly liable for pure economic loss on the grounds that it was not just and reasonable for the enforcer of standards in the interest of the public to be liable for damages if he were to be in error. Given that the Enforcement Concordat makes an express promise of assistance and advice to businesses, and also that this could amount to the provision of consultancy skills on a national basis, it might be thought that the local authority is undertaking to be bound by the advice that is given pursuant to its terms and so founding an estoppel which might be capable of recognition in proceedings for judicial review or an appeal against any executive notice served.

Is there a duty to consult before serving a notice?

4.8 Entitlement to be heard. It can be seen above that some legislation and administrative practices have developed which require consultation before an executive notice is served. In the absence of such recognised procedures, and even where a statute is silent as to a duty to consult the person affected before a notice which affects private rights of property is served, it does not mean that there is never a duty upon an enforcement authority to consult. The principle that a party affected by an administrative act is entitled to be heard is well established (*Cooper v. Wandsworth District Board of Works* (1863) 14 C.B.N.S. 180). The duty will only be implied, however, where the purposes of the statute will be fulfilled by consultation between the executive and the person affected:

"For a long time the courts have, without objection from Parliament, supplemented procedure laid down in legislation where they have found that to be necessary for this purpose. But before this unusual kind of power is exercised it must be clear that the statutory procedure is insufficient to achieve justice and that to require additional steps would not frustrate the apparent purpose of the legislation" (*per* Lord Reid in *Wiseman v. Borneman* [1971] A.C. 297 at 308).

Where consultation must be undertaken, either because it is expressly provided for or because it is required to promote the statutory purpose of the legislation, it must be carried out by local authority employees dispassionately and fairly, so as to give proper weight to representations made by persons affected (*R. v. Camden London Borough Council, ex p. Cran*, [1995] R.T.R. 346).

4.9 Frustration of the statutory purpose. This issue was considered in *R. v. Birmingham City Council, ex p. Ferrero Ltd* [1993] 1 All E.R. 530 in the context of a notice under section 14 of the Consumer Protection Act 1987 (a "suspension" notice preventing the marketing of unsafe goods for a period of six months). The Divisional Court, in finding that there was no duty to consult the trader, took account of the following matters:

   (i) where there was a question of urgency the duty to consult, if it existed, would have to be overridden. This would present the enforcement authority with a serious dilemma in each case which could, but need not, be urgent, and could result in the loss of valuable time;

   (ii) the statutory scheme had provided expressly for consultation in other areas where Parliament had thought appropriate.

   (iii) safeguards were built into the statutory scheme by providing for compensation if it was subsequently found that there was no risk to the public.

The court concluded that consultation would frustrate the statutory purpose, not promote it.

4.10 Deregulation. Although the duty to consult, as such, is not envisaged by the Deregulation (Model Appeal Provisions) Order 1996, as one which should be incorporated in the model provisions for adoption, with or without amendments (see paragraph 1.11 above), if any future legislation is passed which adopts the model appeal provisions, the officer must, except in a case where immediate action is necessary, give to a person who might be the subject of enforcement action (as defined by section 5 of the Deregulation and Contracting Out Act 1994 (see paragraph 1.11 above)) a written notice stating that he is considering taking enforcement action and why, and giving to the recipient of the notice the opportunity to make written representations or oral representations in the presence of a senior officer of the authority. These representations would have to be considered and, if enforcement action is to be taken, further written reasons must be given. These steps would make more open the true position of the prosecuting authority and would also facilitate appeal against the enforcement action were any tribunal to be appointed under the provisions of the Order (Deregulation (Model Appeal Provisions) Order 1996, Sched. 1, Chapter 1). Already, as indicated above, the Deregulation (Improvement of Enforcement Procedures) (Food Safety Act 1990) Order 1996 has introduced a procedure which requires an officer wishing to serve an improvement notice under section 10 of the Food Safety Act 1990 to serve a written notice stating that he is considering serving an improvement notice, setting out the reasons and giving an opportunity to make written or oral representations. Although there is a duty to consider the representations, there is no obligation to give written reasons if the representations are rejected – unlike the Model Provisions Order. Even in the lesser form now applicable in Food Safety cases, this procedure recognises the benefit, if not of consultation prior to the service of a notice, of hearing the counter-arguments before costly litigation or modifications are commenced. Where local authorities have adopted the Enforcement Concordat, officers are required to provide an opportunity to discuss the circumstances of the case and resolve points of difference (see paragraph 2.10 for an explanation of the nature and effect of the Enforcement Concordat, which is intended to replace the provisions of section 5 above), although not with the degree of provision or formality which the trader might have expected under the Model Appeals provisions.

PROCEDURAL VALIDITY OF NOTICES SUBJECT TO APPEAL IN THE MAGISTRATES' COURT

Examples of notices capable of appeal to magistrates

4.11 Three commonly used powers are used to illustrate this type of notice. These are section 10 of the Food Safety Act 1990 (improvement notices), section 14 of the Consumer Protection Act 1987 (suspension notices) and sections 79 and 80 of the Environmental Protection Act 1990 (nuisance abatement notices). Improvement notices and nuisance abatement notices both require the person served to take positive steps to act lawfully. The suspension notice prohibits a trader from selling or supplying (and other related concepts) goods which are subject to the notice. These notices must comply with a number of requirements which can be contrasted. In each case, the notice cannot be issued unless the authority has a certain state of mind; the notice must be served in accordance with the legislative requirements and it must observe the formalities laid down in the statutory provision. Each is subject to appeal to the magistrates and an offence lies if the terms of the notice are not complied with.

State of mind of the issuing authority

4.12 Belief, suspicion and reasonableness.

Improvement Notices. Section 10 of the Food Safety Act 1990 provides that the enforcement authority may serve an improvement notice in respect of the premises or operations of a food business. A notice may be served if the authorised officer of the enforcement authority *"has reasonable grounds for believing"* that the proprietor of a food business is failing to comply with any regulations to which the section applies. The notice should specify the grounds relied upon and set out what is to be done to comply (section 10(1)).

Suspension Notices. By section 14 of the Consumer Protection Act 1987 the enforcement authority may serve a notice if the authority has *"reasonable grounds for suspecting"* that there has been a non-compliance with safety requirements. This notice, similarly, must set out the grounds for the suspicion.

Distinction between the tests. The tests of reasonable grounds for belief and suspicion are not the same as each other. In *Holtham v. Metropolitan Police* (1987), *The Times*, November 28, 1987 the Court of Appeal identified suspicion as a state of surmise or conjecture in which proof was lacking. A requirement that there be reasonable cause for suspicion did not upgrade that notion into a higher test, although the reasonable grounds for reaching the suspicion may be looked at. In *R. v. Hall (Edward)* (1985) 81 Cr. App. R. 260 (a handling case) belief was described as "something short of knowledge. It may be said to be the state of mind of a person who says to himself "I cannot say I know for certain that these goods are stolen, but there can be no other reasonable conclusion in the light of the circumstances, in the light of all that I have heard and seen". Suspicion such as "I suspect that these goods were stolen but it may be on the other hand that they were not" was distinguished.

Contrasting the tests. The use of each test is reflected in the different legislative purposes: section 14 of the 1987 Act, for example, aims to prevent the distribution of goods while steps are taken for forfeiture (see paragraphs 4.41 onwards) or for prosecution. It is a holding procedure, set against background decisions. Its inappropriate use may entitle a trader who suffers loss to obtain compensation (see paragraph 4.45). Section 10 of the 1990 Act, on the other hand, envisages a less urgent trigger for the service of the notice. Other procedures for the service of prohibition notices exist to deal with an immediate and serious risk. Accordingly, the mental standard to be met by the enforcement authority is higher.

Reasonable cause. As with the expression "reasonable cause to believe" it is likely that there must be not only reasonable cause for suspicion but also actual suspicion that there is a non-compliance (see *R. v. Banks* [1916] 2 K.B. 621; *R. v. Harrison* [1938] 3 All E.R. 134; *Nakkuda Ali v. Jayaratne* [1951] A.C. 66).

4.13 Satisfaction. A nuisance abatement notice under section 80 of the Environmental Protection Act 1990 may be served if the local authority is "satisfied" as to certain matters. Presumably, the requirement is for satisfaction on the balance of probabilities rather than to the higher, criminal, standard. Although the word "shall" is used in section 80, this has been held not to exclude a discretion to act in another manner (*Nottinghamshire City District Council v. Newton* [1974] 1 W.L.R. 923).

Is there a remedy for an unlawful state of mind?

4.14 The consequences of the issue of an executive notice where the issuing authority has not achieved the correct mental state will depend entirely on the statutory context. In some legislation the notice may be invalidated (see paragraph 4.16 below). In some legislation (see paragraph 4.15 below) an absence of an appropriate state of mind on the part of the issuer may be quite irrelevant. There are three points at which the question may arise: on an appeal brought by the person upon whom the notice is served, in a prosecution for non-compliance and on an application for judicial review to challenge the validity of the instrument.

On appeal

4.15 Notice not vitiated. An example of a notice the validity of which is plainly not affected merely because the enforcement authority has not had the correct state of mind or has acted unreasonably is furnished by section 14 of the Consumer Protection Act 1987. The power of appeal to the justices enables them to set aside the notice only if they are satisfied that there is no contravention of a safety requirement. Accordingly, the misuse of power by the enforcement authority where there is a contravention of a safety requirement cannot lead to a successful appeal at all. This was confirmed in *R. v. Birmingham City Council, ex p. Ferrero Ltd* [1993] 1 All E.R. 530 in which Taylor L.J., in finding that the appropriate appeal lay to the magistrates and not by way of judicial review to the Divisional Court, said:

> "The provisions [for appeal to the magistrates] aim at withholding goods from the public if there is a reasonable suspicion that they are unsafe. Unless they are then cleared of the danger, it is right that the suspension should remain, even if the process by which the enforcement authority reached its decision was flawed. It cannot be right that dangerous goods should continue to be marketed simply because of some procedural impropriety by the enforcement authority in the process of deciding to issue a suspension notice. Common sense dictates that protection of the public must take precedence over fairness to the trader ... Protection is given to the trader by providing for compensation if there has been no contravention."

4.16 Examples of notices where vitiation is an arguable issue.

Food Safety Act 1990, s.10. In the case of section 10 of the Food Safety Act 1990, the position may be different from that under section 14 of the Consumer Protection Act 1987 because the right of appeal given by section 37 of the Act lies in respect of "the decision ... to serve an improvement notice" and allows the court to cancel or affirm the notice with or without modification. While it is probable that the magistrates court has power to rehear the whole issue and is not limited to reviewing the correctness or otherwise of an authority's decision (*Fulham Metropolitan Borough Council v. Santilli* [1933] 2 K.B. 357, *Stepney Borough Council v. Joffe* [1949] 1 K.B. 599), it does not follow that the court is entitled to affirm a notice which is procedurally invalid. There is no express provision in the Food Safety Act 1990 that the court can transform a notice which on investigation on appeal appears to be procedurally invalid into a valid one by the substitution of its own view. Although the powers of the court to look behind the formal validity of the notice are, it is submitted, greater on appeal than when a defence to an allegation of non-compliance is at issue, the full extent of those powers remains to be determined.

Environmental Protection Act 1990, ss.79 and 80. The genuineness and reasonableness of "satisfaction" of the local authority which serves an abatement notice can, it is submitted, be investigated on appeal, because one of the grounds of the Statutory Nuisance (Appeals) Regulations 1990 is whether the notice was "justified". It is also a ground that there has been "some informality, defect or error or error in, or in connection with the abatement notice". The notion of justification could bear one of two meanings, namely whether the local authority had acted correctly in issuing the summons or whether the outlying circumstances were sufficient to warrant the issue of a notice (regardless of the legality or otherwise of the local authority's decision about them). An informality, defect or error is, it is submitted, wide enough to include an improper state of mind at the time of serving the notice (provided that the improper mental state had not been arrived at maliciously, in which case another ground, such as that of justification would need to be chosen). The consequences of permitting an investigation into the procedural validity of the notice are limited by regulation 2(3) which provides that the court shall dismiss the appeal if satisfied that the informality, defect or error was immaterial. There is no corresponding provision relating to an "unjustified" notice. It has yet to be conclusively determined whether an inadequate state of mind at the time of issuing a notice is a matter which could render the notice unjustified, or whether an innocent mistake is an informality, defect or error. If the latter, would the improper decision to serve a notice be so material (analagous to a pre-condition, the absence of which may be a fundamental flaw in an otherwise valid notice) that the defect was incapable of cure as a matter of law, or would the magistrates need to consider the factual consequences of the impropriety?

On prosecution for non-compliance

4.17 Is an improper state of mind by the enforcement authority a defence? The service of a notice which is unlawful because the enforcement officer did not have the requisite suspicion or belief might be a defence to a prosecution for non-compliance with it, although whether this contention can be raised in a case where the notice is formally valid will depend on the proper interpretation of the statute giving rise to the offence of failure to comply with the notice. In *R. v. Wicks* [1997] 2 All E.R. 801 (which concerned an allegation of bad faith in issuing a notice under planning legislation), Lord Hoffman, while open to the suggestion that there was a wide right for anyone prosecuted under a byelaw to challenge its validity, said:

> "The point at which we absolutely part company [that is, with Counsel for Mr Wicks] is when he submits that this right can be extrapolated to enable a defendant to challenge the vires of every act done under statutory authority if its validity forms part of the prosecution case or its invalidity would constitute a defence. In my view, no such generalisation is possible. The question must depend entirely upon the construction of the statute under which the prosecution is brought. The statute may require the prosecution to prove that the act in question is not open to challenge on any ground available in public law or it may be a defence to show that it is. In such a case, the justices will have to rule upon the validity of the act. On the other hand, the statute may upon its true construction merely require an act which appears formally valid and has not been quashed by judicial review. In such a case, nothing but the formal validity of the act will be relevant to an issue before the justices. It is in my view impossible to construct a general theory of the *ultra vires* doctrine which applies to every statutory power, whatever the terms and policy of the statute."

An allegation that the authority did not satisfy the requirements as to the state of mind for issuing the notice amounts to an allegation that the notice is unlawful and therefore invalid (see paragraphs 4.14 to 4.16 below). To the extent that the argument is available, there is some authority in support of a contention that the defendant may raise arguments as to the validity of a notice even if he could have raised those arguments on appeal but has not done so (*Francis v. Yiewsley and West Drayton Urban District Council* [1958] 1 Q.B. 493), although in the case of *Wicks* the fact that there was an appeal process pointed to a contention of *mala fides* being unavailable as a defence to prosecution, even though the grounds upon which an appeal could be entertained did not include *mala fides*. In the Food Safety Act 1990 there is no express provision that a ground of invalidity cannot be a defence if it could have been raised on appeal but has not been. On the other hand, under the predecessor of section 80 of the Environmental Protection Act 1990 (section 58 of the Control of Pollution Act 1974) the statutory code has been interpreted so as to prevent questions as to the validity of the notice being raised as a defence to prosecution if those questions could have been raised on appeal (see paragraph 4–18 below). There is no reported authority under the Food Safety Act 1990 or the Consumer Protection Act 1987 on this point. It is now clear, however, that in many cases questions of the state of mind of the maker of the notice may not be raised by way of defence to a prosecution for non-compliance with the notice although it seems that if they cannot be raised on appeal, an application by way of judicial review of the decision to issue the notice may be made. In *R. v. Wicks* the House of Lords confined the challenge that may be made on the grounds of invalidity as a defence to prosecution for non-compliance with an enforcement notice under the legislation in question, and indicated that where there was an allegation of bad faith, it might be appropriate to adjourn the criminal proceedings to allow the defendant to apply to the Divisional Court: the procedure which was not permitted in the *Ferrero* case (above).

4.18 Statutory preclusion of a defence.   It is only a small step further to say that the consequence of a matter being capable of consideration in an appeal, may in any event, render it incapable of consideration as a defence. In *A. Lambert Ltd v. Lomas* [1981] 1 W.L.R. 898, the decision in *Francis v. Yiewsley and West Drayton Urban District Council* (above) was distinguished. The defendant was charged under section 58 of the Control of Pollution Act 1974 with failure without reasonable excuse to comply with an abatement notice. He raised the invalidity of the abatement notice as a reasonable excuse for non-compliance. It was held that the scheme of the Act and Regulations (namely the predecessor to the Statutory Nuisance (Appeals) Regulations 1990) made under it was such that the invalidity of the notice could not be raised as a defence in respect of any issue which could have been raised on appeal. In particular the regulations:

(i)   made detailed provisions for the appeal, including many and various grounds;

(ii)   made provision for the quashing or variation of the notice or for dismissal of the appeal;

(iii)   provided for orders to be made as to the burden of costs to be incurred in carrying out the work;

(iv)   required the magistrates to have regard to the ownership and occupancy of any premises and its terms and conditions which made it apparent that the same issues could not be raised as part of a defence.

If it is a correct interpretation of the 1990 Regulations (see paragraphs 4.16 above, 4.35 and 4.36 below) that the state of mind of the enforcement authority is capable of investigation on appeal, it is not capable of being raised as a defence on the ground that the notice is invalid, but it is also clear from the speech of Lord Hoffman in *Wicks* that the reverse does not apply.

Judicial review

4.19 Judicial review. Where complaint is made of the decision to issue an enforcement notice which goes to its regularity, an application may be made for leave to apply for judicial review (*R. v. Wicks* (above)) although see also the approach of the court in *R. v. Ferrero* and *Imperial Tobacco v. Attorney General* [1981] A.C. 718, in which it was decided that judicial review on grounds other than the validity of the instrument giving rise to the offence was not available to challenge an on-going prosecution, see also paragraph 2.23 above in respect of the scope of judicial review abuse of process and the decision to prosecute. In *R. v. Wicks* it was posited that it might be appropriate to adjourn proceedings in the magistrates' court while an application for judicial review was made.

SERVICE OF THE NOTICE

4.20 Acts of the server and the recipient's knowledge distinguished. It is a mistake to equate service of a notice with actual receipt of the document or knowledge by the recipient. This principle has two consequences:

(i) Where express statutory provision specifies the steps which are to be taken to effect service of a document, service may be effected when those steps have been taken, notwithstanding that they may have been ineffective to bring the content of the document to the attention of the intended recipient. So in *Lombard North Central plc v. Power-Hines* [1995] C.C.L.R. 24, a County Court judge refused to set aside a judgement obtained following the posting of a default notice in accordance with section 176(2) of the Consumer Credit Act 1974 to the defendant's last-known address, even though that notice did not come to his attention. His Honour Judge Viljoen commented that the service provision was designed to apply where, through no fault of the sender, the document was not brought to the attention of the intended recipient. It appears that similar reasoning may be adopted even in cases where the failure to comply with the mandatory requirements of the notice constitutes an offence (*R. v. Collett* [1994] 2 All E.R. 372 and paragraph 4–39 below).

(ii) If the notice is served on the wrong person, even though it may have come to the attention of the party interested in its content, the service of the notice may be insufficient. So, in *AMEC Building Ltd v. London Borough of Camden* [1997] Env. L.R. 330, notices were sent to the company secretary of AMEC Construction Ltd, rather than to the appellant, the head office of which was at the same address. AMEC Building Ltd was the company interested in the subject matter of the notice and responded, suggesting that all further correspondence be addressed to AMEC Building Ltd. On a prosecution for failure to comply with the notice, the point was taken that the notice had not been served. The Divisional Court set aside the conviction because the statutory provisions did not permit service on a third party, notwithstanding that the right person might receive the document from the third party. Receipt alone was not a substitution for service.

4.21 Specific provision. Legislation requiring the service of notices usually contains specific provision as to how, and upon whom, the document must be served. Additional powers exist under section 233 of the Local Government Act 1972 in respect of any notice, order or other document required under an enactment to be served by a local authority. Under the Food Safety Act 1990 the notice must be served on the proprietor of a food business and under the Consumer Protection Act 1987 and the Environmental Protection Act 1990 any person committing a contravention of the legislation may be served with the notice. The manner of service and the provisions for problems with service may differ. Section 44 of the Consumer Protection Act 1987, for example, provides that any document required or authorised by a person to be served may be served:

(i) by delivery to his proper address or by sending it by post to him at that address;

(ii) where the person is a body corporate, by serving it in accordance with (i) above on its secretary or clerk;

(iii) where the person is a partnership, by serving it on a person having control or management of the partnership business.

The proper address of a person is his last known address, except that if service is effected on a body corporate, or its secretary or clerk, the proper address is its registered or principal office and if on a partnership by a person having its management or control at the address of its principal office. Similar provisions apply under the Environmental Protection Act 1990 and corresponding but not identical provisions apply under the Food Safety Act 1990, s.50, except that this statute also provides that where it is not practicable after reasonable inquiry to ascertain to whom a document should be addressed it is permissible to serve on "the owner" or "the occupier" by leaving the document with someone at the premises or by affixing it to some conspicuous part of the premises. Section 233 of the Local Government Act 1972 makes similar provision.

4.22 Interpretation Act 1978. Section 7 of the Interpretation Act 1978 provides that in the absence of express provision, service by post is deemed to be effected by properly addressing, pre-paying and posting a letter containing the notice. It further provides that unless the contrary is proved, it is effected at the time the letter would be served in the ordinary course of post. When, then, is it open to the intended recipient to prove that he has not received an executive notice by reliance on section 7 of the 1978 Act? In *Lombard North Central plc v. Power-Hines* (paragraph 4.20 above) His Honour, Judge Viljoen asserted that:

> "the second part [of section 7 of the Interpretation Act 1978, relating to the time at which service would be effected] . . . comes into play and only comes into play in a case where under the legislation to which the section is being applied the document has to be received by a certain time. There is no provision as to time in section 87 of the Consumer Credit Act 1974."

It is easier to understand the logic of this (which is, in turn, derived from the language of Parker L.J. in *R. v. County of London Quarter Sessions Appeals Committee, ex p. Rossi* [1956 1 Q.B. 683) in the light of the structure of the Consumer Credit Act 1974 where the failure to comply within the period specified in section 88 of the Act merely empowers the taking of further action, than it would be were the same reasoning to be applied to executive notices requiring the intended recipient to act under pain of a penalty. See paragraph 4.28 below.

4.23 Failure properly to serve a notice. A notice will have been improperly served if the formalities for communicating its content have not been complied with by the sender, or, in a case where the intended recipient is required by the legislation to have received the notice, where he can prove that he did not receive it. Where there has been no service of the notice at all, there cannot be a prosecution for non-compliance with it, unless the statutory provision is merely directory and not mandatory (see below). Similarly, if the wrong person is served, no prosecution can follow (see paragraph 4.20 above). A failure properly to serve a notice goes to its validity but does not necessarily render it a nullity. In *R. v. London Borough of Greenwich, ex p. Patel* [1985] J.P.L. 851 and *R. v. Collett* [1994] 2 All E.R. 372 (the latter distinguishing a Scottish case, *McDaid v. Clydebank DC* [1984] J.P.L. 574) it was held that the failure to serve an enforcement notice under planning legislation did not render the notice a nullity. These cases were decided by reference to legislation which made express provision for circumstances where a notice was not served, and under which, therefore, the failure to serve the notice was not fatal to the prosecution. The same approach may not be adopted where no legislative consideration is given to non-service.

4.24 Invalid notices. If an improvement notice is not null but is invalid because it has not been served at all (and non-service has not rendered it null) or has been served defectively, this, it is submitted, does not prevent the inadequacy of service being raised as a ground of appeal under the Food Safety Act 1990, and it is likely that a failure to serve a notice under section 80 of the Environmental Protection Act 1990 probably would be "an informality, defect or error". In the latter case, the Regulations provide that the materiality of the failure must be considered (see paragraph 4.16 above). In the former case, if a magistrates court has power in the absence of express provision to affirm an invalid notice (see paragraph 4.36 below), the failure to serve the notice is unlikely to be a ground of cancellation of the notice unless the failure has caused substantial prejudice (see, for example, *Mayes v. Secretary of State for Wales* [1989] J.P.L. 848). Any difficulty caused by an abridgement of time for compliance occasioned by defective service can be overcome by the powers of the magistrates court to modify the notice under section 39 of the Food Safety Act 1990.

4.25 Time. A suspension notice under the Consumer Protection Act 1987, s.14 is effective on service and must expire not later than six months after its date. The period of suspension must be specified in the notice (section 14(1)). A notice under section 10 of the Food Safety Act 1990 must require measures specified in the notice or equivalent measures to be undertaken within a certain period. The abatement notice under section 80 of the Environmental Protection Act 1990 must require an abatement or prohibition or restriction of an occurrence or recurrence of the nuisance (it can be served before the nuisance has occurred) and must require the execution of works or the taking of other steps which are necessary. The Act also provides that the Act "shall" specify the time or times within which the notice shall be complied with. Notwithstanding the mandatory words, a notice may not be materially defective if is fails to specify a time within which the work is to be undertaken (*Strathclyde Regional Council v. Tudhope* [1983] J.P.L. 536). In the absence of any contrary intention, an abatement notice remains effective indefinitely (*R. v. Birmingham Justices, ex p. Guppy* (1988) 152 J.P. 159). For questions of formality see paragraph 4.26 onwards below.

FORMALITY OF THE NOTICE

4.26 **Nullity and invalidity.** Even where there is no prescribed form there is, in each example chosen in this chapter, a statutory requirement for each notice which must be satisfied before the notice will be valid. Where the notice is defective on its face it will be formally invalid and may be null and without legal effect. A notice will be defective on its face if the defect can be ascertained by considering the document in conjunction with the empowering legislation and those facts which are adverted to on the face of the document (for example, an executive notice which refers to the wrong premises may be, as against the true premises, null and unenforceable, even though the intention of the enforcement authority was to identify thee premises in the defendant's possession). Arguably, a notice which is manifestly unreasonable will also be defective on its face (see the speech of Lord Nicholls in *R. v. Wicks* [1997] 2 All E.R. 801). Where the notice can be proved to be defective for some other reason it will be merely invalid, and such invalidity may be incapable of investigation in some types of proceeding (see *R. v. Wicks* (above)). The position in planning cases was summed up by Upjohn L.J. in *Miller Mead v. Minister of Housing and Local Government* [1963] 2 Q.B. 196 at 226 in this way:

> "Now, I think, is the time to draw the distinction between invalidity and nullity. For example, supposing development without permission is alleged and it is found that no permission is required or that, contrary to the allegation in the notice, it is established that in fact the conditions in the planning permission have been complied with, . . . the notice is invalid: it is not a nullity because on the face of it it appears to be good and it is only on the proof of facts aliunde that the notice is shown to be bad . . . But supposing the notice on the face of it fails to specify some period required [by statute]. On the face of it the notice does not comply with the section: it is a nullity and is so much waste paper . . . Supposing then upon its true construction the notice was hopelessly ambiguous and uncertain, so that the owner or occupier could not tell in what respect it was alleged that he had developed the land without permission or in which respect he had failed to comply with a condition, or again, that he could not tell with reasonable certainty what steps he had to take to remedy the alleged breaches. The notice would be bad on its face and a nullity"

A null notice might include one which required steps which are unlawful under other legislation (*McKay v. Secretary of State for the Environment* [1994] J.P.L. 806).

4.27 **Illustrations of want of formality.**

Suspension Notices. Under section 14 of the Consumer Protection Act 1987 a notice must:

(i) specify the period of suspension of trading in goods;

(ii) describe the goods in a manner sufficient to identify them;

(iii) set out the grounds upon which the authority suspects that a safety provision has been contravened; and

(iv) state that there is a right of appeal and the manner in which it can be exercised.

A notice which fails to do these things may be null and therefore without legal effect. If magistrates find that the notice is a nullity, they cannot allow a prosecution for non-compliance to proceed. On the other hand, it is submitted that the magistrates cannot entertain an appeal against a null notice either. The powers of the justices are limited by section 15(3) to setting aside a notice only if they are satisfied that there is no breach of safety requirements but it would be surprising, it is submitted, if the statute intended that the magistrates should be required to uphold a null notice. It was not part of the argument in *R. v. Birmingham City Council ex p. Ferrero Ltd* [1993] 1 All E.R. 530 (see paragraph 4.15 above) that the notice was a nullity. Where the informality is such that the notice may be invalid, but is not null, the *Ferrero* decision would suggest that judicial review may not lie. On the other hand Lord Hoffman's view in *Wicks* (see paragraph 4.26) that there can be no hard and fast rule in this area as to the points which may be taken as to validity in the magistrates' court (see paragraph 4.17 above) must be taken also to apply to the Divisional Court.

Improvement Notices.   In the case of the Food Safety Act 1990, the position is somewhat different. Prescribed forms appear in the Food Safety (Improvement and Prohibition – Prescribed Forms) Regulations 1991 and a Code of Practice issued pursuant to section 40 of the Food Safety Act 1990 sets out the obligations of the enforcement authority. The requirements of the notice are that it must:

(i) state the officer's grounds for believing that the proprietor is failing to comply with the regulations;

(ii) specify the matters which constitute the failure to comply;

(iii) specify the matters which in the officer's opinion, the proprietor must take in order to secure compliance;

(iv) require the proprietor to take those or equally effective measures within a given time (not less that 14 days).

It is important that each step is observed and that the obligations to set out each are not elided. In *Bexley London Borough Council v. Gardner Merchant* [1993] C.O.D. 383 an improvement notice alleging a failure to meet the requirements of regulation 18 of the Food Hygiene (General) Regulations 1970 (the predecessor to the Food Safety (General Food Hygiene) Regulations 1995) stated that "a conveniently accessible wash-hand basin with a supply of hot and cold water or hot water at a suitably controlled temperature is not supplied . . ." This did no more than set out the statutory obligation and allege a non-specific non-compliance. The magistrates held that it was null and void and the Divisional Court upheld their decision. Although no application to amend was made in that case, a null notice could not, it is submitted, be amended by the magistrates on appeal. It remains to be decided whether the power to introduce modifications to a notice will allow a notice which is merely invalid to be upheld on appeal.

4.28 Specifying steps in a notice. Where steps are necessary to abate a nuisance, they must be specified (even though the language of section 80 of the Environmental Protection Act 1990 speaks of "requiring the execution of such works and the taking of such other steps as may be necessary") with reasonable particularity (*Salford City Council v. McNally* [1976] A.C. 379, *Millard v. Wastall* [1898] 1 Q.B. 342, *R. v. Fenny Stratford Justices, ex p. Watney Mann (Midlands)* [1976] 1 W.L.R. 1101, 1106). The last-mentioned case includes an illustration of the difficulty of setting standards. It is, for example, desirable to specify in an abatement notice what decibel level must not be exceeded, but the notice must also state where the decibel level is to be measured. The language of the Food Safety Act 1990, which requires "specification" of the steps to be taken, compares with the planning legislation which preceded it. Because of the serious consequences of a failure to comply, the remedial action cannot be merely described in general terms, or the notice will be invalid. So, in a comparable planning case, an enforcement notice which required the recipient to "install satisfactory sound proofing" and to "take all possible action to minimise the effects created by acrylic paint" was too vague to be enforceable (*Metallic Protectives Ltd v. Secretary of State for the Environment* [1976] J.P.L. 166). It would probably be insufficient, therefore in a food hygiene case to require "the satisfactory cleaning of the premises" or "the prevention, so far as is reasonably practicable, of the entry of birds and the risk of infestation by rats". In a food safety case, the importance of careful specification is magnified because the recipient of the notice is not required to do the works specified as long as he undertakes equivalent works. Undertaking works to an equivalent standard is incapable of performance if the enforcement officers have not sufficiently identified what must be done. Also see *Network Housing Association v. Westminster City Council, The Times,* November 8, 1994 in relation to the specification of works. On the other hand, it has been held (*Budd v. Colchester Borough Council,* New Law, July 29, 1996) that this case is not authority for the proposition that an abatement notice always needs to specify the works to be done or the steps to be taken. It can be sufficient if the notice specifies precisely the result to be achieved, for example, the nuisance abated. The question of the sufficiency of the specification of work to be done is a question of fact to be decided in the circumstances of each case.

4.29 Notices which specify the steps to be taken. Where a notice specifies that steps must be taken and does not require merely that the offensive conduct be ameliorated or discontinued, the failure to carry out the steps set out in the notice is likely to be an offence, notwithstanding that the offensive conduct may in fact have been ameliorated or discontinued by other steps. So in *AMEC Building & Anor v. London Borough of Camden* [1997] Env. L.R. 330, the contention was raised in respect of a nuisance abatement notice that, as there was no finding of a continuation of a statutory nuisance after the date of the service of the notice, there could be no finding of non-compliance. The notice required a schedule of works to be carried out. It had not been. The Divisional Court held that the prosecution was not required to show continuation of the nuisance after the notice in order to establish the offence and, if in fact there was an abatement, an attack on the need for the notice could have been made by appeal.

APPEALS

Procedure

4.30 Manner of appeal. In the future, it is possible that some statutory provisions may permit a right of appeal to a tribunal to be established under the Deregulation (Model Appeal Provisions) Order 1996 although it appears that the current administration has no wish to divert enforcement procedures away from the criminal courts and it therefore seems unlikely that such a tribunal will be established. Now, where there is a right of appeal against an executive notice, it is to existing courts and tribunals. This section deals only with appeals to the magistrates' court. Appeals to the magistrates' court against executive notices are customarily by way of complaint (see paragraph 8.42 below). Because no criminal penalty is attached unless there is a non-compliance (and compliance is usually not required under statutory provisions pending the determination of the appeal although see paragraph 4.32 below in relation to a suspension notice under the 1987 Act), the proceedings in the magistrates court are of a civil character (see paragraph 10.113 below). An appeal against a suspension notice under the 1987 Act, for example, may be made by way of complaint provided that no proceedings for forfeiture or by way of prosecution are afoot. An appeal under section 37 of the Food Safety Act 1990 similarly lies by way of complaint, as does an appeal against an abatement notice. This has the consequence that the procedures and rules of evidence to be applied in the magistrates' court will be different from those applicable in criminal proceedings. On the other hand, where a prosecution or forfeiture proceedings (see paragraph 4.41 below) have already been commenced an appeal against a suspension notice under the Consumer Protection Act 1987 is by application to the court where those proceedings are pending. If the procedure is by way of application in criminal proceedings, the appeal is presumably itself to be regarded as of a criminal rather than civil nature and it is questionable whether criminal rather than civil procedure should govern the trial before the justices in this instance. It would be undesirable for appeals to be conducted disparately merely because a prosecution has been commenced expeditiously.

4.31 Time for bringing an appeal. No time is specified for an appeal against a suspension notice, but an appeal against an improvement notice under the Food Safety Act 1990 must be brought within one month from the date of service of the notice or within the period in which the improvement is to be made, whichever is the earlier (section 37(5)). It is usual to exclude from the calculation of the period the day of service (see, for example, *Dodds v. Walker* [1981] 2 All E.R. 609, *E. J. Riley Investments Ltd v. Eurostile Holdings Ltd* [1985] 3 All E.R. 181). Under section 80(3) of the Environmental Protection Act 1990, on the other hand, the provision makes it clear that the day of service is included in the 21 days allowed for the appeal.

4.32 Effect of entry of appeal. Under the 1990 Act, the effect of an appeal is to stay the operation of the improvement notice. There is no stay under the 1987 Act (the trader's remedy is in compensation, see paragraph 4.37 below) although if an appeal from the magistrates court to the Crown Court is pursued, an order in the magistrates court which sets aside a suspension notice may contain provisions staying the operation pending an appeal. An appeal under section 80 of the Environmental Protection Act 1990 operates as a stay of the notice until the appeal is determined (Statutory Nuisance (Appeals) Regulations 1990).

Powers on appeal

4.33 Upholding the notice or dismissal only. The magistrates' power on appeal under the Consumer Protection Act 1987 is limited to dismissal if the court is satisfied that "there has been" no breach of the relevant safety provisions. This does not on its face appear to allow an appeal where there has been a breach but a modification introduced to goods falling within a general description in the suspension notice has subsequently rendered them safe. It is doubtful whether this is what was intended by the legislature, so that care needs to be taken in the description of the goods in the suspension notice. A suspension notice drafted too widely might properly be the subject of judicial review.

4.34 No power to diminish legislation. Where a statute allows variations of the notice on appeal, the first question is what the power to vary may allow. It is likely in every case that variation will not permit the magistrates to alter the effect of the legislation which is addressed by the notice, although the power to vary the notice may change the manner in which compliance is to be achieved. So, in *Salford City Council v. Abbeyfield (Worsley) Society Ltd* [1993] C.O.D. 384, the respondent, who ran a charitable home, was served with two notices requiring that the food handlers be provided with washable overclothing. Some of the food handlers were unpaid residents of the home. On appeal, the magistrates limited an improvement notice to "all paid employees" carrying out activities "in the kitchen". The Divisional Court found those limitations to be held *ultra vires* because they did not reflect the requirements of the Food Hygiene (General) Regulations 1970: there was no justification for a distinction in the notice between types of person, both of whom were under a legal obligation to comply with the provisions of the Food Safety Act 1990 and the Food Hygiene Regulations.

4.35 Variation and invalidity. As indicated above, the courts' powers to deal with invalidity depend entirely on the construction of the legislation giving rise to the powers. In the absence of statutory provisions which permit, expressly or impliedly, the court to uphold an invalid notice the court will be constrained to allow an appeal on the ground that the notice was invalid. It is not always obvious whether there is an implied power to uphold an invalid notice. For example, there has been no decision which makes clear whether an invalid (as opposed to null) improvement notice under the Food Safety Act 1990 may be upheld by the magistrates (see paragraph 4.16 above). There is certainly no express power which permits the upholding of an invalid notice but on a proper construction of the Act the power granted under section 39 of the Act to make modifications could be construed to allow all or some invalidities to be cured. The position under section 80 of the Environmental Protection Act 1990 may be contrasted, however, because the Statutory Nuisance (Appeals) Regulations 1990 provide a ground of appeal if the notice is not justified or if it is defective, informal or if there is an error in it, or if there is a defect, informality or error in connection with it. Regulation 2(3) prevents the appeal being allowed unless the defect, informality or error is material. This may suggest that an invalidity can be cured by variation where appropriate. The magistrates' powers are to quash or vary the notice or to allow the appeal (Regulation 2(5)).

4.36 Relevant considerations. The Statutory Nuisance (Appeals) Regulations 1990 set out a list of matters to be considered in relation to appeals under the

Environmental Protection Act 1990. These may be relevant matters to be considered in respect of appeals under other statutes, even though the legislation is silent as to the issues to which the magistrates should address themselves (for example, under the Food Safety Act 1990). The general considerations under the 1990 Regulations include:

    (i) that the notice is not "justified". This appears to relate to the position on the merits before the magistrates, but whether it also involves a consideration of whether the local authority could properly have reached the decision to issue the notice is a moot point;

    (ii) that there is a defect, informality or error in, or in connection with the notice;

    (iii) that the authority have unreasonably refused to accept an alternative method of compliance or that the requirements of the notice are unreasonable in character or extent or are unnecessary;

    (iv) that any time for compliance is insufficient;

    (v) that the notice should have been served on someone else.

Where the legislation is silent as to the matters that are to be taken into account, it may mean that the merits of the matter under appeal are to be considered de novo, with the magistrates exercising their discretion as to the matter without the need to consider the conduct of the issuing authority, although it does not then follow that the conduct of the issuing authority cannot also be a ground of appeal (see paragraphs 4.15, 4.16 and 4.24 above).

Compensation

4.37 **Available only where provided for.** Where an enforcement authority serves a suspension notice but there has been no contravention of a safety requirement nor was the exercise of the power attributable to the act or default (for the meaning of this expression see paragraph 7.87) of a person affected, there may be a liability to pay loss or damage to any person affected. In the event of dispute, the calculation of the right to or amount of loss or damage is decided by arbitration (Consumer Protection Act 1987, s.14(8)). Similar provisions exist in a number of different situations, see for example, in section 9(8) of the Food Safety Act 1990, where a dispute as to the amount of compensation payable to an owner of food which is not condemned by magistrates may be determined by arbitration. Where there is no express provision for compensation, none is payable, although in *Weldon v. North Cornwall* [1997] 1 W.L.R. 570, damages in tort were recovered against the local authority for the *ultra vires* activities of an Environmental Health Officer who required substantial expenditure on unnecessary works purportedly in exercise of his powers under the Food Safety Act 1990 (but contrast *Harris v. Evans & Anor* (Court of Appeal April 24, 1998) which is likely to render *Weldon* the exception rather than the rule).

Offences and defences

4.38 **Strict liability.** If there is no qualification in the provision rendering non-compliance an offence, the offence of non-compliance with an executive notice is likely to be one of strict liability. Failure properly to serve a notice may be a defence to a prosecution under some legislation (but see paragraphs 4.20 and 4.23 above), subject to the consideration that failure to raise the matter on appeal (where possible) might be fatal to the defence (see paragraph 4.18 above). On the other hand, in *Porritt v. Secretary of State for the Environment* [1988] J.P.L. 414 a court was prepared to uphold an enforcement notice served only 27 (the Act required 28) days before it was due to take effect. The court held that the error was *de minimis*, that there had been an appeal and there was no evidence of prejudice.

4.39 In cases where the legislation provides that the offence is committed if there is compliance "without reasonable excuse" , such as in section 80(4) of the Environmental Protection Act 1990, the state of mind of the defendant may give rise to a defence. For further consideration of these words see paragraph 6.11. It seems that it is not a defence, however, that the defendant has not carried out the work through shortage of funds (*Saddleworth Urban District Council v. Aggregate & Sand* (1970) 114 Sol.Jo. 931).

Registration

4.40 Registration of improvement and prohibition notices. There is a requirement under section 3 of the Environment and Safety Information Act 1988 for public registers to be kept of some improvement and prohibition notices. The entries must appear in each case: within 14 days of the date of serving the notice for notices where there is no right of appeal; within 14 days of the expiry of the time for appealing if no appeal has been lodged and within 14 days of the disposal of the appeal in cases where an appeal is brought. The legislation applies to improvement and prohibition notices under the Health and Safety at Work, etc., Act 1974 but not if the notice is for the protection solely of persons at work, under the Fire Precautions Act 1971 (though not improvement notices under this legislation), the Safety of Sports Grounds Act 1975, the Food and Environment Protection Act 1985, the Environmental Protection Act 1990 and the Radioactive Substances Act 1993.

FORFEITURE ORDERS AND CONDEMNATION

Forfeiture orders

4.41 Nature of forfeiture. In English statutes, forfeiture can have two functions, as a penalty, and as a means of protection of the public by disposing of offending products. Although forfeiture is usually by order of the court, some statutory provisions may give powers to enforcement officers to forfeit offending items or to seize and detain items which may in due course be subject to forfeiture proceedings before the court (see paragraph 4.43 below).

4.42 Forfeiture as a penalty. An example of forfeiture utilised as a penalty could be seen in section 21(6) of the Wildlife and Countryside Act 1981 which provides that where a person is convicted of an offence under Part I of the Act (Protection of Wildlife) any bird, nest, egg animal, plant or other thing in respect of which the offence was committed shall be forfeit and also provides for the discretionary forfeiture of any vehicle, animal or weapon used to commit the offence. The power of forfeiture in this instance is exercisable by the court and arises only after there has been a conviction. These provisions also deter the creation of a "black market" in natural plants, animals, eggs, etc., which have been illegally acquired. The provision permitting the forfeiture of vehicles, etc., does not appear to require them to belong to the convicted defendant. By analogy with the cases decided in respect of powers exercisable by the Commissioners of Customs & Excise, indeed, it would appear that forfeiture of vehicles etc. can in principle be ordered in the absence of any mens rea on the part of the owner (*Customs & Excise Commissioner v. Air Canada* [1991] 2 Q.B. 446). A failure to inquire into whether there was any intention to aid the commission of an offence by an owner other than the defendant before making a forfeiture order, would, however, be perverse. Moreover, no such order should be made without permitting the owner an opportunity to be heard. Section 21(2) of the Video Recordings Act 1984, by contrast, makes specific provision that the owner of or person otherwise interested in a video recording shall, if he applies, be heard before an order can be made to forfeit it. The opportunity to make representations to the Commissioners of Customs and Excise and thereafter to take judicial review proceedings meant that the English provisions as to forfeiture under the Customs and Excise Management Act 1979 were not contrary to the European Convention on Human Rights (*Allgemeine Gold- und Silberscheideanstalt v. United Kingdom* (1986) *The Times,* October 25, 1986).

4.43 Executive powers of search and detention in respect of forfeiture provisions. It is necessarily the case that these powers are different in every statute, so that in each case, the powers must be scrutinised jealously. By way of example, under section 29(6) of the Consumer Protection Act 1987, an authorised officer of an enforcement authority has power to seize and detain goods which he has reasonable grounds for suspecting will be subject to forfeiture under section 16 of the Act. (For a discussion on the expression "reasonable grounds for suspecting" see paragraph 4.12 above: these powers do not arise under all legislation where there is a mere suspicion. By way of an instance where the power to seize only arises if the offence has been committed, see section 18(1) of the Petroleum (Consolidation) Act 1928.) The enforcement officer is also entitled, as a requirement under a suspension notice (see paragraphs 4.12 and 4.37 above) to be kept informed about the whereabouts of goods subject to the notice. This enables an officer of an enforcement authority to be sanguine as to the enforcement of any forfeiture order which might be made. An application for forfeiture can be made whether or not goods have been made the subject of a suspension notice or detained and whether or not a prosecution has been commenced. If a prosecution has been commenced or an appeal made against a suspension notice, an application for forfeiture can be made in that court. If no such proceedings have been commenced, the order for forfeiture should be sought by way of complaint (s.16(2)). For procedure by way of complaint see paragraphs 8.42 and 10.113 below.

4.44 The order. An order can be made before trial of any offence under the Consumer Protection Act 1987 only if the magistrates court is satisfied that there has been a contravention of a safety provision. It appears that, in theory, an order can be made before the hearing of a prosecution although, as it is likely that the same issues will arise in the forfeiture proceedings as in the trial, this is very undesirable. The court may give directions as to the destruction of the forfeited items and, instead of ordering destruction there is a power to permit their release for reconditioning and repair or sale as scrap (section 16(7) and section 46(7)(a) and (b)) on condition that any costs order or order for payment of expenses of the proceedings be met. Appeal against a forfeiture order lies to the Crown Court.

4.45 Release of detained goods. An application for the release of detained goods under the Consumer Protection Act 1987 lies to the magistrates court by way of complaint if no proceedings are extant and by way of application in the proceedings if they are. The magistrates may not order release of the goods unless they are satisfied that proceedings had not been brought within 6 months from their seizure or that proceedings had been brought but concluded without a forfeiture order. Where goods have been seized and no forfeiture order is made, the enforcement authority may be liable to pay compensation in respect of loss or damage caused to any person provided that the detention was not due to his neglect or default. For the meanings to be attached to these words see paragraphs 7.44 and 7.87 below.

Condemnation

4.46 Section 9 of the Food Safety Act 1990. The condemnation of unfit food has long been a part of the scheme of the regulation of the supply of food. Condemnation is analogous to forfeiture. The procedure is that an authorised officer of a food authority may give notice to a person in charge of food that it is not to be used for human consumption and is not to be removed or is to be removed only to some specified place or, in the absence of such a notice, the officer may seize and remove it to bring it before a justice of the peace. It is an offence knowingly to contravene the requirements of a notice. Where a notice is served, the authorised officer has 21 days within which to determine if the food complies with food safety requirements. If he is satisfied that the food contravenes food safety requirements, he may apply to a justice of the peace for a condemnation order. He must condemn the food if, after hearing evidence, he is of the view that a food safety requirement is contravened. Section 9(5) makes it clear that any person who might be liable to prosecution in respect of the food is entitled to be heard and to call witnesses. The Court of Session has held that the magistrate acts in a judicial capacity *Humphrey v. Errington* (unreported), although an earlier case, *R. v. Cornwall Quarter Sessions, ex p. Kerley* [1956] 1 W.L.R. 906, had decided that the magistrate was acting in an administrative capacity to review the decision of the authorised officer. Even where the magistrate is exercising an administrative function he must act fairly (*R. v. Birmingham City Justices, ex p. Chris Foreign Foods (Wholesalers) Ltd* [1970] 3 All E.R. 945). If the court refuses to condemn the food, the food authority may be liable to pay compensation to the owner for its depreciation in value resulting from the action taken by the authorised officer.

4.47 Failed prosecutions. Where there has been a prosecution which has failed, the seeking of a condemnation order could be an abuse of process. See, by analogy, *R. v. Haringay Magistrates Court, ex p. Cragg, The Times,* November 8, 1996 and paragraph 10.43 below.

4.48 Right of appeal. There is no right of appeal against the making of a condemnation order although the procedure may be subject to judicial review. For instance, it appears that in *Humphrey v. Errington* (unreported) the refusal of the sheriff to allow expert evidence to be called was said by the Court of Session to be a denial of natural justice. This would appear to be comparably justiciable in the courts of England and Wales.

CHAPTER 5

Civil Proceedings to Enforce the Law

LOCAL AUTHORITIES

5.1 Civil proceedings. The enforcement of regulatory offences is not limited solely to proceedings in the magistrates' court or Crown Court. Apart from those occasions (not covered in this book) where executive notices can be subject to appeals in the civil courts, prosecuting bodies sometimes resort to civil proceedings where the criminal law is insufficient to achieve the level of compliance required. This chapter looks at those occasions when an injunction will be available as an adjunct to the process of proper enforcement, particularly in relation to local authorities as the enforcement authority and also to those occasions when defendants may be able to obtain an injunction to preclude misconduct by prosecuting authorities as well as considering the tort of misfeasance in public office.

5.2 Section 222 of the Local Government Act 1972. Where a local authority initiates civil proceedings in an endeavour to enforce the law in the area for which it is responsible it does so purportedly in the interest of the public it serves. In the ordinary way, proceedings which are for the public good are required to be commenced by the Attorney General of his own motion or by way of relator action, because the Attorney General is the only person recognised by public law as entitled to enforce the law for the public good. An illustration of this principle was the case of *Gouriet v. Union of Post Office Workers* [1978] A.C. 435 in which the House of Lords confirmed that an individual was not entitled to a declaration that particular conduct would be unlawful. Lord Wilberforce commented "the distinction between public rights, which the Attorney General can and the individual (absent special interest) cannot seek to enforce, and private rights is fundamental in our law". So under the Local Government Act 1933, s.276, the power to bring prosecutions did not include an express provision that civil proceedings could be instituted in its own name, with the consequence that the authority was bound to seek the consent of the Attorney General to commence an action (*Prestatyn U.D.C. v. Prestatyn Raceway Ltd* [1970] 1 W.L.R. 33). Section 222 of the Local Government Act 1972 which replaced the earlier section provides that "Where a local authority consider it expedient for the promotion and protection of the interests of the inhabitants of their own area, they may prosecute or defend or appear in any legal proceedings and, in the case of civil proceedings, may institute them in their own name . . .". This provision applies to those councils in England appearing in Schedule 1 of the 1972 Act (as amended) and, in Wales, in Schedule 4, and confers a general power to bring proceedings provided that they fall within the wide scope of that section.

5.3 **Scope of section 222.** In *Stoke on Trent Council v. B & Q (Retail) Ltd* [1984] 1 A.C .754, the powers conferred by section 222 were considered by the House of Lords. It was contended that the words "in their own name" were not intended to enlarge the powers conferred on a County Council to enable it to enforce matters for the public good otherwise than through the auspices of the Attorney, which it would otherwise not have been able to do. The House of Lords did not uphold that argument. Lord Templeman, with whom their Lordships concurred, drew attention to the fact that the power enabled the authority to act only if they considered it "expedient for the promotion and protection of the interests of the inhabitants of their area", a consideration which could be examined on an application for an injunction both as to whether it had been exercised rationally in the *Wednesbury* sense (*Associated Provincial Picture Houses v. Wednesbury Corporation* [1947] 1 K.B. 223) and in the context of the court's ordinary power to consider applications for equitable and discretionary remedies. Lord Roskill drew attention in this context to the entitlement of the local authority to decline to enforce the law if the likely burden of costs would not be in the public interest, so limiting the apparently wide words of Donaldson L.J. in *R. v. Braintree District Council, ex p. Willingham* (1982) 81 L.G.R. 70, in which it appeared to be suggested that considerations of the cost of enforcement were not relevant to the taking of a decision not to prosecute.

5.4 **Other powers.** In other instances, where the local authority is clearly entrusted with a particular responsibility or duty, it may be empowered to sue or be sued in its own name because the statutory provision itself, by reason of the imposition of the responsibility, confers a sufficient interest on the local authority. An example arose in *London County Council v. South Metropolitan Gas Company* [1904] 1 Ch. 76, where it was held that the local authority was entitled to seek an injunction in its own name to prevent a gas company from refusing entry for inspection purposes on a Sunday because the local authority had the responsibility to carry out the inspection and therefore a sufficient interest in the proceedings to be an initiator of them in its own right. It is in every case a question of construction of the applicable provisions whether the legislation imposes a special responsibility such as to enable proceedings in the name of the responsible party or whether the public interest in enforcement of the provisions can only be served by involvement of the Attorney General. In *Hampshire County Council v. Shonleigh Nominees Ltd* [1970] 1 W.L.R. 865 the court held that a County Council which was permitted by the Highways Act 1959 to "assert and protect the rights of the public to the use and enjoyment of [the highways in their area]" were not, without express words, entitled to assert those rights without the fiat of the Attorney General. The contrast between these two cases is that in the latter it was the public interest with which the local authority was concerned, whereas in the former, it was the local authority's own private responsibility for obtaining entry to enforce which was in question. In *Kirklees Borough Council v. Wickes Building Supplies Ltd* [1992] 3 All E.R. 717, the provisions of section 71(1) of the Shops Act 1950 read together with section 222 of the Local Government Act 1972 were held to enable the institution of civil as well as criminal proceedings. Section 71(1) provided: "It shall be the duty of every local authority to enforce within their district the provisions of this Act and of the orders made under those provisions, and for that purpose to institute and carry on such proceedings in respect of contraventions of the said provisions and such orders as aforesaid as may be necessary to secure observance thereof". The appellant argued that because in 1950, the enforcement of the criminal law by injunction was unknown, the scope of that section could not be so wide as to include a reference to enforcement by civil proceedings, and, that, because section 222 did not impose a duty to take proceedings, but only a power to do so in the public interest, section 71(1) did not authorise the initiation of those proceedings. The House of Lords rejected that argument and upheld the decision in *R. v. Braintree Urban District Council, ex p. Willingham* (1982) 81 L.G.R. 70.

5.5   Relator actions.   A relator action must be brought in any instance where section 222 of the 1972 Act does not apply. This requires the consent of the Attorney General (or the Solicitor General if the Attorney is not available) and the proceedings are brought in the name of the Attorney. If the Attorney decides not to consent, it appears that this decision is not justiciable (*London County Council v. Attorney General and others* [1902] A.C. 165). This principle was re-affirmed in dicta of the House of Lords in *Gouriet v. Union of Post Office Workers* [1978] A.C. 435. In other contexts, the discretion of the Attorney General has been held to be incapable of challenge in the courts (in relation to his power to consent to a fresh inquest and his decision whether to institute proceedings for contempt: see *R. v. Attorney General, ex p. Ferrante* [1995] C.O.D. 18, *R. v. Solicitor General, ex p. Taylor* (1995) 8 Admin. L.R. 206).

5.6   The geographical restriction of section 222.   The fact that the power under section 222 of the Act is limited to the promotion or protection of the interests of the inhabitants of the local authority's own area sometimes poses a problem for local authorities. Taking proceedings against a "rogue" trader who operates from a base outside the area of the local authority, or who sometimes operates within the area of the local authority but sometimes operates elsewhere and whose trade is carried on exclusively by mail order throughout the country could be risky if the local authority has no evidence from disappointed customers within its own territory. It is not necessary for the benefit to inhabitants of the area of the local authority to be exclusive, however. The inhabitants of the area of the local authority may be benefited by a proceeding which also promotes or protects the interests of the inhabitants of other areas (*Solihull Metropolitan Borough Council v. Maxfern* [1977] 1 W.L.R. 127). Where a local authority is unable to produce evidence which suggests that the interests of its own inhabitants are affected, it can refer to the details of the complaint to the Office of Fair Trading for action (if any) under the powers of the Director General.

5.7   What is the test for jurisdiction to grant the injunction.   Many injunctions were obtained by local authorities prior to the Sunday Trading Act 1994 to prevent unlawful trading on Sundays, contrary to the provisions of the Shops Act 1950, so that a significant number of the decided cases have addressed the problems to which this legislation gave rise.

In circumstances where the unlawful conduct constitutes an offence, the authorities are not always consistent as to what test needs to be applied before a superior court will be willing to act. In particular, three questions arise: first, does there need to have been prior criminal proceedings which have proved ineffective, secondly, must the alleged defendant be "flagrantly and deliberately flouting the law" or will a mere intention to act otherwise than in accordance with the law be sufficient, and thirdly, must it be plain that there is no defence?

Must there have been prior criminal proceedings?

It is very common for an injunction to follow previous unsuccessful attempts at discouragement of offenders by way of prosecution. This was a pattern under the Shops Act 1950, where the profits to be made from unlawful trading rendered insignificant the prospects of prosecution with the small fines that could be imposed under the Act. In *Stafford Borough Council v. Elkenford* [1977] 1 W.L.R. 324, Bridge L.J. commented:

> "We have been urged to say that the court will only exercise its discretion to restrain by injunction the commission of offences in breach of statutory prohibitions if the plaintiff authority has first shown that it has exhausted the possibility of restraining those breaches by the exercise of the statutory remedies. Ordinarily no doubt that is a very salutary approach to the question, but it is not in my judgment an inflexible rule.

The reason why it is ordinarily proper to ask whether the authority seeking the injunction has first exhausted the statutory remedies is because in the ordinary case it is only because those remedies have been invoked and have proved inadequate that one can draw the inference, which is the essential foundation of the court's discretion to grant an injunction, that the offender is, in the language of Oliver J. [in the court below] "deliberately and flagrantly flouting the law". In an appropriate case it may be possible:

> ". . . to draw that inference before there has been any resort to statutory remedies at all. It would have to be an exceptional case. It would have to be shown that the scale of the operations which the defendants were carrying on and the plan of their proposed operations were such that it could be legitimately inferred that they would continue unless and until effectively restrained by law. In some cases it may be apparent from the start that the profits the defendants are likely to make are such that nothing short of an injunction will be effective to restrain them. Finally, of course, in such a case it must be plain beyond doubt that there is no defence to a prosecution under the statute."

These words were cited in part with approval by Lord Templeman, with whom the other members of the Appellate Committee expressed their agreement, in *Stoke on Trent v. B & Q (Retail) Ltd* (above). It follows, therefore, that there need not have been previous criminal offences, but where there have been no such offences, the stringent requirements imposed by the courts before an injunction can be granted may be difficult to satisfy.

Must the defendant have been deliberately and flagrantly flouting the law?

It is clear from the above passage, that the shorthand reference to the test in *Stoke on Trent v. B & Q (Retail) Ltd* (above) described it as a "deliberate and flagrant flouting of the law". The reason for stringency was explained by Lord Templeman at page 776:

"The right to invoke the assistance of the civil court in aid of the criminal law is a comparatively modern development. Where Parliament imposes a penalty for an offence, Parliament must consider the penalty is adequate and Parliament can increase the penalty if it proves to be inadequate. It follows that a local authority should be reluctant to seek and the court should be reluctant to grant an injunction which if disobeyed may involve the infringer in sanctions far more onerous than the penalty imposed for the offence. In *Gouriet v. Union of Post Office Workers* [1978] A.C. 435 at 481 Lord Wilberforce said that the right to invoke the assistance of civil courts in aid of the criminal law is "an exceptional power confined, in practice, to cases where an offence is frequently repeated in aid of a, usually, inadequate penalty . . . or to cases of emergency . . .".

But even before the decision in that case, the lower courts had begun to develop the principle further. In *Kent County Council v. Bachelor (No 2)* [1979] 1 W.L.R. 213 it had been held that the county council had power in it's own name to institute proceedings to restrain breach of a tree preservation order. Talbot J. had referred not only to the existence of a duty to make tree preservation orders, but argued that because the Council's duties went further, so did their powers to restrain by injunction, so that the court was not only concerned with the Council's duty to prevent a breach of the criminal law, but also with their duty to preserve areas of natural beauty. This was an approach reinforced by the later decision in *Runnymede Borough Council v. Ball* [1986] 1 W.L.R. 353, which was said by Purchas L.J. to have been in accord with the spirit and intent of the speech of Lord Templeman, if not necessarily with its precise words. In that case the activities of the defendant (creating a caravan site without planning consent and ignoring stop notices and enforcement orders) were held to be at the least "a threat to the proper exercise by the plaintiff of its duties as a local planning authority to protect the interests of the inhabitants of its area" and "something more than a mere infringement of planning control". In *Kirklees Borough Council v. Wickes Building Supplies Ltd* [1992] 3 All E.R. 717 Lord Goff referred to the above passage from the speech of Lord Templeman and commented that the test as described by the formula "deliberate and flagrant flouting" was too narrow and did not cover cases of emergency. He said:

". . . quite apart from the fact that such a statement does not accommodate cases of emergency – cases where the defendant's unlawful conduct could, unless restrained, cause serious and irreparable harm before trial, as for example, where the defendant threatens to cut down a tree in breach of a tree preservation order – in other cases it is usually not so much the flagrancy of the breach as the fact that the defendant intends to persist in offending unless restrained by an injunction, which justifies the invocation of that form of relief".

Lord Goff cited the decision in *City of London Corp. v. Bovis Construction Ltd* (1988) [1992] 3 All E.R. 679 in support of that proposition. In that case, the local authority wished to restrain the activities of some contractors upon whom a notice had been served under section 60 of the Control of Pollution Act 1974 (requirements as to the way development was to be carried out) breach of which would have constituted an offence. A number of informations had been issued, but there had been no hearing to establish whether or not there had been breaches of the notice. Whether or not there were breaches, it was apparent from the evidence filed in support of the injunction that there was a prima facie case of nuisance by noise emanating from the development works, although there was also substantial evidence that, far from a "deliberate and flagrant flouting" of the law, the defendants were endeavouring to comply, but the siting of the works they were required to do, and the complexity of the undertaking was such that there had been lapses in their control systems. O'Connor L.J. had in the *Bovis* case adopted the reasoning of Purchas L.J. in *Runnymede Borough Council v. Ball* [1986] 1 W.L.R. 353 and said:

> "I think that there is a difference between what I think can be called pure public law cases such as Sunday trading and cases like the present where enforcing the public law notice is no more than a convenient method of protecting the inhabitants of their area from a nuisance."

He had concluded that it was not necessary to show the commission of a criminal offence, although the nature of the offence alleged was relevant to the form of injunction to be granted. The injunction was "to restrain Bovis from 'failing without reasonable excuse to comply with paragraph 1 and the schedule . . . of the section 60 notice dated . . .' ". Bingham L.J. in the same case formulated a three-fold guide for the grant of an injunction at the behest of an enforcement authority. The guiding principles, he said, were:

(i) that the jurisdiction is to be invoked and exercised exceptionally and with great caution;

(ii) that there must be something more than a mere infringement of the criminal law before the assistance of civil proceedings can be invoked and accorded for the protection and promotion of the interests of the inhabitants of the area;

(iii) that the essential foundation for the exercise of the court's discretion is not that the offender is deliberately and flagrantly flouting the law but the need to draw the inference that the defendant's unlawful operations will continue unless and until effectively restrained by the law and that nothing short of an injunction will be effective to restrain them.

It is submitted that an approach to the granting of injunctions which is dependent on drawing a distinction between "pure public law" (such as Sunday Trading) and the protection of the public is to set up a distinction which is hard to draw, and the three-fold test of Lord Justice Bingham should be regarded as universally applicable.

Must it be plain that there is no defence?

This was considered in *Kirklees Metropolitan Borough Council v. Wickes Building Supplies Ltd* [1992] 3 All E.R. 717. It was argued that as a prerequisite to the grant of an injunction in support of the criminal law it must be plain that there was no defence, and until that had been determined in favour of the applicant, the court was not entitled to progress to apply the principles applicable to the grant of interlocutory relief laid down in *American Cyanamid Co. v. Ethicon Ltd* [1975] A.C. 396. This argument would have applied the principle laid down by Bridge L.J. in the passage cited above in *Stafford Borough Council v. Elkenford* [1977] 1

W.L.R. 324, but it was not accepted by the House of Lords. The conduct of the litigation had been such that the House of Lords had been persuaded to refer to the European Court under Article 177 of the Treaty of Rome the question whether the restriction on Sunday trading was a breach of Article 30 (see paragraph 6.40 below). If the restriction was a contravention of Article 30, it would have meant that it was unlawful. That issue had not been determined by the European Court, and, in the meantime, the local authority sought an injunction to stop Sunday trading. The Appellate Committee referred to the previous authorities and decided that the existence of a possible defence was not a bar to the power to grant of an injunction, but where an interlocutory injunction was sought, it was a matter to be taken into account in the exercise of the discretion whether the injunction should be granted. Notably, in this case, the House of Lords thought that the challenge to the Shops Act 1950 under Article 30 was very likely to fail.

5.8 The interlocutory injunction. In nearly every case where an injunction is sought by an enforcement authority, it is an interlocutory injunction which is needed. In the main, actions commenced for the purpose of supporting the interlocutory relief do not come to trial and the order for costs made when the injunction is granted recognises the reality that after the grant of the interlocutory injunction, no further significant costs may be incurred, although if the proceedings are not discontinued, in the ordinary way, a person who has obtained an injunction has an obligation to push forward expeditiously with the hearing (*Hong Kong Toy Centre v. Tony U.K., The Times* January 14, 1994).

Where an interlocutory injunction is sought, the power which the High Court exercises is that now conferred by section 37 of the Supreme Court Act 1981 to grant an injunction where it is just and convenient. It follows from this that if the court is persuaded that it is otherwise a case for the court to exercise its jurisdiction to grant an injunction, the court must then go on to consider the criteria laid down in *American Cyanamid v. Ethicon* [1975] A.C. 396, namely, whether there is a serious issue to be tried (an issue which may very often have been encompassed in the considerations affecting the determination if there is jurisdiction) and where the balance of convenience may lie. In determining the balance of convenience, the court is very likely to have regard to two material principles:

(i)   the fact that the plaintiff purports to act in the public interest. In those circumstances, the court should consider whether the *American Cyanamid* principles need to be qualified (see, for example, *Swift v. Inner London Education Authority* [1978] 1 All E.R. 411 – a case brought against a public body where the balance of convenience might, were the defendant not a public body acting in the public interest, have lain in favour of the plaintiff).

(ii) the fact that the interlocutory injunction, in a regulatory case, is likely to decide the whole action. In those circumstances, the relative strength or weakness of the parties' cases should be determinative of whether an injunction should be granted rather than the balance of convenience (*Newsweek Inc. v. British Broadcasting Corporation* [1979] R.P.C. 441, *Cambridge Nutrition v. British Boadcasting Corporation* [1990] 3 All E.R. 523). Where the opposition to the grant of an injunction arises out of a contention that European law is contrary to national law, the Court must also apply principles other than those in *American Cyanamid*, in that the court should endeavour to make its own assessment of the strength of the challenge and grant or refuse the injunction accordingly (*Factortame Ltd v. Secretary of State for Transport* [1991] 1 A.C. 603).

5.9   The undertaking in damages.   In the ordinary way, an applicant for an injunction is required to give an undertaking in damages in respect of any loss which the respondent suffers as a consequence of the injunction if in due course it transpires that the injunction ought not to have been granted. It had long been the case, however, that the Crown had not been required to give an undertaking in damages in law enforcement proceedings. This issue was re-considered at length in the case of *Hoffman-La Roche & Co. AG v. Secretary of State for Trade and Industry* [1975] A.C. 295 in which the impact of the Crown Proceedings Act 1947 on the common law principles was addressed. The House of Lords drew a distinction between those cases where the Crown was asserting a proprietorial right and those where the litigation was to prevent a subject from breaking the law where that breach would be harmful to the public or a section of the public. It propounded the principle that where the Crown was charged with the duty of enforcement in the public interest, the Court should consider the propriety of requiring an undertaking in damages in the light of the circumstances of each case. In the circumstances of that case, in which the Crown sought to restrain Hoffman-La Roche from charging for drugs in excess of an order approved by Parliament but which the drug company challenged as *ultra vires*, no undertaking in damages was required. In *Kirklees Borough Council v. Wickes Building Supplies Ltd* [1992] 3 All E.R. 717, the House of Lords considered whether the same principle could be applied to local authorities. In the Court of Appeal it had been decided that the discretionary power of the court not to require an undertaking in damages was "a privilege of the Crown alone". The House concluded, however, that there was no material distinction to be drawn between the position of the Crown as a law enforcer and a local authority. In the *Kirklees* case, no undertaking in damages was required.

5.10   European law and the undertaking in damages.   In the *Kirklees* case, consideration was also given to whether there was an obligation to require an undertaking in damages because the challenge which the defendant made was that the national law was contrary to Article 30 of the Treaty of Rome. In particular, B&Q (Retail) Ltd placed weight on the decision of the European court in *Francovich v. Italian Republic* [1992] I.R.L.R. 84 which renders the United Kingdom liable for damage caused to individuals as a result of a failure to implement European law. The House of Lords found that this consideration did not assist B&Q. If the United Kingdom government is to be held responsible for a failure to implement European law, there was no justification for an obligation to make good losses arising from that failure to be imposed on a local authority.

5.11   Ancillary powers (detention and preservation of property).   The Rules of the Supreme Court make provision for ancillary orders for the detention preservation of property, etc., and for the taking of samples. The need for such powers in regulatory cases must be limited, because of the powers granted in the legislation which imposes the duty to enforce. In principle, however, these powers would also be available to a proper plaintiff.

PROCEEDINGS BY OTHER ENFORCERS

5.12   Proceedings by other enforcers should, providing that the right to enforce the law in its own name by injunction can be established (see paragraphs 5.2 to 5.5.

above), concerning enforcement of the same considerations be subject to criminal law by injunction as do local authorities.

PROCEEDINGS AGAINST ENFORCEMENT AUTHORITIES

5.13 Injunction: Judicial review and action. Where proceedings brought by an individual or group of individuals concern an issue of public law, and there is no allegation of infringement of private rights, the proceedings must be commenced by judicial review (*O'Reilly v. Mackman* [1983] 2 AC. 237). Even if the action is properly brought by judicial review the applicants must nevertheless show that they have sufficient *locus standi* to bring the action (*Gouriet v. Union of Post Office Workers* [1978] A.C. 435). Order 53 rule 3(10) of the Rules of the Supreme Court allows for the grant of an interlocutory injunction, the approach of the court to which is similar to that applied in actions begun by writ under Order 29 rule 1, that is, the court will look at the principles applicable in *American Cyanamid* (paragraph 5.8 above) but will modify those principles by reference to the public interest subject matter of the action. It is now established that by virtue of section 21(2) of the Crown Proceedings Act 1947 it is not permissible to obtain an injunction against the Crown (*R. v. Secretary of State for Transport, ex p. Factortame Ltd (No. 1)* [1990] 2 A.C. 85), although this does not apply in cases where an interlocutory injunction is sought to prevent the implementation of national law which is contrary to E.C. law (*R. v. Secretary of State for Transport, ex p. Factortame Ltd (No. 2)* [1991] A.C. 603). There is no prohibition from obtaining an interlocutory injunction against a local authority in a proper case.

5.14 Cause of action. An individual or organisation which has been specifically injured by an actionable act or omission of a local authority may seek an injunction in an action begun by writ without joining the Attorney General even if there is a public law element to his claim (*Barrs v. Bethell* [1982] Ch. 294, *Marriott v. East Grinstead Gas Co.* [1909] 1 Ch. 70). It is axiomatic that such a plaintiff must have a cause of action upon which the application for an injunction may hinge. Clearly, if there is a claim for breach of contract or negligence, the cause of action is plain. In *Weldon v. North Cornwall District Council* [1977] 1 W.L.R. 570 the cause of action rested upon a negligent misstatement, when an environmental health officer served a notice requiring unnecessary works upon which the recipient relied, although there was no question in this case of the seeking or grant of injunctive relief. In *Harris v. Evans & Anor*, April 24, 1998, CA, the decision in *Weldon* (above) was distinguished on the grounds that it was not just and reasonable for those responsible for the enforcement of statutes for the public good to be liable to an award of damages for pure economic loss. In such instances, the case for injunction to prevent unlawful requirements by enforcement authorities might be all the stronger. In recent years the tort of misfeasance in public office has regained prominence having fallen virtually into desuetude. In circumstances where there is a cause of action, the individual or organisation can in principle seek an interlocutory injunction restraining the unlawful conduct of the prosecuting authority. In such circumstances however, the court will place considerable weight upon the fact that the prosecuting authority purports to be carrying out a public duty, so an interlocutory injunction is unlikely to be granted except in a very clear case.

5.15   Misfeasance in public office.   Recent authorities have affirmed the tort of "Misfeasance in public office" which provides a remedy in damages for unlawful actions by an authority or officer of an authority if either:

(i) the authority or person has actual malice towards the plaintiff (*Jones v. Swansea City Council* [1990] 1 W.L.R. 1453); or

(ii) the authority or person knew that it or he was acting unlawfully and it was foreseeable that his actions would damage the complainant *(Bourgoin S.A. v. Ministry of Agriculture* [1986] Q.B. 716); (*Three Rivers District Council v. Bank of England (No. 3)* [1996] 3 All E.R. 558).

"Public office" does not describe only those situations where the authority is acting in the public interest, but also where it is acting in a private law capacity (*e.g.* as a landlord, for instance: see the *Jones* case (above)). Care needs to be taken where the tort is alleged to be that of an employee of an authority. If he has acted unlawfully, especially if he has acted with malice, his actions may be a "frolic of his own" for which his employer is not liable (see *Racz v. Home Office* [1994] 3 All E.R. 737, HL).

5.16   Declaration.   A declaration is a remedy which is only obtainable as a final remedy: there is no such thing as an interlocutory declaration. It is nonetheless available in both judicial review proceedings and as an equitable remedy in an action bought against an enforcement authority by writ.

5.17   Damages.   Damages are available as a remedy in judicial review proceedings if they have been claimed in the applicant's statement in support of his application for leave to seek judicial review and if they would have been available had the action been commenced by writ (Order 53, rule 7) and are in a proper case, available in an action begun by writ.

CHAPTER 6

Some Juridical Issues Affecting Regulatory Offences

SCOPE OF THIS CHAPTER

General issues

6.1 This chapter deals with some general issues which are of particular relevance to the assessment of the prospects of success in a prosecution as well as the considerations which may affect the decision to prosecute and the understanding of the nature of the offence alleged. Each offence has, of course, different evidential requirements and different questions of construction will arise. The following discussion includes these common considerations:

   (i) the incidence of the burden of proof;

  (ii) the question whether the prosecution has to prove any particular state of mind, and, if so, to what extent *mens rea* is relevant in different offences;

 (iii) areas of conflict between European law and domestic law

 (iii) concepts which appear in many trading offences;

 (iv) the interpretation of regulatory offences;

  (v) delegated legislation;

(vii) codes of practice.

THE INCIDENCE OF THE BURDEN OF PROOF

The golden thread principle and its exceptions

The principle

6.2 It was established in *Woolmington v. DPP* [1935] A.C. 462 that the burden of proof in respect of all the elements of a criminal charge fall upon the prosecution except in cases of insanity or where a statutory defence arises. Viscount Sankey L.C. at pages 481–482 expressed "the golden thread principle" thus:

> "Throughout the web of English criminal law one golden thread is always to be seen, that it is the duty of the prosecution to prove the prisoner's guilt subject to what I have already said as to the defence of insanity and subject also to any statutory exception. If, at the end of and on the whole of the case there is a reasonable doubt created by the evidence given either by the prosecution or the prisoner as to whether the prisoner killed the deceased with a malicious intention, the prosecution has not made out the case and the prisoner is entitled to an acquittal. No matter what the charge or where the trial the principle that the prosecution must prove the guilt of the prisoner is part of the common law of England and no attempt to whittle it down can be entertained".

Woolmington concerned a defence of accident raised to rebut a charge of murder. It was not directly concerned with statutory offences or defences, but it can be said to form the point of departure for the consideration of the approach to all criminal and quasi-criminal offences.

Express statutory exception

6.3 Scope. The scope of the statutory exception referred to in *Woolmington* was considered by the Court of Appeal in *R. v. Edwards* [1975] Q.B. 27. Lawton L.J. expressed the view of the court that the exception was "limited to offences arising under enactments which prohibit the doing of an act save in special circumstances or by persons of specified classes or with special qualifications or with the licence or permission of specified authorities". This formulation (which was described by Lord Griffiths in *R. v. Hunt* [1987] A.C. 352 at 375 to 376 as "an excellent guide to construction rather than as an exception to a rule") appears to suggest that only where the offence is statutory in nature does the exception apply, and then only if the limitation of the scope of the offence falls into one of the categories described. This restricted view of the position appears to accept the contention put in argument in that case that the common law exception was accurately reflected by the predecessor of section 101 of the Magistrates Courts Act 1980. It followed therefore that the question upon whom the burden lay could not be determined differently depending upon the choice of summary or Crown Court jurisdiction. In relation to regulatory offences the question of the incidence of the burden of proof may be of considerable importance particularly because of the "technical" nature of the defences which are customarily run.

Magistrates' Courts Act 1980, s.101

6.4 Application. Section 101 provides that in a summary trial, the burden of proving any "exception, exemption, proviso, excuse or qualification whether or not it accompanies the description of the offence or matter of complaint in the enactment creating the offence . . ." lies on the defendant. The section imposes a burden on the defendant where there is a derogation from an enacting clause. It does not apply where the derogation is part of the description of the offence (*R. v. Hunt* [1987] 1 A.C. 352, *Nimmo v. Alexander Cowan & Sons* [1968] A.C. 107 per Lord Wilberforce in his dissenting speech at 128–130) and it does not apply to a saving, which is a provision taken not to confer or detract from an existing right or prohibition (*Ealing London Borough Council v. Race Relations Board* [1972] A.C. 342). A saving frequently begins "Nothing in this Act (or section) shall . . .".

6.5 Construction of the statutory provisions. It appears, moreover, that the section does not apply where it is the definition of the prohibited conduct which is qualified rather than the offence. By analogy, in *Westminster City Council v. Croyalgrange* [1986] 1 W.L.R. 674, paragraph 6 of Schedule 3 of the Local Government (Miscellaneous Provisions) Act 1982 prohibited "Subject to the provisions of this schedule" use of premises as a sex establishment. It further provided that there were three situations in which premises could be used, in particular where there was a licence in force from the Council. On the face of the paragraph, it would appear that the situations in which premises could be used were within the wider definition of a proviso argued for by Bennion (see paragraph 6.7 below) or were an exemption. The offence of knowingly causing or permitting prohibited use arose under paragraph 26 of the schedule. The directors of the company contended that they had believed that the company had a licence. Lord Bridge described reliance by the prosecution on section 101 of the Magistrates Courts Act 1980 as "quite misconceived". He added "The exceptions and exemptions under Schedule 3 to the 1982 Act qualify the prohibition created by paragraph 6, not the offence created by paragraph 20(1)(a)". Further consideration was given to the scope of section 101 of the Act in *Polychronakis v. Richards and Jerrom Ltd, The Times*, November 19, 1997. The Divisional Court, in rejecting the contention that the words "without reasonable excuse" where they appeared in section 80(4) of the Environmental Protection Act 1990, passed the burden of proving the excuse and its reasonableness to the defendant, said that the application of section 101 was extremely limited and confined to extremely rare circumstances and was not designed to interfere with the fundamental rule of criminal law that it was for the prosecution to prove the elements of the offence. For further discussion of this case see paragraph 6.11 below.

6.6 Definitions of proviso. Despite the decision in *Polychronakis* (above), the language of section 101 is very wide. A definition of the terms referred to in section 101 could be advanced as follows:

 (i) an exception reduces the scope of the applicable facts;

 (ii) an exemption identifies a sub-class which could qualify for treatment as part of a larger class, but is nonetheless excluded;

 (iii) a proviso is usually understood to mean that the words "provided that" limit the effect of a preceding "enactment clause".

 (iv) an excuse is a matter of exculpation (which would have supported the prosecutor's arguments in *Polychronakis* (above));

 (v) a qualification is something in the nature of a defence which cuts down the width of the enacting clause (*Nimmo v. Alexander Cowan & Sons Ltd* [1968] A.C. 107).

6.7 Notably, Francis Bennion (Statutory Interpretation, (3rd ed., p. 493)) whilst discussing provisos appears to group all of the above categories within the generic term "proviso" and discusses their drafting format. He offers as an alternative to the words "provided that" the expression "so however". He comments that limitation of the enacting clause can be achieved by commencing it with the words "Subject to subsection . . ." or by commencing a subsequent limitation with the words "notwithstanding anything in subsection . . .". He adds that many contemporary draftsmen would not use language which underlines the presence of the limitation at all, on the basis that it must be obvious from their placement that there is a derogation from the enacting clause. Although this practice is apparently a matter of form, it is largely not welcomed by practitioners. What is obvious to the draftsman is not always correspondingly clear to the practitioner and when it is the substance and effect of the legislation itself which is in issue, a point of certainty is welcome. For further discussion, see paragraphs 6.10 and 6.11 below.

Construction of the statute as a whole places burden on defendant

6.8   Burden of proof on the defendant.   The decision in *R. v. Hunt* [1987] 1 A.C. 352 has determined that in trials on indictment a comparable exception applies not only where a statutory provision expressly states that the burden is to lie upon the defendant (such as Trade Descriptions Act 1968, s.24 "it shall . . . be a defence for the person charged to prove.") but also where, as a matter of construction of the statute, a burden is imposed on the defendant. For this to occur, there need not necessarily be an exemption, proviso, etc., but that will be the usual circumstance in which the statute casts a burden on the defendant (*R. v. Hunt* (above) *per* Lord Griffiths at page 375 to 376. It follows:

(i) that the transference of the burden of proof to the defendant is not limited to cases where this is linguistically obvious; and

(ii) where the burden of proof is on the prosecution, it may need to put forward evidence to negative a possible defence.

As Lord Griffiths commented "The real difficulty in these cases lies in determining upon whom Parliament intended to place the burden of proof".

6.9   *Hunt* concerned an offence of possession of a class A drug (for a discussion whether "possession" is a notion describing a certain mental state, see paragraph 6.51, below). Regulation 4(1) of the Misuse of Drugs (Safe Custody) Regulations 1973 provided that it was not an offence to possess a mixture which contained less than a specified proportion of the drug. The analyst's certificate relied upon by the Crown omitted to specify the proportion of the drug in the mixture which had been found. The defendant had submitted that there was no case to answer because the prosecution had not negatived the possible defence that the defendant had been in possession of less than the prohibited quantity. The House of Lords upheld his argument. A number of pointers to determining the proper construction were adverted to in the speeches of Lords Griffiths and Ackner.

Pointers to construction

6.10   Form and placement.   In the absence of express provision, the clearest guidance to the incidence of the burden of proof is the form and placement of the alleged exception or proviso. So, where the statute provides that some conduct is prohibited, and subsequently qualifies it by permitting the prohibited conduct in certain circumstances, the burden of proving the applicability or otherwise of the qualification is likely to be within the exceptions rule (*per* Lord Griffiths at p. 374). An example might be Radioactive Substances Act 1993, s.9: "No person shall . . .

keep, use, lend or let on hire mobile radioactive apparatus . . . unless he is registered . . . or is exempted from registration . . .". It is likely that the burden of proving registration or exemption lies on the defendant.

6.11   **Substance and effect.**   Construction of a provision is more difficult where the words of qualification are contained in the description of the offence itself. In *Nimmo v. Alexander Cowan & Sons Ltd* [1968] A.C. 107, a civil court (although it was acknowledged that, because the statutory provision created an offence as well as a tort, the same problem would present itself to a criminal court) had to determine whether the burden rested on the defendant to bring evidence to establish that he had taken all reasonable steps to provide and maintain a safe place of work or whether the plaintiff (or prosecution) had to prove that it was reasonable practicable for the defendant to make the workplace safe. Section 29(1) of the Factories Act 1961 provided that: "There shall, so far as is reasonably practicable, be provided and maintained safe means of access to every place at which any person has at any time to work, and such place shall, so far as is reasonably practicable be made and kept safe for any person working there". By a majority of three to two, the House of Lords decided that the burden of proving reasonable practicability was imposed on the defendant. Lord Pearson made clear that it was the substance and effect of the enactment as well as its form which mattered when considering upon whom the burden of proof lies. This is, of course, a consideration which is of particular importance when considering regulatory offences, which are generally to be construed by reference to their object (see paragraphs 6.71 to 6.73). In contrast to this decision, in *Polychronakis v. Richards and Jerrom Ltd, The Times*, November 19, 1997, the Divisional Court had to consider the incidence of the burden of proof in relation to an appeal against conviction for an offence under section 80(4) of the Environmental Protection Act 1990 (contravention of an abatement notice). The offence specifies that "if a person upon whom an abatement notice is served, without reasonable excuse, contravenes or fails to comply with any requirement or prohibition imposed by the notice, he shall be guilty of an offence". The Divisional Court placed emphasis on the fact that there were separate subsections containing separate defences which expressly placed the burden on the defendant to prove the material giving rise to the defence and also upon the limited application of section 101 of the Magistrates' Courts Act 1980 (see paragraph 6.5 above).

6.12   **Onerous burden.**   in *R. v. Putland & Sorrell* [1946] 1 All E.R. 85, the Consumer Rationing (Consolidation) Order 1944, article 4 provided that a person "shall not acquire rationed goods . . . without surrendering . . . coupons". The burden of proving that no coupons were surrendered for the acquisition of some silk stockings lay with the Crown. In *R. v. Oliver* [1944] K.B. 68, the defendant was prosecuted for selling sugar without a licence contrary to the following article of the Sugar (Control) Order 1940: "Subject to any directions given or except under and in accordance with the terms of a licence permit or other authority granted by or on behalf of the Minister no . . . wholesaler shall by way of trade . . . supply . . . any sugar". This provision was held to cast the burden of proving that he had a licence on the defendant.

6.13   The distinction between these two cases, expressed by Humphreys J. in *Putland & Sorrell* as a broad distinction between a statutory prohibition against doing an act and a statutory prohibition against doing an act otherwise than in a particular way, was criticised by Lawton L.J. in *R. v. Edwards* [1975] Q.B. 27. Lord Griffiths in *Hunt* similarly declined to adopt the distinction preferred by Humphreys J. and distinguished these cases by reference to the ease or otherwise by which the defendant could discharge the burden putatively cast upon him. Lawton L.J. in *Edwards* had previously described this means of distinction as "not substantial enough".

6.14   Lord Griffiths placed considerable weight on the argument that it would be unlikely, as a matter of construction, that Parliament's intention was to impose a burden on the defendant that it would be hard for him to discharge. He said at page 374:

> "I regard this consideration [the ease or difficulty that the respective parties would encounter in discharging the burden] as one of great importance for surely, Parliament can never lightly be taken to have intended to impose an onerous duty on a defendant to prove his innocence in a criminal case, and the court should be very slow to draw such an inference from the language of a statute".

6.15   Practical consequences.   Whereas Lord Griffiths appeared to have in mind primarily the danger of placing a heavy burden on the defendant, Lord Ackner in the same case approached the issue from the other point of view. He argued at page 383 that if the grammatical construction appeared to place a burden on the prosecution which was "particularly difficult or burdensome with the consequence that the purpose of the legislation would be significantly frustrated, then this would be a relevant consideration to weigh against the grammatical form".

6.16   Seriousness of the offence.   Lord Griffiths at page 378 was motivated to conclude any ambiguity in the statute in favour of the defendant because the offence was "among the most serious in the criminal calendar" and absolute. It follows that if the offence had not involved Class A drugs the House of Lords may have placed substantially less significance upon its absolute nature.

6.17   Status of the offence.   On the other hand, if an offence requires *mens rea*, this, in some cases, may militate in favour of the burden of proving all elements of the offence resting on the prosecution. D.J. Birch in her article "Hunting the Snark: the Elusive Statutory Exception" [1988] Crim.L.R. 221, argues that if the offence is one requiring *mens rea*, an exception which may affect the mental element, *e.g.* "without lawful excuse", will be "pulled" into the prosecution's obligation as a matter of construction, such that no burden will rest on the defendant. An alternative view is that the practical consequence of the burden of proving the defendant's state of mind may, in some cases, be the same as negativing the excuse relied upon by the defendant. See, for example, *R. v. Smith (David)* [1974] 1 Q.B. 354. Moreover, an offence requiring full *mens rea* is habitually regarded as more serious than an absolute offence, such that the burden should lie on the prosecution. It is worth noting also that Francis Bennion in his article "Statutory Exceptions: A Third Knot in the Golden Thread" [1988] Crim.L.R. 31 appears to suggest that the exceptions rule applies only to offences of strict liability and that the decision in *Westminster City Council v. Croyalgrange* [1986] 1 W.L.R. 674 is comprehensible on that basis.

6.18   Licensing cases.   Provisions by which the holder of a licence is permitted to perform an otherwise prohibited act are customarily construed to impose a burden on the defence, even where the language of the section does not obviously show an exception, proviso, etc. This is apparent by an examination of the authorities which were referred to in *Hunt* and, indeed, it was argued by the appellant (but not accepted by their Lordships) that licensing cases were *sui generis*. A further example is *Guyll v. Bright* [1987] R.T.R. 104 (decided before the House of Lords' decision in *Hunt*) in which the authorities were similarly reviewed.

A Mental Element?

Determining whether the offence involves *mens rea*

6.19   Meaning.   What is an offence involving *mens rea*? It is one in which the prosecution must prove that the accused had a particular state of mind as to some or all of the elements of the *actus reus* (for the converse see L. H. Leigh "Strict and Vicarious Liability" (1982) p. 1). An offence where the prosecution need prove no *mens rea* is a "strict liability" or "absolute" offence. Although Professor Leigh (above) ascribes to the expression "strict liability" the meaning that it may be indefeasible by any defence, the two expressions are frequently used interchangeably, and are used as such in this work. How can an offence requiring *mens rea* be distinguished from an absolute offence? Many statutory provisions are silent as to whether *mens rea* is required. The consideration which predominates is the degree of "criminality" addressed by the statute. For that reason, regulatory offences are usually found to be offences of strict liability unless the statutory provision expressly provides otherwise.

6.20   There are three distinct situations:

(i) offences of "full *mens rea*";

(ii) offences where a mental element is described in legislation but does not apply to every element of the *actus reus*;

(iii) offences where no mental element is prescribed but the nature of the *actus reus* implies a particular mental state.

The criteria for deciding into which class an offence falls are discussed in paragraphs 6.30 to 6.35 below.

True criminality versus prohibition under a penalty

6.21   Presumption where offence truly criminal.   Offences of full *mens rea* are found both where the statutory provision is silent as to the need for the prosecution to prove a mental state and where the provision expressly makes reference to some state of mind, whether it be knowledge, recklessness, fraud, dishonesty, intention or other intellectual ingredient. In regulatory offences, for the reasons set out in paragraphs 6.22 and 6.23 below, express provision is usually required in the legislation before *mens rea* will be imputed.

6.22   The legal reasoning is as follows. Where the Act is silent, the court must ask whether the offence is of a truly criminal nature. If it is, there is a presumption that *mens rea* in some form is an essential element of the offence. In *Sweet v. Parsley* [1970] A.C. 132 at page 149 Lord Reid said:

". . . it is firmly established by a host of authorities that *mens rea* is an essential ingredient of every offence unless some reason can be found for holding that that is not necessary.

It is also firmly established that the fact that other sections of the Act expressly require *mens rea*, for example, because they contain the word "knowingly" is not in itself sufficient to justify a decision that a section which is silent as to *mens rea* creates an absolute offence. In the absence of a clear indication in the Act that an offence is intended to be an absolute offence, it is necessary to go outside the Act and examine all relevant circumstances in order to establish that this must have been the intention of Parliament. I say "must have been" because it is a universal principle that if a penal provision is capable of two interpretations, that interpretation which is most favourable to the accused must be adopted."

For an instance where the absence of the word "knowingly" in contrast to its presence in other provisions of the same Act led the House to decide that an offence under the Medicines Act 1968 was absolute, see *Pharmaceutical Society of Great Britain v. Storkwain Ltd* [1986] 1 W.L.R. 903.

6.23 Lord Reid in *Lim Chin Aik v. The Queen* [1963] A.C. 160, distinguished offences which "are not criminal in any real sense, but are acts which in the public interest are prohibited under a penalty" (*per* Wright J. in *Sherras v. De Rutzen* [1895] 1 Q.B. 918)" in the following way:

"It has long been the practice to recognise absolute offences in this class of quasi-criminal acts and one can safely assume that when Parliament is passing new legislation dealing with this class of offences, its silence as to *mens rea* means that the old practice is to apply."

This frequently-cited passage suggests that where the Act is silent one of two presumptions can be raised: one which infers *mens rea* if the offence is truly criminal; and one which repudiates *mens rea* if it is not. This interpretation of the passage was rejected by Lord Diplock, however, who expressed the view at page 163 that the presumption that *mens rea* was to be proved by the prosecution should not be displaced even in the case of an act which is not truly criminal unless "there is something that the person on whom the obligation is imposed can do directly or indirectly, by supervision or inspection, by improvement of his business methods or by exhorting those whom he may be expected to influence or control, which will promote the observance of the obligation". Lord Diplock's approach was preferred by the Privy Council in *Gammon (Hong Kong) Ltd v. A.G. of Hong Kong* [1985] A.C. 1. As most regulatory offences are drafted with the object of the enforcement of proper systems of activity, this consideration is rarely addressed in practice.

6.24 What is a truly criminal offence?. An offence of conspiracy to commit an absolute offence is always an offence requiring *mens rea*, because the offence is the agreement, rather than the commission of the statutory wrong. Therefore, an agreement to do an act which is not unlawful cannot be converted into an agreement to do an act which is unlawful by reason of facts of which the defendant is unaware (*Churchill v. Walton* [1967] 2 A.C. 224) although an agreement to do an act which is unlawful will not, of course, cease to be a criminal conspiracy by reason of the fact that the parties did not know that the intended conduct was contrary to the law. In respect of the statutory offence itself, the characterisation of the offence as "truly criminal" or otherwise, is much more difficult. Professor Sir John Smith describes this notion as a distinction "invented by the courts and the criteria for its application are not stated and difficult if not impossible to ascertain. Presumably it all depends upon the degree of stigma which the court believes would attach to a conviction" ([1986] Crim.L.R. 696). There are, however, some pointers to construction.

6.25 Pointers to construction. In determining whether an offence which is silent as to any mental state requires full *mens rea* or merely proscribes certain conduct under a penalty, there are a number of well-recognised, albeit overlapping, indicia.

6.26 The subject matter of the legislation. In some areas of statutory intervention in human activities, it is presumed by the nature of the area of activity that the offence will be one of strict liability. Examples of these are consumer protection and safety (*Tesco Stores Ltd v. Nattrass* [1972] A.C. 153); health and safety (*Nimmo v. Alexander Cowan & Sons* [1968] A.C. 107); building regulations (*Gammon* (above)); environmental protection and planning (*Maidstone Borough Council v. Mortimer* [1980] 3 All E.R. 552).

6.27 The language. Clearly the insertion of a word bearing *mens rea* can in some cases be determinative in favour of full *mens rea*. However, in some cases, the word importing the mental element applies only to one element of the offence and the offence is "semi-strict" (see paragraph 6.31 below).

6.28 The structure of the act and other provisions. The Act must be read as a whole and its ambit and intention construed in the light of that. There are, however, some areas which are frequently referred to as guides to the correct construction. These include:

(i) *Due Diligence.* If the Act gives rise to a due diligence defence which applies to the section creating the offence, it is unlikely that the offence requires *mens rea*, because the two provisions are inconsistent (see *Pharmaceutical Society of Great Britain v. Storkwain Ltd* [1986] 1 W.L.R. 903). This is far from conclusive, however. In the Trade Descriptions Act 1968, the due diligence defence (section 24) is available to an offender charged with recklessly making a statement which is false under section 14(1)(b) which is an offence of full *mens rea*.

(ii) *Third Party offence.* Where there is a third party offence (see paragraphs 7.81 onwards), this leans against a construction that the principal offence is other than one of strict liability because the purpose of such offence is to bring the "moral offender" before the court. If the offence requires *mens rea*, the principal is a "moral offender".

(iii) *Regulation-making power.* Where the regulation making power (if any) contains provisions that are inconsistent with an offence under the Act or under the Regulations requiring *mens rea*, that is a strong pointer. See *Storkwain* (above).

(iv) *Other offences.* It is relevant, also, to look at the other offences: as the court did so in both *Sweet v. Parsley* and *Storkwain* (see paragraph 6.22 above).

(v) *The sentence imposed for the offence.* In *R. v. Wells St Magistrates Court, ex p. Westminster City Council* [1986] Crim.L.R. 695 the offence of undertaking unauthorised works to a listed building was held not truly criminal although the prosecutor had pressed for trial on indictment and the offence was punishable even on summary conviction by three months imprisonment. In *Gammon* (above) Lord Scarman considered the significance of the penalty in deciding whether the offence is truly criminal. The ordinance under consideration provided for a punishment of three years imprisonment. Lord Scarman said:

> ". . . there is nothing inconsistent with the purpose of the ordinance in imposing severe penalties for offences of strict liability. The legislature could reasonably have intended severity to be a significant deterrent, bearing in mind the risks to public safety arising from some contravention . . . It must be crucially important that those who participate in or bear responsibility for the carrying out of works in a manner which complies with the requirement of the ordinance should know that severe penalties await them in the event of any contravention or non-compliance with the ordinance by themselves or anyone over whom they are required to exercise control".

On the other hand, Lord Morris of Borth-y-Gest considered that the range of possible punishments assisted in determining whether the offence was one of *mens rea* in *Sweet v. Parsley*. It is proper to conclude that the punishment is a factor but is far from being determinative.

6.29 Legislative purpose. Before concluding that an offence of strict liability has been created, the court should be satisfied that the legislative purpose is carried forward by the creation of a strict liability offence (*Gammon* (above)).

The nature of the mental element in offences of true mens rea

6.30 What state of mind is imputed?. Where an offence creates full *mens rea*, it does not necessarily follow that the mental element is uniform in each offence. The traditional formulation is "an honest and reasonable belief in the existence of facts which, if true, would make the act charged innocent". See, for example, Lord Diplock in *Sweet v. Parsley* (above). Since the decision of the House of Lords in *DPP v. Morgan* [1976] A.C. 182, it is possible to derive three propositions relevant to the state of mind imputed in a regulatory offence which requires *mens rea*:

(i) *Different Meanings Mens rea* may have different meanings in different offences: (*per* Stephen J. in *R. v. Tolson* (1889) 23 Q.B.D. 168 at page 187). Some offences, for example, will not be committed unless there is knowledge, belief or intention, or dishonesty or recklessness. Difficulties arise with words such as "cause" or "permit" which are capable of bearing meanings which suggest knowledge and otherwise. Whether a statutory offence is one of *mens rea*, and if so, the type of *mens rea* imputed can be ascertained only on the face, or by construction or interpretation of the particular legislation giving rise to the offence.

(ii) *Subjective Test:* Where a statute provides for a certain state of mind to be shown, that state of mind must be shown to a subjective standard. So in *Wilson v. Inyang* [1951] 2 K.B. 799 a non-registered medical practitioner was charged with wilfully and falsely using the title "physician" contrary to the Medical Act 1858. The Divisional Court upheld the decision of the magistrate that the defendant was entitled to be acquitted and held that where a defence of no *mens rea* was raised, the prosecution had to show that he did not honestly believe that he was permitted to use the title, rather than the lesser burden of showing either that he did not believe it or that he had no reasonable grounds for so doing. In *DPP v. Morgan* (above) this case was explained by Lords Hailsham and Edmund Davies as an example of the burden on the Crown to show the subjective quality of falsity and wilfulness.

In *Westminster City Council v. Croyalgrange* [1986] 1 W.L.R. 674, Lord Diplock's exposition of the common law rule in *Sweet v. Parsley* (above) was tentatively modified to omit the reference to belief on reasonable grounds where the allegation against the defendants was that they "knowingly" caused or permitted prohibited behaviour. Where the requirement of *mens rea* is for knowledge of the *actus reus*, the deliberate shutting of the eyes to an obvious means of knowledge (constructive knowledge) may equate to actual knowledge (*Roper v. Taylor's Central Garages (Exeter) Ltd* [1951] 2 T.L.R. 284 at page 288, *per* Devlin J.).

(iii) *Subjective and Objective Test* The quality of the mental element is variable according to the nature of the crime. Where the offence is one of *mens rea* and the nature of the intention falls to be determined, the question whether the prosecution must show merely the absence of the requisite state of mind on reasonable grounds, or must go further and show that there was no such state of mind irrespective of whether the holding of that state was reasonable or unreasonable, will depend upon the mental element inherent in the crime. The statute creating the offence in *R. v. Tolson* (1889) 23 Q.B.D. 168 was categorised in *DPP v. Morgan* [1976] A.C. 182 as a statute creating an absolute offence which the presumption in favour of *mens rea* rescued and was so distinguishable from the common law offence of ulterior intent, such as rape. In such cases where no specific intent is involved, the classic formulation of the defence as "an honest and reasonable belief in the existence of facts, which, if true, would make the act charged innocent" (the objective test) applies. Presumably, this formulation would govern every regulatory offence but does not govern a non-regulatory offence of ulterior intent, such as rape (*DPP v. Morgan* (above)) where the mental element to be proved is the absence of any honest (even if unreasonable) belief that the victim did not consent.

Semi-strict liability

6.31 Not every statutory provision which cannot be proved without satisfying a persuasive burden as to the defendant's state of mind is an offence of full *mens rea*. In the case of regulatory offences, the proper construction of the statutory provision may be that the *mens rea* is limited to one aspect only of the *actus reus*. Such offences are frequently referred to as "semi strict". A classic example is section 14(1) of the Trade Descriptions Act 1968, which provides:

"It shall be an offence for an person in the course of any trade or business

(a) to make a statement which he knows to be false

(b) recklessly to make a statement which is false

as to any of the following matters . . ."

6.32 Although at first sight this appears to create an offence of full *mens rea*, the House of Lords in *Wings v. Ellis* [1985] A.C. 272 found that the offence under section 14(1)(a) is semi-strict. Knowledge in that subsection was referable only to the falsity of the content of the statement when the offence was committed (that is, when the statement in a travel brochure was read by the prospective customer), even though the defendant was unaware that the statement was false when the brochure was promulgated. In contrast, the offence under section 14(1)(b) is of full *mens rea* because "recklessly" within the context of the Trade Descriptions Act 1968 means having no regard to the truth or falsity of the statement (*MFI Warehouses v. Nattrass* [1973] 1 W.L.R. 307).

6.33 It was acknowledged by Lord Scarman that in order to conclude that knowledge within section 14(1)(a) related only to the falsity of the statement, the offence had to fall within that class of act which is prohibited under a penalty in the public interest:

"It [this interpretation] involves, of course, construing the offence as one of strict liability to the extent that the offence can be committed unknowingly, ie. without knowledge of the act of statement: but this is consistent with the social purpose of a statute in the class to which this Act belongs."

6.34 *Wings v. Ellis* (above) can be contrasted with *Westminster City Council v. Croyalgrange* (above) where the submission that "knowledge" related only to the use of the premises as a sex establishment was rejected on the construction of the legislation as a whole, which was, in any event, regarded as a penal statute.

Mental element implicit in the actus reus

6.35 Some offences which would otherwise be absolute require a state of affairs which can only exist if there is an accompanying state of mind. An example may be the notion of possession, which can arise under the general criminal law only if a person is aware that he has the item (*Kirkland v. Robinson* [1987] Crim.L.R. 643). Many offences which are acknowledged to be offences of strict liability include a requirement of possession. An example is section 10 of the Consumer Protection Act 1987, whereby a person is guilty of an offence if he possesses for supply goods which fail to comply with the general safety requirement. Where there is an offence of selling goods in certain circumstances, the meaning of sale is sometimes given an extended definition to include "in possession for the purposes of sale" (see, for example, the Food Labelling Regulations 1996, regulation 2). If "possession" is to carry the same meaning in regulatory offences, the defendant or someone for whom he is liable under the criminal law must know that the offending item is within his power. Notwithstanding this, it does not appear that the knowledge of custody of the offending item must be shown to be that of the directing mind and will of the principal (see paragraphs 7.23 to 7.49 below) because the offence is absolute.

CONFLICTS BETWEEN EUROPEAN LAW AND DOMESTIC LEGISLATION

6.36   The interface of domestic legislation and European law.   European law impinges on regulatory offences in a number of ways. Most obviously, much regulatory legislation implements European directives on consumer and other affairs, whether by way of subordinate legislation enacted to conform with European requirements or by way of primary legislation. In relation to consumer affairs, this gained greater prominence after the Single European Act 1986, because it introduced an amendment – Article 100a which reflects Article 100 on the approximation of laws affecting the establishment and functioning of the common market making specific provision for consumer protection. An example of the legislation which is subordinate to existing legislation but which introduces new Community standards is the Food Safety (General Food Hygiene) Regulations 1995, which are made under the Food Safety Act 1990 and implement most of Council Directive 93/43/EEC of June 14, 1993 on the hygiene of foodstuffs and those parts of Council Directive 80/778/EEC of July 15, 1980 (the Water Quality Directive) which relate to the use of water in food production. An example of new primary legislation is Part II of the Consumer Protection Act 1987, which implemented Directive 85/374 [1985] O.J. L210/29 (the Product Liability Directive).

The programme of implementation of European law is not a seamless whole, however, despite constant moves towards harmonisation. As regulatory law has developed piecemeal, with much still remaining from our own legal tradition (particularly in the area of weights and measures) there remain areas of confrontation between European law and domestic law. Moreover, not all directives have at any point in time been implemented, or have been implemented only in part or unsatisfactorily.

A prosecutor should always consider whether there might not be a "European defence" to any action on the part of a prospective defendant particularly if it appears to be a deliberate step taken to confront domestic legislation. The prosecutor, when taking the decision to prosecute, should ensure that the full implications of a prosecution involving a controversial point of European law are fully understood. Where a local authority are the prosecutor, this should embrace both the financial and political considerations of the prosecution. It scarcely needs to be said that prosecutions which involve several tiers of appeal and perhaps a reference to the European Court of Justice are significantly more costly than those which are resolved at the first hearing by a guilty plea in the magistrates' court.

Directly applicable European law

Treaties

6.37   Treaties.   In particular, the question sometimes arises whether domestic legislation offends against a principle of European law having direct effect.

> ". . . every national court must, in a case within its jurisdiction, apply Community law in its entirety and protect rights which the latter confers on individuals and must accordingly set aside any provision of national law which may conflict with it, whether prior or subsequent to the Community rule" (*Amministrazione delle Finanze v. Simmenthal* (106/77) [1978] E.C.R. 629)

Infringement of European law can occur where there is an infringement of an Article under the Treaties or other European legislation with direct effect. A notorious example of a defence of infringement in the consumer context arose in the "Sunday trading" cases in the 1980s and early 1990s. The culmination of these cases, before the introduction of new legislation in the form of the Sunday Trading Act 1994, was *Stoke on Trent City Council v. B&Q* [1993] A.C. 900 in which it was alleged that domestic legislation (the Shops Act 1950) offended against Article 30 of the Treaty of Rome and was therefore unlawful. The case was referred for the consideration of the European court by the House of Lords under Article 177 of the Treaty of Rome. In fact, the European Court of Justice decided that Article 30 was not infringed on a point of proportionality. Because the Shops Act 1950 pursued a legitimate aim under community law, and the restriction was not excessive in pursuit of that aim, there was no infringement. Many other instances exist over a vast range of topics and points of law can arise that are as justiciable in the magistrates court as in the European Court of Justice.

6.38   Treaty provisions which might have an effect on the lawfulness of regulatory offences.   The mostly commonly considered provisions which might have an impact on some domestic legislation are set out below. These are by no means intended to suggest that other relevant treaty provisions could not be relied upon in regulatory cases, and, as with other areas of this work are intended as pointers to aspects of further research, rather than as an exhaustive explanation of issues of European law.

Fiscal Barriers

6.39   Fiscal barriers.

Article 12

> "Member States shall refrain from introducing between themselves any new customs duties on imports or exports or any charges having equivalent effect . . .."

Article 95

> "No Member State shall impose, directly or indirectly, on the products of other Member States any internal taxation of any kind in excess of that imposed directly or indirectly on similar domestic products.
>
>   Furthermore, no Member State shall impose on the products of other Member States any internal taxation of such a nature as to afford indirect protection to other products."

Both these articles, which deal with fiscal matters, prohibit trade barriers raised by revenue differences. It is the effect of any charge or tax and not its purpose to which the courts must have regard, and the disputed tax cannot be justified by reference to Article 36, which is an available protection in relation to physical barriers but not as to fiscal ones (*Commission v. Italy* [1969] E.C.R. 193). In the case of differential taxation, this is permissible and not contrary to Article 95 if the differences can be justified by the pursuit of an economic policy which is not itself contrary to the provisions of the Treaty and other European law (*Chemial Farmaceutici v. DAF* [1981] E.C.R. 1). Indirect protection fell for consideration in

Commission v. U.K. [1983] 3 C.M.L.R. 512, in which the different taxation systems applied to wine and beer (products thought of by the European Court as capable, in part, of meeting the same market) were held to be discriminatory and in breach of Article 95. In the case of importers, it is permissible for States to impose a fee for services legitimately offered to importers, but not if the effect of those fees is to cause an unwarranted interference with free trade (*Commission v. Italy* (above); *Besciani v. Amministrazione Italiana delle Finanze* [1976] E.C.R. 129; *Commission v. Belgium* (C–294/81) [1983] E.C.R. 281).

Quantitative Restrictions

Article 30

"Quantitative restrictions on imports and all measures having equivalent effect shall, without prejudice to the following provisions, be prohibited between Member States".

Article 34

"Quantitative restrictions on exports and all measures having equivalent effect shall, without prejudice to the following provisions, be prohibited between Member States".

6.40   These two provisions, taken together, cover the trading rules enacted by Member States which are capable of hindering, directly or indirectly, actually or potentially, intra-Community trade (*Procueur du Roi v. Dassonville* [1974] E.C.R. 837). This does not mean, merely because there is a difference between a restriction in one jurisdiction and that in another or others, that Article 30 (or 34) will have been infringed. If the national rules apply equally to goods within its jurisdiction, whatever their origin, there will have been no infringement (*Keck and Mithouard* [1993] E.C.R. I–6097), but if the national rules applied to domestically produced goods, for example, are more restrictive than the rules of other parts of the community or applied to imports from other parts of the community it seems likely that there will be an Article 30 defence to an allegation of infringement of domestic legislation (Keck and Mithouard) above.

Examples of challenges relevant to consumer legislation

(i) *Criminal proceedings against Ricardo Tasca* (C–65/75) [1976] E.C.R. 291: a price fixing scheme which meant that imports could only be sold at a loss would be illegal under Article 30. Also see *Openbaar Ministerie v. Van Tiggele* [1978] E.C.R. 25.

(ii) *Rewe-Zentrale A.G. v. Bundesmonopolverwaltung fur Branntwein* [1979] E.C.R. 649 (the *Cassis de Dijon* case): a provision of German law fixed a minimum alcoholic content for various categories of alcoholic drinks – which minimum was higher than the alcoholic content of cassis. The Court was asked, *inter alia,* whether measures having an effect equivalent to quantitative restrictions on imports contained in Article 30 . . . were to be understood so that traditional products of other Member States could not be put into circulation within the State in which the measures were applied. The Court observed that whereas disparities between national laws were justifiable "so far as those provisions may be recognised as being necessary in order to satisfy mandatory requirements relating in particular to the effectiveness of fiscal supervision, the protection of public health, the fairness of commercial transactions and the defence of the consumer", the requirements in question did not serve a purpose which was in the general interest and such as to take precedence over the requirements of the free movements of goods, which constitutes one of the fundamental rules of the Community. See also, on this topic *Ministere Public v. Deserbais* [1988] E.C.R. 4907 (Edam cheese); *Commission v. Germany* [1987] E.C.R. 1227 (beer). It is difficult to know what is encompassed by "mandatory requirements" within the *Cassis de Dijon* formula.

(iii) *Commission v. Ireland* [1981] E.C.R. 1625: Irish legislation; the Merchandise Marks Order 1971, required imported goods bearing motifs or in the shape of items which suggested that they were Irish, to bear also an indication of origin, or the marking "foreign". The Irish government defended this restriction in the interests of consumers and commercial fairness between manufacturers. The Court said: [10] ". . . the Court has repeatedly affirmed (in . . . Case 120/78 *Rewe* [1979] E.C.R. 649, . . . in case 788/79 *Gilli and Andres* [1980] E.C.R. 2071 . . . in Case 130/80 *Kelderman* [1981] E.C.R. . . . that 'in the absence of common rules relating to the production and marketing of the product in question it is for Member States to regulate all matters relating to its production, distribution and consumption on their own territory, subject, however, to the condition that those rules do not present an obstacle . . . to intra-Community trade and that it is only where national rules, which apply without discrimination to both domestic and imported products, may be justified as being necessary in order to satisfy imperative requirements relating in particular to . . . the fairness of commercial transactions and the defence of the consumer that they may constitute an exception to the requirements arising under Article 30". The Court then found the Order discriminatory and in contravention of Article 30.

(iv) In *Commission v. Denmark* [1988] E.C.R. 4607, the Court had to balance the aim of the protection of the environment with the free movement of goods. The court weighed up the measures taken to achieve the aim of protecting the environment (requiring sale in certain sizes of disposable cannisters, with a small exception for importers), and found that the prohibition, taken with the paucity of the exception, was disproportionate. Accordingly, the "mandatory requirements" of the domestic law could not displace the requirements of Article 30.

(v) *Commission v. UK* [1985] E.C.R. 1202: the Trade Descriptions (Origin Marking)(Miscellaneous Goods) Order 1981 was challenged by the Commission. This legislation required certain types of goods (clothing and textiles; domestic electrical appliances; footwear; cutlery) to bear an origin marking. The U.K. government contended that the Order complied with Article 30 because it affected both domestically produced and imported goods, and that the origin marking assisted consumers to ascertain the true value of the goods. The Court found that the origin marking would have the effect of encouraging domestic consumers to favour domestic products, and so was not in accordance with the requirements of Article 30. Notably, where the imported product is favoured by national laws, there may be no infringement *(Nederlandse Bakkerij v. Edah* [1986] E.C.R. I–3395) but this proposition must now be considered in the light of *Criminal Proceedings against Keck and Mithouard* [1993] E.C.R I–6097.

(vi) *Apple and Pear Development Council v. Lewis* [1983] E.C.R. 4083: In this case, a distinction was drawn between the promotion of a national product by a Member State (contrast *Commission v. Ireland* [1982] E.C.R. 4005 in which a Government-led "Buy Irish" campaign was held to be contrary to Treaty obligations) and promotions by producers themselves or an association of producers. Following this case, "Commission Guidelines for Member States' Involvement in Promotion of Agricultural and Fisheries Products – Article 30 Aspects [1986] O.J. C–272/3" were published.

(vii) *Societe d'Importation Edouard Leclerc- Siplec v. TFI Publicite SA and M6 Publicite SA* [1995] E.C.R. I–179: French television channels prohibited advertising by the distribution sector. It was contended by importers of fuel that this impeded sales opportunities for imported fuels. The Court reaffirmed that where a Member State impedes access to the market place, but not in such a way as to favour domestic products above imported ones, Article 30 does not apply. An interesting feature of this case was the Opinion of the Advocate General, who recommended that the test of the applicability of Article 30 should depend on the extent of restriction on access to the market place, rather than on comparative restrictions.

(viii) *Verein Gegen Unswesen in Handel und Gewerbe Koln v. Mars GmbH* [1995] E.C.R. I–1923. In this case, the German authorities were precluded from prohibiting packaging which was lawful in England. Suggestions that the packaging was inaccurate and misleading were not a justification for its prohibition, because those aspects could be regulated by domestic legislation.

(ix) *Criminal Proceedings against Pistre, Barthes, Milhau and Oberti* (C–321/94 to 324/94) (unreported) New Law, May 7, 1997. French legislation which was intended to promote the interests of producers from mountain areas was held to be discriminatory, and contrary to Article 30. It could not be justified under any of the grounds under Article 36 (below) because the description "Mountain" was not an indication of provenance, and therefore was incapable of being an industrial or commercial property of the goods.

6.41 *Article 36*

The provisions of Articles 30 to 34 shall not preclude prohibitions or restrictions on imports, exports or goods in transit justified on grounds of public morality, public policy or public security; the protection of health and life of humans, animals or plants; the protection of national treasures possessing artistic, historic or archaeological value or the protection of industrial or commercial property. Such prohibitions or restrictions shall not, however, constitute a means of arbitrary discrimination or a disguised restriction on trade between Member States.

(i) In *Commission v. U.K.* [1982] E.C.R. 2793, the United Kingdom had made an import ban on poultry meat and eggs shortly before Christmas 1981. The purpose of this was said to have been as an effort to prevent the spread of Newcastle disease (foulpest). The court found that the United Kingdom had been promoting its commercial interests and the steps taken to prevent the spread of Newcastle disease were disproportionate to the steps which needed to be taken to achieve the same stated objective. Article 36 did not, therefore, assist the Government in defending an allegation of breach of Article 30.

(ii) *Officier van Justitie v. Sandoz* [1983] E.C.R. 2445: Dutch authorities refused to permit the sale of muesli bars marketable in Belgium and Germany on the basis that it contained vitamins which were dangerous to health. The Court, while upholding the principle that, in the absence of harmonisation, Member States were permitted to legislate on the areas of public health, concluded that there was a duty to assess whether there was in fact such a risk as to justify the prohibition. It is legitimate for a Member State to insist on secondary testing if the testing process of the importing Member State does not meet its genuine concerns, although the Member State is required as part of a continuing process to assess to what extent its approvals system can be justified by Article 36 (*Frans-Nederlandse Maatschappij voor Biologische Producten* [1981] E.C.R. 3277). The Member State can also justify its position in an appropriate case, notwithstanding that there are is also a Community directive which imposes minimum requirements, but reserves the decision to the Member State whether stricter controls may be necessary (*Rewe Zentralfinanz GmbH v. Landwirtschaftskammer* [1975] E.C.R. 843) but where there is harmonising legislation without such a reservation, there can be no reliance on Article 36 (*Oberkreisdirektor v. Moorman* [1988] E.C.R. 4689). Also see *Campus Oil Ltd v. Minister for Industry and Energy* [1984] E.C.R. 2727 in relation to public security.

Free movement of Services

6.42   Free movement of services.

Article 59 governs the free movement of services. It provides: "Within the framework of the provision set out below, restrictions on the freedom to provide services shall be progressively abolished during the transitional period in respect of nationals of Member States who are established in a State of the Community other than that of the person for whom the services are intended."

This principle is closely allied to Article 52 which sets out the right, to be progressively applied, to establish undertakings in other Member States. These provisions have been extended by Directive 73/148 on the Abolition of Restrictions on Movement and Residence within the Community for Nationals of Member States with regard to Establishment and Provision of Services. This has had an impact on cross-border qualifications but, in the regulatory context, particular significance in the field of financial services.

(i) *Commission v. Germany* [1986] E.C.R. 3755: German laws required all providers of insurance services to have a permanent establishment in Germany and to be authorised by the German state. This meant that it was significantly more expensive for insurers who would otherwise only provide services in Germany occasionally, because they were required to provide a fixed place of business there. The Court found that the German requirements could be compatible with Articles 59 and 60 only if it was established that there were imperative reasons relating to the public interest which justified the restrictions. The Court found that there were particular reasons relating to the insurance market (namely the need for consumers to be able to enforce the insurance contract) why special protections could be applied, but found that a blanket requirement that there be a permanent establishment on German soil was not proportionate to the need. Authorisation procedures, however, were upheld. Proportionality is an issue in relation to the provision of services as it is elsewhere (*Collectieve Antennevoorzienin Gouda and Others v. Commissariat voor de Media* [1991] E.C.R. I–4007).

(ii) *Alpine Investments BV v. Minister van Financien* [1995] E.C.R. I–1141: Alpine Investments (a provider of financial services) was prevented by Dutch law from making unsolicited calls to potential customers by telephone without their written consent. The Court rejected the argument that as this prohibition applied as much to Dutch national business as to non-national business, Article 59 did not apply. The analogy with *Keck and Mithouard* (above) was rejected because inability to make direct contact was 8an intra-Community hindrance. The Court did, however, accept that it was not disproportionate for a Member State to prohibit cold calling in order to protect investor confidence in national financial markets.

Competition

6.43   Articles 85 and 86.   These articles, which are referred to only broadly here, set out the basis of European competition policy, preventing anti-competitive practices in so far as it affect trade between member states, such as many forms of exclusive distributorship agreements (*Etablissements Consten SA and Grundig GmbH v. Commission* [1966] E.C.R. 299). It needs to be remembered that even an agreement which appears to be confined to one Member State may affect trade between Member States (*Co-operatieve-Stremsel-en Kleauselfabriek v. Commission* [1981] E.C.R. 851) and the agreement need not be formal or binding in law (*ACF Chemiefarma v. Commission* [1970] E.C.R. 661).

Advertising

6.44   Conflicts between national law and Community regulation concerning advertising have given rise to the use of Article 30 as a basis for defeating the legality of the national law. An example of this was *GB-INNO v. CCL* [1990] E.C.R. I–667, in which a national law which prohibited the provision of certain information to consumers was held to be incompatible with Article 30 because it prevented the free movement of goods. Additionally, directives (see below) made under the auspices of Article 100 and 100a (concerning the approximation of provisions which affect the establishment or functioning of a common market) control advertising: the "misleading advertising" directive (Directive 84/450) is enforced by the provisions of domestic legislation and also by the OFT. The "comparative advertising directive" (Council Directive 97/55) is likely to be implemented by changes to the Control of Misleading Advertisments Regulations 1988. In addition there are directives concerned with advertising tobacco and broadcasting and distance selling.

Regulations

6.45   Regulations.   Regulations of the Community are given direct effect by Article 189 of the Treaty of Rome.

Article 177

6.46   Article 177.   The reference procedure is available to determine disputes arising out of the Treaties and so ensure uniform application throughout the Community, not to determine points of national law. National courts have jurisdiction to decide when a reference to the European Court of Justice should be made. Article 177 is not a means of redress to parties before national courts, but a means of assisting national courts to come to a conclusion. National courts need only make a reference if the point is necessary for them to reach a decision, and they need not do so where the resolution of the point is obvious (Case 283/81 *CILFIT* [1982] E.C.R. 3415). Lower courts can make a reference if the circumstances require it: subject to the preceding observations, higher courts must. In *Irish Creamery Milk Supplier v. Government of Ireland* [1981] E.C.R. 735, the Court of Justice commented that the legal context within which the reference is to be made should be determined so that the Court of Justice can place the interpretation in the correct context. The national court's decision when to make the reference is to be determined by considerations of procedure and efficiency.

European law applicable vertically

Directives

6.47   Directives.   Although Article 189 suggests that Directives, unlike Regulations, may not have direct effect, that is an oversimplification. In *Pubblico Ministero v. Ratti* [1979] E.C.R. 1629, a directive required Member States to introduce legal rules as to the packaging and labelling of solvents. This had to be done by December 1974. It was not. In a criminal prosecution, the defendant relied upon his compliance with European requirements under the Directive, which was in breach of the requirements of the national law. It was held that a Member State could not rely upon its national law against an individual in circumstances where there had been a failure to comply with the obligations under the Directive. In contrast, where the deadline for implementation of the Directive has not yet passed, a Defendant cannot claim a defence on the basis of compliance with the Directive. This principle was taken further in a civil case, *Marshall v. Southampton Area Health Authority* [1986] E.C.R. 732, in which the European Court decided that where a Member State had failed to implement a directive, and if the Directive was in its terms sufficiently clear and unconditional, the national court could declare national law inapplicable and ineffective as against the Member State. Also see *El Corte Ingles SA v. Blasquez Rivero* [1996] E.C.R. I–1281. This principal is called "vertical" applicability. The notion of the State encompasses local authorities (*Fratelli Costanzo v. Milano* [1989] E.C.R. 1839) and publicly owned bodies (*Foster v. British Gas* [1990] E.C.R. I–3133). Although an individual can rely upon an unimplemented Directive as against an emanation of the Member State, the reverse is not true. In *Officier van Justitie v. Kolpinghuis Nijmegen* [1987] E.C.R. 3969, the European Court concluded on a reference under Article 117 that Dutch authorities may not rely in a criminal prosecution upon the provisions of a Directive which had not been implemented. Also see *Criminal Proceedings against Arcaro* [1997] All E.R. (E.C.) 82 and paragraph 6.75 below. Directives are not applicable horizontally (*i.e.* between private citizens) in the absence of express implementation (*Faccini Dori v. Recreb Srl* (C–91/92) [1994] E.C.R. I–3325).

6.48   Interpretation.   See paragraphs 6.74 to 6.76 below. The approach of the European Court to questions of interpretation can be referred to as "indirect applicability" of European law.

Remedies for non-implementation of European law

6.49   Damages.   In addition to the defence which unimplemented Directives may provide in criminal proceedings, an individual who has suffered loss in consequence of the failure to implement European directives within the requisite period may claim reparation (*Francovich v. Italian State* [1991] E.C.R. I–5357). This possibility arises if:

   (i)   the purpose of the directive is to grant rights to individuals;

   (ii)   the content of those rights can be divined by reference to the Directive; and

   (iii)   there is a causal link between the breach of the State's obligations and the loss suffered (*Faccini Dori v. Recreb Srl* (C–91/92) [1994] E.C.R. I–3325).

CONCEPTS WHICH APPEAR FREQUENTLY IN REGULATORY OFFENCES

6.50   Issues considered.   There are many characteristics of regulatory offences which are shared in common between regulatory statutes, even though those statutes do not have common origins and could not necessarily be regarded as part of a single code. Some of these characteristics are considered in this section. Recurrent themes in regulatory offences include offences dependent upon sale, possession for sale, etc., offences arising from the dissemination of inaccurate information in the course of business; offences arising from the failure to provide prescribed information and offences relating to the failure to achieve a general standard. Moreover, some regulatory offences give rise to a particular difficulty in that the same conduct may give rise to a very large number of offences concerning different aggrieved persons.

Recurrent themes in regulatory offences

6.51   Offences dependent upon sale, possession for sale, supply.

Sale: This refers to the contract by which goods are exchanged for money. There is no sale unless there is a promise to exchange goods. Where sale is a critical issue to the offence, the legislation giving rise to the offence frequently allows for an extended definition. An example is in the Food Safety Act 1990, section 2:

   "(1) For the purposes of this Act–

   (a)   the supply of food, otherwise than on sale, in the course of a business; and

   (b)   any other thing which is done with respect to food and is specified in an Order made by the Ministers."

In criminal offences a purported sale of goods may be deemed to have occurred, even though no goods meeting the description were in fact supplied. An example of this is *Meah v. Roberts* [1978] 1 All E.R. 97, where the requested product was lemonade, but what was supplied was caustic soda. An offence of "sale" of lemonade was charged and proved.

A mere offer to supply is not a sale, and much legislation directs itself to including this aspect with the notion of sale.

Supply   This envisages the passing of possession from one person to another without the need for a commercial transaction, although the offence taken as a whole may impose a requirement that the supply be in the course of business before an offence can be committed. See, for example, *Wadham Kenning Motor Group Ltd v. East Sussex County Council* (unreported), December 3, 1997 (D.C.). It is important to recall that many statutory definitions of the word "supply" are extended to include the notion of having in possession for sale or supply – and not always consistently, even within legislation covering the same area. Because an Act defines supply, it should not always be assumed that regulations made under that Act will contain the same definition. Contrast, for example, the meaning of supply within the Consumer Protection Act 1987 with that in the Toy Safety Regulations 1995.

Possession for supply or sale   This is likely to require a person to have some physical control over the goods in question and the means of disposal of them. Where a defendant has separated goods in his possession so that they shall not be sold, the fact that he has had them in possession for sale will not be sufficient. They must be separated from the balance of the stock as a matter of fact and not merely as a matter of intention.

6.52   Knowledge.   In regulatory offences, a requirement that the prosecution must prove that a defendant had knowledge may not mean that it must be shown that he had knowledge of every aspect which comprises the offence. So in *Wings Ltd v. Ellis* [1985] 1 A.C. 272, the prosecution need only show that the defendant knew that the content of the statement was false – even though he might have been quite unaware of its making (see paragraphs 6.32 to 6.34 above). Exactly the same construction as that in section 14(1)(a) might be interpreted differently in a different offence. So, for instance, in section 47 of the Financial Services Act 1986:

> "(1) Any person who makes a statement, promise or forecast, which he knows to be misleading, false or deceptive or dishonestly conceals any material facts . . . is guilty of an offence if he makes the statement, promise or forecast or conceals the facts for the purpose of inducing or is reckless as to whether it may induce another . . . to enter or offer to enter into etc. an investment agreement . . .."

It is quite likely that the comparable words "makes a statement . . . which he knows to be . . . false" means that the person must both know that the statement is made and that it is false when it is made. Moreover, if the offence is one of full *mens rea*, only the person who has made the statement (rather than someone employing that person) is likely to be guilty of an offence.

Knowledge may include "wilfully shutting one's eyes to the truth" (*Warner v. Metropolitan Police Commissioner* [1969] 2 A.C. 256 *per* Lord Reid at 279) and see

Wing v. Nuttall (1997) 161 J.P. 701. This issue is, however, usually regarded as a matter of evidence of actual knowledge rather than of law (*Westminster City Council v. Croyalgrange* [1986] 1 W.L.R. 674).

6.53   Recklessness.   It is an offence contrary to section 14(1)(b) of the Trade Descriptions Act 1968 recklessly to make a statement as to certain matters concerning services which is false. This is an offence of full *mens rea*. Other offences of recklessness abound in the criminal statutes whether regulatory or otherwise (see, for another regulatory example, section 44 of the Environmental Protection Act 1990). Recklessness does not connote dishonesty, albeit that it is a state of mind of greater indifference to the outcome of activity that mere negligence but it is not usually equated with knowledge or implied knowledge. Under the general law, recklessness is contrasted with the foresight of the ordinary prudent man. So if the circumstances were such that the ordinary prudent man sharing the same characteristics, age and sex of the defendant, would have foreseen that a likely outcome, and more than just a slight risk, would be the prohibited event, a defendant is reckless who either fails to give thought to the risk, or, having thought of the risk, nevertheless takes the chance that the prohibited event would occur (*R. v. Lawrence* [1982] A.C. 510). If the offence is one requiring *mens rea*, a company is only liable for this offence if a person who is part of the directing mind and will of the company can be shown to have been reckless as to the accuracy of a statement, or if the making of the statement had been delegated to an employee who was reckless (*Airtours plc v. Shipley* (1994) 158 J.P. 835). However, some care needs to be taken in considering the state of mind of a person capable of being the directing mind and will. A complete failure to carry out any sort of checks on an inferior employee may amount to recklessness on the part of the person to whose actions the company's liability can be attributed. An example of this arose in *Wing v. Nuttall*, above, in which the Court of Appeal determined that an employer who failed to make checks on his drivers' tachograph charts in order to confirm that they were complying with the requirements relating to driving hours was reckless. In the circumstances of this case, this recklessness was a "shutting of the eyes", and so amounted to implied knowledge.

Offences arising from the dissemination of incorrect information in the course of business

6.54   The information conveyed: False and misleading statements.   There are many instances of offences designed as deterrents to protect the public from being misled and prejudiced by information furnished by traders. The offence of applying a false trade description to goods for sale contrary to section 1(1)(a) of the Trade Descriptions Act 1968 is one example. Others include the making of a false or misleading statement as to services provided in the course of business contrary to section 14 of the Trade Descriptions Act 1968, the giving of a misleading price indication contrary to section 20 of the Consumer Protection Act 1987 and conveying information which is false or misleading in a material respect contrary to section 46 of the Consumer Credit Act 1974.

6.55   What does the advertisement, brochure, etc. state?   The first step in considering any advertisement or other conduct by which information is conveyed, is to ascertain precisely what the advertisement or conduct indicates and then to evaluate its lawfulness. The significance of this process was underlined in *Jenkins v. Lombard North Central* [1983] C.C.L.R. 15, in which stickers bearing the name and logo of the advertiser, which was a company providing a wide range of financial services, had been placed on cars. The question was whether the fact that the advertiser was a company which was well-known as providing credit facilities indicated that the company was willing to provide credit in respect of the cars. The Divisional Court concluded that the matter had to be decided by looking at the advertisement itself and not through extraneous knowledge. In contrast, in *R. v. Warwickshire County Council ex p. Johnson* [1993] 1 A.C. 583, where the issue to be determined was not as to the meaning of the price indication but whether the price indication was misleading, that could be judged by reference to subsequent events. Lord Roskill, with whom the other members of the House agreed, emphasised that the only method of testing whether a price indication was misleading was whether it was in fact complied with.

6.56   What is the assertion made?   The assertion made need not be in express terms. For example, in *British Airways Board v. Taylor* [1976] 1 W.L.R. 13, BOAC (an airline operator) confirmed a passenger booking for specified flights for which a ticket had already been purchased. When the confirmation letter was sent, seats on the relevant flights were available. Because BOAC operated a policy of overbooking the flights, when the passenger arrived for the flight there was no seat available and he could not be carried. BOAC was charged with recklessly making a statement which was false contrary to section 14(1)(b) of the Trade Descriptions Act 1968. The House of Lords concluded that the letter and ticket, taken together, could be understood as a statement of fact that the booking was certain, whereas, because of the overbooking policy, that statement was false. Therefore, even though BOAC did not expressly state that the booking was certain, and even though the nature of the express words in the ticket and letter were in the nature of a promise as to the future (which can be neither true nor false – see *Beckett v. Cohen* [1973] 1 All E.R. 120) there was an implied statement as to the time at which the service was to be provided. Whether express words contain an implied statement is a question of fact to be determined by the magistrates court or jury as the case may be (*R. v. Clarksons Holidays* (1972) 57 Cr. App. R. 38; *R. v. Sunair Holidays Ltd* [1973] 1 W.L.R. 1105; *British Airways Board v. Taylor* above). A false implied statement as to existing fact may be made if the information is inaccurate even where the statement contains a reservation that the promises contained in it made may be subject to change (*R. v. Avro plc* [1993] Tr. L. 83).

6.57   Does the assertion fall within the prohibited topic?   The statute delimits the offence to which it gives rise by prescribing the information to which the communication must relate. So, in relation to section 1 of the Trade Descriptions Act 1968, the prohibition is upon the making of a false trade description. A trade description is apparently defined exhaustively in section 2, but that has not prevented much argument as to what will and will not fall within the prohibited category. For instance, a trade description must be a description of fact. So the words "extra value" on a chocolate bar was not a trade description because "value" was not a matter capable of ascertainment of truth or falsity (*Cadbury Ltd v. Halliday* [1975] 2 All E.R. 226). The same consideration is true of a "statement" within section 14 of the Act which is, by definition, a matter the truth or falsity of which is susceptible of proof. So "information" in an advertisement would seem, by definition, to exclude a mere puff. Telling the difference is not always easy, however. In *Robertson v. Dicicco* [1972 R.T.R. 431 the description "beautiful car" was interpreted by the Divisional Court as relating to its fitness for purpose, strength, performance, behaviour or accuracy within section 2(1)(d) of the Act. "Immaculate condition" was also held by the Divisional Court as being capable of being a trade description, although the case was remitted to the magistrates to determine to what the description related (*Kensington London Borough v. Riley* [1973] R.T.R. 122).

Similar problems have arisen under section 14 of the 1968 Act: a refund was not within the definition of services (*Dixons v. Roberts* (1984) 148 J.P. 513) although the failure to honour a money back guarantee was (*Ashley v. Sutton London Borough Council, The Times* December 8, 1994).

6.58 Disclaimers and inconsistent assertions. It is important to distinguish a disclaimer which is in fact part of the statement and prevents it from being false, from a disclaimer which is merely a defence. Applying a disclaimer where a false statement has been applied by the defendant to goods and, by analogy, services, cannot always give rise to a "defence" but a disclaimer may result in a prosecution failure to prove the offence. An offence of applying a false trade description cannot in general be defended by reliance upon a disclaimer, although an offence of supplying goods to which a false trade description has been applied may be defended in this way as part of a due diligence defence (*R. v. Southwood* [1987] 1 W.L.R. 1361, [1987] 3 All E.R. 556). In the last-mentioned case, the defendant had "zeroed" the odometer. This was held to be the application of a false trade description. A disclaimer defence was held to be unavailable:

> "The "disclaimer", assuming it to be in the terms of those in the instant case, would be saying: "This is a false trade description. I assert that it is a false trade description and because I assert that it is a false trade description it ceases to be a false trade description applied to goods, and consequently I am not guilty of a contravention of section 1(1)(a)". The assertion does not cause the description to be any less false than it was originally, nor does it cause the description to cease to be applied to the car."

per Lane L.C.J. at page 1365.

Moreover, that offence is committed when the trade description is applied with a view to a supply or prospective supply (for instance when the odometer is "zeroed") so that a subsequent disclaimer when the vehicle came to be sold would be too late (*Newman v. Hackney London Borough Council* [1982] R.T.R. 296). The reasoning of these decisions was followed in *Newham London Borough Council v. Singh and Sandhu* [1988] R.T.R. 359, although the Divisional Court added that, whilst a disclaimer could not be a defence under section 1(1)(a), it could be evidence of disassociation of an odometer reading from the car, to support a contention that there had been no application of a false trade description.

Increasingly, the Divisional Court appears anxious to ensure that prosecutions for false or misleading statements are not founded on part only of the material available to the customer (see *R. v. Bull* below). Two situations can be distinguished from the broad policy of *R. v. Southwood* (above):

1. Where the effect of adding an inconsistent description or oxymoron is to make clear that certain language does not carry a traditional or familiar meaning, no offence is committed. In *Wolkind v. Northcott Pura Foods Ltd* (1987) 151 J.P. 492 a product called "Pura Vegetable Lard" which was described as containing "vegetable lard - 100 per cent vegetable oils",

was the subject of a prosecution under section 1(1)(b). It was contended, with the support of various dictionary definitions that "lard" meant "pig fat". The Divisional Court refused to allow a prosecution appeal because they did not accept that the Crown Court (which had acquitted on appeal) had been satisfied either that "lard" meant only pig fat, nor that "vegetable lard" was a false description. The Divisional Court set itself against curtailing the development of new and possibly innovative uses of words.

2. Where the words are such as to make it clear that no reliance is placed on the false description so that the "disclaimer" can be taken as part of the trade description itself. In *R. v. Bull* [1996] 160 J.P. 240, a false mileometer reading inserted in a sales invoice immediately adjacent to a highlighted statement that the odometer reading was to be taken as false, meant that there was no case to answer on a charge of applying a false trade description to goods under section 1 of the Act. The disclaimer was part of the trade description and the description was not, therefore, false. This approach to disclaimers had been criticised in a prosecution appeal in *London Borough of Ealing v. Taylor* [1995] 1159 J.P. 460, but the court declined to interfere in the finding of the magistrates. The test for the efficacy of a disclaimer is whether the disclaiming words are "as bold, precise and compelling" as any they are intended to negate (*Norman v. Bennett* [1974] 1 W.L.R. 1229, *Smallshaw v. PKC Associates Ltd* (1995) 159 J.P. 654). For further discussion of this topic see paragraphs 9.4 to 9.8 below.

The time factor

6.59 When is the assertion made? Where information is conveyed to a large number of people by posters, fly-sheets, books or other media, traders are at particular risk of multiple prosecutions in the event that the advertisement is flawed. In the context of section 14(1)(b) of the Trade Descriptions Act 1968, this was addressed by the Court of Appeal in *R. v. Thomson Holidays* [1974] 1 Q.B. 592. The defendants, having been prosecuted and convicted in relation to a false statement in a travel brochure which had been acted upon by one complainant, raised a defence of autrefois acquit in respect of the same false statement in another copy of the same brochure which had been the subject of a separate complaint, or, it was said, it was an abuse of process and oppressive to bring a further prosecution. The Court of Appeal, relying on dicta in *Sunair Holidays v. Dodd* [1970] 1 W.L.R. 1037, held that the true construction of section 14 of the Act was that a statement was made when it was read. This was re-affirmed in the House of Lords in *Wings Ltd v. Ellis* [1985] 1 A.C. 272. Their Lordships described the circumstances in which a statement might be made in different ways, although each rejected the notion that communication of the statement was a necessary limitation on the way in which a statement might be made. Lord Hailsham at page 285 said of a statement in a brochure:

"When in the course of a trade or business, a brochure containing a false statement is issued in large numbers through a chain of distribution involving several stages, and intended to be read and used at all or some of the stages, it does not follow that it is only "made" at its ultimate destination. It may be "made" when it is posted in bulk, when the information is passed on by telephone or in smaller batches by post, and when it is read by the ultimate recipient, provided that at each stage what happens is in accordance with the original intention of the issuing house".

The notion of intention in that passage is presumably, not to introduce any element of *mens rea* into the offence, but to define the category of persons to whom a statement may be made. Lord Brandon at page 298 made clear his view that the statement was a continuing or repeated one which continued to be made so long as it remained without effective correction. This aspect of the decision in *Wings* was further taken up in *R. v. Avro plc* (above) in which the Divisional Court held that an offence was committed when an airline ticket was read even though it had been issued previously to the passenger. In *National Homecare Ltd v. Berkshire County Council*, New Law DC Com 58, July 13, 1996, the Divisional Court considered the position of a statement which may have been a contractual statement, accurate when first read by the recipient but which became incorrect while the contract between the company and the recipient was in force. It was held that the statement was of a continuing nature, so that even though the statement was accurate when first made, it became false and the company could be convicted when the recipient refreshed his memory from the document. It was a question of fact to be derived from all the circumstances how long any statement continues. The consequence of this decision is that the assertion in *Beckett v. Cohen* [1972] 1 W.L.R. 1593 that section 14(1) of the 1968 Act has no application to statements which amount to promises with regard to the future has to be approached with some care. It is not clear whether only a written statement can be continuing, or whether an oral promise is also to be regarded as continuing for the period for which the promise is contractually bound to endure. Where there is a written promise as to the future which is capable of being a continuing statement, it seems that the maker of the promise will be at risk of prosecution if it is dishonoured. Where that written statement is contained in a standard text or advertisement for use with a substantial number of customers, clients or others, an offence may be committed in respect of each customer.

6.60 Although the above discussion relates to section 14 of the Trade Descriptions Act 1968, the problem of the continuing nature of an advertisement also relates to other statutory provisions. Section 46 of the Consumer Credit Act 1974 refers to "an advertisement . . . which . . . conveys information which in a material respect is false or misleading". There is no authority which determines whether this section creates a continuing offence, but, by analogy with *Wings* and applying a purposive construction (see paragraphs 6.71 below), the point is more than arguable. In section 6 of the Trading Stamps Act 1964, express guidance is given in the statutory provision: ". . . an advertisement issued by way of display or exhibition in a public place shall be treated as issued on every day on which it is so displayed or exhibited . . .". Correspondingly, section 20 of the Consumer Protection Act 1987 provides that a price indication which has become misleading after it was given (and in respect of which all reasonable steps to prevent continuing reliance are not taken by the person who has made the statement in the course of his business) shall give rise to an offence. It seems, however, that the offence involves publication to a person (whether or not that person must always be identified is a moot point: see paragraphs 8.14 and 10.4 below) and not mere display (*R. v. Birmingham Justices, ex p. Matthews and others* (1996) 104 I.T.S.A. 11 M.R. 24.

6.61   Nor are "advertisements" and brochures the only illustrations of the problems associated with exposure of services and products to a general public. In a typical supermarket situation, problems of multiple offences are posed by shelf-edge and other labels. In *Gateway Foodmarkets Ltd v. Devon County Trading Standards Officer* [1989] C.O.D. 342, some tins of cat food were adjacent to a marker which showed cat food at 36p. Some individual tins were priced at 38p. The information alleged eight counts of offering goods for sale at a price less than that at which they were in fact offered contrary to section 11 of the Trade Descriptions Act 1968 (now repealed and replaced by section 20 of the 1987 Act). The Divisional Court upheld the magistrates' convictions of all counts in that the goods offered were the individual tins, not the overall display.

6.62   **Offences of "applying" a statement.** These may be contrasted with offences of making statements. In *VAG (U.K.) Ltd v. Lancashire County Council* New Law, DC, March 14, 1996 the offence of applying a false trade description was held not to be of a continuing nature. So a description in a motor car handbook describing an anti-theft device could not be "applied" after the anti-theft device had ceased to be provided with cars of that sort.

The nature of falsity and misleading

6.63   **False and misleading.** What is misleading may not be false and vice versa. In *Metsoja v. H. Norman Pitt* (1989) 153 J.P. 485 the Divisional Court found that there was a prima facie case against a trader who had given information about credit which was literally true but which might mislead. Not all statutes make reference to both concepts, however. Whereas section 14 of the Trade Descriptions Act 1968 relates to statements that are false as to the nature of services (although see section 14(2)), section 20 of the Consumer Protection Act 1987 relates to price indications that are misleading and section 46 of the Consumer Credit Act 1974 refers to information which is false or misleading. This appears to create two separate offences.

6.64   **Trade Descriptions Act 1968, s.14.** "False" is defined in the Trade Descriptions Act 1968 in relation both to false statements under section 14 but also in relation to false trade descriptions under section 1 as meaning "false" to a material degree. This excludes, therefore, *de minimis* inaccuracies and excesses of caution. Section 3(2) of the Act, however, for the purposes of section 1 also defines "false" as including "misleading" but, as can be seen above, it does not follow that the same meaning can be traced into section 14. Of note, though, is that section 14(2)(a) provides that "anything likely to be taken for such a . . . statement as to [any of the matters specified in subsection (1)] as would be false shall be deemed to be a false statement as to that matter". This seems to mean that a statement which is misleading as to its subject matter may be a false statement, but the scope of this provision is hard to understand. It has a parallel in section 3(2) of the Act. An additional clue is that the sidenote is "false or misleading statements as to services, etc.," but this must be treated with care. The modern view is that sidenotes may be an aid to construction of the text, although they can be but poor guides because they are no more than a pointer to the main subject matter (*per* Lord Reid in *D.P.P. v. Schildkamp* [1971] A.C. 1 at page 10). Where the sidenote refers to something not expressed in the section, the reader is put on enquiry "but the answer may be that the drafter chose an inadequate signpost, or neglected to alter it to match an amendment made to the clause during the passage of a Bill" ("Statutory

Interpretation" Francis Bennion, (2nd ed. at p. 513). No distinction between what is false and what is misleading was drawn in the decision in *Thomson Travel v. Roberts* (1984) J.P. 666. This case concerned a statement in a brochure which described an area of sand retained by a concrete wall from which one gained access to the sea as a "beach". Although the Court looked at the effect on the mind of the reader, the same conclusion could have been reached by the court if it had assessed the factual accuracy of the statement.

6.65 In essence, the distinction between the two notions ought to be that falsity is a question of factual inaccuracy, whereas the determination of what is misleading involves looking into the mind of a notional recipient of the information to decide whether the information gives the wrong impression. The test of what is misleading is that in *Sweeting v Northern Upholstery Ltd* (1983) 2 Tr.L. 5, namely, whether there is a reasonable likelihood of ordinary people being misled. Forbes J. at page 9 said that the Act "requires a shopkeeper, and this seems to me to be important, to take pains to avoid possible ambiguities, and if they are not resolved an offence is committed." It follows that an offence is not committed if the words are clear. Where a statement is expressed in a specialist area, the test for what is misleading may incorporate the degree of sophistication which might reasonably be expected of the reader. So, in *Southwark London Borough v. Time Computer Systems, The Independent*, July 14, 1997, an advertisement in "What PC" magazine which showed software boxes with computer hardware for sale as a package, but also contained a footnote showing that the boxes were optional extras because the software came pre-loaded, was not misleading to those likely to be reading that magazine. The question is one of fact (*R. v. Adams, The Times*, January 26, 1993).

Offences of failing to provide prescribed information

6.66 Some provisions require specified information to be communicated to a consumer or other person. An example of this is to be found within the Consumer Credit (Advertisement) Regulations 1989, which set out detailed requirements for advertisements for credit. The Consumer Credit (Agreements) Regulations 1983 are another example. The consequences of failure may be both civil and criminal. There may be an offence, and also the credit may be irrecoverable. As with other regulatory areas, detailed consideration of the statutory requirements is necessary to see if there has been a non-compliance. Moreover, particular care needs to be taken with the form of any information which follows the breach alleged. See, for example, the difficulties which arose in *Carrington Carr Ltd v. Leicester County Council* [1994] C.C.L.R. 14.

Offences of failure to achieve a general standard

6.67 Increasingly, regulations made pursuant to European harmonising legislation are aimed at setting standards to be attained rather than making prohibitions which limit a pre-existing freedom. Offences may be committed if the standard is not attained. So, for example, the Management of Health and Safety at Work Regulations 1992, regulation 3(1) requires that "every employer shall make a suitable and sufficient assessment of–

(a) the risks to the health and safety of his employees to which they are exposed whilst they are at work; and

(b) the risks to the health and safety of persons not in his employment arising out of or in connection with the conduct by him of his undertaking, for the purpose of identifying the measures he needs to take to comply with the requirements and prohibitions imposed upon him or under the relevant statutory provisions." Section 33 of the Health and Safety at Work Act etc. 1974 renders the failure to comply with regulations an offence. This regulation, as with the other provisions of the same enactment must be interpreted in the light of the Framework Directive, which also sets broad objectives. A Code of Practice assists with its practical interpretation – in broad terms. While "suitable" has its feet in previous legislation, sufficiency appears to be a highly subjective notion, such that a willing and compliant employer may have considerable difficulty in identifying what, precisely, he must do. For instance, if there is an accident concerning equipment not referred to in his risk assessment because it was not thought to be a risk, will his risk assessment by definition be insufficient? The Approved Code of Practice (paragraph 9) suggests that only significant risks need to be the subject of the risk assessment, but what appears significant after an accident is quite different from what may seem significant when the employer tries to identify and quantify the risk with the benefit only of what he can foresee. It is likely that the offences under the regulations are absolute, so that intention, negligence and knowledge presumably play no part.

Where the question of what is "suitable" or "sufficient" is raised, the burden of proof appears to be on the prosecution to show that whatever steps are necessary have not been taken.

6.68   The same notion of risk assessment has been introduced in other areas where there is an element of risk of injury to the public or sections of the public, see for example, regulation 4(3) of the Food Safety (General Food Hygiene) Regulations 1995 and see paragraphs 9.23 to 9.25 (application of due diligence defences to HACCP systems) and paragraph 6.74 (interpretation of legislation based on European directives).

Multiplicity of offences

6.69   One of the matters which may affect a decision to prosecute is whether the prospective defendant has been prosecuted before in relation to the same conduct. In the case of offences which arise through advertising or the publication of circulars and brochures for dissemination to the general public, this raises particular problems of multiplicity and interpretation.

6.70   Multiple prosecutions.   The Court in *R. v. Thomson Holidays Ltd* [1974] 1 Q.B. 592 addressed the considerations which apply to multiple prosecutions. The Court rejected the submission on behalf of the defendants that the second prosecution should be stayed and also that the penalty in respect of the second prosecution should be nominal. Particular reference was made to the provisions of section 30 of the Trade Descriptions Act 1968 (now repealed and replaced by section 130 of the Fair Trading Act 1973: see paragraph 8.41 below). The court suggested that the object of that provision was to enable (then) the Department of Trade and Industry to collect information about intended prosecutions and give advice about them and, by so doing, prevent oppressive numbers of prosecutions based upon the same course of conduct. If that was the function then of the DTI it is now the function of the Director General of Fair Trading under section 130 of the 1973 Act. The court did accept, nonetheless, that there might come a time when to go on prosecuting would become oppressive so that proceedings should be stayed or penalties imposed nominal. That time had not come after one prosecution. In *Wings* (paragraph 6.59, above) Lord Hailsham commented (at page 285) that the finding that the same conduct by the defendant could result in many offences did not mean that "a prosecution policy of excessive zeal involving repeated attempts to convict a firm in respect of each separate communication of an individual copy of a brochure ought to meet with anything but reprobation from the courts. That must depend on the circumstances." In practice, repeated prosecutions tend to emanate from different prosecuting authorities, although prosecuting authorities are generally aware, through their information network, of the progress of prosecutions in other areas of the country and are often content to await the outcome of an on-going prosecution elsewhere.

INTERPRETATION OF REGULATORY OFFENCES

Legislation with no European influence

6.71 Domestic legislation. There are two conflicting principles which the courts have frequently referred to when interpreting the statutory language which expresses regulatory offences with no origin in European law. It is not clear which principle predominates and there is no conclusive authority. This difficulty is made more confusing by an increasing enthusiasm to move to a purposive interpretation of all legislation, whether European in origin or not, whether penal or otherwise.

Penal provisions Traditionally, it is axiomatic that any ambiguity should be resolved in favour of the defendant: "It is a universal principle that if a penal provision is capable of two interpretations, that interpretation which is most favourable to the accused must be adopted" (*Sweet v. Parsley* [1970] A.C. 132 *per* Lord Reid at p. 149). This principal was also applied by Goff L.J. in *Newell v. Hicks* (1984) 148 J.P. 308, in which he declined to extend the meaning of the word "facility" to include the provision of goods in a criminal statute even though he accepted that the word facility might carry an extended meaning in commercial circles. Similar reasoning in respect of the same section had been applied by Woolf J. in *Westminster City Council v. Ray Alan (Manshops) Ltd* [1982] 1 All E.R. 771.

Purposive construction: The second principle is that regulatory legislation falls to be construed according to its purpose so far as the wording may reasonably permit. The resolution of ambiguity therefore is in favour of implementing the statutory object of protecting the public or the consumer as the case may be (see Lord Scarman in *Wings plc v. Ellis* [1985] 1 A.C. 272 at page 295). In *Tesco Ltd v. Nattrass* [1972] A.C. 153 Lord Diplock made clear his view that the aim of the protection of the public was to be tempered by the expectation that "Parliament intended (the Trade Descriptions Act 1968) to give effect to a policy of consumer protection which does have a rational and moral justification" (at pp. 196-197). The principle of construction in favour of promotion of the philanthropic object of legislation also follows that applied in the field of factory legislation (*Harrison v. National Coal Board* [1951] 1 All E.R. 1102, *Thurogood v. Van den Berghs and Jurgens Ltd* [1951] 2 K.B. 537 at 548, *McCarthy v. Coldair Ltd* [1951] 2 T.L.R. 1226, *Norris v. Syndic Manufacturing Co. Ltd* [1952] 2 Q.B. 135 at 142).

6.72 Modern purposive construction. Although the two principles referred to above continue to co-exist, the courts increasingly favour the adoption of a "purposive" approach to all legislation:

"The days have long passed when the courts adopted a strict-constructionist view of interpretation which required them to adopt the literal meaning of the language. The courts now adopt a purposive approach which seeks to give effect to the true purpose of legislation and are prepared to look at much extraneous material that bears upon the background against which the legislation was enacted"

per Lord Griffiths in *Pepper v. Hart* [1993] A.C. 593 at page 617. Thus the purposive approach taken by some courts in relation to regulatory legislation may be difficult to displace. It is important, however, correctly to identify its purpose, namely that which reflects "the intention of Parliament" to be derived from the language of the statute, its context, subject matter, effects and consequences and the spirit and reason which underlies it.

6.73 Construing defences. Where a doubt may arise about the scope of a defence to an absolute offence, the courts should avoid a restrictive interpretation which will hinder the defence. In *Rochdale Metropolitan Borough Council v. F.M.C. (Meat) Ltd* [1980] 1 W.L.R. 461 where the prosecution sought to apply a construction which restricted the express wording of section 115 of the Food and Drugs Act 1955 Woolf J. commented that such an interpretation "would not be justified in the case of a section which provides a defence to criminal offences, many of which are absolute offences and not dependent upon any lack of care of the alleged offender." In the recent case of *Coventry City v. Lazarus* (1996) 160 J.P. 188, the meaning of the words "information supplied" were construed in favour of the Defendants because the statutory provisions were penal.

Legislation with a European influence

6.74 European directives and English and Welsh Regulations. The interpretation of legislation which is intended to implement European legislation follows different rules. Provided that the English legislation can reasonably be interpreted so as to conform to the European legislation (*Webb v. EMO Air Cargo (UK) Ltd* [1993] 1 W.L.R. 49; *Duke v. GEC Reliance Systems Ltd* [1988] I.C.R. 339) and the result envisaged by the Directive is clear (*per* Lord Keith in *Duke* above), the courts must apply a construction which promotes that purpose. This position is so, even if the legislation for interpretation precedes its European counterpart (*Marleasing SA v. La Comercial Internacional de Alimentacion SA* [1990] E.C.R. I–4135; *Faccini Dori* [1994] E.C.R. I–3325). In order to determine the result intended by the European legislation it is necessary to look both at the wording of any relevant directive but also at any construction placed on it by the European Court of Justice. This purposive construction is less constrained by the statutory language than is the purposive construction of domestic legislation. In *James Buchanan & Co. Ltd v. Babco Forwarding and Shipping (U.K.) Ltd* [1977] 2 W.L.R. 107 at page 112 Lord Denning described how European Judges:

"adopt a method which they call in English by strange words – at any rate they were strange to me – the "schematic and teleological" method of interpretation. It is not really so alarming as it sounds. All it means is that the judges do not go by the literal meaning of the words or by the grammatical construction of the sentence. They go by the design or purpose . . . behind it.

When they come upon a situation which is to their minds within the spirit – but not the letter – of the legislation, they solve the problem by looking at the design and purpose of the legislature – at the effect it was intended or sought to achieve. They then interpret the legislation so as to produce the desired effect. This means they fill in gaps quite unashamedly, without hesitation. They ask simply: what is the sensible way of dealing with this situation so as to give effect to the presumed purpose of the legislation? They lay down the law accordingly".

6.75 **Criminal cases.** It has been held without argument in the Divisional Court that this purposive approach applies to criminal cases in the same fashion as it does to civil matters (*Ken Lane Transport v. County Trading Standards Officer of North Yorkshire* [1995] 1 W.L.R. 1416, although, interestingly, in *Criminal Proceedings against Vessoso and Zanetti* [1990] E.C.R. 1-1461, the Advocate General took the view that a purposive construction may be inapplicable in criminal cases. He said:

"That rule [that national courts be required to interpret their national law in the light of the wording and purpose of the directive] must, in my view, be qualified in criminal proceedings where the effect of interpreting national legislation in that way would be to impose liability where such liability would not arise under the national legislation taken alone. The reason for that qualification is that an excessive interpretation of penal legislation runs counter to the fundamental principle of legality (*nullum crimen, nulla poena sine lege*). It is established that, in the absence of implementing legislation, a directive cannot, of itself, have the effect of determining or aggravating the liability in criminal law of persons who act in contravention of the directive: see Case 14/86 *Pretore Di Salo v. persons Unknown* [1987] E.C.R. 2545; *Kolpinghuis Nijmegen* [1987] E.C.R. 3969. In my view, similar principles apply where a Member States has introduced legislation to give effect to a directive but that legislation, although creating criminal liability does not specify clearly and unambiguously all the circumstances in which the liability arises. I do not consider that as a matter of Community Law, to interpret domestic legislation in the light of the wording and purpose of directives where the result would be to impose criminal liability which would not otherwise arise. It is for the referring courts to decide whether the national legislation at issue here can be interpreted consistently with the relevant directives, without resorting to an extreme interpretation which would be contrary to the principle of legality."

This argument by the Advocate-General was not the subject of comment by the court, who appeared to apply a purposive construction without deciding the point. Then, in *Criminal Proceedings against Arcaro* [1997] All E.R.(E.C.) 82, the Court of Justice revisited the question and determined that a purposive construction was to be applied to criminal legislation in so far as the criminal legislation reflected the directive. That construction, however, reached a limit where the national legislation had not implemented all of the Directive. It was not open to a court dealing with the case of an individual (as opposed to an emanation of the State) to disapply a provision which contravened a directive nor could reference to Community law which had not been transposed into the directive aggravate a criminal liability.

6.76   Capability of interpretation in accordance with European legislation.   It is not always straight-forward to determine whether legislation is intended to be fully compliant with European legislation. By way of an example of difficulty, the Food Imitations (Safety) Regulations 1989 were intended to implement Directive 87/357/EEC. Prior to the European Directive, there had been domestic regulations which dealt with goods which resembled food, but these regulations had not extended to "products intended for use to represent food in a dolls house or other model scene or setting". The 1989 Regulations included an exemption for these products. No such exemption appears in the Directive. Presumably an English court would not be able to ignore the exemption because it flew in the face of the Directive. In *European Commission v. United Kingdom* [1997] All E.R.(E.C.) 481, the European Court of Justice was called upon to determine whether Part I of the Consumer Protection Act 1987 had implemented the Defective Products Directive (EEC 85/374 on the approximation of laws, etc., concerning liability for defective products) – the contention being that the English legislation had provided a "state of the art" defence which was subjective in quality, whereas the directive had only allowed for such a defence on objective grounds. The Court was required to construe the legislation as a whole, and, in so doing, it paid particular attention to the provisions of section 1(1) of the Act which expressly provided that the relevant provisions should be interpreted in accordance with the directive. In so doing, the Court commented that the Commission had stressed particular terms without looking at the overall impact of the legislation.

Contempt of statute

6.77   It is extremely rare that, albeit that there are no plain words to that effect, it is contended that an offence has been created under primary legislation. Occasionally, it is argued that a criminal offence is created either on the construction of a statute alone or by virtue of an almost obsolete doctrine known as "contempt of statute". The Law Commission recommended the abolition of the latter (Law Commission Report on Conspiracy and Criminal Law Reform (HC Paper) No. 176 (1976) para. 6.5) but this has not come about and, indeed, was relied upon unsuccessfully by the private prosecutor in *R. v. Horseferry Road Magistrates Court, ex p. Independent Broadcasting Authority* [1987] Q.B. 54, in which it was contended that the Broadcasting Act 1981 created a criminal offence in section 4(3): "it shall be the duty of the Authority to satisfy themselves that the programmes broadcast...do not include [subliminal communications]". No penalty was provided for, although the magistrates court clerk was persuaded to issue a summons. The Divisional Court quashed the summons, holding that:

   (i)   contravention of the section was not said to be an offence;

   (ii) mandamus would lie to enforce the duty, so that finding the existence of an offence would not lend efficacy to an otherwise toothless statute;

   (iii) as the provision required the Authority to satisfy itself as to the broadcast matter, it imposed a subjective obligation which was unlikely to give rise to an offence.

   (iv) the doctrine of contempt of statute was only a rule of construction, and in considering if there was an offence of breach of statutory duty, the court would have regard to whether the requirement was mandatory or prohibitory, whether the statute was ancient or modern, and whether there was any other means of enforcing the duty. In the case of a mandatory duty, imposed by a modern statute and enforceable by judicial review it was an irresistible inference that Parliament did not intend an offence to be created.

6.78 It would not be right to say, however, that the doctrine has no modern significance. In *Rathbone v. Bundock* [1962] 2 Q.B. 260, the question was whether an offence was "under Part I" of the legislation: the offence-creating section clearly was, but the penalty was not. The Divisional Court relied upon the doctrine of contempt of statute to bolster its decision that an offence can occur without provision for a penalty. In a later case of *R. v. Lennox-Wright* [1973] Crim.L.R. 529, the doctrine was the only way of establishing an offence where a subsection of the Human Tissue Act 1961 provided that no-one other than a fully qualified medical practitioner could remove part of a body. A lay person who forged his credentials and removed the eyes of a corpse committed an offence.

6.79 It may be that the doctrine can be applied more frequently than it is relied upon in aid of interpretation and can assist arguments as to powers to be found in subordinate legislation (see paragraph 6.80 onwards, below).

DELEGATED LEGISLATION

Statutory instruments

6.80 These include all statutory Orders in Council and rules, regulations and other legislation made by Ministers of the Crown pursuant to powers granted by statute and which are (in the case of all Acts since 1948) expressed to be exercisable by statutory instrument (Statutory Instruments Act 1946).

6.81 **Regulations.** Much delegated legislation which is produced by the machinery of State is by way of regulations, made under specific powers contained in the "enabling provisions" of the Act. The power in the Act will usually provide that "The Secretary of State may by regulations" . . . legislate for the detail thought desirable to make the primary legislation operate more smoothly (*Utah Construction and Engineering Property Ltd. v. Pataky* [1966] 2 W.L.R. 197). In some cases, the apparent discretion confers a mandatory obligation: "may" means "must" (*Pargan Singh v. Secretary of State for the Home Department* [1993] A.C.) By section 5 and Schedule 1 of the Interpretation Act 1978, the expression "the Secretary of State" means one of Her Majesty's Principal Secretaries of State, and it is for the Prime Minister to say which functions are to be carried out by each one. Any change is made by a Transfer of Functions Order made pursuant to section 1 of the Ministers of the Crown Act 1975.

6.82 Regulations made under this power are frequently drafted by the Government Department for which the Minister is responsible, although in some cases, particularly where the regulations are especially complex or intended to be enacted at the same time as a piece of primary legislation, the Office of the Parliamentary Counsel will be responsible for their production pursuant to detailed instructions received from the relevant Government Department.

6.83 **Rules.** The term "rules is usually reserved for procedural requirements, such as rules of court. As with regulations, rules are frequently drafted by the

Government Department with responsibility for the subject matter rather than by Parliamentary Counsel.

6.84 Orders. This expression includes orders made by the Privy Council pursuant to a statutory power (Orders in Council), which tend to be concerned with the regulation of professional conduct, but often is a piece of legislation expressing an executive act, such as a commencement order. Where an enabling power confers power to make an order, the Statutory Orders (Special Procedure) Acts 1945 and 65 generally applies. This requires advertising of the order, consideration of petitions against it and a resolution by Parliament in respect of it.

6.85 Proving delegated legislation. An important practical consideration is that delegated legislation should be proved by the production of the Queen's Printers' copy of it. In *R. v. Koon Cheung Tang* [1995] Crim.L.R. 813 the point had been taken in the Divisional Court that the prosecution in the court below had failed to prove the regulations, but relied upon a photocopy. As no objection had been taken in the court below, the Divisional Court would not allow this ground of appeal.

Scope of delegated legislation

6.86 Infra vires. The regulations which can be drawn must not exceed the powers conferred expressly or impliedly by the enabling legislation nor must the powers be exercised irrationally in the *Wednesbury* sense. If the regulations exceed the scope of the powers or are irrational, they will be *ultra vires* and void. See, for example, *R. v. Customs and Excise Commissioners, ex p. Hedges & Butler Ltd* [1986] 2 All E.R. 164 in which the regulations allowed for "supplemental provisions" thought necessary for the protection of the Revenue. It was held that this could not permit a new and radically more extensive scheme of powers. (Also, see *R. v. Secretary of State for Health, ex p. U.S. Tobacco International Inc.* [1992] 1 All E.R. 599.) Regulations may not contain an offence unless the primary legislation expressly or impliedly permits it. For a contrast between implied and express permission, for example, section 26(3) of the Food Safety Act 1990, which provides that the regulations may "provide that an offence under the regulations may be tried in the manner specified; and . . . include provisions under which a person guilty of such an offence shall be liable to such penalties . . . as may be specified" which does not state in terms that an offence may be created, but it is obvious because trial and penalties may be provided for, contrasts with section 12(5) of the Safety of Sports Grounds Act 1975 which provides "Regulations . . . may provide that a breach of the regulations shall be an offence punishable as provided by the regulations . . ." In the latter provision the offence is created by the primary legislation, taking effect once the regulations are made, but the subject matter of the offence and penalty falls to be determined by reference to the regulations. In *R. v. Secretary of State for Trade and Industry, ex p. First National Bank plc* [1990] C.C.L.R. 94 and 105, the Divisional Court and the Court of Appeal upheld the power of the Secretary of State to require in the Consumer Credit (Advertisements) Regulations 1989 a warning that "Your home is at risk if you do not keep up repayments on a mortgage or other loan secured on it". The applicant for judicial review had contended that this went beyond the parent power to regulate so that "an advertisement conveys a fair and reasonably comprehensive indication of the nature of credit facilities offered", and was irrational. Even though the power to include warnings which differentiated between secured and unsecured lending (which might also put a borrower's home at risk) was not expressed, the Court of Appeal found that the power to make regulations was not limited by the words in the parent Act that the regulations "shall contain" the requisite material and was not to be read as though the words said "shall only contain". Broadly speaking, the Courts will be slow to draw an inference that the Secretary of State has exceeded his powers when regulations are made and will not intervene unless it is shown that the Secretary of State has "gone outside the four corners of the Act or has acted in bad faith" (*per* Lord Guest in *McEldowney v. Forde* [1971] A.C. 632 at 643F and also see *Nottinghamshire County Council v. Secretary of State for the Environment* [1986] 1 A.C. 240).

6.87 Consultation. Regulation-making powers frequently contain a requirement for consultation. See, for example, section 3 of the Deregulation Act 1994 (see paragraph 1.11 above). Where that duty is contained, the consultation must be genuine: a genuine invitation for comment and a genuine consideration of the responses (*R. v. Secretary of State for Social Services, ex p. Association of Metropolitan Authorites* [1986] 1 W.L.R. 1).

6.88 Venue for challenging delegated legislation. It is a principle of English law that delegated legislation must be presumed to be valid unless or until declared either invalid or incompatible with E.C. law (*Factortame v. Secretary of State for Transport* [1990] 2 A.C. 85 *per* Lord Bridge at 141). The declaration, to be effective, must be by a court of competent jurisdiction – but what is a court of competent jurisdiction? The function of courts dealing with private law rights and public rights is different (*O'Reilly v. Mackman* [1983] 2 A.C. 237, *Davy v. Spelthorne Borough Council* [1984] A.C. 262).

The Divisional Court. The Divisional Court, dealing with a supervisory jurisdiction over the exercise of power (see paragraphs 12.32 onwards, below), is certainly a court in which a challenge may properly be made. Subordinate courts or tribunals do not necessarily enjoy such powers. So in *Chief Adjudication Officer v. Foster* [1991] 3 All E.R. 846, a social security commissioner was held to be precluded from finding that the Income Support (General) Regulations 1987 were in part *ultra vires* because he was confined to considering whether the tribunal's decision (from which he sat in appeal) was erroneous in point of law. The issue should have been referred to the Divisional Court, but it does not follow that all tribunals will have no power to determine issues as to jurisdiction.

Other courts. On the other hand, if regulations are unlawfully made and invalid, it may be unfair to preclude a defendant to proceedings from relying on their invalidity. This is particularly the case where the defendant may be subject to a criminal penalty. Accordingly, the criminal courts have permitted the consideration of the validity of delegated legislation. See paragraph 6.92 below relating to challenge to the validity of byelaws.

6.89 Severance of unlawful provisions. Where possible, a court may sever an unlawful part of delegated legislation from parts which are properly made. It is not a blue-pencil test (*Dunkley v. Evans* [1981] 1 W.L.R. 1522). In that case, the court ignored the provisions in the West Coast Herring (Protection of Fishing) Order 1978 so far as they applied to Northern Ireland although it was not possible to delete parts of the order to leave a text which made sense. Ormrod L.J. adopted the following test:

"Unless the invalid part is inextricably interconnected with the valid, a court is entitled to set aside or disregard the invalid part, leaving the rest intact."

He later added:

"We can see no reason why the powers of the court . . . should be restricted to cases where the text of the legislation lends itself to judicial surgery or textual amendment by excision."

On the other hand, the question of textual severance may be a guide to whether the delegated legislation can be upheld or not. Lord Donaldson M.R. in *Chief Adjudication Officer v. Foster* [1991] 3 All E.R. 846 referred to not "doing violence" to the text.

6.90 Test for severance. The matter was considered in relation to the Greenham Common byelaws in *DPP v. Hutchinson* [1990] 2 A.C. 783. The House of Lords found that byelaws under the Military Lands Act 1892 (which states that no right of common could be interfered with) were *ultra vires* because they purported to prevent commoners from exercising certain rights. Although the applicant was not a commoner, the byelaws were held to be incapable of severance. Lord Bridge said that usually both "textual severability" and "substantial severability" would be required before a byelaw which was invalid in part could be upheld. By substantial severability, is meant that the severance must create no difference in substance in its purpose, operation and effect. Lord Bridge, with whom three or four other Lords agreed, went on to argue that the test of textual severability is not to be rigidly upheld if to do so would unreasonably defeat the legislator's principal purpose, but substantial severability must be the test in all cases.

Byelaws

6.91 Meaning. The term "byelaw" refers to delegated legislation which is made by local authorities, commons commissioners, public utilities and other public bodies. They are principally to deal with local issues and are limited to a small geographical area. Many local byelaws are "good rule and government" byelaws made under the provisions of the Local Government Act 1972, s.235 which allows a district council or London Borough Council to make byelaws for the good rule and government of the area represented and for the suppression of nuisances. Other powers exist under section 231 of the Public Health Act 1936 and section 76 of the Public Health Act 1961 and under many Clauses Acts and Private Acts.

6.92 Invalidity a defence? Can a defendant challenge the validity of a byelaw as a defence to a prosecution? In *DPP v. Bugg* [1987] Crim.L.R. 625, the High Court held that magistrates had been wrong to acquit a defendant on the ground that the byelaws had not been proved by the prosecution to be valid. If this approach were upheld, it would mean that a different consideration applied, depending upon whether the delegated legislation was a byelaw or made by way of regulation or other statutory instrument (*Factortame* (above)). The High Court confirmed that the validity of the byelaws should be assumed unless the contrary is shown and further accepted that criminal courts had power to decide the issue (rather than allow an adjournment for the matter to be decided in the Divisional Court). Similarly, in *R. v. Reading Crown Court, ex p. Hutchinson* [1988] Q.B. 384

the High Court accepted that criminal courts had power to determine the validity of byelaws if the point was raised by way of defence to a criminal charge. This view has now been upheld in the House of Lords in the case of *Boddington v. British Transport Police* [1998] 2 W.L.R. 639, and the earlier case of *Bugg and Greaves v. Director of Public Prosecutions*, [1993] Q.B. 473 overruled. In the *Bugg* case, an issue arose as to the lands apparently identified under byelaws made under the Military Lands Act 1892. The defendants alleged that the byelaws were insufficiently precise as to the land covered and therefore *ultra vires* on the grounds of uncertainty. The Divisional Court had found that the byelaws were too vague and said, too, that it was proper to raise the issue as a defence to proceedings in the magistrates court but Woolf L.J. in giving the judgement of the court distinguished between procedural validity (that is, that arising where there has been a procedural non-compliance in the making of the byelaw) and substantive validity (that is, where its terms go beyond the power under which it was made or it is otherwise unreasonable). Substantive validity was said to be capable of examination in the criminal courts, whereas procedural invalidity could be investigated only in the Divisional Court. This decision had drawn the reasoning relating to byelaws into line with the reasoning previously expressed in *R. v. Waverley District Council, ex p. Hilden and others* (1988) 152 L.G.R. 190, *Avon County Council v. Buscott* [1988] Q.B. 656 and *Plymouth City Council v. Quietlynn Ltd* [1988] Q.B. 114, relating to other forms of delegated legislation. However, it was vigorously criticised by the House of Lords in *R. v. Wicks* [1997] 2 All E.R. 801 before overrule in *Boddington*. It therefore follows that the powers of the criminal court will extend to an investigation of the jurisdiction of the regulating body to make the regulations, whether the ground for challenge appears on the face of the delegated legislation or otherwise. The power of the Court to intervene on the ground of an excess of jurisdiction is the same whether the delegated legislation is in the form of a bye-law or otherwise.

6.93   Power of the court.   The power of the court to intervene in the case of byelaws is, however, wider in respect of other grounds than it is in relation to other forms of delegated legislation. The courts are entitled to look both at the scope of the power purportedly exercised when the byelaws were made, but also at the likely reasonableness of its exercise. That said, the courts should assume when considering the validity of byelaws that the powers claimed in the byelaws will be applied reasonably and not capriciously or in bad faith. In *Kruse v. Johnson* [1898] 2 Q.B. 91, Lord Russell of Killowen said at page 99:

> "They [byelaws] ought to be supported if possible. They ought to be, as has been said, "benevolently interpreted" and credit ought to be given to those who have to administer them that they will be reasonably administered".

Also, in *Walker v. Stretton* (1896) 60 J.P. 164, Russell L.C.J. referred to the need to construe generously local legislation that dealt with local matters and not "pick holes" in it. The justices findings in relation to a local matter are of particular importance (*Everton v. Walker* (1927) 91 J.P. 125).

6.94   Circumstances in which byelaws will be unlawful.   There are a number of areas in which successful challenges to the validity of byelaws have been made, although the following illustrations should not be taken as a comprehensive list. Examples, however, are:

(i) *Repugnance to the general law:* An offence under byelaws of using obscene language in a public place or land adjacent thereto was held to be repugnant to the general law because it was not limited to occasions when it was used to the annoyance of the public in *Strickland v. Hayes* [1896] 1 Q.B. 290. On the other hand, in *Getel v. Rapps* [1902] 1 K.B. 160, a tramway byelaw which omitted similar words was found not to be invalid. In the light of *Kruse v. Johnson* (above), the former case may have been wrongly decided because the width of the byelaw is to be determined in relation to the prospect of unreasonable enforcement by the local authority. Also see *Mantle v. Jordan* [1897] 1 Q.B. 248 and *Brabham v. Wookey* (1901) 18 T.L.R. 99. In *Powell v. May* [1946] K.B. 330, an example of repugnance was furnished where a local law prevented betting in a public place but did not replicate the defences made available by the general law to a person charged.

(ii) *Uncertainty:* If it is not possible to determine the scope of a prohibition contained in a byelaw, the byelaw may be unreasonable. The precise circumstances when a byelaw will be struck down for uncertainty is, however, not clear. In *Kruse v. Johnson* (above at page 108) Mathew J. described certainty in the context of byelaws as containing "adequate information as to the duties of those who are to obey" whereas in *Fawcett Properties Ltd v. Buckingham County Council* [1961] A.C. 636 at page 676, Lord Denning, speaking of the certainty of statutes said: "But when a statute has some meaning, even though it is obscure, or several meanings, even though there is little to choose between them, the courts have to say what meanings the statute is to bear, rather than reject it as a nullity". In *Percy v. Hall, The Times*, May 31, 1996 the Court of Appeal preferred (obiter) the test in *Fawcett*, namely that the byelaw would be struck down only if it was impossible to attribute any sensible meaning to it. Peter Gibson L.J. commented that it was wrong in principle that there should be a different meaning of certainty which was dependent upon whether the legislation in question was primary or a byelaw. Earlier cases in which the certainty of a byelaw was addressed may not have fulfilled the *Fawcett* test, although the byelaws might have been otherwise unreasonable when ascribed their literal meaning. In *Scott v. Pilliner* [1904] 2 K.B. 855 a byelaw which purported to prohibit selling any paper devoted wholly or mainly to the probable result of races, steeplechases or other competitions was held to be uncertain and unreasonable. A byelaw which provided that no person should annoy passengers in the public streets was similarly uncertain (*Nash v. Finlay* (1901) 66 J.P. 183).

(iii) *Prohibition too wide:* Where the prohibition would cover matters not intended to be subject to control, the byelaw may be *ultra vires*. In *Johnson v. Croydon London Borough* (1886) 16 Q.B.D. 708, a byelaw which prohibited the playing by anyone other than the army of any musical instrument in the street on a Sunday was held to be unreasonable because it allowed no qualification or exception in any circumstances.

(iv) *Byelaws may not legalise prohibited conduct:* In contrast to the above decision, a byelaw which prevented the playing of a noisy instrument or preaching in the street on a Sunday without a licence from the mayor, was unlawful because it would enable the mayor to permit a nuisance, which would be unlawful: alternatively, the byelaw would prohibit actions which were not nuisances (*Munro v. Watson* (1887) 51 J.P. 660). By analogy, in *Yabbicom v. King* [1899] 1 Q.B. 444, it was held that a local authority has no power to sanction building plans which are not in accordance with the byelaws and any purported approval of the plans would be inoperative.

(v) *Byelaws may not oppressively or gratuitously deprive a person of his private rights:* In considering one persons "rights", however, the effect on the liberties of people on neighbouring ground is relevant. So, in *Derham v. Strickland* (1911) 75 J.P. 300, a person committed an offence prohibiting the touting for hackney carriages in the public thoroughfare even though he stood on private ground. In *Teale v. Harris* (1896) 60 J.P. 744 a byelaw which prevented the keeping or management, to the annoyance or disturbance of residents of fairground equipment adjacent to or near a street or public place was upheld. Also see *DPP v. Hutchinson* (above).

(vi) *Other instances of unreasonableness:* Other instances would be where the byelaws operated "partially and unequally between different classes", if they were manifestly unjust, or disclosed bad faith. See Lord Russell C.J. in *Kruse v. Johnson* [1898] 2 Q.B. 91 at 99.

Other delegated legislation

6.95 There is no limit on the nomenclature to be employed by the legislature to describe delegated legislation. A not uncommon example of another type of delegated legislation is where the enabling Act provides for the creation of "a scheme", for example, under the Job Release Act 1977, s.1. Another is "direction". By section 12 of the Fair Trading Act 1973, the Secretary of State may give directions to the Director General of Fair Trading.

Codes of Practice

6.96 It has become increasingly common in regulatory statutes to control the detail of the exercise of statutory activities by the use of Codes of Practice. These Codes of Practice may have a legislative origin in so far as they may be made by Order in Council, or may be laid before Parliament after issue. Some codes can only be issued after consultation with interested parties: section 40(4) of the Food Safety Act 1990, by way of example, provides:

"Before issuing any code under this section, the Ministers or the Minister shall consult with such organisations as appear to them or him to be representative of interests likely to be substantially affected by the code."

Presumably a failure to consult would mean that the Ministers in charge of its issue had acted *ultra vires* – a consideration likely to have effect only in a small number of cases because the effect of the code is only to give administrative guidance, although it is guidance which a court or prosecutor is required to consider, but not necessarily follow. Under section 40 of the Food Safety Act 1990, the matters to be covered by the Code or Codes made under it are "recommended practice as regards the execution and enforcement of [the] Act and of regulations and orders made under it". Section 40 also makes express provision that:

". . . every food authority–

(a) shall have regard to any relevant provision of any such code; and

(b) shall comply with any direction which is given by the Ministers and Minister and requires them to take any specified steps in order to comply with such a code"

An interesting feature of the Codes of Practice issued under this Act is that "official" material is included in bold type alongside a commentary which is not a part of the Code itself. Quite what status in the courts this departmental guidance has is yet to be determined. The Divisional Court were willing to look at the departmental guidance in *Bexley London Borough Council v. Gardner Merchant Ltd* [1993] C.O.D. 383, but no reference was made to the significance of this material in the decision of the Divisional Court.

6.97 A power to make Codes of Practice under section 25 of the Consumer Protection Act 1987, however, makes them specifically referable to the questions to be decided by a court as to whether an offence has been committed. Sub-section (2) provides that:

A contravention of a code approved under this section shall not of itself give rise to any criminal or civil liability, but in any proceedings against any person for an offence under section 20 [misleading price indications]

(a) any contravention by that person of such a code may be relied upon for the purpose of establishing that that person committed the offence or of negativing any defence; and

(b) compliance by that person with such a code may be relied upon in relation to any matter for the purpose of showing that the commission of that offence by that person has not been established or that that person has a defence."

Accordingly, in this instance and other where the same applies, observance of the Code of Practice is an important part of establishing and defending the legality of conduct in a conceptually complex area.

CHAPTER 7

Prosecuting the Correct Defendant

PROBLEMS OF LEGAL PERSONALITY

The nature of the problem

7.1 Correct identification. The prosecutor must correctly identify both himself and the defendant in the information, summons or warrant which sets out the allegation which the defendant is to face (for the procedure for commencement, see Chapter 8 below). He must identify himself because a defendant is entitled to know the identity of his accuser and that his accuser has the authority to prosecute him. He must identify the defendant correctly, so that the person against whom the allegations are made is truly before the court.

7.2 Commercial premises. It frequently occurs in cases where the person to be prosecuted carries on business from commercial premises which have been inspected by enforcement officers, that the prosecuting authority errs in naming the defendant accurately. Sometimes this may be a mere mistake as to the proper name of an individual or company, but commonly mistakes have arisen from bringing the wrong company before the court. Groups of companies give rise to a particular difficulty. Often companies may organise themselves so that they are identified by a trading name which does not mirror the name of the company which is carrying out the trading operation. Similarly, the best known name is often that of the holding company. The staff may be employed by a company other than the trading arm of the group and the land and buildings may be held by yet another company. Taking a hypothetical example, the chain of shops may have a trading name "Mirage", the holding company may be Mirage Stores plc, the trading operations carried out by Mirage Stores Limited and the staff employed by Mirage Services Limited. In that situation, where the offence to be charged is levelled against the person carrying on the business, it is important that the company named is Mirage Stores Limited. Prosecuting Mirage Stores plc will result in the wrong defendant being brought before the court (*Salomon v. Salomon Ltd* [1897] A.C. 22). There is no authority which suggests that a holding company is carrying on the business of its subsidiaries. Magistrates are likely to be powerless to remedy the defect (paragraphs 7.5 to 7.7 below). Where the offence is triable either way and the case has reached the Crown Court before the prosecution are alerted to the defect, the Crown Court will have no power to prefer an indictment against any party who has not been committed to the Crown Court by the magistrates court or been the subject of a voluntary bill of indictment (Administration of Justice (Miscellaneous Provisions) Act 1933, s.2(2)).

7.3   **No obligation to assist the prosecutor.**   If a prosecutor has proceeded against the wrong party, this may not always be apparent at an early stage in the case. The defendant company, if it is not a party carrying on the business, is under no obligation (unless asked, for which see paragraphs 7.10 to 7.16 below) to give the name of the company truly carrying on the business and may simply challenge the prosecution case at trial on the basis that it is not the proper defendant.

The effects of a mistake

An error in the name of the defendant

7.4   **Misdescription.**   A mere misdescription of a defendant who has otherwise been correctly identified, such as a mistake as to his first name or a reference to the wrong address will not result in the failure of the prosecution (*R. v. Norkett, ex p. Geach* (1915) 139 L.T. Jo. 316; *Allan v. Wiseman* [1975] R.T.R. 217). In the first case the wrong Christian name was given, in the second, the wrong surname. The general rule is that no objection shall be allowed to any defect in the substance or form of any information, complaint, summons or warrant nor may objection be taken if there is a variance between the contents of an information, summons or warrant and the evidence adduced at the hearing (Magistrates Courts Act 1980 s.123). The effect of this section is that the validity of an information, summons or warrant is not impugned by a minor departure from the document setting out the allegations in the case presented to the court. If the variation is, however, substantial, it may be unjust to proceed without an amendment and the court may require the prosecution to amend the information, summons or warrant (*Garfield v. Maddocks* [1974] Q.B. 7). A court has a discretion whether or not to allow an amendment. Failure to amend in circumstances where an amendment is required may result in any subsequent conviction being quashed (*Hunter v. Coombs* [1962] 1 All E.R. 904. The test is whether justice will be done between the parties *R. v. Newcastle-upon-Tyne Justices ex p. John Bryce (Contractors) Ltd* [1976] 1 W.L.R. 517. In that case, a prosecutor was allowed to amend an information to allege a different offence arising out of the same facts even though the time limit for the commencement of fresh proceedings for the new offence had already expired. (Also see *R. v. Scunthorpe Justices ex p. M, The Times*, March 10, 1998; *R. v. Newcastle-upon-Tyne Magistrates' Court, ex p. Poundstretcher Ltd* (New Law 498031901, March 3, 1998.) If the defendant has been misled by the variance (for example, because he had not arranged for evidence to meet a substituted allegation or a change in the name of the defendant) the court must allow an adjournment (Magistrates Courts Act 1980, s.123(2)).

Identification of the wrong defendant

7.5   **Amendment not possible.**   Where the defendant is not merely wrongly named but wrongly identified, amendment is not permissible. If the wrong party altogether is before the court it is not a defect in the substance or form of the document, but a defect which goes to the root of the prosecution. So, using the example given above, if the prosecution has wrongly brought Mirage Stores plc (an existing company) before the court, the court cannot regard this merely as a technical error and substitute Mirage Stores Limited by permitting an amendment. In *Aldi GmbH & Co. KG v. Mulvenna*, (1995) 159 J.P. 717, the Divisional Court held that section 123 of the Magistrates Courts Act 1980 could not be relied upon where the wrong defendant had been named in the information. In that case an English registered company was prosecuted under section 20 of the Consumer Protection Act 1987 for misleading price indications. Before the magistrates, evidence was given that the stores in question were run by a German registered partnership and that the English company merely supplied goods to the partnership. The prosecution were permitted by the magistrates to amend the information to substitute the retailer as the defendant and a retrial before a different bench was directed. The Divisional Court on an application for judicial review (for the procedure on challenges to the magistrates' decisions see paragraphs 12.31 to 12.40 below) held that the magistrates were not entitled to amend.

In *Marco (Croydon) Ltd v. Metropolitan Police* [1984] R.T.R. 24, the Divisional Court held that the magistrates had gone wrong in substituting Marco (Croydon) Ltd for the company, A. J. Bull Ltd, named in the information.

7.6   Determination of the issue.   Determination whether the prosecution has named the wrong party or merely misdescribed the intended defendant may often be a matter of evidence rather than a fact accepted by both sides. Where the named company is not an existing company, there will be strong evidence that there has been a mere misnomer. The prosecution's intention is likely to have been to prosecute the company operating out of the specified business premises. In *Marco (Croydon) Ltd* a distinction was drawn between bringing the wrong party to court and a case where the right person had received the summons, and known it was for him, and so was not prejudiced in any way. Allowing the prosecution to obtain a conviction against the wrong party (for instance, a defunct company) is not an abuse of the process of the court: *R. v. Headley, The Times*, February 15, 1995.

7.7   Unless the time limit for commencing proceedings against the true defendant has expired (see paragraphs 8.19 to 8.24 below), the prosecution, having failed to secure a conviction of the wrong defendant, may proceed against the proper party. The consequences of having chosen the wrong defendant are those, in the main, of wasted costs and wasted time. The prosecution may, in an obvious case, find that an order for costs is made against it in favour of the wrongly named party (for costs see Chapter 13, below).

Wrongly naming the prosecutor

7.8   In *Rubin v. DPP* [1989] 2 All E.R. 241, information was laid by "the Thames Valley Police" which was an unincorporated body and not a legal personality with authority to lay an information. The prosecutor should have been named as the police officer. Amendment was allowed by the magistrates and upheld in the Divisional Court because, on the facts, no one was misled. The accused could have found the name of the prosecutor by a simple enquiry. It followed that no injustice was done to him. For discussion of the authority to prosecute, see paragraphs 2.31 above onwards.

DISCOVERY OF THE TRUE DEFENDANT

General

7.9 It is not always straightforward to ascertain who is the company carrying on business at the premises in question. The prosecutor needs to be able to satisfy himself from his own investigations and to call evidence to prove that the named defendant is the party who should be charged. It has already been seen (Chapter 3) that many statutory provisions contain powers of search and seizure and that where such powers exist enforcement officers can require the production of books and records and take copies of them. In many cases, these may provide information as to the true defendant, but in other cases, may just serve to mislead the enforcement officer. For example, where the books and records seen by him are those relating to the operation of a due diligence system (see paragraphs 9.13 below onwards), the documents seen may only have been headed with the trading style, in the example, "Mirage", and not the name of the legal personality who is to be prosecuted.

Similarly, the enforcement authority may enter into correspondence with the company which, in the example given, is likely to be handled at group level. In consequence, the stationery of the company responding to the enforcement officer's letters and requests for information is likely to be that of the holding company and not of the trading company. What steps, then, can be taken?

Requesting information

Voluntary provision of information by a non-defendant

7.10 It is not uncommon for enforcement officers in correspondence with a holding company to ask the holding company to identify the trading company operating from business premises. Latterly, some local authorities even render a questionnaire to deal with this problem. Sometimes a reply is voluntarily given. It does not follow, however, that any reply or exchange of correspondence will become admissible in evidence. If the holding company has supplied information, the need to adduce it as evidence will be not so much to resolve a dispute as to which is the operating company but to satisfy the burden which rests on the prosecution to show that the company named in the information was, in fact, that carrying on the business there.

7.11 Admissibility under Criminal Justice Act 1988, s.24. If the holding company replies to the effect that another company is the true defendant, this assertion is hearsay and, at common law, inadmissible against the other company so identified. In some limited circumstances a document obtained in this way may become admissible under Criminal Justice Act 1988 s.24, although these situations in connection with regulatory offences will be rare. The section allows the admission of evidence of statements in documents where:

(i) the document was created or received by a person in the course of a business, trade, profession or other occupation (or as the holder of a paid or unpaid office); and

(ii) the supplier of the information (whether or not the maker of the document) had or may reasonably be supposed to have had personal knowledge of the information given in the statement

(iii) every person through whom the information was supplied was acting in the course of a trade, business, profession or other occupation or was an office holder.

If the document came into existence for the purposes of pending or existing criminal proceedings or as part of a criminal investigation, such a statement will not be admissible unless its maker is unfit to attend court; or is outside the United Kingdom and it is not reasonably practicable to secure his attendance; or he cannot be found; or the statement must have been given to an authorised enforcement officer and the person who made the statement is frightened to give evidence or is being "kept out of the way"; or the maker cannot reasonably be expected to have any recollection of the matters contained in the statement. (Criminal Justice Act 1988, ss.23, 24). Few of these considerations apply in practice in the case of individuals or companies charged with regulatory offences. If any does apply, a letter naming another company as the proper defendant may be admissible against that company and, with the leave of the court, can be admitted in evidence. The court has to consider whether the admission of the statement is in the interests of justice (Criminal Justice Act 1988, s.26).

7.12 **Failure to supply information.** The extent to which a person who is not to be prosecuted for the offence under investigation is required to respond to a request for information is considered in paragraphs 3.21 to 3.25 above. Where the statutory provisions create an offence of obstruction for a failure to give such information and assistance as an enforcement officer may reasonably require (see, for example, Consumer Protection Act 1987, s.32; Food Safety Act 1990, s.33(1)(b)) the failure by a holding company to identify a subsidiary which is trading from specified premises may amount to an offence of obstruction. The fact that the subsidiary may be prosecuted is unlikely, it is submitted, to be a "reasonable cause" for failing to supply information (see paragraphs 3.21 to 3.25 above). A proviso that a person shall not be required to incriminate himself cannot assist a holding company who is required to incriminate a subsidiary. Of course, if the company required to provide information is itself at risk of prosecution as a principal or accessory (see paragraphs 7.50 below onwards), the effect of the proviso may be that it can decline to state who should be prosecuted, although see the suggestion in *Walkers Snack Foods Ltd v. Coventry City Council, The Times,* April 9, 1998, that a company cannot claim the privilege at all and paragraph 3.24.

Requesting information from a potential defendant

7.13 **Police and Criminal Evidence Act 1984.** Additionally, if the prosecutor has grounds to think that the company of whom he requests information may be the party to be named as the defendant, he should, in requesting information, administer a caution in accordance with Code of Practice C.10 (Code of Practice for the Detention, Treatment and Questioning of Persons by Police Officers) (see paragraphs 3.26 above onwards). Because section 34 of the Criminal Justice and Public Order Act 1994 permits an inference to be drawn from the silence of a person accused in respect of a matter about which he might reasonably have been expected to furnish information, the caution must advise the suspect that a failure to answer any question about something which is later advanced in evidence by the defence may be relied upon to detract from the truth of the defence (Criminal Justice and Public Order Act 1994, s.34). The form of the new caution cannot be relied upon to displace positive evidence but the fact that no reply or contradiction is put forward in interview will permit the court to draw certain inferences. For further discussion, see paragraph 3.36 above.

7.14 Business Names Act 1985, s.4(1)(a). An interesting conflict with the protection offered by the common law against self-crimination and the protection provided by the Code of Practice and caution may be occasioned in some cases by the impact of the Business Names Act 1985 s.4(2). Section 4(1)(a) of the Act requires a person to whom the Act applies to state on all business letters, written orders for goods or services, invoices, receipts and written demands for payment of debts the following details:

  (i) in the case of a partnership, the name of each partner;

  (ii) if an individual, his name;

  (iii) if a company, its corporate name.

The Act applies to any person who has a place of business in Great Britain and who carries on business in Great Britain under a name which does not consist of the names of all the partners, the surname of the individual or the corporate name of the company, as the case may be. Section 4(2) requires a person to whom the Act applies to provide the same details in writing to someone "with whom anything is done or discussed" who asks for them. Failure to supply the details is an offence.

The scope of these words appears wide. It is possible that an enforcement officer may be able to bring himself within the category of a person with whom matters are discussed if he has visited the business premises and conversed with authorised staff about compliance with the legislation which it is his duty to enforce. The *Shorter Oxford Dictionary* (1993 edition) gives among the meanings of discuss: "investigate or examine by argument, talk about (a topic) to, with, or *with* another person". This may suggest that there has to be co-operation in the communication by the prospective defendant: a mere request in the absence of input from the company may not suffice but the point is arguable. Accordingly, without more, a letter requesting details required to be placed on the stationery may not invoke the requirement under s.4(2).

7.15 Express provision to remove common law privilege?. On the other hand, the fact that the requirement to provide information in the context of a criminal prosecution may remove the prospective defendant's privilege against self-crimination, may be a reason for a narrower interpretation of "anything done or discussed" to limit it to the purview of a business adventure (although see *Walkers Snack Foods Ltd v. Coventry City Council, The Times*, April 9, 1998, which suggested that the privilege was limited to individual not corporate defendants). It is a principle of construction of legislation in cases where more than one meaning can be found that express language is necessary to take away a clear right or alter a clear principle of law. In *Leach v. R.* [1912] A.C. 305 the Criminal Evidence Act 1898 s.4 did not take away the common law privilege of a wife to decline to testify against her husband because there was not a "clear, definite and positive enactment" *per* Lord Atkinson at 311.

7.16 If the provision does assist an enforcement officer considering prosecution, however, he may in some cases be able, by a letter addressed (in the hypothetical example) to "Mirage" at the trading premises, to elicit whether the business is a sole proprietorship, partnership or company and obtain the name and address of the prospective defendant.

Requesting information from an employee

7.17   An employee who is not to be prosecuted for an offence may be asked to provide information about his employer. Where the statutory provisions enable enforcement officers to prosecute an employee for obstruction if the employee fails to reply to a proper request, the request may have some teeth, but see paragraphs 3.21 to 3.25 above.

No estoppel

7.18   Any information received by the prosecutor as a response to a request is no more than, at most, an item of evidence. It is not unknown for a person (such as a holding company) to admit in correspondence that it is the proper defendant, when, in reality, it is not the trading arm of the group of companies (see for example, the facts in *Aldi GmbH & Co. KG v. Mulvenna* (above)). Subsequently, there may be a retraction of tthat admission. There is no estoppel in criminal proceedings. Indeed, even a previous conviction against the holding company cannot prove (considerations of admissibility apart) that it is the proper defendant (*D.P.P. v. Humphrys* [1976] 2 All E.R. 497). Any assertion in a document is not, therefore, conclusive of the issue.

Business Names Act 1985, s.4(1)(b)

7.19   In addition to the obligations described in paragraph 7.14 above, a person to whom the Act applies must also display at any business premises to which customers and suppliers have access a notice in a prominent position stating the name[s] and address[es] which are required by section 4(1)(a) (see paragraph 7.14 above) to appear on certain types of stationery. Accordingly, strong evidence of the true defendant is available to a prosecutor at the premises of the business itself. It is an offence to fail to show the notice (Business Names Act 1985 s.4(6)).

Local Government (Miscellaneous Provisions) Act 1976, s.16

7.20   This provision gives to a local authority a power to serve a notice upon the occupier of any land or a person with an interest of an owner or manager or a letting agent of any land requiring the person on whom the notice is served to give details of his interest and the details of the owner, occupier, etc. The recipient of the notice must provide the information within 14 days. Failure to do so is an offence.

The power may be exercised "where, with a view to performing a function conferred on it by any enactment, the authority considers that it ought to have information connected with any land . . .". Where the local authority is a prosecuting authority under any legislation, it would appear that the power may be exercised on its behalf by an enforcement officer employed by it.

Land Registry Searches

7.21   The register of any title which is registered land can now be searched by any person (compulsory registration of title applies throughout England and Wales, but only occurs on a disposition of the property: nearly all property is now registered but there remain some titles which are not). A prospective prosecutor may make an official or personal search of the register and obtain copies of any documents referred to in the register which are in the registrar's custody (Land Registration Act 1925, s.112 as amended by Land Registration Act 1988, s.1). The registrar has a discretion to allow inspection of other documents if they are in his possession. It is important to remember, however, that not all interests appear in the register, for example, short leases or licences, so that an entry in the register can rarely amount to more than part of the investigative process.

Other registers and enquiries

7.22   An inspection of other registers can be undertaken in difficult cases. Every local planning authority must keep a register of planning applications (Town and Country Planning Act 1990, s.69). Some types of business activity are required to be registered or licensed by a controlling body. For example, nursing homes are required to be registered and the persons behind the organisation must be declared on the application for registration (Nursing Homes and Mental Nursing Homes Regulations 1984, Sched. 2); public houses and consumer credit businesses, financial advisers etc. must at present be licensed. Where these situations exist, more detailed information may be available upon which to base a prosecution.

PRIMARY OFFENDERS

General

7.23   It is commonly the case where statute has created absolute offences (see paragraphs 6.19 to 6.35) that the same set of facts give rise to more than one offence and more than one offender – often both the employer and the person carrying out the illegal activity or making the omission which forms the offence. A statute which specifies that "No person shall" or "A person who" may hold in its sights more than one category of defendant. The wide scope of such words may be limited to a more specific target by interpretation of the legislation in question.

A person

7.24   **Meaning.** The Interpretation Act 1978 provides that unless the contrary intention appears, a person includes a body of persons whether corporate or unincorporated (section 5 and Schedule 1). In modern statutes, where only a natural person is intended to be referred to, the drafting practice is to describe such persons as an individual, or expressly to make provision that a person is to mean a natural person only. Where no express definition of "person" is provided in the statute, its scope must be determined by reference to the principles for interpretation of statutes. It must be remembered that even where there is an interpretation clause, it does not follow that where a word is used more than once in a statute it will always bear the same meaning. In *Meux v. Jacobs* (1875) L.R. 7 HL 481, Lord Selborne concluded that in that case the meaning ascribed to some words by an interpretation clause could be displaced by repugnancy in the context of their use or in the sense.

7.25   **Context may exclude the wrongdoer.** There are some instances, moreover, where the words "a person" or "any person" may expressly exclude the alleged wrongdoer from liability for an offence. These instances arise where the accused is both perpetrator and victim. A clear example of where this occurs as a matter of drafting is section 20 of the Consumer Protection Act 1987 but it also arises in many other statutory provisions. In *R. v. Arthur (No. 2)* [1968] 1 Q.B. 810 the court held that the words "any person" could not apply to the defendant in an offence that "whoever shall unlawfully and maliciously set fire to any dwelling house, any person being therein, shall be guilty of felony". Because the defendant was the only person in the house, he was not guilty. (Also see *Cooper v. Motor Insurer's Bureau* [1983] 1 W.L.R. 592, *R. v. Dunbar* [1982] 1 All E.R. 188 and *John v. Matthews* [1970] 2 Q.B. 443.)

7.26 Qualification. The words "any person" may be qualified by their immediate context. In *R. v. Warwickshire C.C. ex p. Johnson* [1993] A.C. 583, the House of Lords, interpreting the expression "A person shall be guilty of an offence if, in the course of any business of his, he . . ." under section 20(1) of the Consumer Protection Act 1987 decided that a store manager could not fall within the section. This is a contrast with the expression "any person who, in the course of a trade or business, (a) applies . . ." etc, which, where it appears in section 1 of the Trade Descriptions Act 1968, includes an employee acting within the scope of his employment (*Coupe v. Guyett* [1973] 1 W.L.R. 669).

7.27 Construction as a whole. Guidance in identifying a person to be prosecuted is to be derived from the construction of the legislation as a whole and, in some cases by contrast with other legislation (see paragraph 1.10). In *Hotchin v. Hindmarsh* [1891] 2 Q.B. 181, DC a foreman who sold diluted milk on behalf of his employer was held to be a person to whom section 6 of the Sale of Food and Drugs Act 1875 applied. That provision specified that "No person shall sell to the prejudice of the purchaser any article of food . . .". The court, looking at the statute as a whole, and determining that some other provisions of the legislation penalised individuals who occasioned the breach of the law, held that the penal legislation contemplated particular unlawful acts rather than concerning itself with questions of contract. So, even though the employee was not party to the contract of sale, he sold the milk:

> "In my opinion a person who takes the article in his hand and performs the physical act of transferring the adulterated thing to the purchaser is a person who sells within this section . . . If any person transgresses against the provisions of section 6, be he principal or agent, he falls within that section" (*per* Lord Coleridge).

This decision was followed in *Melias v. Preston* [1957] 2 Q.B. 380 (a decision as to the meaning of "actual offender" in the context of the defendant's employer's conviction for selling or having in his possession for sale certain food). The "actual offender", the employee, was brought before the court under a third party procedure (see paragraph 7.83 below). The reasoning in *A Walkling Ltd v. Robinson* 46 T.L.R. 151 which had held that goods were not in the possession of a servant and were not sold by him was not followed. In *Walkling* the defendant was an employer who had sought to blame his servant to establish a defence to the charge against him.

7.28 Unincorporated associations. There are uncharted waters where the "person" who has committed the offence is an unincorporated association. Where an Act is silent, the Interpretation Act 1978 will, in theory, render an unincorporated association liable for the commission of an offence and some statutes make express provision that an unincorporated association shall commit an offence. An example is the Surrogacy Arrangements Act 1985. Like a company, an unincorporated association can only act through its members but unlike a company, there is no readily available formula to determine who should be regarded as its directing mind and will. So, in *John v. Matthews* [1970] 2 Q.B. 443 it was held that a members club could not be liable for a false description made to a member because the club consisted of the totality of the members and could not therefore make a false trade description to itself. Some modern statutes expressly provide for the prosecution of an unincorporated association in its own name with provision for the payment of a fine from its own funds (see Banking Act 1987, s.98; Insurance Companies Act 1982, s.92). For the position in relation to a company see paragraphs 7.33 below onwards.

7.29 Partnerships. Arguably, a partnership can be prosecuted under the name of the partnership (although there is no authority expressly to this effect), or one or more partners can be prosecuted in their individual names. The latter course is preferable where the partnership is small to simplify enforcement or where imprisonment might be an appropriate remedy. If the offence is one requiring *mens rea*, consideration may need to be given to whether it is the named individual who is truly criminally liable (see paragraphs 7.46 to 7.48 below). As with unincorporated associations, potential problems may be averted by an express stipulation of the liability of partners (see, for example, Banking Act 1987, s.98(6)).

7.30 Agents. Like a servant, a professional agent may attract liability for an act that he does on behalf of his principal (*Fletcher v. Sledmore* [1973] R.T.R. 371, *May v. Vincent* (1990) 98 I.T.S.A. 10 M.R. 20). The offence of giving a misleading price indication makes it clear that an agent acting in the course of his business (but not a servant) can commit an offence (*R. v. Warwickshire C.C., ex p. Johnson* [1993] A.C. 583). An agent will not attract liability in every case where his principal has committed an offence, however. Each case will depend upon its own facts and the interpretation of the legislation. In *Lester v. Balfour Williamson* [1953] 2 Q.B. 168, a broker who had never had possession of goods was not liable for a breach of the Pre-Packed Food (Weights and Measures: Marketing) Order 1950.

LIABILITY FOR SERVANTS AND AGENTS

Liability of a principal for acts of servants or agents

7.31 Generally. A particular problem presents itself where an employer is prosecuted for acts of his servant. It is a clear principle that a person cannot evade responsibility for prohibited conduct by employing another to do it on his behalf. Where another acts innocently on his behalf, the procurer is liable as a principal (*R. v. Tyler* (1838) 8 C. & P. 616). Where an agent acts voluntarily for his principal, both may be participants in a joint enterprise or conspiracy or the employer might be an accessory to an offence committed by his employee and vice versa.

7.32 Vicarious liability and the duty to prevent the offence. More difficult is the situation where the employer is charged for an offence committed by his employee or agent of which he had no knowledge. The extent to which vicarious liability is a notion recognised by the criminal law remains open to debate (see, for example, *National Rivers Authority v. Alfred McAlpine Homes (East) Ltd* [1994] 4 All E.R. 286 and further discussion at paragraph 7.40 below). The employer may, however, be expressly or impliedly made liable for the acts of his employees by statute, whether this is described as vicarious liability or not. In the case of absolute offences, particularly in the field of consumer protection, the implication that the employer is liable for the acts of his employees is very strong:

> "Consumer protection, which is the purpose of statutes of this kind, is achieved only if the occurrence of the prohibited acts or omissions is prevented. It is the deterrent effect of penal provisions which protects the consumer from the loss which he would sustain if the offence were committed. If it is committed he does not receive the amount of any fine. As a taxpayer he will bear part of the expense of maintaining a convicted offender in prison.
>
> The loss to the consumer is the same whether the acts or omissions which result in his being given inaccurate or inadequate information are intended to mislead him, or are due to carelessness or inadvertence. So it is the corresponding gain to the other party to the business transaction with the consumer in the course of which those acts or omissions occur. Where, in the way that business is now conducted, they are likely to be acts or omissions of employees of that party and subject to his orders, the most effective method of deterrence is to place upon the employer the responsibility of doing everything which lies within his power to prevent his employees from doing anything which will result in the commission of an offence.
>
> This, I apprehend, is the rational and moral justification for creating in the field of consumer protection, as also in the field of health and safety, offences of "strict liability" for which an employer or principal, in the course of whose business the offences were committed, is criminally liable, notwithstanding that they are due to acts or omissions of his servants or agents which were done without his knowledge or consent or were even contrary to his orders."

(*per* Lord Diplock in *Tesco Supermarkets Ltd v. Nattrass* [1972] A.C. 153 at page 194B-E).

Where the principal is a company

7.33 **The problem.** A corporate body presents a particular problem because it can only act through living persons. It therefore follows that if a company is ever to be convicted of an offence, it must be because the company is notionally accepting responsibility for the acts or omissions of its employees. In *Tesco v. Nattrass* (above) at page 170E-G Lord Reid said:

> "A corporation must act through living persons . . . Then the person who acts is not speaking or acting for the company. He is acting as the company and his mind which directs his acts is the mind of the company. There is no question of the company being vicariously liable. He is not acting as a servant, representative, agent or delegate. He is an embodiment of the company or, one could say, he hears and speaks through the persona of the company. It must be a question of law whether, once the facts have been ascertained, a person in doing particular things is to be regarded as the company or merely as the company's servant or agent. In that case, any liability of the company can only be statutory or vicarious liability".

Accordingly, where the offence is an absolute offence and the statute contains no provision which enables the employer to allege as a defence that the offence was committed as a consequence of the act or default of another (invariably a due diligence defence: see below), the employer will not escape liability on the basis that the acts of the employee were not those of the directing mind and will of the corporation (*R. v. British Steel plc* [1995] 1 W.L.R. 1356, *R. v. Gateway Foodmarkets Ltd* [1997] 3 All E.R. 78).

7.34   Offences with a mental element.   Where the offence requires full *mens rea* (see paragraphs 6.19 to 6.34 above), a company will normally only be liable for the acts of employees if (i) the statute intends that there should be vicarious liability. Usually this will require clear language, such as that found in Licensing Act 1964, s.163: "a person shall not . . . either himself or by his servant or agent . . ."; or (ii) the directing mind of the company had the requisite mental element or (iii) if there had been a delegation of functions such that the delegate was truly to personify the company.

> "Normally, the board of directors, the managing director and perhaps other superior officers of a company carry out the functions of management and speak and act as the company. Their subordinates do not. They carry out orders from above and it can make no difference that they are given some measure of discretion. But the board of directors may delegate some part of its functions of management giving to their delegate full discretion to act independently of instructions from them. I see no difficulty in holding that they have thereby put such a delegate in their place so that within the scope of the delegation he can act as the company. It may not always be easy to draw the line but there are cases in which the line must be drawn....In some cases the phrase alter ego has been used. I think it is misleading. The person who speaks and acts as the company is not alter. He is identified with the company. And when dealing with an individual, no other individual can be his alter ego. The other individual can be a servant, agent, delegate or representative but I know of neither principle nor authority which warrants the confusion (in the literal or original sense) of two separate individuals"

(*per* Lord Reid in *Tesco v. Nattrass* (above) at page 171F-G).

7.35   Rules of attribution.   The analysis referred to in the paragraph above must now be considered in the light of the Privy Council decision in *Meridian Global Funds Management Asia Ltd v. Securities Commission* [1995] A.C. which doubted whether the "directing mind and will" test was universally applicable to all statutes. (That the test is not universally applicable has been borne out by *R. v. Gateway Foodmarkets Ltd* (above) in which on a true construction of the Health and Safety at Work etc., Act 1974, no distinction was to be drawn between the acts of the employee and of the employer.) In *Meridian* the Privy Council commented that the ratio decidendi in *Tesco v. Nattrass* was that an employee was capable of being "another person", not that his state of mind could not be attributed to his employer. In *Meridian*, a company had failed to notify an interest in other securities acquired by two of its employees. These employees were authorised to do the deal by which the securities had been acquired, but they were not directors or delegates. Lord Hoffman, giving the opinion of the Privy Council advanced the following scholarly analysis:

> (i) it is a necessary part of corporate personality that there are rules by which acts of individuals are attributed to the company;

(ii) the primary rules of attribution are to be found in the constitutional documents of the company and implied by company law;

(iii) these are supplemented by general rules of attribution in order to enable the company to do business. Such rules include estoppels or ostensible authority in contract or vicarious liability in tort;

(iv) any statement about what a company had or had not done is necessarily a reference to its rules of attribution because there is no such thing as a company as such;

(v) there would be cases where the primary and general rules of attribution would not describe the company's obligations. Those cases are generally true of the criminal law which ordinarily impose liability for the *actus reus* and the *mens rea* of the defendant himself;

(vi) in such cases, a court might decide that the imposition of liability was not limited to its own acts and mind or it might decide that liability could only arise on the basis of its primary rules of attribution, namely if the act giving rise to liability is specifically authorised by a resolution of the board or a unanimous resolution of the shareholders;

(vii) in many cases neither of the above would be appropriate and a special rule of attribution would have to be applied to the particular substantive rule;

(viii) the rule of attribution to be applied was a matter of construction and interpretation of the substantive rule;

(ix) the "directing mind and will" formula would often be the most appropriate description of the person designated by the attribution rule;

(x) in the *Meridian* case, the person whose knowledge counted as the knowledge of the company was the person who acquired the relevant interest;

(xi) the fact that the employee did not tell the company because he was acting corruptly could not affect the company's liability.

It is likely that under the Trade Descriptions Act 1968, the "directing mind and will formula" will continue to be adopted, but this may not apply to other statutes. The application of the reasoning in *Meridian* makes the decision in *Tesco Stores Ltd v. Brent London Borough Council* (see paragraph 7.42 below) easier to understand.

7.36 Delegates. It was not apparently argued in *Meridian* (above) that the dishonest employees were delegates, merely that they were authorised. The delegate does not customarily fall within the primary rule of attribution outlined by Lord Hoffman, nor is he part of the "directing mind and will". The difficulty of accommodating the delegate within the rules of attribution was acknowledged by Lord Diplock in *Tesco v. Nattrass* (above). He warned of the danger of substituting the vivid metaphor of Denning L.J. in *H. L. Bolton (Engineering) Co. Ltd v. T. J. Graham & Sons Ltd* [1957] 1 Q.B. 159, 172, 173 (contrasting the "brains and nerve centre" of a company with its hands) for the powers laid down in the articles of association of the company. He said:

"The decision in that case [*Bolton*] is not authority for extending the class of persons whose acts are to be regarded in law as the personal acts of the company itself, beyond those who by, or by action taken under its articles of association are entitled to exercise the powers of the company".

He departed from dicta to the contrary in *The Lady Gwendolen* [1965] P. 294 (where Willmer L.J. suggested that the traffic manager of a company might be its alter ego for the purposes of its shipping business). Lord Hoffman on the other hand, regarded *The Lady Gwendolen* as illustrative of a case where "the directing mind and will" formula was wrongly treated as though it was a test to be religiously applied. In the context of delegation of functions, Lord Diplock's approach seems a curious insistence upon formal considerations. If the articles of association permit a delegation of functions, the company will be liable for the acts of the delegate. If there has been an unlawful delegation of functions contrary to the articles of association, it is difficult to see why the unlawfulness of the delegation should provide protection to the company.

7.37 Where *mens rea* not attributable. An example of the prohibition on attributing an employee's *mens rea* to the employer arose in *Air Tours v. Shipley* (1994) 158 J.P. 835. In that case a company was charged with recklessly making a false trade description to the effect that a hotel had an indoor swimming pool when it did not. The responsibility for producing the brochure in which the statement appeared rested with a product manager who was not a director of the company. There was a company errata policy. The magistrates held that the company had delegated the responsibility to produce the brochure to the product manager. The Divisional Court allowed the appeal. The product manager was a mere employee with no discretion to act independently of the directors. She was "a cog in the machine". The judgment of Mann J. in *Wings Ltd v. Ellis* [1984] 1 W.L.R. 772 (approved in the House of Lords at [1985] A.C. 272) was still good law despite contrary indications in *Yugotours Ltd v. Wadsley* [1988] Crim.L.R. 623. The Divisional Court confirmed that where an offence requires *mens rea*, in the absence of guilty participation by a directing mind of the company, the company cannot be liable for the reckless act of an inferior employee.

7.38 Fraud. As was apparent in *Meridian*, where an individual whose state of mind is attributed to the company acts fraudulently, the company will not be released from liability – even if the fraud was directed at the company itself. In *Moore v. Bresler Ltd* [1944] 2 All E.R. 515 the secretary and general manager and a sales manager sold some of the company's goods for their own benefit and made false entries in the purchase tax returns. The company, as well as the individuals, were convicted of making false returns with intent to deceive. Contrast the rare situations where the employee can be shown to be acting outside his authority (see paragraph 7.41 below).

7.39 Semi-strict liability. If the offence is "semi-strict" (see paragraphs 6.31 to 6.35 above) or the mental element is contained only within a word which also defines the *actus reus*, it is treated for these purposes as though it were an absolute offence in the full sense.

7.40 Absolute offences. Where the offence does not require *mens rea*, a company will generally be liable for the acts of its employees within the scope of their employment (see paragraph 7.33 above). This assertion encompasses situations where the employee is a delegate and where statute makes unambiguous provision for vicarious liability but it is not limited to those situations. It does not follow as a matter of course that the fact that an employer is liable means that there is vicarious liability. Professor Sir John Smith at [1993] Crim.L.R. 612 argues that vicarious liability only arises where an employee acts and the employer is liable for that act. In contrast, where the employer is impressed with the duty to prevent the occurrence of certain events or conditions, that is a distinct concept. The tendency in recent cases has been to elide the two ideas. See, for example, the reasoning of Staughton J. in *Seaboard Offshore Ltd v. Secretary of State* [1993] 3 All E.R. 25 at pages 31–32. In *National Rivers Authority v. Alfred McAlpine Homes (East) Ltd* [1994] 4 All E.R. 286, the Divisional Court similarly failed to draw a distinction and purported, in a case under the Water Resources Act 1991, to find that the employer was vicariously liable for the acts of his employee. The court interpreted an earlier decision, *Alphacell v. Woodward* [1972] A.C. 824, as provoking this conclusion. Professor Sir John Smith argues (above) that in *Alphacell* there was no act for which the employer was vicariously liable, and it is significant that the speeches in the earlier case do not adopt the language of vicarious liability.

In the same way as the employee may perform acts for which the employer is bound, an authorised employee's admissions may also provide evidence against it. In *Edwards v. Brooks (Milk) Ltd* [1963] 3 All E.R. 62 the status of a depot manager of a dairy company was such that his authority to speak on behalf of the company was presumed. His employer was bound by what he had said and the admissions he made were not hearsay.

7.41   Acts outside the scope of employment.   The employer is not liable for his employee without limit, however. He is not liable for any acts performed by the employee which are outside the scope of his employment, although a mere contention that the employee was not authorised will be insufficient. In *Whittaker v. Forshaw* [1919] 2 K.B. 419 the defendant, who had only authorised his daughter, aged 13, to deliver milk, was not liable because she had been intimidated by an inspector into making an unauthorised sale. (Also see *Winter v. Hinckley & District Industrial Co-operative Society* [1959] 1 All E.R. 403, *Goodfellow v. Johnson* [1966] 1 Q.B. 83). Moreover, it seems that where the court finds that statute intends the imposition of vicarious liability for the acts of an employee, it may not extend that liability for the acts of every employee. In *Seaboard Offshore Ltd v. Secretary of State* [1993] 3 All E.R. 25 an employer was not liable for failing to take all reasonable steps within the meaning of s.31 of the Merchant Shipping Act 1988 where no evidence was given about the management system governing the conduct of the employee who actually committed the offence.

7.42   Ignorance and statutory defences.   Where there is a statutory defence to the effect that the offence has been committed by "another person" and the employer has acted with due diligence, an employee may be "another person" provided that he is not such a person as personified the company (*Tesco v. Nattrass* above). It may follow from the persuasive authority of *Meridian* that the court will not recognise a divide between an employer and inferior employee in every case where a defence relies upon the employer having no guilty knowledge. In *Tesco Stores Ltd v. Brent London Borough Council* [1993] 2 All E.R. 718, an employer was held vicariously liable for the employee's guilty knowledge because, were the employer not to be so liable, he could rarely be convicted under the Video

Recordings Act 1984. The apparently contrary decision in *Camden London Borough Council v. Fine Fare Ltd* (unreported) February 2, 1987, DC, was distinguished. Professor Sir John Smith at [1993] Crim.L.R. 612 suggests that *Tesco Stores Ltd v. Brent London Borough Council* was wrongly decided, but that view was expressed before the report of the persuasive decision in *Meridian*.

Where the principal is an individual

7.43 Crimes involving a mental element. The question whether an individual can ever be liable for the acts and omissions of an agent in an offence requiring full *mens rea* remains open. (For a discussion of the meaning of full *mens rea* see paragraph 6.30 above). In *Tesco v. Nattrass* (above) Lord Reid at page 171G doubted that an individual could be liable for acts delegated to another (see paragraph 7.29 above). In his speech at page 173G he referred to *Magna Plant v. Mitchell* (unreported April 27, 1966 DC) in which Parker C.J. had said:

> "Knowledge of a servant cannot be imputed to the company unless he is a servant for whose actions the company are criminally responsible, and as the cases show, that only arises in the case of a company where one is considering the acts of responsible officers forming the brain, or in the case of an individual, a person to whom delegation in the true sense of delegation of management has been passed."

Lord Reid registered his disagreement with the idea that an individual could be liable for acts delegated to another. He commented that the recognition that an individual might be so liable had been recognised in licensing cases (see *Vane v. Yiannopoulos* [1965] A.C. 486) but that was, in his view, anomalous. The opinion of Lord Reid appeared to be shared by Lords Morris of Borth-y-Gest and Diplock and by Viscount Dilhorne.

7.44 Alter ego. Lord Pearson embraced the concept that an individual could have an alter ego. He said, in the context of section 24 of the Trade Descriptions Act 1968 that:

> "In the case of an individual defendant his ego is simply himself, but he may have an alter ego. For instance, if he has only one shop, and he appoints a manager of that shop with full discretion to manage it as he thinks fit, the manager is doing what the employer would normally do and may be held to be the employer's alter ego. But if the defendant has hundreds of shops, he could not be expected personally to manage each one of them and the manager of one of his shops cannot, in the absence of exceptional circumstances be considered his alter ego" (*Tesco v. Nattrass* (above) pp. 192G–193A).

Accordingly, in that instance, Lord Pearson argued, the employer would be liable for the acts and mind of his manager.

7.45 Absolute offences. Where the offence is an absolute offence, the position is the same as that pertaining to a company. An individual will be liable for the criminal activity of an employee notwithstanding that he might have entrusted the employee with the responsibility of avoiding the offence (*Tesco v. Nattrass per* Viscount Dilhorne at 186A-C). Semi-strict offences and offences where the actus reus involves proof of some mental state are treated as absolute offences for this purpose. See Paragraphs 6.31 to 6.35 above.

Partnerships

7.46   Offences requiring full *mens rea*.   Where the defendant is the partnership itself, there is no reason why the same rules should not apply to a partnership as to a company, that it to say, it should be liable for the acts of its employees where there has been a delegation by one of the partners or where a statutory provision expressly imposes vicarious liability or (perhaps) where a partner has acted with complicity in the commission of the offence. Moreover, the principles expressed in *Meridian* (above) may be adapted to extend liability to cover the mental state of an authorised agent.

7.47   Individual partners.   Where an individual partner is prosecuted, he could not be made liable for the acts of an employee of the partnership unless either the statute expressly or impliedly provides for vicarious liability or:

(i)   there had been a delegation by him of responsibility to that employee and

(ii)   an individual can be liable for the acts of his delegate (see paragraph 7.44 above).

A more interesting question is whether one partner can be made liable for the acts and omissions of a co-partner. There is little conclusive authority. In *Davies v. Harvey* (1873–74) L.R. 9 Q.B. 433 the appellant was held liable for the acts of his partner who, without his knowledge, supplied property to be given in parochial relief. The appellant was a guardian of the Poor Laws and so not entitled to profit from such property. His partner was not. Blackburn J. at page 438 appeared to accept that guilty knowledge was a necessary part of the offence charged, but considered that knowledge by a co-partner was sufficient to found a conviction because the statute envisaged vicarious liability.

> "The . . . question we are asked is whether the furnishing or supplying of goods by the co-partner was a supply of goods by the defendant . . . Now the goods were ordered by the appellant's partner . . . within the scope of the partnership authority for the profit of both partners. If this section made the supplying of goods a crime, I should say that required something more than that the goods had been supplied under a general authority given to a partner to make the co-partner liable for a crime; but when we look at the object of the section and its language I think it forbids the supplying of goods by a guardian for his own profit and on his own account; whether that be done through the agency of a partner, or a manager or a servant, the mischief is certainly the same. I agree that, in order to make the supply of goods an offence, it must be shewn that the partner or manager entrusted with authority by the co-partner or manager was aware that he was dealing with the supply of goods given in parochial relief. I think it is necessary that knowledge should in that sense be brought home to a guardian: I do not think it is necessary to show that he had personal knowledge, it is sufficient to constitute the offence if the partner or manager who supplied the goods had knowledge".

Lush J. adopted similar reasoning.

In the absence of a construction of the statute to infer vicarious liability, this case seems to suggest that a partner will not be liable for the actions of his co-partner in an offence requiring *mens rea*.

7.48   In *Parsons v. Barnes* [1973] Crim.L.R. 537, the Divisional Court expressed the view that there was no general proposition that one partner was necessarily responsible for the acts or omissions of his co-partner in a prosecution under the Trade Descriptions Act 1968, s.14, resting their decision instead on a finding that the appellant had acted in concert with his manifestly guilty partner. The partnership in question had been informal in nature, but there is no reason to think that any distinction should be drawn on the ground of formality. Moreover, in *Northamptonshire County Council v. Rose & Sargent*, 497031901 New Law, March 24, 1998, an advertisement contained a false indication as to the supply of services contrary to section 13 of the Trade Descriptions Act 1968 or a false statement as to services contrary to section 14 of the Act. The prosecution had called no evidence to show whether either of the defendants had placed the order. The Divisional Court held that the inference to be drawn when an advertisement advertised a business and that business consisted of two men in partnership, was that both men had authorised the advertisement. This inference could be rebutted by evidence to the contrary. See also *Garrett v. Hooper* [1973] Crim.L.R. 61.

7.49   Absolute offences.   Where the offence is one of strict liability, it seems that a partner will be liable for the acts or omission of his co-partner. The appellant in *Clode v. Barnes* [1974] 1 W.L.R. 544, a motor trader, was unaware that his partner had incorrectly told a purchaser that a car had a new engine. He was jointly charged with his partner with contravening section 1 of the Trade Descriptions Act 1968. It was held that section 1 required no *mens rea* and the court found no answer to the proposition that the appellant was a joint supplier.

ACCESSORIES

7.50   Where appropriate, an accessory may (arguably) be prosecuted for a trading offence, whether that offence is absolute or requires *mens rea*. In the magistrates court a person who "aids, abets, counsels or procures the commission by another of a summary offence" shall also be guilty of that offence and may be tried by a court of competent jurisdiction. It is not necessary to describe the secondary offender as an accessory. He may be described as a principal (Magistrates Court Act 1980, s.44). The position is the same in the case of offences to be tried in the Crown Court (Accessories and Abettors Act 1861, s.8; Criminal Law Act 1967, s.1).

7.51   The origins of these classes of accessory are of little modern practical interest save that they have followed the classes of offender recognised by the law relating to felonies. It is said that the use of these words do not describe different offences (*Stacey v. Whitehurst* (1865) 29 J.P. 136, *Gough v. Rees* (1929) 94 J.P. 53. Although each category of offender is different from another (*Attorney General's Reference (No. 1 of 1975)* 61 Cr. App. R. 118), the fact that the accessory can be and is often charged as a principal means that in most cases the precise type of assistance which is alleged has been furnished does not need to be categorised in the information. There must have been an offence committed by the accessory, however, so that the incidents of each class cannot be entirely forgotten.

7.52   Although charging accessories for regulatory offences is an option open to prosecutors, it rarely happens, even when to charge the offender who has occasioned the crime as an accessory would represent the justice of the offence. The reason for this may be that most modern statutes contain express provision for prosecution of secondary offenders (see paragraphs 7.60 to 7.89 below). The fact that express provision is made does not necessarily oust the more general jurisdiction arising under Magistrates Courts Act 1980, s.44 or Accessories and Abettors Act 1861, s.1, although it is an arguable proposition as a matter of construction. Nor is it the case that to charge an accessory with an offence it is also necessary to charge the principal offender (*R. v. Millward* (1994) 158 J.P. 1091). There, the accessory was convicted even though the principal offender had been neither arrested or tried. So, for example, in *R. v. Warwickshire County Council ex p. Johnson* [1993] A.C. 583, whereas the prosecution failed to obtain a conviction against a shop manager charged under section 20 of the Consumer Protection Act 1987 because he had not given a misleading price indication "in the course of any business of his", the local authority might have succeeded against him had the case against him been put that he was an aider and abettor of the commission of an offence by his principal. It is likely that a prosecution in reliance on Magistrates Courts Act 1980, s.44 or the Accessories and Abettors Act 1861, s.1 against an accessory can succeed even though a principal offender is acquitted either because he has successfully relied upon, or would be entitled to acquittal because of, a due diligence defence (*R. v. Bourne*, 36 Cr. App. R. 125, *Hui Chi-Ming v. R.* [1992] 1 A.C. 34).

Aiders and abettors

Presence

7.53   Aiding and abetting is appropriately charged against a person who was both present at the *actus reus* and participated in it. If a person was not present at the *actus reus*, he is, by traditional analysis, not an aider and abettor, although he could in some cases be a counsellor or procurer. So, in *Bowker v. Premier Drugs Co Ltd* [1928] 1 K.B. 217 a wholesale merchant charged with aiding and abetting a retailer was entitled to be acquitted of selling food to the prejudice of a purchaser contrary to the Sale of Food and Drugs Act 1875 because:

(i)   the wholesaler was not present at the sale ; and

(ii) there was no evidence that he knew the composition of the goods, nor that it would be sold without a warning as to its true nature.

7.54   Latterly, some authorities appear to suggest that presence immediately prior to the conduct which constitutes the offence may be sufficient. In *National Coal Board v. Gamble* [1959] 1 Q.B. 11, the defendant's employee had loaded too much coal on to the principal offender's lorry, knowing that it was overweight and that the principal offender intended to drive it in that condition on the road. Devlin J. said:

"A person who supplies the instrument for a crime or anything essential to its commission aids in the commission of it; and if he does so knowingly and with intent to aid, he abets it as well and is therefore guilty of aiding and abetting. I use the word "supplies" to comprehend giving, lending, selling or any other transfer of the right of property. In a sense, a man who gives up to a criminal a weapon which the latter has a right to demand from him aids in the commission of the offence as much as if he sold or lent the article. But this has never been held to be aiding in law . . . In the transfer of property there must be either a physical delivery or a positive act of assenting to the taking."

This excerpt corresponds with the reasoning of McCullough J. in *Blakely v. DPP* [1991] R.T.R. 405. In the light of these authorities, it must be questionable whether *Bowker* (above) would today be decided the same way, at least in respect of the requirement for presence at the sale by the retailer. In *Brookes v. Retail Credit Cards* [1986] Crim.L.R. the Divisional Court declined to find "constructive presence" by a consumer credit business at the premises of an unlicensed ancillary credit business by virtue of the presence there of a display box containing the respondent's terms of business. The court doubted the need for presence at the scene of the crime and commented that many crimes have no "scene".

Participation

7.55 Negligence. A defendant will not be guilty of aiding and abetting a principal offender if his conduct is merely negligent. In *Callow v. Johnstone* (1900) 64 J.P. 823 a veterinary surgeon who had negligently certified unsound meat to be sound was not guilty of aiding and abetting the exposure of unsound meat for sale. Similarly, an employer's failure to enforce against his employee a requirement to produce his records within 7 days does not, of itself, amount to aiding and abetting, counselling or procuring the non-delivery (*Cassady v. Reg Morris (Transport)* [1975] R.T.R. 470, but contrast the attitude of the court in *R. v. J. Alford Transport Ltd, The Times*, March 31, 1997).

7.56 Encouragement. The act of participation can be encouragement of the commission of the offence. In *Tuck v. Robson* [1970] 1 W.L.R. 741, DC a licensee was convicted of aiding and abetting customers drinking intoxicating liquor after hours by taking no active step to compel the customers to leave. In a similar vein, where the allegation is one of aiding and abetting an absolute offence, the degree of participation which the prosecution must prove is not the commission of acts which the secondary offender intended to result in the commission of the offence, but the intention to do acts which enabled the crime to be committed, whether or not the aider and abettor held the commission of the crime itself as his intent (*R. v. J. Alford Transport Ltd, The Times*, March 31, 1997).

Counsellors and procurers

7.57 Counselling and procuring are offences which can be committed without the presence of the accused at the *actus reus*. The offence of counselling involves advising that an offence should be committed, followed by the commission by another of the primary offence. Procurement involves bringing about a course of conduct which might not otherwise have occurred and does not require any measure of agreement between the principal offender and the accessory (*Attorney General's Reference (No. 1 of 1975)* 61 Cr. App. R. 118).

The mental element

7.58 In an offence of being an accessory to a strict liability offence, the accessory must be aware of sufficient circumstances of the actus reus and must intend his actions to aid the actus reus (*R. v. Woolworth (FW) & Co.* [1974] 46 D.L.R. 3d 345 Ontario, CA; *National Coal Board v. Gamble* [1959] 1 Q.B. 11, *R. v. J. Alford Transport Ltd, The Times*, March 31, 1997). In an offence involving *mens rea*, an accessory must intend a crime of the nature committed, but it is not necessary for him to intend the exact crime (*R. v. Bullock*, 38 Cr. App. R. 151, *R. v.*

Bainbridge, 43 Cr. App. R. 194). It is an open question to what extent suspicion that an offence may occur will be sufficient *mens rea* to commit an offence as an accessory.

7.59   It follows that an employer might be liable as an accessory to an offence committed by his employee, at any rate where the employee has followed instructions or acted within a defective system of work. Correspondingly, where an employee occasions his employer to commit an offence, the employee is eligible for prosecution as an accessory to his employer's offence. In respect of these two situations most statutes make express provision for the prosecution of a secondary offender.

STATUTORY EXTENSION OF LIABILITY TO SECONDARY OFFENDERS

Generally

7.60   It is now customary for statutes which provide for the commission of an offence by a company also to make provision for the prosecution of its officers. This is so, whether the offences created by statute are offences requiring *mens rea* or are offences of strict liability. Additionally, where a statute creates offences of strict liability, there is frequently provision for prosecution of the true offender. In many instances, both provisions may be contained in the same statute, for example, sections 20 and 36 of the Food Safety Act 1990, sections 20 and 23 of the Trade Descriptions Act 1968, section 40(1) and (2) of the Consumer Protection Act 1987. The need for express reference to the potential liability of an officer is that, for the purposes of a prosecution, an individual who is part of the directing mind of the company personifies it (*Tesco Stores Ltd v. Nattrass* [1972] A.C. 153). He cannot therefore be "another person" for the purposes of a provision fixing a third party with liability.

Offences committed by officers, etc., of the body corporate

7.61   The forms of drafting which extend criminal liability for acts of a company to its directors are frequently replicated in statutes dealing with widely different subject matter. Although it is necessary to bear in mind that each time that a provision appears it must be construed in the context of the legislation in which it has been inserted, in the main, these provisions, in their standard forms, are intended to convey the same meanings to each new statute (see paragraph 1.10 above).

7.62   **Usual form.**   The most common form of provision is as follows:

"Where an offence [punishable] under this Act committed by a body corporate is proved to have been committed with the consent and connivance of, or to be attributable to any neglect on the part of any director, manager, secretary or other similar officer of the body corporate, or any person purporting to act in such capacity, he, as well as the body corporate shall be guilty of that offence and shall be liable to be proceeded against and punished accordingly."

See, for example, section 20 of the Trade Descriptions Act 1968, section 52 of the Registered Homes Act 1984, section 108 of the Electricity Act 1989, Schedule 1 of the Hallmarking Act 1973, section 24 of the Slaughterhouses Act 1974.

"An offence [punishable] under this act committed by a body corporate"

7.63   Primary offence must have been committed. Where an officer of a company is charged as a secondary offender it is important to establish that the primary offence was covered by the scope of the section imposing liability on the officer. The description of the offences which trigger the liability of officers, etc., of a company varies, of course, from statute to statute. The difference between the reference to offences "under this Act" and offences punishable under an enactment (for an example of the latter see section 35 of the Plant Varieties and Seeds Act 1964) is that the latter may include offences which are created under other legislation but for which the sanction is prescribed in the Act in question. Where offences are created under subordinate legislation the general rule is that they are, for the purpose of obedience or disobedience, a provision of the parent Act so that the expression "an offence under this Act" may include offences under subordinate legislation of the Act (*Willingale v. Norris* [1909] 1 K.B. 57 at 64 *per* Lord Alverstone). The rule is not of universal applicability, however, and some statutes distinguish between offences "under the Act" and offences under subordinate legislation. An example is the scheme of food legislation, where a reference in the Food Safety Act 1990 to an offence under the Act may not refer to an offence under the regulations (*United Dairies (London) Ltd v. Beckenham Corporation* [1961] 1 All E.R. 579 at 584). In some statutory provisions specific reference is made to an offence under the Act and to subordinate instruments, for example, section 110 of the Agriculture Act 1970.

7.64   Prosecution not necessary. The legislative trigger is only that the offence shall have been committed, however. It does not require that there shall have been a prosecution under the Act, still less a conviction. In *R. v. Dickson* [1991] B.C.C. 719 Leggatt L.J. stated at p722G:

> "We . . . accept . . . that the appellants could, even in the absence of the company, have been found guilty of the relevant offences upon proof that the company had committed the substantive offences. In many cases, if not most, that would be an undesirable course for the prosecution to adopt because it would involve proof of the commission of an offence by what, on that footing, would be an absent party"

In that case, leave to prosecute a company in liquidation had not been sought, so that the proceedings against the primary offender were void. That did not invalidate proceedings against the secondary offender.

By analogy, in *R. v. Donald* (1986) 83 Cr. App. R. 49 a person assisting a principal offender to impede apprehension or prosecution contrary to section 4 Criminal Law Act 1967 could be convicted even though the principal offender was, at the time, neither arrested nor tried. There must, however, be admissible evidence of the commission of the offence (*R. v. Spinks* 74 Cr. App. R. 263) and if all the elements of the principal offence cannot be proved, the secondary offender cannot be convicted. In *Coupe v. Guyett* [1973] 1 W.L.R. 669, DC, the defendant was a car repair workshop manager who recklessly made a false statement in a business invoice. The owner of the business (the defendant's employer) was charged with contravening section 14(1)(b) of the Trade Descriptions Act 1968 and an information was preferred against the defendant under section 23 of the Act (a third party liability section: see paragraphs 7.81 to 7.89 below). Section 23 applied "where the commission by any person of an offence" was due to another's act or default. As the recklessness of the defendant employee could not be attributed to the owner, she was acquitted on the grounds that the offence had not been made out. Correspondingly, the Divisional Court held that the defendant was entitled to be acquitted because no primary offence had been committed.

7.65   Primary offender's statutory defence not relevant.   The position would have been different had the offence been made out but the owner acquitted because of the impact of a defence under section 24 (a due diligence defence: see paragraphs 9.13 to 9.39). In *Tesco Stores Ltd v. Nattrass* [1972] A.C. 152, Lord Diplock at 195F-G makes clear what the term "the commission of an offence" means in relation to offences of strict liability:

> "The section [section 24 of the Trade Descriptions Act 1968] refers to a stage in the proceedings at which the prosecution have proved facts necessary to constitute an offence of strict liability on the part of a principal. This is all that is incumbent upon the prosecution to prove. The onus then lies upon the principal to prove facts which establish a defence under the subsection."

Lord Diplock's observations were adopted in *Coupe v. Guyett* (above) to apply to an offence requiring *mens rea*. See also *Cottee v. Douglas Seaton (Used Cars) Ltd* [1972] 1 W.L.R. 1408.

7.66   Guilt.   In some legislation, the reference to the commission of an offence is replaced by the words "where a body corporate is guilty of an offence". See, for example, Indecent Displays (Control) Act 1981, s.3, Water Resources Act 1991, s.217. This is capable of more than one meaning. It may mean merely that the body corporate has committed an offence, or it may mean that the body corporate would have been convicted (that is, that no defence would have availed it) or it may mean that there has in fact been a conviction of the body corporate. In some statutes, the juxtaposition of the expression "has committed an offence" and "is guilty of an offence" suggests that the two are not intended to be synonymous. So, the Water Resources Act 1991, s.217(1) makes provision for the liability of directors where the company is guilty of an offence, whereas, in contrast, section 217(3) makes provision for the liability of third parties in terms of the commission of an offence. Where different language is used in the same section there is a prima facie inference that the draftsman intended the language to have a different effect (*Hadley v. Perks* (1866) L.R. 1 Q.B. 444). A similar contrast, but not so stark, appears in the Agriculture Act 1970 where section 110 makes reference to the guilt of a body corporate whereas section 81 makes reference to the commission of an offence by any person.

7.67   Commission, deeming.   On the other hand, section 81 also provides that the secondary offender "as well as the body corporate" shall be guilty of an offence. This suggests that "guilty of an offence" means no more than the word "committed [an offence]". The alternative interpretation would lead to an absurdity. Nor, where it appears in some statutes, does a deeming provision assist. It is the secondary offender who is "deemed" to have committed an offence (whatever this may mean: either he has or he has not), not the body corporate. See Betting and Gaming Duties Act 1981, s.27, Radioactive Substances Act 1948, s.8(5), Agricultural Marketing Act 1958, s.48. If it is correct to interpret the words "is guilty of an offence" to mean "has been convicted of an offence" this may have a consequential effect on the meaning of the word "guilt" where it refers to the secondary offender.

7.68 Where the primary offender has been convicted of an offence, the prosecution may rely upon the certificate of conviction as evidence of the commission of an offence. It is open to the defence to show that, notwithstanding the conviction, the offence was not committed (section 74(2) and (3) of the Police and Criminal Evidence Act 1984).

Consent and connivance

7.69   Mens rea.   It remains unclear what state of mind is sufficient to render an officer of a company guilty of an offence. In *Southend Borough Council v. Alan John White* (1991) unreported (ref. CO/470/90) Nolan L.J., addressing the question whether a director had acted neglectfully said:

> "He appears to have acted quite deliberately and consciously in what he did. I find it hard to see what he can be said to have neglected. His conduct might have been charged as consent or connivance to the falsification performed by the company through his agency."

This appears to suggest that consent and connivance may relate to positive conduct, but can the expression also include acquiescence? See paragraphs 7.71 below).

7.70   "And" and "or".   It is interesting to note that whereas section 20 of the Trade Descriptions Act 1968 refers to consent and connivance, some provisions refer to consent or connivance. It seems that "and" is to be read conjunctively, so that both consent and connivance are required (*Boulting v. Boulting* (1864) 3 Sw. & T. 329 at 335). Where the word "or" is used, this probably to be read disjunctively: it will be sufficient if the prosecution prove one or the other.

7.71   Consent.
Acquiesence. Does consent involve acquiesence? This question was answered in the negative in *Bell v. Alfred Franks and Bartlett Co. Ltd* [1980] 1 All E.R. 356 in relation to consent or acquiescence within the meaning of the Landlord and Tenant Act 1954, s.23(4). Where a statutory provision refers to both notions, however, and expresses them as alternatives, there is an inference that one is not inclusive of the other. On the other hand, in a rape case consent includes reluctant acquiesence (*R. v. Olugboja* [1981] Q.B.). The Oxford Dictionary includes compliance and permission amongst the definitions given for consent. In *Huckerby v. Elliott* [1970] 1 All E.R. 189 Ashworth J., discussing at 194, a provision in the general form of officer's liability, adopted the stipendiary magistrate's definition of consent as follows: "It would seem that where a director consents to the commission of an offence by his company, he is well aware of what is going on and agrees to it".
Knowledge.   Is knowledge an essential part of consent? The above quotation suggests so. Similarly, in *Re. Caughey ex p. Ford* (1876) 1 Ch. D. 521 at 528, Jessel M.R. said in relation to "consent and permission" under the Bankruptcy Act 1869 "Those words imply knowledge. You cannot consent to a thing unless you have knowledge of it". On the other hand, proof of "constructive knowledge" may be sufficient to show consent. Constructive knowledge may be demonstrated, for example, where the defendant has shut his eyes to some material fact which

occasions the commission of an offence, or where there has been connivance or, perhaps, where there has been negligence. See *Mallon v. Alan* [1964] 1 Q.B. 385 *per* Lord Parker C.J. at page 394. In *Attorney General's Reference (No. 1 of 1995), The Times*, January 30, 1996 the Court of Appeal held that the state of mind that had to be proved against a director charged with consent to the acceptance by a company of a deposit without an authorisation or licence from the Bank of England was that he knew the material facts which constituted an offence and that he agreed to the company conducting its business on the basis of those facts. It was not necessary for him specifically to have addressed his mind to the absence of an authorisation or licence. The court also observed that a person who believed erroneously that a licence had been obtained was not consenting to the commission of the offences by the company. Contrast *Westminster City Council v. Croyalgrange Ltd* [1986] 1 W.L.R. 674. (Also see *Knox v. Boyd* (1941) J.C. 81 at 88, *Taylors Central Garages (Exeter) Ltd v. Roper* (1951) J.P. 445 at 449, 450.)

7.72 **Connivance.** The meaning of connivance in the context of divorce has given rise to a number of authorities, all of which indicate that for there to be connivance, there must be a degree of encouragement (*Churchman v. Churchman* [1945] P. 44, *Douglas v. Douglas* [1951] P. 85. In *Huckerby v. Elliott* (above), in contrast, Ashworth J. agreed with the description by the stipendiary magistrate of conduct amounting to connivance:

> "Where [the director] connives at the offence committed by the company he is equally well aware of what is going on but his agreement is tacit, not actively encouraging what happens but letting it continue and saying nothing about it".

7.73 **Approval.** In some older provisions, the language, instead of making reference to connivance, makes reference to "approval". An example is section 48 of the Agricultural Marketing Act 1958. The question whether approval necessitates knowledge was determined affirmatively in *Davis v. Leicester City Council* [1894] 2 Ch. 208, a case which did not involve criminal liability.

"Attributable to any neglect"

7.74 **Meaning of neglect.** Does "neglect" involve opprobrium, or does it, in this context, merely mean failure? Under the Merchant Shipping Act 1894 "neglect of duty" was held to mean merely omission to perform it (*Deacon v. Evans* [1911] 1 K.B. 571). On the other hand, in *R. v. McMillan Aviation Limited and McMillan* [1981] Crim.L.R. 785, the director of a company bought a car on behalf of the company, advertised it for sale and then negotiated the sale with a prospective customer. The car had a false odometer reading. The director admitted in an interview that he had not checked the reading with the previous owner. It was held that "neglect" suggested a failure to do something that he ought to have done. To prove neglect it was necessary to show either that he knew of the falsity of the trade description or that he had reasonable cause to suspect its falsity. In the latter situation, he would have had a duty as a director to take steps to see if it was false or not. On that test, the director was acquitted. In *Lewin v. Bland* [1985] R.T.R. 171, the managing director of a garage was not guilty of neglect where he had delegated work to senior staff and had expected them to carry out his instructions. He had not checked that the staff had done so. This decision was distinguished in the later case of *Hirschler v. Birch* [1987] R.T.R. 13 in which one of two co-directors asked the other to make enquiries as to the legality of a product they were proposing to market and then relied absolutely upon his assurances. He was guilty of neglect when it transpired that the product was illegal. Consideration was given to the same wording as it appears in section 37 of the Health and Safety etc. Act 1974 in *Wotherspoon v. H.M. Advocate* [1978] J.C. 74. It was said at page 78 that neglect "in its natural meaning pre-supposes the existence of some obligation or duty on the part of the person charged with neglect" so that "the search must be to discover whether the accused has failed to take some steps to prevent the commission of an offence by the corporation to which he belongs if the taking of those steps either expressly falls on or should be held to fall within the scope of the functions of the office which he holds".

7.75   Attribution is not causation.   The provision does not require that the neglect is causative of the offence by the company, but is attributable to it. It follows that a failure to take remedial action may fall within the ambit of the secondary offence just as much as may action or inaction which occasions the commission of the offence. In *Wotherspoon* (above) it was held that:

> "any degree of attributability would suffice and in that sense it is evident that the commission of a relevant offence by a body corporate may well be found to be attributable to failure on the part of each of a number of directors, managers or other officers to take certain steps which he could and should have taken in the discharge of the particular functions of his particular office".

"Any director, manager, secretary or other similar officer of the body corporate or any person purporting to act in any such capacity"

7.76   Officers.   The object of the provision is to enable the conviction of a "directing mind" of the company, and "director, manager, secretary," etc., must be interpreted in that light (see *Lennard's Carrying Co. Ltd v. Asiatic Petroleum Ltd* [1915] A.C. 705 *per* Viscount Haldane at page 713 and paragraph 7.48 above). So in *R. v. Boal* [1992] 1 Q.B. 591, the Court of Appeal instigated and allowed an appeal against conviction on the grounds that a manager of a book store (Foyles) was not a manager of the body corporate. A small number of statutes, such as the Betting and Gaming Duties Act 1981 make reference to a "general manager" in order to overcome the possibility that a junior manager may be prosecuted. Management, moreover, is likely to mean taking an active part in running the business and not merely concurring in the trade which is involved in the business (*R. v. Miles* [1992] Crim.L.R. 657).

7.77   Shadow Officers.   The reference to a person purporting to act in the capacity of an officer is designed to overcome the decision in *Dean v. Hiesler* [1942] All E.R. 340 in which it was held that a person who acted in the capacity of a director but who was not appointed in accordance with the articles of association was not a director of the company and could not be proceeded against under emergency legislation. Few modern statutes do not contain the extension of liability to such a person, although there are some older provisions, for example, section 48 of the Agricultural Marketing Act 1958, where the issue may continue to arise.

7.78   Shadow directors.   In respect of a company registered on or after November 1, 1929 all companies other than private companies must have at least two directors and a private company must have at least one (Companies Act 1985, s.282). This, of course, refers to directors who have been formally appointed. In some recent statutes also, specific reference is made to shadow directors in addition to persons acting in the capacity of officers of the company (for example, Insurance Companies Act 1982, ss.91 and 96, Companies Act 1985, s.733).

7.79 Statutory undertakers. Additionally, provision is usually made in modern statutes to extend liability to members of a statutory undertaking (for example, Wildlife and Countryside Act 1981, s.8) and, where the affairs of a body corporate are managed by its members, to the members (for example, Consumer Protection Act 1987, s.40(3)). Where appropriate, provision can also be made for making individuals liable for offences committed by an unincorporated association (for example, Banking Act 1987, s.98(7)).

"Shall be guilty"

7.80 For a discussion of the meaning of the word "guilty" see paragraph 7.66 above. It is usually the case that a secondary offender liable under the above section or a variation of it may himself take advantage of any due diligence provision, although whether this is so where there is a "deeming" provision (see paragraph 7.67 above) must be harder to determine in the absence of express words. Clearly, if the word "guilty" connotes certain conviction, a due diligence defence cannot apply. If it is synonymous with commission of the offence, any due diligence defence would not appear inconsistent, but, if the words "consent", "connivance", neglect" have meanings which describe knowledge and approbation of the primary offence, the occasions when the due diligence defence could result in acquittal must be rare.

Offences committed by third parties

7.81 Usual form. As with the provision rendering an officer of a body corporate liable for an offence committed by a company, so does statute frequently provide that a third party may be liable for an offence committed by another due to the act or default of the third party. The most common formulation of this third party offence is as it appears in section 23 of the Trade Descriptions Act 1968:

> "Where the commission by any person of an offence under this Act is due to the act or default of some other person that other person shall be guilty of the offence and a person may be charged with and convicted of the offence by virtue of this section whether or not proceedings are taken against the first mentioned person."

7.82 This provision is commonly to be found in statutes which also have a form of due diligence defence (see paragraphs 9.13 to 9.39 below). In the Trade Descriptions Act 1968, the due diligence defence (section 24 of the Act) allows an accused person to rely upon the act or default of "another person". The two provisions may operate in tandem, so that if the primary offender throws the blame under section 24 of the Act on to another person, that person can also be prosecuted. For this reason, and to allow the prosecutor to investigate, most due diligence defences require notice of a defence which blames another to be served prior to the hearing.

The third party and the actus reus

7.83   The third party offence usually does not appear to require the prosecution to prove that the secondary offender committed the *actus reus*, only that the *actus reus* was committed by the primary offender due to the act or default of the third party. The first part of the third party offence makes it clear that where the commission of the offence is due to the act or default of another, that other can be prosecuted. The section does not create a new offence but extends liability. The other person can be prosecuted only for "the" offence, that is, the offence which would have been committed by the primary offender. The question whether the provision envisaged that the secondary offender had to have committed the *actus reus* did not fall for decision in *Tesco v. Nattrass* (above), although, had the store manager been charged under section 23 of the Act, the issue might have arisen directly. It did arise in *Meah v. Roberts* [1978] 1 All E.R. 97 where a waiter inadvertently supplied caustic soda to a customer who had ordered lemonade because a representative of a brewery company had put the caustic soda into a lemonade bottle after cleaning the pumps. The brewer's representative was brought before the courts under the third party procedure available under section 113 of the Food and Drugs Act 1955. (This procedure was the usual way of bringing a third party before the court, and cast the burden of proving the case against the third party on the primary defendant. In virtually all statutes, it has been replaced by a form comparable to Trade Descriptions Act 1968, s.23, although there are some instances, such as under the Slaughterhouses Act 1974, where the procedure lingers into the present day.) Section 113 permitted the conviction of the secondary offender of "the offence", namely that with which the primary offender was charged. The brewer's representative therefore contended that as he had not sold or supplied the caustic soda, he could not be convicted of selling or supplying lemonade which was unfit or not of the nature, substance or quality demanded by the customer. Wein J. dismissed this argument.

7.84   In *Olgeirsson v. Kitching* [1986] 1 All E.R. 746, the question does not appear to have been addressed again and section 23 was treated as though it rendered another person guilty of "an" offence, rather than made him liable for "the" offence. The facts were that the appellant (who was not a motor trader) had sold a car to a dealer, knowing that the odometer reading was false and making a misrepresentation as to the car's true mileage. The dealer subsequently sold the car, and when the misrepresentation was discovered, reported the facts to a trading standards officer. It is an offence under section 1 of the 1968 Act for a person in the course of a trade or business to apply a false trade description to goods or to supply goods to which a false trade description is applied. The question for the Divisional Court was whether the appellant could be convicted, as he was not acting in the course of a trade or business. McNeill J. summarised the appellant's arguments:

> ". . . that section 23 has no application . . . that the section should be read so as to include after the words "some other person" some such words as "who is engaged in or connected with the trade or business of selling motor cars". . . . Counsel . . . accepts that section 23 is not so limited in terms, but submits that on a proper construction . . . it is and the words there should be so read. He contends that Parliament must have intended the construction . . . because this is a statute which is designed to protect the citizen from the trader . . ."

The appellant's conviction was upheld in reliance upon *Meah v. Roberts* (above) and the construction of the provision by reference to the words "the offence" was not, apparently, considered.

7.85   To depart from the effect of that decision and to limit the scope of the section to traders and not their employees, section 40 of the Consumer Protection Act 1987 adopts the words "act or default committed by some other person in the course of any business of his" (*R. v. Warwickshire County Council, ex p. Johnson* [1993] A.C. 583).

7.86   In contrast, the principal offence must have been committed, or the secondary offender cannot be convicted, even though he may have conducted himself reprehensibly (*Coupe v. Guyett* [1973] 1 W.L.R. 669).

Act or default

7.87   **Meaning.**   Do these words import a notion of *mens rea*? Are they expressions which are neutral descriptions of conduct, or do they carry a pejorative meaning? This question was not concluded in *Sedgwick v. Ernest Ostler Ltd* [1963] Crim.L.R. 109 where a false description on an invoice by a supplier of a substance as "marzipan" may have occasioned a retailer to describe the substance falsely to his customers. It was held that as there was no real evidence that the retailer had relied upon the description in the invoice, there was room for real doubt that there had been an act or default which occasioned the offence. This case is an illustration of the need for the prosecution to call evidence to show that all the elements of the third party offence are established. It is arguable that default carries a meaning which suggests a failure to do that which he was required to do, but "act" does not. In *Tesco Ltd v. Nattrass* [1972] A.C. 153 *per* Lord Diplock at 196:

> "In the expression "act or default" in section 23 and in paragraph (a) of section 24(1) [of the Trade Descriptions Act 1968] the word "act" is wide enough to cover any physical act of the other person which is causative of the offence. But the use of the word "default" instead of the neutral expression "omission" connotes a failure to act which constitutes a breach of a legal duty to act. A legal duty to act may arise independently of any contract or it may be a duty owed to another person arising out of a contract with him". Lord Diplock then made it clear that a breach of the other person's contract of employment fell within the scope of "default". This appears consistent with other authorities. In *Lamb v. Sunderland and District Creamery Ltd* [1951] 1 All E.R. 923 Lord Goddard at page 925 expressed the view that the act or default must be a wrongful act or default, but a wrongful act or default was no more than one which constituted an offence. The decision in *Noss Farm Products v. Lillico* [1945] 2 All E.R. 609 similarly required conduct which was wrongful at the time when it was committed. Also see *Tarleton v. Nattress* [1973] 1 W.L.R. 1261.

Mens rea or negligence need not be proved if the original offence does not require *mens rea* or negligence (*Lindley v. George W. Horner & Co. Ltd* [1950] 1 All E.R. 234, *Lester v. Balfour Williamson Merchant Shippers Ltd* [1953] 2 Q.B. 168; *Fisher v. Barrett & Pomeroy (Bakers) Ltd* [1954] 1 W.L.R. 351). Also see *K. Lill Holdings Ltd t/a Stratford Motor Co. v. White* [1979] R.T.R. 120 (disapproved on its facts in *R. v. Southwood* [1987] 1 W.L.R. 1361).

Other expressions

7.88   For a discussion of the meaning of the words "person" see paragraphs 7.24 to 7.27 above; "commission of an offence/shall be guilty", paragraphs 7.63 to 7.68 and 7.80 above; "an offence under this Act", paragraphs 7.63 to 7.64.

Defences

7.89   If the legislation provides that the primary offender may have a defence of due diligence it is usual for a secondary offender to have a similar defence. Where the secondary offender is an employee, will it be sufficient for him to state that he was following the instructions of his employer?

CHAPTER 8

Commencing Proceedings

COMMENCING THE PROSECUTION

The first steps

8.1 Classification of offences. Criminal offences (except that of failing to surrender to custody under section 6(1) of the Bail Act 1976 and those commenced by the preferment by a High Court Judge of a Bill of Indictment) begin in the magistrates' court. There are three categories (excluding a fourth category of summary offence introduced by the Criminal Justice Act 1988 which can be tried on indictment where the facts of the offence are the same as an indictable offence to be sent to the Crown Court) of criminal offence: those which are "indictable", that is, can be tried on indictment whether because they can only be tried thus (like murder) or because they can be tried either on indictment or summarily in the magistrates' court. Offences which can be tried either summarily or on indictment form the second category, known as offences "triable either way" and offences triable only in the magistrates' court are "summary offences" (Interpretation Act 1978, Sched. 1).

8.2 There are no regulatory offences which are indictable only, but many are "either way" offences. The classification is important because different procedural provisions may apply, depending upon whether the offence alleged is triable either way or summary only.

8.3 Arrestable offences. In addition to the classification above, some offences are "arrestable". This description applies to offences for which a person may be arrested without a warrant and, in relation to regulatory offences, applies only if the offence carries a maximum term of imprisonment of five years or more (Police and Criminal Evidence Act 1984, s.24). Few regulatory offences fall within this category and those which do not are commenced by the laying of an information in the magistrates court. This is followed by the issue of a summons to require the defendant to attend court or, in the case of regulatory offences, infrequently, a warrant for the arrest of the defendant (see paragraph 8.6 below).

Laying an information

8.4   Formality.   Unless an arrest warrant is sought, the information need not be in writing or on oath (Magistrates' Courts Act 1980, s.1(3)). An oral application made *ex parte* to a magistrate is sufficient to enable a summons to be issued. Alternatively, the information may be laid in writing before a magistrate or a justices' clerk or any person who has been appointed by the committee of magistrates for the area in question to assist the justices' clerk and has been authorised by the clerk in writing (Justices' Clerks Rules 1970 (S.I. 1970 No. 231 as amended). It is usual for the information to be laid by post in the form prescribed in Form 1 of Schedule 2 of the Magistrates' Courts (Forms) Rules 1981 (S.I. 1981 No. 553 as amended. The information is "laid" when it is received in the office of the clerk to the justices (*R. v. Manchester Stipendiary Magistrate, ex p. Hill* [1983] 1 A.C. 328). "Receipt" includes, where there is a computer link between the prosecutors' office and the clerk to the justices, the feeding in of the information at the prosecutor's office, even though this is not printed out on the same date (*R. v. Pontypridd Juvenile Court, ex p. B and others* [1985] Crim.L.R. 842 and commentary thereto. The Magistrates' Courts (Forms) Rules 1981 provide only that the prescribed form be used or a form "to like effect . . . with such variation as the circumstances may require". The information will be sufficient provided that it complies with rules 4 and 100 of the Magistrates' Courts Rules 1981. In *R. v. Kennett Justices, ex p. Humphrey and Wyatt* [1993] Crim.L.R. 787, the information took the form of a letter to the clerk to the justices advising of further allegations to be put to the defendant and enclosing copies. It was held that the letter and enclosure satisfied the rules and the information had been validly laid.

8.5   Some enactments require an information to be laid before two or more justices. By section 1(7) Magistrates' Courts Act 1980, a single magistrate has power to issue a summons or warrant, notwithstanding such express provision in an earlier enactment.

When a warrant may be issued

8.6   Provided that the information is in writing and on oath, a warrant for the arrest of a person may be issued only if the offence is punishable with imprisonment, or indictable or if the person's address is not sufficiently established to enable a summons to be served. Clearly, these provisions can only be effective where the defendant is an individual.

Territorial jurisdiction

8.7   Power to issue.   There is no power to issue a summons or warrant if there is no territorial jurisdiction (Magistrates' Courts Act 1980, s.1). So, the information must:

   (i) relate to an offence committed or suspected to have been committed within the commission area of the magistrate (MCA 1980, s.1(2)(a)), or

   (ii) if the interests of the better administration of justice so require, relate to a person who should be charged with another person who is to be proceeded against within the commission area (or is in custody in the area) (MCA 1980, s.1(2)(b)). If consideration is not given to this aspect at the time of the issue of the summons or warrant, this provision cannot be relied upon subsequently to found jurisdiction (*R. v. Abergavenny Justices, ex p. Barratt* [1993] Crim.L.R. 785). Or

(iii) if the person resides in the area (unless the offence is summary only, when that ground alone will not give the magistrate jurisdiction to issue a summons, although a warrant returnable at an appropriate court may be issued) (MCA 1980, s.1(2)(c), s.1(5)(a),(b)) or

(iv) if an enactment gives jurisdiction (MCA 1980, s.1(2)(d)), or

(v) if the offence was committed outside England and Wales. Where the offence is summary only the court must be the one which would have had jurisdiction were the offender before it (MCA 1980, s.1(2)(e)) (*e.g.* offences under the Merchant Shipping Act 1894).

If an offence is in fact within the magistrates' courts' jurisdiction, but the information or summons is wrongly worded so that it suggests otherwise, the information is not bad *ab initio* and can be amended (*R. v. Ormskirk Magistrates' Court, ex p. Battistini* [1990] Crim.L.R. 591).

Exercising the discretion to issue a summons or warrant

8.8 **Judicial character of discretion.** Once the information has been laid, the magistrate, justices' clerk or authorised appointee (see above) has a discretion whether to issue the summons or, where appropriate, warrant. The discretion must be exercised judicially (*R. v. Manchester Stipendiary Magistrate, ex p. Hill* [1983] 1 A.C. 328, *R. v. Wilson, ex p. Battersea Borough Council* [1948] 1 K.B. 43).

> "It would appear that [a magistrate] should at the very least ascertain: (1) whether the allegation is of an offence known to the law and if so whether the essential ingredients of the offence are prima facie present; (2) that the offence alleged is not "out of time"; (3) that the court has jurisdiction; (4) whether the informant has the necessary authority to prosecute" *per* Lord Widgery C.J. in *R. v. West London Metropolitan Stipendiary Magistrate, ex p. Klahn* [1979] 1 W.L.R. 933.

The above is not an exhaustive list. In *R. v. Bros* (1901) L.T. 581 the court concluded that a magistrates' court was entitled to look at whether the allegation was made vexatiously. See also *R. v. Leeds Justices, ex p. Hanson* [1982] Q.B. 892, *R. v. Redbridge Justices, ex p. Whitehouse* (1992) 94 Cr.App.R. 332. It is also clear that the magistrate or his clerk (or appointee) may refuse to issue a summons where it is plain that there is another form of abuse of the process of the court (*R. v. Clerk to the Medway Justices, ex p. DHSS* [1986] Crim.L.R. 686). In exceptional circumstances, the decision maker may seek additional information:

> "In the overwhelming majority of cases the magistrate will not need to consider material beyond that provided by the informant. In my judgment, however, he must be able to inform himself of all relevant facts. Mr Woolf, who appeared as *amicus curiae,* and to whom the court is indebted for his assistance, submitted that the magistrate has a residual discretion to hear a proposed defendant if he felt it necessary for the purpose of reaching a decision. We would accept this contention.

"The magistrate must be able to satisfy himself that it is a proper case in which to issue a summons. There can be no question, however, of conducting a preliminary hearing. Until a summons has been issued there is no allegation to meet; no charge has been made. A proposed defendant has no *locus standi* and no right to be heard. Whilst it is conceivable that a magistrate might seek information from him in exceptional circumstances it must be entirely within the discretion of the magistrate whether to do so." (*R. v. West London Metropolitan Stipendiary Magistrate, ex. p. Klahn* [1979] 1 W.L.R. 934 at page 936).

Clearly, not all facts which may later result in the dismissal of the information will be known to the person to whom the decision to issue the summons falls and it will be only in exceptional cases that it will be justifiable to seek further information prior to the issue of the summons.

8.9 Private prosecutions. Where a private prosecution is brought, it is usual for special care to be taken by the magistrates court. If the private prosecutor is not charged with the enforcement of certain provisions (such as a local authority), the information is likely to be required to be made orally so that enquiries can be made by the justices to ensure that the procedure is not an abuse of the process of the court. If the Crown Prosecution Service or other authorised prosecutor has already proceeded against the defendant in respect of the same facts, a summons should be issued at the behest of some other prosecutor only in the most exceptional circumstances (*R. v. Tower Bridge Metropolitan Magistrates' Court, ex p. Chaudry* [1994] 1 All E.R. 44). It is important to avoid the issue of a summons merely to satisfy an ulterior motive of the prosecutor (*R. v. Bury Justices, ex p. Anderton* [1987] Crim.L.R. 638).

Offence must be known to law

8.10 Ordinary language. Rule 100 Magistrates' Courts Rules 1981 provides only that the offence be described in ordinary language without necessarily stating all the elements of the offence. Words like "knowingly" or "wilfully" may in some cases be omitted as technical (*Lomas v. Peek* [1947] 2 All E.R. 574 – but contrast *Waring v. Wheatley* (1951) 115 J.P. 630, where the omission of the word "wilful" in the information resulted in the quashing of a conviction). The offence must be identifiable. It is insufficient merely to recite preambulatory matters which must have occurred before the offence can have been committed if the offence is not then alleged (*Gorman v. Plaice* [1969] 1 All E.R. 62).

In *Hunter v. Coombs* [1962] 1 All E.R. 904 the information alleged an offence which had been repealed and replaced. The conviction of the defendant was quashed on the ground that the information was defective. Potentially, this situation could have been averted before the issue of the summons had the justices' clerk spotted the error. See also *R. v. Folkestone Justices, ex p. Kibble* [1993] T.L.R. 103 and *Meek v. Powell* [1952] 1 K.B. 164, but contrast *Jones v. Thomas* [1987] Crim.L.R. 133, where the information had referred to a provision "as amended" whereas it had been substituted by a later provision. The case was remitted for hearing on the grounds that rule 100 was satisfied.

8.11 Information must not be duplicitous. Magistrates may not proceed to trial of an information which charges more than one offence (Magistrates' Courts

Rules 1981, r.12). In *Carrington Carr Ltd v. Leicestershire County Council* (1994) 158 J.P. 570, Mantell J. identified 5 categories of case which can be found in the authorities.

(i) Where an offence refers to more than one category of activity of mental state. An example of this occurred in *Mallon v. Allan* [1964] 1 Q.B. 385 where an information alleged both that a bookmaker "admitted to or allowed to remain" on his premises a person who was under age. As a matter of construction of the legislation, two offences were created and the information was duplicitous and bad. Similarly, an information alleging an offence of emitting smoke or steam to occasion reasonable grounds for complaint by the public or the passengers under certain byelaws was duplicitous and bad because it failed to allege whether the public or the passengers were inconvenienced (*Cottrell v. Lempriere* (1890) 24 Q.B.D. 634). In contrast, in *Davis v. Loach* (1886) 51 J.P. 118, an allegation under a similar provision alleging the emission of smoke and steam was not duplicitous. In every case, it is a question of construction of the legislation whether the count alleges one offence or more than one. See also *Shaw v. DPP* [1993] 1 All E.R. 918, *Bastin v. Davis* [1950] K.B. 579.

(ii) Where a count alleges more than one offence disjunctively or in the alternative;

(iii) A single act is charged but the offence can be committed in more than one way – for example, driving under the influence of drink or drugs;

(iv) Where a count purports to be only one offence but on the evidence more than one offence is revealed (*Jemmison v. Priddle* [1972] 1 Q.B. 489, *DPP v. Merriman* [1973] A.C. 584). In these cases, it may be necessary to look at witness statements to decide the point (*R. v. Greenfield* [1973] 3 All E.R. 1050);

(v) Where a single act is charged but can be supported by a number of particulars, for example, obtaining by deception where there are several misrepresentations. In this last class, the count is not bad for duplicity. By way of further example, an information that a defendant "has on and since a specified day used his land in contravention of an enforcement notice' is not bad for duplicity because the information only alleges a single offence, even though each day of the contravention could have, in a differently worded information, given rise to a separate offence (*Hodgetts v. Chiltern District Council* [1983] 2 A.C. 120).

8.12 Consequence of duplicity. If the information alleges more than one offence, it will not be void, although a conviction upon a duplicitous information may be quashed. By an amendment to Magistrates' Courts Rules 1981 r.12(3), if the court finds that the information is duplicitous, it is required to call upon the prosecutor to elect the offence upon which he wishes to proceed and the remaining offence or offences are to be struck out. Thereafter, the magistrates must proceed to try the altered information afresh. This is likely to involve reference of the case to a differently constituted bench.

8.13   Information must refer to the legislation creating the offence. Rule 100 requires that the Act or instrument under which the offence arises must be referred to. Where the offence is created by subordinate legislation, it is customary to refer both to the provision of the parent act which enables the offences to have been created and the delegated legislation itself. If the legislation is not identified this can be fatal. An example is *Atterton v. Browne* [1945] K.B. 122 in which allegations against the respondent arose under a third party offence (see paragraphs 7.81 to 7.89 above). The form of the summons suggested that she had sold diluted milk to certain named persons, whereas she had sold milk only to the Milk Marketing Board and caused an intermediary to commit an offence on sale to a consumer. The Divisional Court upheld the decision of the magistrates to dismiss the informations. Because vital particulars were missing, the summonses were so defective and inaccurate as to have been misleading. If the summons had referred to the provisions of the legislation or explained the detail of the allegation, the defendant would have understood what charge she had to meet.

8.14   Reasonable particulars. The information should give such particulars as are necessary for giving reasonable details as to the nature of the allegation. Failure to give full particulars does not always render the information defective as application for further particulars may be sought by the defendant subsequently (*R. v. Aylesbury Justices, ex p. Wisbey* [1965] 1 All E.R. 602). The failure to give adequate particulars may, in a serious case, render the information defective, and no such information should be issued. For example, in *R. v. Birmingham Justices, ex p. Matthews and another* [1996] 104 I.T.S.A. 11 M.R 24 informations were laid alleging breaches of section 14 of the Trade Descriptions Act 1968. Some of the informations failed to indicate why statements made were said to be false. Others failed to identify to whom the statements were alleged to have been made. In both cases, the Divisional Court held that the omissions were so fundamental that the information were null. This decision should be contrasted with that in *Jevons v. Cosmoair* (February 13, 1997, DC) in which the same points were made as in the *Matthews* case. It was held on the facts of the second case that it was clear on the facts to whom the statements were alleged to have been made and also clear why it was alleged that those statements were false. The informations should have been amended.

The information must have been laid in time

8.15   If a summons is issued in circumstances where there is doubt whether the informations was laid in time, it must be dismissed (*Lloyd v. Young* [1963] Crim.L.R. 703). In a proper case the magistrate, his clerk or an authorised appointee (see paragraph 8.4 above) may refuse to issue the summons or warrant.

8.16   Summary offences. If the offence is summary only and there is no express provision in the statute or regulations creating the offence, section 127(1) of the Magistrates' Courts Act 1980 will apply. This prohibits a magistrates court from trying information unless the information was laid within six months from the commission of the offence. If a conviction is obtained in respect of an information laid out of time, it may be set aside on appeal (see Chapter 12 below). In some instances where there is prejudice this rule may prevent amendment of the summons to allege a new offence after six months has expired (*R. v. Pain, R. v. Jory, R. v. Hawkins* (1986) 82 Cr. App. R. 141) but see *R. v. Newcastle on Tyne*

Justices, ex p. Bryce (Contractors) Ltd [1976] 1 W.L.R. 517, *R. v. Scunthorpe Justices, ex p. McPhee, The Times* March 9, 1998 and *R. v. Newcastle Upon Tyne Magistrates' Court, ex p. Poundstretcher Ltd*, New Law, March 3, 1998.

8.17   Express provision.   If the offence is capable of trial on indictment, there is no general statutory limit preventing prosecution at any time, although many regulatory offences are subject to a limitation laid down in the legislation creating the offence. An example, which is repeated with slight variations only in many statutes and statutory instruments, can be found in section 19 of the Trade Descriptions Act 1968. Section 19(2) expressly extends the period within which a summary offence may be tried to 1 year from the date of commission of the offence and section 19(2) provides in relation to either way offences that no prosecution shall be commenced after 3 years from the date of commission of the offence or 1 year from its discovery by the prosecutor. Failure to observe the provision can be fatal. In *R. v. Pain* (above) a defendant charged with conspiracy to defraud agreed that he would plead guilty instead to conspiracy to breach the terms of the Trade Descriptions Act 1968. An appeal on the basis that the substitution of the charges took place more than 1 year after the discovery of the facts by the prosecutor was upheld.

8.18   "Offences under the Act".   It is important to be clear that the time limit provision applies to the offence charged. In some instances, offences arising under subordinate legislation will have a different time limit from the offences under the parent act. This may not be immediately obvious, particularly where the subordinate legislation creates summary offences and is silent as to the time within which the proceedings may be brought. The expression "offences under the Act" is potentially capable of describing both offences under primary legislation and offences under subordinate legislation made pursuant to it (*Willingale v. Norris* [1909] 1 K.B. 57 at 64). It does not follow that the expression will embrace offences under subordinate legislation in every instance, however. An example where the expression "offences under the Act" does not include offences under subordinate legislation arises in the Food Labelling Regulations 1996, where summary offences are created. The Food Safety Act 1990, to which, by virtue of the Interpretation Act 1978, the Food Labelling Regulations are subordinate, contains provisions limiting prosecution of offences "under the Act" in section 34. These provisions do not apply to the offences under the Food Labelling Regulations 1996 which are governed by the shorter limitation under section 127 Magistrates' Courts Act 1980 (paragraph 8.16 above). This is because the 1990 Act provides that the regulations may specify punishment; the maximum punishment envisaged under the Act is greater than the maximum punishment specified under the Regulations; and historically, there is a distinction drawn in the drafting of food and drugs legislation between offences under the Act and offences under the regulations. This instance demonstrates the importance of construing the powers of both the Act and regulations as a whole in order to determine their true effect.

8.19   Commencement of proceedings.   Proceedings are commenced for the purposes of a limitation provision when the information is laid (see paragraph 8.4 above) not when the summons is served (*Abraham v. Jutson* (1962) 106 Sol. Jo. 880, *Beardsley v. Giddings* [1904] 1 K.B. 847).

8.20 Commission of the offence. It is unusual for there to be doubt as to the date of commission of an offence. Occasionally, however, problems arise where the offence involves more than one activity. An example is the third party offence (see paragraphs 7.81 to 7.89 above) where the allegation is that a secondary offender has by his act or omission occasioned the commission of an offence by a primary offender. Time begins to run at the date of the commission of the offence by the primary offender, not at the date of the secondary offender's conduct (*Concentrated Foods v. Champ* [1944] K.B. 342). Similar reasoning will apply to the liability of officers, etc., for offences committed by a body corporate (see paragraphs 7.60 to 7.80), and to an offence of aiding and abetting, counselling or procuring (paragraphs 7.50 to 7.59) (*Gould Co. Ltd v. Houghton* [1921] 1 K.B. 509, *Homolka v. Osmond* [1939] 1 All E.R. 154).

8.21 Discovery of the offence. The question when the offence has been discovered frequently arises. Discovery is generally understood to mean the point at which all the facts material to the allegation are known to the prosecutor (*London Borough of Newham v. Co-op Retail* (1985) 149 J.P. 421, *Brookes v. Club Continental* (1982) 1 Tr. L. 126, *R. v. Beaconsfield Justices, ex p. Johnson and Sons Ltd* (1985) 149 J.P. 535). There are three important rules: the prosecutor himself must have knowledge of the offence; he must have sufficient knowledge to cause time to begin to run, but he need not have proof; and where the offence is repeated or is of a continuing nature, the prosecutor may rely upon an offence committed on a later day than the date upon which he first learnt of the same offence.

8.22 The prosecutor must know of the offence. The discovery must have been made by the prosecutor and not (where the prosecutor is a local authority) merely by an employee of the same Council. In *R. v. Shrewsbury Magistrates' Court, ex p. Simon Dudley Limited*, [1997] I.T.S.A. M.R. 30, the question arose whether the knowledge of a fire officer and assistant chief solicitor was sufficient to fix the prosecutor with knowledge of an offence. The local authority had agreed to buy a fire engine from the defendants. It was delivered in July 1991 and problems were found, which were discussed between the defendants, the fire officer and the assistant chief solicitor. The Deputy Chief Trading Standards Officer heard about the problems for the first time during a radio broadcast on May 21, 1992. On May 20, 1993 the Chief Trading Standards Officer laid informations under section 1 of the Trade Descriptions Act 1968. The defendants alleged that the prosecution was out of time under s.19 of the 1968 Act. The Divisional Court found that the prosecution was not out of time. The scheme of delegation by the Council gave the Chief and Deputy Chief Trading Standards Officers authority to prosecute (see paragraphs 2.27 to 2.40 above), so that they, and not the County Council were the prosecutors. Moreover, even if the Council had been the prosecutor, knowledge of the facts by the fire officer and solicitor, without knowledge of their significance would not cause time to begin to run. A similar approach was followed in *Swan v. Vehicle Inspectorate* (1996) 161 J.P. 293, in which the defendant appealed to the Divisional Court on the basis that information was out of time. The time limit was six months from the date on which sufficient evidence, in the opinion of the prosecutor, was known to him to enable the proceedings to be issued. A traffic examiner had interviewed the defendant in respect of driving while disqualified, but he did not have authority to determine whether the defendant should be prosecuted. The decision to prosecute was made by the senior traffic examiner, who did not learn of the offence until a point within the six month period. The mere fact that the investigator has apparent authority does not mean that the person investigating was the prosecutor. It seems to follow from this that if it is intended by a defendant to take a point as to the moment of knowledge by the prosecutor, it will be necessary to identify the person with authority to prosecute, perhaps by reference to the resolutions or standing orders of the enforcement authority.

8.23 Sufficient knowledge does not equate to proof. The Divisional Court held that a prosecutor was out of time where he was aware that an offence had been committed but was not aware of the exact body who had committed it (*Brooks v. Club Continental* (1982) 1 Tr. L. 126. Similarly, a prosecutor could not contend that he had insufficient proof albeit that he knew of the commission of the offence and who had committed it so as to enable him to delay the date of "discovery" (*R. v. Beaconsfield Justices, ex p. Johnston Sons Ltd* (1985) 149 J.P. 535). On the other hand, in *R. v. Stoke on Trent Magistrates' Court, ex p. Leaf Ltd.* (November 6, 1997, Divisional Court) the Divisional Court confirmed that proceedings were not out of time when the prosecutor calculated that time ran from the date when he obtained an "official" certificate of analysis that he could rely upon in court, even though he had previously been in possession of an informal analysis which suggested what the likely "official" test would say.

8.24 Repeated and continuing offences. If the prosecutor is informed of an offence and subsequently carries out an investigation and finds evidence of the commission of the same offence on a later day, and the later allegations form the basis of the prosecution, the defendant cannot generally complain that the prosecutor could have proceeded earlier. In *Newham London Borough v. Co-operative Retail Services Limited* (1985) 149 J.P. 421 magistrates had held that informations were time-barred because a complaint had been made to the consumer protection service on August 31, 1982. On September 8 and 9, 1982 an officer of the council attended the store about which the complaint had been made and collected evidence. Information alleging an offence on September 9, 1982 was laid on September 8, 1983. The Divisional Court allowed the prosecution appeal. Similarly, facts which give rise to a continuing offence were considered in (*R. v. Thames Metropolitan Stipendiary Magistrate, ex p. Hackney London Borough Council* (1994) 158 J.P. 305) in which food hygiene offences discovered in September 1989 were persisting in March 1990. The Council proceeded in respect of the offences discovered in March 1990. It was held by the Divisional Court that the offences were of a continuing nature and therefore that the limit did not prevent proceedings in respect of the later date.

There must be no apparent abuse of process

8.25 Patent abuse. Abuse of the process of the court can take many forms, most of which will not be known to the court at the stage when the summons or information is issued. (See paragraphs 10.26 to 10.47 below for a discussion of the scope and nature of abuse of the process of the court and its consequences.) In some cases where facts coming to the attention of the justices or their clerk indicate an abuse of process, it will be the court's duty to inquire, and if appropriate, to refuse to issue the summons (*R. v. Liverpool Stipendiary Magistrate, ex p. Ellison* [1990] R.T.R. 220, *R. v. Clerk to the Medway Justices, ex p. DHSS* [1986] Crim.L.R. 686, *R. v. Bury Justices, ex p. Anderton* (1987) N.L.J. 410). This is particularly so where the abuse arises from the wrongful manipulation of court procedures. In cases of delay (see paragraph 8–27 below) the court may need to be more circumspect. The summons could properly be issued and the matter argued between the parties at trial or at a specially convened hearing. It is now accepted that magistrates, at least when sitting as a court of summary trial (and perhaps when sitting as examining magistrates have the power to stay proceedings which are an abuse in relation to matters directly affecting the fairness of the trial of the defendant (*Bennett v. Horseferry Road Magistrates' Court* [1993] 3 All E.R. 138 but see the speech of Lord Lowry, particularly at 166 to 169). Wider considerations are not matters for the magistrates' court but for the Divisional Court. These matters should not be considered before the issue of the summons (see paragraphs 10.30 to 10.34 below for a more detailed consideration).

8.26 Enquiries. If the justices, their clerk or authorised appointee (see paragraph 8.4) considers that there are exceptional circumstances in which a further enquiry should be made, such an enquiry may be made. In *R. v. West London Metropolitan Stipendiary Magistrate, ex p. Klahn* (above) the Divisional Court considered that the decision maker would be entitled to make enquiry of the prospective defendant. More commonly, further information is sought from the prospective prosecutor. In *R. v. Clerk to Medway Justices, ex p. DHSS* [1986] Crim.L.R. 686 the prospective defendant had, apparently, admitted a fraud. The papers were passed to another government department, where they were retained for 110 days before being returned. The information was submitted 12 days later. The justices' clerk refused to issue a summons without an explanation from the DHSS Regional Solicitor's office. He sent a letter. The letter was not answered. The period within which proceedings could be brought had not expired. The DHSS sought judicial review of the decision of the clerk not to issue a summons. The Divisional Court expressed the view that in most cases it was preferable that the question of abuse of process should be dealt with in open court after the issue of the summons rather than *ex parte*, but that the clerk was entitled to refuse to issue the summons even though the period within which the prosecution could be brought had not expired. Moreover, he was entitled to take into account the fact that no reply had been forthcoming to his letter of enquiry.

8.27 Delay within the period for commencing the prosecution. The most frequently alleged abuse of process is excessive delay in issuing the proceedings leading to prejudice to the defendant, even where any statutory limitation has not expired. In an obvious case, the decision-maker may initiate inquiries but the court should be wary about acting at this stage. In some cases prejudice may be presumed from delay, without the need for specific evidence to be given about it, however. (*R. v. Bow St Metropolitan Stipendiary Magistrate, ex p. Cherry* (1990) 154 J.P. 237). In *Daventry District Council v. Olins* [1990] Crim.L.R. 414 the prosecutor failed to lay an information for some months after the discovery of an offence under the Food Act 1984. The defendant alleged that there was an abuse of process even though the time limit for proceeding had not expired. The Divisional Court upheld the decision of the magistrate that there had been an abuse of process: of particular significance was the fact that the defendant for a substantial period had no details of the complainant and it is a matter of particular prejudice that the allegation was based upon an anonymous complaint. This case may illustrate an instance where the court would have been justified in making enquiries before the issue of the summons. Of no significance was the fact that the defendant may have experienced distress and anxiety by the delay.

8.28   Although there is no different principle to be drawn between regulatory offences and "true" crime (see paragraph 10.46 below), delay in notifying the defendant of the allegation can be of particular importance where regulatory offences are concerned if there was no contemporaneous interview or correspondence, because the passage of time is likely to render it difficult to recall the circumstances surrounding the sale or supply or other facts upon which the prosecution base their allegation. That is prejudicial to a defendant, even though a prosecutor may believe that he has a cast-iron case. If there has been correspondence between the prosecution and the defendant prior to the issue of the summons, or if the defendant has been interviewed and warned orally, any potential prejudice may have been allayed because the defendant has been given an opportunity to isolate the incident and investigate the allegations. In the absence of an enquiry at the stage of issuing the summons, the court is unlikely to be aware of sufficient facts to exercise a discretion against issue of the summons.

Preliminary requirements should have been met

8.29   It is the duty of the clerk or whoever issues the summons to ensure that all preliminary requirements have been met. Where proceedings can only be issued with the consent of a Minister or by a particular person, the clerk should ensure that this has been done. Where there is a duty to serve a notice prior to the commencement of proceedings (see paragraph 8.38 onwards, below) the clerk must ensure that this has been done (*Price v. Humphries* [1958] 2 Q.B. 353). Where there is a restriction on prosecution unless some administrative hurdle has been overcome or the proceedings have been instituted by an authorised person, the issue of the summons by the clerk gives rise to the presumption that the proceedings have been commenced regularly, which, if it is to be challenged, must be specifically raised before the close of the prosecution case by the defence (*Price v. Humphreys* (above), *Anderton v. Frost* [1984] R.T.R. 106). If the challenge is mounted, the burden of disproving it lies on the prosecution.

Issuing the summons

8.30   The summons must be signed by a person authorised to exercise the discretion (Magistrates' Courts Rules 1981, r.98 and Justices' Clerks Rules 1970 as amended. It is permissible to "rubber stamp" the summons with a facsimile of the signature of the person issuing the summons provided that consideration has properly been given by that person to the information and a decision taken (*R. v. Gateshead Justices, ex p. Tesco Stores Ltd* [1981] Q.B. 470). In *R. v. Hay Halkett, ex p. Rush* [1929] 2 K.B. 431 it was held that the absence of a signature on the summons was a mere formal defect and did not render the summons invalid.

8.31   The summons must state the matter contained in the information and give the defendant details of the place and time to appear before the court. The usual form is in Magistrates' Courts (Forms) Rules 1981, Schedule 2, Form 2, but, comparably with the form of the information, the important requirement is that Rules 98 and 100 of the Magistrates' Courts Rules 1981 are complied with. A single summons may be issued in respect of numerous informations but the matters in the informations must be set out in the summons and the summons is then treated as though it were several summonses, one in respect of each information (Magistrates' Courts Rules 1981, r.98(3)).

8.32 Some statutory provisions require that service of the summons shall occur within a specified time (for example, Road Traffic Offenders Act 1988, s.1) but most do not. Where a statutory provision requires the proceedings to be issued within a given time, a summons may be issued after the expiry of the period on the basis of an information laid within time. Where the first summons is not proceeded upon, a second summons may be served (*Brooks v. Bagshaw* [1904] 2 K.B. 798).

Service of the summons or execution of the warrant

8.33 The summons must be served in one the following ways pursuant to the Magistrates' Courts Act 1980 although express provision may be made in some statutes for service in another fashion.

8.34 A corporation. If the defendant is a body corporate with a registered office in the United Kingdom, the summons must be served by post or by delivery to the registered office. If the body corporate has no such registered office, the summons should be served at any place where it trades or conducts its business (Magistrates' Courts Rules 1981, r.99(2)). Unless the contrary is shown, a summons sent in a properly addressed, pre-paid envelope is deemed to have been effected at the time when the letter would have been delivered in the ordinary course of post (Interpretation Act 1978, s.7).

8.35 An individual or unincorporated body. A summons may be served on any person other than a corporation by delivering it to him, by leaving it with some person at his last known or usual place of abode or by sending it by post to his last known or usual place of abode. The summons may also be sent by post to an address provided by the recipient other than his last known or usual place of abode (Magistrates' Court Rules 1981, r.99(1) and (8)). If no alternative address is provided by the defendant, it is not good service to leave or post the summons to his place of business (*R. v. Lilley, ex p. Taylor* (1910) 75 J.P. 95, *R. v. Rhodes, ex p. McVitie* (1915) 79 J.P. 527). In respect of an offence which is summary only, a summons sent by post is then deemed to have been served in the ordinary course of post (Interpretation Act 1978, s.7). In respect of an offence triable either way, a summons which is left at premises or sent by post is not treated as proved if the defendant fails to appear, unless evidence is given as to service. A letter purporting to come from the defendant may be relied upon as proof (Magistrates' Courts Rules 1981, r.99(2)) and evidence may be also be admitted by a declaration in solemn form (Magistrates' Courts Rules 1981, r.67).

8.36 Warrant. This must direct the police constables for the area to arrest the defendant (Magistrates' Courts Rules 1981 r.96). The warrant must contain the name or a description of the person to be arrested and must contain a statement of the offence or the ground upon which the arrest warrant has been issued.

8.37 The consequences of defective service. Where a person appears before the magistrates without raising an objection that the service of a summons or warrant was defective, any irregularity is treated as cured (*R. v. Hughes* (1879) 4 Q.B.D. 614). The defendant should, however, be informed of his right to object to the defect because he cannot be taken to have waived a right to object that he did not know he had (*R. v. Essex Justices, ex p. Perkins* [1927] 2 K.B. 475. If a defendant merely attends before the magistrates in answer to the summons to draw to their attention the defect in the summons and then withdraws, he will not be deemed to have waived any irregularity (*Pearks, Gunston & Tee Ltd v. Richardson* [1902] 1 K.B. 91). Where the defect in a warrant is a defect in form only, the magistrates must not accede to an application to treat it as a nullity. If the defect is substantial, the magistrates should allow an amendment with or without an adjournment (Magistrates' Court Act 1980, s.123 and see paragraphs 10.4 to 10.8 below). If the defect (even if procedural) goes to the root of the process, the summons may be void. In *Dixon v. Wells* (1890) 25 Q.B.D. 249 a conviction under the Sale of Food and Drugs Act 1875 was quashed where a defendant had appeared under protest that the summons was technically defective because it was issued by a person who had not (under the procedure then employed) heard the complaint. The same objection would now be open in respect of the laying of the information.

Proceedings which require prior notice

8.38   Some prosecutions cannot be commenced unless certain administrative steps have already been taken to make the defendant aware that he is to be, or might be, prosecuted. An example arises under the Weights and Measures Act 1985, s.83 which applies to most proceedings under or having effect under Parts IV and V of the Act and to many offences under the Trade Descriptions Act 1968. That provision limits the time within which the prosecution can be brought and further provides that an offence shall not be instituted unless notice in writing giving the date and nature of the offence charged has been served on the defendant (except in the case of street traders) within 30 days "beginning with the date when evidence which the person proposing to institute the proceedings considers is sufficient to justify a prosecution for the offence came to his knowledge". Section 83(5) provides for a certificate to be conclusive evidence of the date when the offence first came to the prosecutor's knowledge.

8.39   It is the nature of the offence which must be brought to the attention of the prospective defendant. He is not entitled to a draft of the information. In *Milner v. Allen* [1933] 1 K.B. 698, a road traffic case, a notice made reference to the offence of driving in a manner dangerous to the public. In fact, the defendant was charged with the lesser offence of driving without due care and attention. The magistrates held that the notice was adequate and the defendant had suffered no prejudice because he had adequate notice of the essential facts in the case. Under the Weights and Measures Act 1985, by way of a different example, the notice is, on the face of it, to be served after the prosecutor has decided what offence is to be charged and not, as in *Milner v. Allen*, merely 14 days after the incident alleged. This may suggest that a greater degree of particularity is needed in relation to these trading offences. In any event, if the train of investigation by the defendant of the offence alleged has been prejudiced by misleading indications in the notice, it is difficult to see that continuation of the prosecution can be fair.

8.40   Although the latest time for serving the notice is before 30 days from the time when the prosecutor has sufficient knowledge, the beginning of the time when the period is to run is not fixed by those words. In *Bakerboy (Hot Bread) v. Barnes* (March 23, 1984, unreported) the defendant was summoned in respect of offences under the Weights and Measures Act 1963 alleged to have occurred on July 13, 1982. A notice was served on August 11, 1982 and the prosecutor certified he had knowledge sufficient to justify the prosecution on September 10, 1982. The information was laid on November 11, 1982. It was held on appeal that the notice was valid because, although it could not be served after the period, the notice need not be served within the 30 day period referred to.

8.41   In some cases, notice must be given to an official but not to a defendant. So a prosecuting authority must give notice under section 130(1) of the Fair Trading Act 1974 in respect of some prosecutions (namely, section 23 of the Fair Trading Act 1973, offences under the Trade Descriptions Act 1968 other than section 28(5) and section 29, under Part III Consumer Protection Act 1987, under section 1 or paragraph 6 of Schedule 1 of the Property Misdescriptions Act 1991 and under section 2 of the Timeshare Act 1992) to the Director General of Fair Trading, together with a summary of the facts upon which the charges are founded. The clerk or other person issuing the summons should satisfy himself that notice has been given (see paragraph 8.29 above) although the statute appears to suggest that the duty is owed to the Director General, not the accused, so failure to give the notice cannot be relied upon as a ground of defence (see "Notice of Intended Proceedings – A Matter Between the Authority and the Director" R. Carruthers and A. Fidler and "Notification of Intended Proceedings to the Director General" N.J. Marsh (1985) ITSA M.R. 239–40).

CIVIL PROCEEDINGS

The complaint

8.42   Civil proceedings, such as those by way of appeal against an administrative notice (see Chapter 4, above) are begun by complaint. A complaint may be made in writing or orally, and, like an information, need not be on oath (Magistrates' Courts Rules 1981, r.4). Where the complaint is in writing, there is a prescribed form (Magistrates' Courts (Forms) Rules 1981, Form 98) and requires the name and address of the complainant and the defendant to be set out, together with short particulars of the complaint. Unlike a criminal information, it may contain several matters of complaint (*Tyrrell v. Tyrrell* (1928) 92 J.P. 45).

The summons

8.43   After the complaint is made, a justice of the peace, his clerk, or anyone authorised in the manner prescribed by the Justices' Clerks Rules 1970 (as amended) (see paragraphs 8.4 above) must apply his mind to the complaint and go through the judicial process of deciding whether process should ensue (*R. v. Brentford Justices, ex p. Catlin* [1975] 2 W.L.R. 506 at 512). As with consideration of an information, the decision is a judicial function and cannot be delegated (*R. v. Manchester Stipendiary Magistrate, ex p. Hill* [1983] 1 A.C. 328 and see paragraphs 8.8 to 8.29 above). The principal matters to which the justice of the peace, his clerk or authorised official must direct his mind are:

(i)   whether the court has prima facie power to make the order asked for;

(ii) whether the court has territorial jurisdiction; and

(iii) whether the complaint has been made, so far as appears, within any limitation of time.

Jurisdiction

8.44   In the absence of any power contained in a statute directing particular matters to particular courts, a magistrates court has jurisdiction "if the complaint relates to anything done within the commission area for which the court is appointed or anything left undone that ought to have been done there, or ought to have been done either there or elsewhere and relates to any other matter arising within that area" (Magistrates' Courts Act 1980, s.52).

Service

8.45 A summons requires the defendant to attend and sets out shortly the matter of complaint. The provisions for service of a summons issued following a complaint are identical to those in respect of a summons following the laying of an information (see Magistrates' Courts Rules 1981, rule 99 and paragraphs 8.33 to 8.37 above).

CHAPTER 9

Defences

THE NATURE OF DEFENCES

9.1 Defences which the prosecution must disprove. The defences discussed here can have one of two effects. One type of defence is a matter which, if raised, casts the burden back on to the prosecution to prove that it does not apply. If the prosecution cannot disprove the matter, the accused is entitled to acquittal. The so-called "disclaimer defence" (see paragraph 9.3 below) can fall into this category (*R. v. Hammerton Cars Ltd* [1976] 1 W.L.R. 1243 at 1248–49) but is not always analysed as so falling, because it can also be part of a due diligence defence (see paragraphs 9.2, 9.3 and 9.27 below). Recognised categories of common law defences, such as that of duress or necessity (in so far as they may apply to regulatory offences) similarly require the prosecution to prove that they cannot avail the defendant in the particular case.

9.2 Statutory defences and defences of exception, etc. which the defendant must prove. The second category is the statutory defence arising either from a proviso or other exception (see paragraphs 6.6 and 6.7) or from express legislation directing that, upon proof of certain matters, the defendant is to be acquitted. The "due diligence" defence falls into this category (see paragraphs 9.13 onwards, below).

9.3 Disclaimer defences. So-called "disclaimer defences" may fall into one or both of the above categories. They apply where the giving of false or misleading information by one person to another constitutes an offence, and, to counteract the falsity or misleading nature of the information furnished, the person providing it has distanced himself from affirming its accuracy in some way. A question which frequently arises is whether such a defence can stand alone to defeat the prosecution case, or whether the disclaimer can be merely evidence relied upon to prove the statutory offence of due diligence. In the first instance, the defence is no more than an assertion that when the circumstances are viewed as a whole, the prosecution cannot prove that the offence has been committed (see paragraph 9.4 below). In the second instance, where the offence involves dissemination of inaccurate information, a disclaimer, even if falling short of that required to controvert an express representation to the contrary, may form an important item of evidence in establishing a due diligence defence. A due diligence defence to an allegation of making false representations is likely to fail if a disclaimer could have been given but was not (see paragraph 9.27 below).

COMMON LAW DEFENCES

Disclaimers as common law defences

9.4   Background.   Although applicable to any case where the offence turns on the communication of prohibited statements, offers, advertisements or invitations, historically the "disclaimer defence" developed its significance in trade descriptions cases where sellers of cars were troubled by their helplessness in the face of prosecutions for passing on second hand cars which had been "clocked" by a previous owner. By virtue of the decision in *Stoodley v. H.W. Thomas & Sons Ltd* [1945] K.B. 413 and *Wickens Motors (Gloucester) Ltd v. Hall* [1972] 3 All E.R. 759 the odometer reading is a trade description and a false odometer reading is therefore an offence under section 1 of the Trade Descriptions Act 1968. In *Tarleton Engineering Co. Ltd. v. Nattrass* [1973] 1 W.L.R. 1261, Weir J. in the Divisional Court put forward the view that a disclaimer could negate an otherwise false trade description, provided that the disclaimer was part of the material available to the purchaser at the time of negotiation or supply. This was followed in subsequent authorities, and a principle was established in *Norman v. Bennet* [1974] 1 W.L.R. 1229 where Widgery L.C.J. asserted:

> "I think that where a false trade description is attached to goods, its effect can be neutralised by an express disclaimer or contradiction of the message contained in the trade description. To be effective, any such disclaimer must be as bold, precise and compelling as the trade description itself and must be as effectively brought to the notice of any person to whom the goods may be supplied. In other words, the disclaimer must equal the trade description in the extent to which it is likely to get home to anyone interested in receiving the goods.
>
>   To be effective as a defence to a charge under section 1(1)(b) of the Act any such disclaimer must be made before the goods are supplied . . . Can a supplier who has made a false trade description protect himself by withdrawing the description before delivery? He certainly should not be able to do so and I think the answer to that problem is that the words "is applied" in section 1(1)(b) mean "is applied at the time of supply or has been so applied in the course of negotiations leading to such supply"."

Accordingly, "disclaimer defences" have been available to meet an allegation under section 1(1)(b) of the Trade Descriptions Act 1968 (supplying goods to which a false trade description has been applied) but not that under section 1(1)(a) of the Act (applying a false trade description) (*R. v. Southwood* [1987] 1 W.L.R. 1361, although see *Newham London Borough v. Singh and Sandhu* (1987) 157 J.P. 239 and *R. v. Shrewsbury Crown Court, ex p. Venables* [1994] Crim.L.R. 61, at paragraph 9.8 below). It is important always to recall that *Norman v. Bennet* (above) and other cases which have followed it, must not deflect attention from the true reasoning. The cachet, "disclaimer defence", compounds a misconception that in these circumstances there is a type of defence that the defendant must prove. Rather it is that where a disclaimer is applied, the offence may not have been committed (*R. v. Hammertons Cars Ltd* [1976] 1 W.L.R. 1243). If the false element of a description is only part of the information available to the purchaser of goods, and if also the false part of the information has been negated in its impact on the purchaser by words which undermine reliance on it, the description, taken as a whole, may not be false either at all or to any material degree, although some words may be. The prosecution has to prove the offence. In the circumstances suggested, there may be no trade description which is materially false.

9.5 Construction of the circumstances as a whole. Following that argument through, therefore, there ought to be no prohibition upon the availability of the "defence" to a seller who has applied a false trade description: rather it should be a matter of fact that a disclaimer is unlikely to undermine a deliberate attempt to deceive by the application of a false description, and the passage from the judgement of Widgery L.C.J. should be interpreted in that light. It was recognised in *R. v. Southwood* (above) that in the main, section 1(1)(a) of the Trade Descriptions Act 1968 is aimed at the unscrupulous trader rather than the mistaken one, and where that is the case, it was accepted that no disclaimer should protect from an attempt to deceive. In the unusual circumstances, however, where a trade description can be both applied and undermined at the same time or in the course of the same negotiations, it is submitted that no false trade description is given and there is no justification for denying the defence. This line of thought was recognised in a case which concerned a disclaimer but did not concern a false trade description. In *Alliance and Leicester Building Society v. Babbs* (1993) 12 Tr.L. 105 a 9 year old boy was sent a document inviting him to apply for a personal loan with his statement of account. It is an offence under Section 50(1)(a) of the Consumer Credit Act 1974 to send, with a view to financial gain, a document to a minor inviting him to borrow money. It was not the policy of the defendant to lend money to people under 18 and its computer programme was designed to prevent error. In the document sent there was a form of disclaimer described by Wright J. as "in italics and in, we should say, regrettably small print" stating "The right to decline any application is reserved. Loans are not available to applicants under 18 years of age". The Divisional Court found *(inter alia)* that the document construed as a whole was not an invitation to a minor for him to borrow money.

9.6 Application of this principle. The Divisional Court has latterly had to address the same contention in relation to an offence under section 1(1)(a) of the Trade Descriptions Act 1968. In *R. v. Bull* (1996) 160 J.P. 240, a mere disclaimer was distinguished from a statement which negates the effect of what would otherwise be a false trade description. Where a car dealer had inserted an odometer reading in a form, he had applied (as an item of evidence taken alone) a false trade description because the car had travelled more miles than showed on the odometer. He therefore appended a note to the entry to the effect that the odometer reading was not to be taken as accurate because he could not verify its truth. It was held on appeal that the magistrates should have found that there was no case to answer. The note was to be read as part of the description (namely that the odometer showed a certain figure) and there was no evidence that this note taken as a whole was false.

It remains to be seen whether the courts will limit this case to its precise facts (namely that the description was limited to what the odometer of the car stated) or whether there will be a more general acceptance that the disclaimer can in some cases apply to section 1(1)(a) as well as to section 1(1)(b) of the Trade Descriptions Act 1968.

9.7 What is a sufficient disclaimer? Each case turns on its own facts, although Lord Widgery's expression "bold, precise and compelling" *(Norman v. Bennett* (above)) has taken root as the test to be applied for sufficiency *(Gerard*

Francis Smallshaw v. PKC Associates Ltd (below)). The requirement that a false trade description and, by analogy, other false statement shall be "neutralised" requires, by reason of that test, significant steps to be taken.
Guideline principles may be:

(i) It is not enough that a selling agent puts a general disclaimer on a noticeboard (*Zawadski v. Sleigh* [1975] R.T.R. 113);

(ii) A casual remark in the course of oral negotiations will not be sufficient, nor "small print" in a document (*R. v. Hammertons Cars Ltd* [1976] 1 W.L.R. 1243).

(iii) The disclaimer must be proximate. In *Waltham Forest London Borough Council v. T. G. Wheatley (Central Garage) Ltd* [1978] R.T.R. 333, the Divisional Court found that a disclaimer notice which read "the mileage on secondhand cars cannot be guaranteed accurate and are sold subject to that undertaking" was inadequate. They stressed the need for the disclaimer to be proximate to the false description. On the other hand, a sticker placed over the odometer which read: "Trade Descriptions Act 1968. Dealers are often unable to guarantee the mileage of a used car on sale. Please disregard the recorded mileage on this vehicle and accept it as an incorrect reading" was a clear dissociation of the odometer from the car (*Newham London Borough v. Singh and Sandhu* (1987) 152 J.P. 239). In *Gerard Francis Smallshaw v. PKC Associates Ltd* (1995) 159 J.P. 654 magistrates construed a leaflet advertising travel insurance (which, if read alone, would have contained a false statement) with the certificate of travel insurance and had decided that if the two documents were read together, there was no false statement contrary to section 14 of the Trade Descriptions Act 1968. The Divisional Court found that they had applied the wrong test. The magistrates should have asked themselves, not whether a person reading the two documents together would be likely to be misled, but whether a person reading the leaflet would be likely to be misled. The other document was relevant to the question whether the person who read the leaflet would have been misled.

9.8 Written descriptions and oral disclaimers. Previously decided cases are of limited help in predicting the approach a court may adopt towards a disclaimer where it has been given only orally and there has been a written description. However, each case must turn on its own facts. The general principle is thought to be that in *Lewin v. Fuell* [1990] Crim.L.R. 658 where it was said that an oral disclaimer was incapable of negating a written false trade description. In contrast, the Divisional Court in *Bury Metropolitan Borough Council v. Real* [1993] C.O.D. 375 upheld the justices' view that the evidence pointed "overwhelmingly" to their conclusion that the oral negotiations made it clear that no trade description was applied to a motor vehicle by reason of the odometer reading. Similarly:

(i) On unusual facts in *R. v. Shrewsbury Crown Court, ex p. Venables* [1994] Crim.L.R. 61, the Divisional Court held that supply to a motor dealer who does not rely upon and is not affected by the odometer reading could neutralise its falsity by virtue of "the understanding between" the buyer and seller.

(ii) In *Kent County Council v. Price* (1993) 12 Tr.L. 137 an oral disclaimer, coupled with a notice describing T shirts bearing brand names as "Brand Copy", was sufficient to negate the effect of a false description.

Necessity and duress

9.9 It is not absolutely clear whether the common law defences of necessity and duress are always available to defendants charged with strict liability offences. Presumably, these defences may apply to statutory offences of full *mens rea*, insofar as they are not negated by the statutory provision giving rise to the offence.

9.10 Necessity. Necessity is synonymous with the expression "duress of circumstances" and is closely related to the defence of duress by threats (see paragraph 9.9 below). Although its precise scope is uncertain, it appears to be available only if, from an objective standpoint, the defendant can be said to be acting to avoid death or serious injury (*R. v. Willer* [1987] R.T.R. 22; *R. v. Conway* (1979) 88 Cr. App. R. 159; *R. v. North* (1979) 88 Cr. App. R. 343). In *R. v. Pommell* [1995] 2 Cr. App. R. 608, the Court of Appeal (Crim. Div.) accepted the comments of Professor Sir John Smith ([1992] Crim.L.R. 172 in relation to the decision in *R. v. Bell* [1992] R.T.R. 335) that:

> "All the cases so far concerned road traffic offences, but there are no grounds for supposing that the defence is limited to that kind of case. On the contrary, the defence, being closely related to the defence of duress by threats, appears to be general, applying to all crimes except murder, attempted murder and some forms of treason."

9.11 Absolute offences. To that list of exceptions, it may be necessary to add some absolute offences, despite that necessity has been recognised as a defence in at least some road traffic cases. In *Cichon v. DPP* [1994] Crim.L.R. 918, the Divisional Court held that there was no defence of necessity available in the case of a prosecution under the Dangerous Dogs Act 1991 for allowing a pit bull terrier to be in public place without a muzzle, even though the owner of a dog had removed the muzzle out of concern for the health of the dog. Because the prohibition was an absolute offence which did not allow the making of a value judgement between what was good for the dog and what was good for the public, the court concluded that Parliament could not have intended that a defence of necessity should apply. This reasoning is consistent with a notion that mistake and duress are defences which negate *mens rea* and so have no place where liability is strict. On the other hand, the Law Commission (Law Com. No. 218) described necessity as a defence where the defendant's freely adopted conduct was justified. Where the latter definition is adopted, it is hard to see why an absolute offence should prevent there being a defence of necessity at common law. In *DPP v. Harris* [1995] 1 Cr. App. R. 170, McCowan L.J. took the view that there was a defence of necessity to a charge of reckless driving, but inclined to think that there was no defence of necessity to the charge of driving without due care and attention, because the notion of "due" care took into account all the considerations including the necessity. Curtis J., on the other hand, thought that the defence of necessity should be available on the lesser charge because, if it was available for a more serious charge, there was no justification for its exclusion in relation to a lesser substitute.

9.12 Duress. Duress is fear of death or grievous bodily harm induced by threat or, perhaps, loss of liberty. It is not clear whether the threat must be to the defendant (*Lynch v. DPP for Northern Ireland* [1975] A.C. 653). This is an issue which rarely arises in regulatory cases. Self-defence is not considered for the same reason.

STATUTORY DEFENCES

The due diligence defence

General

9.13 Rules of attribution. Many regulatory offences now carry with them the opportunity for the defendant to prove on the balance of probabilities that he has satisfied certain criteria which entitle him to acquittal (often a "due diligence" defence). Where there is no due diligence defence, for example, because the offence itself contains the essence of the defence – such as an offence which is committed by conduct which is "without reasonable excuse" (see paragraph 9.46 below) the employer cannot necessarily evade liability by drawing a distinction between the "directing mind and will of the company" and the employee responsible for the misconduct (*R. v. British Steel plc* [1995] 1 W.L.R. 1356 and see paragraphs 7.33 onwards, above). In such circumstances, the employer is likely to be liable for the acts of the employee except where the offence charged makes it clear that the position is otherwise. Examples of the latter might be where the offence alleges expressly or inferentially that a company did not have a certain policy. An instance of implied provision might have been thought to be where it is alleged that an employer had failed to provide a safe system of work (section 2 of the Health and Safety at Work, etc., Act 1974). Arguably, this could be contrasted with a failure to conduct the undertaking safely – the charge faced by the defendant in *R. v. British Steel plc.* (above). The fact that an employee might not have complied with company rules so that an accident occurred would not mean that no sufficient system had been provided: it would merely mean that the employee had not followed it. The Court of Appeal rejected this argument in *R. v. Gateway Foodmarkets Ltd* [1997] 2 Cr. App. R.40, holding that the general purpose of the legislation was such that it should be interpreted as imposing liability on the employer even where the failure was that of an employee. Accordingly, the steps taken to guard against an accident "so far as is reasonably practicable" meant steps taken by the employer and employee on his employer's behalf.

The existence of a due diligence defence, on the other hand, is usually an indication that the rules of attribution are such that the conduct of a junior employee will not, in the context of the defence, be attributed to the employer. The absence of a due diligence defence in the Health and Safety at Work etc. Act 1974 was a factor which the Court of Appeal weighed very heavily in *R. v. British Steel plc.* (above).

9.14 Common form. A common modern form of the due diligence defence appears in Section 21(1) of the Food Safety Act 1990:

"In any proceedings for an offence [under . . . this Part . . .] it shall . . . be a defence for the person charged to prove that he took all reasonable precautions and exercised all due diligence to avoid the commission of the offence by himself or by a person under his control."

This form sets out the general principle, although the test is further expanded and exemplified by subsequent subsections.

9.15 General defence in two parts? Although the test is two-limbed, in practice a distinction is often difficult to draw between reasonable precautions and due diligence. The authorities rarely distinguish between the two notions. Indeed, in *Texas Homecare v. Stockport Metropolitan Borough Council* (1987) 152 J.P. 83, the Divisional Court rejected the contention that the defence under section 24(3) of the Trade Descriptions Act 1968 that a person "did not know or could not with reasonable diligence have ascertained" that a false trade description had been applied to goods imposed a lower standard than that of taking all reasonable precautions and exercising all due diligence. (This case has attracted some criticism, in particular that the earlier decision in *Baker v. Hargreaves* (1981) 125 Sol. Jo. 165, which deals with the difference between section 24(1) and (3), was not referred to (see [1987] Crim.L.R. 709 (note). The *Texas* case has been cited with approval in *R. v. Sutton and Khalil* (unreported, Transcript No. 95/4458/W5).

Generally, however, taking all reasonable precautions is understood to mean setting up a system which will avoid the commission of the offence and exercising all due diligence means taking such appropriate steps as will ensure that the system is implemented.

9.16 The form of the general defence is, in the Food Safety Act 1990, then expanded by examples of the way in which the general principle can be satisfied, and in particular may address the test to be applied where the defendant alleges that the offence was caused by someone who was not under his control. In the Food Safety Act 1990, these further illustrations encompass some of the factual situations which are spelt out in some earlier legislation as matters which must be proved in addition to the due diligence element (for the meaning of which see paragraphs 9.19 onwards, below). Section 21 provides:

"(2) Without prejudice to the generality of subsection (1) above, a person charged with an offence under section 8, 14 or 15 above who neither-

(a) prepared the food in respect of which the offence is alleged to have been committed; nor

(b) imported it into Great Britain,

shall be taken to have established the defence provided by that subsection if he satisfies the requirements of subsection (3) or (4) below.

(3) A person satisfies the requirements of this subsection if he proves-

(a) that the commission of the offence was due to an act or default of another person who was not under his control, or to reliance on information supplied by such a person;

(b) that he carried out all such checks of the food in question as were reasonable, or that it was reasonable in all the circumstances for him to rely on checks carried out by the person who supplied the food to him; and

(c) that he did not know and had no reason to suspect at the time of the commission of the alleged offence that his act or omission would amount to an offence under the relevant provision.

(4) A person satisfies the requirements of this subsection if he proves -

(a) that the commission of the offence was due to an act or default of another person who was not under his control, or to reliance on information supplied by such a person;

(b) that the sale or intended sale of which the alleged offence consisted was not a sale or intended sale under his name or mark; and

(c) that he did not know and could not reasonably have been expected to know, at the time of the commission of the alleged offence that his act or omission would amount to an offence under the relevant provision."

Burden and standard of proof

9.17 Evidence. The burden of proving a due diligence defence lies on the defendant. The standard is that he must show on the balance of probabilities that he has satisfied the statutory criteria (*R. v. Carr Briant* [1943] K.B. 607, *Robertson v. Watson* (1949) J.C. 73, *R. v. Jenkins* (1923) 87 J.P. 115, *R. v. Swaysland* [1987] B.T.L.C. 299, but compare *Cant v. Hartley & Sons Ltd* [1938] 2 All E.R. 768). This requirement will almost invariably mean that the defendant must give evidence in order to establish the defence, but see *Westminster City Council v. Turner & Gow* (1984) 4 Tr.L. 130 where the defendant was acquitted by magistrates on the grounds of due diligence without having given evidence. The Divisional Court held that the defendant was entitled to rely on evidence given by other parties (particularly, in this case, their employee who was convicted).

9.18 Expert evidence. In some cases the onus of calling evidence will require the defendant to call evidence not only as to what he has done but also to the standard to be applied to what he has done. This is now acknowledged to be the case where the due diligence defence rests on the sampling of goods. Expert evidence should in nearly all cases be called to show that there is a statistical significance in the sample chosen. Proof can be made by calling an expert in the field. So, in *Dudley Metropolitan Borough Council v. Roy Firmin Ltd* (1992) unreported (CO/1541/91), where the defendant wished to show that it had taken all reasonable precautions and exercised all due diligence to import only goods which complied with an inflammability requirement, the Divisional Court restored the conviction of the magistrates (overturned in the Crown Court) on the ground that the defence should have called independent statistical evidence to prove that the sample of goods tested was adequate. In *P & M Supplies (Essex) Ltd v. Devon County Council* (1991) 156 J.P. 328 the Divisional Court expressed the same view. Where there is a relevant British Standard for the number of samples, that may be referred to (*London Borough of Sutton v. David Halsall plc* (1994) 14 Tr.L.R. 2). In the last-mentioned case the Divisional Court remitted the matter for sentencing because the method of testing did not comply with the British Standard. Compliance with a British Standard must not, however, be substituted for compliance with the legislative requirement (*Balding v. Lew Ways Ltd* (1995) 14 Tr.L.R. 344).

The nature of the defence

9.19 Diligence a question of fact. There is no legal standard of diligence: it is always a question of fact (*R. C. Hammett Ltd. v. Crabb* (1931) 145 L.T. 638). The Divisional Court or Court of Appeal will intervene (see Chapter 11 below) only if there is insufficient evidence to support a finding of fact (*Rogers v. Barlow & Son* (1906) 94 L.T. 519; *R. C. Hammett Ltd v. Beldam* (1931) 95 J.P. 180; *Pearce v. Cullen* (1952) 96 Sol. Jo. 132). In the Court of Appeal the conviction must be rendered "unsafe" before it can be overturned. Each case must turn on its own facts because what is reasonable will depend on individual circumstances so that, for example, Neill L.J., in finding that there was an obligation for the defendant retailers to make inquiry as to the precautions taken by their suppliers in a case where they had received and sold frozen steak wrongly described as "rump" (it was an inferior cut known as "silverside"), hinted that the size and organisation of the defendant business might in another case vary so as to make the failure to inquire other than "a glaring gap in the evidence adduced by the respondent company" (*Amos v. Melcon (Frozen Foods) Ltd* (1985) 149 J.P. 712). The risk to the public interest if there is a non-compliance may also be a relevant factor.

9.20 Proving the steps. It is unlikely ever to be sufficient to do nothing, however (*Sutton London Borough v. Percy* (1971) 135 J.P. 239), so a defendant must always be in a position to prove something positive about his procedures, even where that procedure involves reliance on another. In *Riley v. Webb* (1987) 151 J.P. 372 the defendants had obtained a blanket assurance from their supplier that all goods supplied would comply with statutory requirements, and had made observance a condition of their contract. It was held that reliance on a blanket assurance of another was insufficient, although the court suggested that if a specific assurance relating to the goods in question had been obtained by the retailer, the test might have been satisfied (also see paragraph 9.27 below). A similar instance under the Control of Pollution Act 1974 arose in *Durham City Council v. Connors (Peter) Industrial Services Ltd, The Independent,* June 4, 1992, where the court held that a contractor who collects waste from others cannot benefit from a due diligence defence in respect of the disposal of toxic waste if he did not ask about the nature of the waste collected.

9.21 Who must be diligent? Where the defendant is a company, the diligence must generally have been exercised by a person or persons embodying the directing mind and will of the company (*Tesco Supermarkets Ltd. v. Nattrass* [1972] A.C. 153). An employee, even an employee in a managerial capacity such as the store manager in *Tesco v. Nattrass* (above), can be "another person" for the purposes of the defence although, of course, he will be a person who is under the control of the defendant.

9.22 Blaming an employee. Where the defendant wishes to allege that the offence was due to the conduct of his employee, he will need to adduce evidence proving that his employee was properly selected, trained and supervised (*Knowsley Metropolitan Borough Council v. Cowan* (1991) 156 J.P. 45, and paragraph 9.27 below). Moreover, wherever the statute requires that notice be given to the prosecutor of a person whose "act or default" is said to have occasioned the offence, the employer must in most circumstances ensure that notice is given naming the employee as the true perpetrator (for occasions where the notice must be served, see paragraphs 9.28 to 9.32 below).

Risk assessment systems and due diligence

9.23 Risk assessment. It is not clear, however, how comfortably the principles appropriate to due diligence defences (for which see paragraph 9.26, below), and indeed the strict statutory language, lie with the "risk assessment" approach derived from European directives and embraced in much modern regulatory provision which involve dangers to health and safety. This is an important consideration, because new regulations may implement the "risk assessment" approach, yet leave available the statutory due diligence test in the event of infringement of considerations of "sufficiency" or "adequacy" of the actions of the defendant. This can be illustrated by reference to, say, the Food Safety (General Food Hygiene) Regulations 1995.

9.24 The Contrast. The "risk assessment" approach requires the employer to carry out an assessment of areas of his operation to identify those circumstances in which maximum controls are required so as not to constitute a danger to the public. Where the operation is less hazardous, lesser controls can be implemented. In relation to food safety in particular, the system implemented in this way is often known as a HACCP system – Hazard Analysis and Critical Control Points. Almost by definition, the carrying out of a risk assessment, and graduating the response in accordance with the degree of seriousness of a risk is a displacement of the literal offence/due diligence approach to the employer's responsibilities. The first has in mind an appraisal of the business activities of the employer with an overall objective of safety. The second is a piecemeal approach, with avoidance of individual, often related, but sometimes unrelated offences as its aim. The only manner in which it is permissible to prioritise activities in the "due diligence scheme" is by reference to the concept of "reasonableness" or appropriateness ("due") – it being perhaps reasonable and appropriate to take some steps and not others.

9.25 Tensions. In some areas, these two approaches co-exist in a way which reveals the unsatisfactory nature of the graft. Food Safety is an example and two instances may serve to illustrate the nature of the problem.

Regulation 4(3) of the Food Safety (General Food Hygiene) Regulations 1995 requires that the food proprietor undertakes an assessment of the risks inherent in his processes. Regulation 4(3) provides:

> "A proprietor of a food business shall identify any step in the activities of the food business which is critical to ensuring food safety and ensure that adequate safety procedures are identified, implemented, maintained and reviewed on the basis of the following principles —
>
> (a) analysis of the potential food hazards in a food business operation;
>
> (b) identification of the points in those operations where food hazards may occur;
>
> (c) deciding which of the points identified are critical to ensuring food safety ("critical points");
>
> (d) identification and implementation of effective control and monitoring procedures at those critical points; and

(e) review of the analysis of food hazards, the critical points and the control and monitoring procedures periodically and whenever the food business's operations change."

Provisions which are designed to guide the conduct of enforcement officers and afford a protection to those required to operate HACCP appear in the regulations. Regulation 8 provides:

"(2) In executing and enforcing these Regulations, a food authority shall-

    (a) ensure that-

        (i) food premises are inspected with a frequency which has regard to the risk associated with those premises, and

        (ii) inspections include a general assessment of the potential food safety hazards associated with the food business being inspected;

    (b) pay particular attention to the critical control points identified by food businesses to assess whether the necessary monitoring and verification controls are being operated;

    (c) give due consideration to whether the proprietor of a food business has acted in accordance with any relevant guide to good hygiene practice which has been-

        (i) forwarded by the Secretary of State to the Commission pursuant to Article 5.5 of the Directive [Council Directive 93 No. 43 of June 14, 1993 on the hygiene of foodstuffs] unless the Secretary of State has announced that it no longer complies with article 3 of the Directive, or

        (ii) developed in accordance with article 5.6 and 7 of the Directive and published in accordance with Article 5.8 of the Directive."

Paragraph (c) of the Regulations does not provide a defence in its own right, but enables the non-statutory guides to be referred to in conjunction with a due diligence defence. No doubt the obligation of the food authority to concentrate on the critical control points may also serve to focus attention on the risk assessment rather than due diligence approach. Notwithstanding this, the requirements of the due diligence defence and particularly the requirement that "all" reasonable precautions and due diligence is taken, appear to demand a more concentrated approach to each potential offence, rather than to the risks appropriate to the process. This problem is exacerbated where the risk assessment approach has consequences for ancillary legislation. For example, regulation 44(d) of the Food Labelling Regulations 1996 makes it an offence to sell food after a "use by" date relating to it. The Food Labelling Regulations 1996 apply, *inter alia*, section 21 of the Food Safety Act 1990 (the due diligence defence). This has the consequence that whereas the statutory defence requires that all due diligence and all reasonable precautions should be exercised to avoid the commission of *that* offence, the circumstances giving rise to the offence may have been classified as of low risk under the risk assessment, such that virtually no steps outside ordinary operations have been deemed necessary. By reference to established cases and guideline principles (see below), taking no steps to avoid the offence charged would seem to be inappropriate and would not appear to give rise to a defence. An example of how this could arise (and some food outlets have, it appears, followed the policy outlined below) is as follows:

Gloria Supermarkets Ltd have a policy of attaching a "use by" date to all their foodstuffs, notwithstanding that some food is of a longer shelf life than that for which a "use by" date is frequently used. It is an offence to sell food after the "use by" date has expired. There is no offence of selling food after a "best before" marking has expired. Gloria Supermarket's management's purpose is to guarantee maximum stock rotation and ensure that greater care is taken by staff. But because the food is, in fact, not causative of a danger to the consumer if eaten after the use by date, the HACCP practices appropriate to high risk foods (such as the keeping of written records, individual responsibility by staff, etc.) are not adopted. The "HACCP" factor shows a low risk (because the food could have been classified as longer life, and is safe) but there are clearly more steps which could have been taken *to avoid the commission of the offence* and an offence under the Food Labelling Regulations 1996 has, arguably, been committed.

How is the court to approach this? It is submitted that the approach of the courts to this issue needs to be sufficiently imaginative to distinguish the guideline principles applicable to conventional situations from those different considerations which arise in the "risk assessment" arena. It is a difficulty inherent in the governance of regulatory standards in criminal courts, that the court does not enjoy the overview which makes this sort of decision easier to make. The decision-maker (particularly if a lay magistrate or judge: stipendiary magistrates can attain a greater degree of familiarity with the subject matter) may have no framework of comparable situations within which to place the issue which it has to decide. The court is asked by the prosecution to concentrate its attention to a single issue. The principles to be gleaned from existing caselaw and academic writers are easy to deduce. The reasons for the departure from those principles are significantly more difficult and may involve reliance on argument as to the efficacy of procedures and expertise which is outside the spotlight shone by the prosecution on the offence itself. This tension can only be to the disadvantage of businesses, and not clearly to the advantage of the consumer.

The HACCP system is one of systematised reasoning. Where a food proprietor is responsible for production of food it occasions a careful look at risks of the recipe, the cooking, handling, presenting and keeping the food, among other considerations. The proprietor of a food business commits an offence by virtue of regulation 6 if he fails to comply with regulation 4(3). But what is the offence envisaged by regulation 4(3)? Its language contains three mandatory elements:

  (i) to identify any step in the activities of the food business which is critical to ensuring food safety;

 (ii) to ensure that adequate safety procedures are:

    (a) identified

    (b) implemented

    (c) maintained

    (d) reviewed

(iii) on the basis of the HACCP principles set out in the above paragraph.

It follows that it is not "offence" but "offences" which are envisaged by regulation 4(3) – at least 6 of them, and perhaps more. These should be charged separately by individual informations under the regulations. What if there is a slip-up and a customer is poisoned? Will that be an offence of failing to implement and maintain an adequate safety procedure? If so, will a due diligence defence (applied to the offence by regulation 7) assist? It must be very doubtful whether the due diligence defence has anything to add to the notion of "adequacy" contained in the offence itself. How can a defendant have taken all reasonable precautions if the hygiene procedures themselves are inadequate? If they are not inadequate, no offence has been committed. Food proprietors should not be disconsolate, yet, however. It remains to be established whether the burden of proving inadequacy will lie on the prosecution (see Chapter 6 above). If it does, the defendant may be in a better position than he would be if he were left to utilise the due diligence defence. The issues in which the failure is alleged would need to be made clear to the court in the course of the prosecution opening, and it would not be left to the magistrates (or jury) to determine whether they are satisfied on every single one of the vast range of issues which have to be raised as part of a conventional due diligence defence and are put in the course of cross-examination (see Chapter 10 below for considerations of procedure).

Guideline due diligence principles

9.26 Diligence and Precautions. The precautions to be taken depend upon the subject matter in question, the size and resources of the defendant, the risk to be guarded against and all the other circumstances. Notwithstanding that different considerations must apply in different cases, a number of relevant considerations are addressed repeatedly in authorities concerned with due diligence defences to trading offences. It is important, however, not to omit the requirement of reasonableness in considering the guidelines set out below. The test is not that *all* precautions and *all* diligence must be taken and observed, but that all *reasonable* precautions and *due* diligence should be taken (see, for instance, the emphasis on this point in *Carrick v. Taunton Vale Meat Co. Ltd* (1994) 158 J.P. 347).

9.27 Guideline principles. These include the following:

(1) *Identifiable system:* there should be an identifiable "due diligence" system in operation. Good systems:

    (a) involve taking appropriate care in the selection, regular instruction and supervision of staff (*Knowsley Metropolitan Borough Council v. Cowan* (1991) 156 J.P. 45; *Baxters (Butchers) Ltd v. Manley* (1985) 4 Tr. Law 219);

    (b) are written down, so that staff can refer to them. The books or manuals recording the system should also be available to the staff for reference when required. Copies of the book kept at Head Office only, or at the owner's home, may be of little assistance, and the mere sending of changes of staff instructions to outlets of the business with no instructions for managers may be insufficient (*Baxters (Butchers v. Manley* (above);

    (c) should cover all aspects of the business subject to regulation and must be implemented;

    (d) should be flexible; for example, a failure to give information to employees about a fault in production precluded successful reliance on the defence (*Bucknall v. F. W. Stevenson Ltd* (1948) DC, unreported);

(e) should involve checks by senior staff and records kept of those checks (*Baxters (Butchers) Ltd v. Manley* (1984) above).

(f) should demonstrate a chain of supervision from senior management to junior staff (*Amos v. Melcom (Frozen Foods) Ltd* [1985] 149 J.P. 712; *Horner v. Sherwoods of Darlington Ltd* (1989) 154 J.P. 299; *R.C. Hammett Ltd v. London County Council* (1933) 49 T.L.R. 209);

(g) require that the responsibilities of directors, managers and employees should be stated in writing and acknowledged by them;

(h) must identify faults and correct them (*McGuire v. Sittingbourne Co-operative Society Ltd* (1976) 140 J.P. 306);

(2) *Assessment of Risks:* Notwithstanding the difficulties addressed above, the due diligence system should usually, even in the absence of a statutory requirement to do so, address an assessment of the risk of infringement of the law. Where statute requires an assessment of risks to health or safety, this assessment must have been carried out adequately, and the due diligence defence will fail if it has not been (see paragraph 9.23 onwards, above).

(3) *Published advice:* Even in the absence of a statutory requirement to have regard to other publications (such as that envisaged by regulation 8(2)(c) of the Food Safety (General Food Hygiene) Regulations 1995), regard should be had to published advice about due diligence systems, where available. This must be so in particular where there is an industry code which has been backed by the Office of Fair Trading (see paragraphs 1.16 above), but also in other situations. For example, LACOTS has produced many guidance documents such as "Due Diligence Guidance on Package Travel" in 1994, the Health and Safety Executive produce guidance in many spheres and in the area of food, voluntary industry guides to good hygiene practices have been developed by trade associations, such as the National Association of Master Bakers, the British Retail Consortium, the National Association of British Market Authorities, etc.

(4) *Reasonable precautions must be taken:* The standard is a high one, but the court must not confuse the taking of *all* precautions with the taking of *all reasonable* precautions (*Carrick v. Taunton Vale Meat Co. Ltd* (1994) 158 J.P. 347). An dramatic illustration of this difference also arose in relation to the service of a prohibition notice under the Health and Safety at Work etc. Act 1974. In this, a prohibition notice was served on Howlett's zoo following the death of a zookeeper which occurred when he was cleaning the tiger's enclosure. It was the policy of Howlett's zoo to allow their tigers to roam freely, whereas the local authority contended that Howletts could have secured the tigers during the cleaning process. The High Court affirmed the decision of the Industrial Tribunal to set aside the notice because the statutory intention was not to render all dangerous working practices illegal (*Howlett's and Port Lympne Estates Ltd v. Langridge* (unreported) January 29, 1996). Any reasonable precaution

which can be taken, however, must be taken (*Marshall v. Herbert* 1963 Crim.L.R. 506; *Garrett v. Boots the Chemists Ltd* (1980) DC unreported; *Marshall v. Herbert* [1963] Crim.L.R. 506). In *Gale v. Dixon Stores Group* (1994) 6 Admin. L.R. 497 the Divisional Court found that a procedure which was put in place after the commission of the offence would have been a reasonable precaution to have taken beforehand, even though the magistrates had dismissed the information. Indeed, prospective defendants should be warned that putting a procedure into place after an incident may be relied upon by the prosecutor as evidence of "shutting the stable door after the horse has bolted", although failure to correct a mistake will be an illustration of an absence of due diligence. In *Oldham Metropolitan Borough v. First Choice Travel Ltd* (1997) 105 I.T.S.A. 1 M.R. 24, a holiday company which discovered an error in its brochure price had not exercised due diligence to prevent the offence of failing to give the true price of a package holiday, contrary to the Package Travel Regulations, because it had not issued and circulated an erratum slip.

(5) *Reliance:* Total reliance cannot be placed on warranties or general assurances from suppliers and others although some measure of reliance is impossible to avoid. Indeed, many due diligence defences make references to reliance upon information supplied by another.

Where there is reliance on, say, a supplier, the reliability of his assurances should, where possible, have been assessed (see paragraph 9.20 above). In this context, the standard of enquiry to be expected of the owner of a corner shop will be very different from that expected of a chain of superstores. In some statutes, such as the Food Safety Act 1990, s.21, the case for reliance is spelled out. In section 21(3) anyone other than an importer or manufacturer can satisfy the due diligence test if he shows that the act or default was due to someone not under his control and that he either carried out reasonable checks or that it was reasonable to rely upon the checks carried out by his supplier. Moreover, he must not know or have reason to suspect that his act or omission would be an offence (*Hicks v. S. D. Sullam* (1983) 147 J.P. 493). In the last-mentioned case, the Court drew particular attention to the fact that the supplier's agent who had purportedly carried out tests on which the defendant had relied was outside the jurisdiction in the Far East. See also *Garrett v. Boots the Chemists Ltd* (above); *Sherratt v. Geralds the American Jewellers* (1970) 114 Sol. Jo. 147; *Hurley v. Martinez & Co. Ltd* (1990) 154 J.P. 821 (where the Divisional Court declined to upset the magistrates' acquittal, stating that the question to be asked in the case of a retailer of wines was whether the risk of the offence which had been committed (alcoholic content wrongly stated on the label on the bottle) was so large as to demand that a small local supplier should arrange for sampling – particularly bearing in mind the nature and expense of analysis and the number of lines which would need to be tested).

The defence of due diligence introduced by the General Product Safety Regulations 1994, implementing the Product Safety Directive, Dir. 92/59, similarly makes clear that reliance upon information provided by someone else will be insufficient unless reliance was reasonable in all the circumstances.

(6) *Sufficiency of testing:* Where the testing of the safety or compliance of a product is of relevance, the tests must be sufficient. In *Rotheram Metropolitan Borough Council v. Rayson (U.K.) Ltd* (1989) 153 J.P. 37 the sample of crayons tested for its lead content was too small and the system was unsatisfactory because the analyst only reported to the defendant if he found a fault. This meant that the defendant could not be reassured that the sampling had been carried out unless he heard of a fault. He therefore had evidence of non-compliance, but not of compliance to the requisite standard. Where a sampling system is relied upon, it seems that expert evidence is necessary to prove the adequacy of the sample (see paragraph 9.18 above).

(7) *Reliance on prosecutor no defence:* It is not sufficient to rely upon the prosecutor, but paradoxically it may also be insufficient if his advice is not sought on the issue giving rise to the offence. In *Taylor v. Lawrence Fraser (Bristol) Ltd* (1977) 121 Sol. Jo. 757 an importer supplied a shop with a toy which had too high a lead content. He did not carry out tests himself but relied upon a contention that his premises were opposite a trading standards department which had taken samples from time to time. It was held that he was not entitled to shuffle off his responsibility on to the enforcement authority. On the other hand, in *Coventry City Council v. Lazarus* [1996] C.C.L.R. 5, the Respondent was charged with a breach of the Consumer Credit (Advertising) Regulations 1989 in relation to certain advertisements. The Respondent's defence was that he relied upon legal advice provided by the Retail Motor Industry Federation and had exercised all due diligence. The Divisional Court remitted the case to the magistrates with a direction to convict because, although the court accepted that legal advice was information for the purposes of the defence section, the Respondent had not exercised due diligence because he could have sought the advice of the Trading Standards Department before publication.

An additional consideration, particularly where a business has a number of outlets, is that satisfaction by one authority with a due diligence system can be evidence as to the reasonableness of the system. It is not unknown for a defendant to call a local authority witness, perhaps from the Home Authority of the business (if there is one) to testify as to the adequacy of the system in place in circumstances where another local authority has expressed dissatisfaction. Indeed, this is a factor which it appears in practice that the magistrates may weigh heavily.

(8) *Disclaimer:* Where an offence concerns a false description to which a disclaimer could have been applied, the failure to give a disclaimer or warning is likely to be treated as a failure to use all reasonable precautions (see paragraph 9.3, above).

(9) *Employees:* Where an employee is prosecuted for an act or default which has occasioned the employer to commit the offence, what standards must he achieve to establish a due diligence defence? Will it be enough if he establishes that he complied with his employer's inadequate instructions, or that he was not told by his employer to remedy an unsatisfactory situation? The answer must depend on the facts in each case.

Notice of an allegation of act or default

9.28 Notice to the prosecution. It is common for legislation to provide that where the defence involves an allegation that the offence was committed because of the act or default of another or sometimes because of reliance on another, notice must be given to the prosecution. Failure to give the notice will preclude the defendant from relying upon the defence unless the Court gives leave. An example is Section 39(2) of the Consumer Protection Act 1987:

> "Where in any proceedings against any person [for an offence to which this section applies] the defence [that he took all reasonable precautions and exercised all due diligence to avoid committing the offence] involves an allegation that the commission of the offence was due–
>
> (a) to the act or default of another; or
>
> (b) to reliance on information given by another,
>
> that person shall not, without the leave of the Court, be entitled to rely on the defence unless, not less than seven clear days before the hearing of the proceedings he has served a notice . . . on the person bringing the proceedings".

It should be noted that not all requirements to give notice are as relaxed. The requirement for notice specified in some other provisions, *e.g.* the Food Safety Act 1990, provides that notice must be given at least seven clear days before the hearing *and*, if the defendant has previously appeared before a court in connection with the offence (*i.e.* there has been an earlier remanded hearing) within one month of his first appearance. In relation to the latter requirement, presumably if there is an adjournment of the case in the absence of either the defendant or his lawyer, the one month period will not begin to run, but if the lawyer attends although the remand is otherwise in the absence of the defendant, time will run – attendance of the lawyer being treated as the attendance of the defendant for this purpose. Since the purpose of this provision is to enable the prosecution to take steps to interview the third party and, where appropriate, proceed against him (see paragraphs 7.81 onwards, above) the introduction of this requirement may prevent in some cases notice being served after the expiry of a time limit (see paragraphs 8.15 to 8.24) within which to prosecute the true defaulter.

In the rare case where the offence is said to have been caused by the wholly legitimate conduct of another person (including an employee), so that there is (arguably) no "act or default" (see paragraph 7.87 above) it would seem to follow that (again, arguably) no notice need be served. There is no authority on the matter. In a case where this issue might arise, there may be a balance to be drawn between the perceived tactical advantage of "keeping the Defendant's powder dry" and the risk that in due course the court might determine that "act or default" in this provision merely describes causation, and so not permit the relevant evidence to be given or might decline to be persuaded by it because no notice had been served.

9.29 Requirements of the notice. The notice under the Consumer Protection Act 1987 is required to "give such information identifying or assisting the identification of the person who committed the act or default or gave the information as is in the possession of the person serving the notice at the time he serves it". Comparable requirements exist under other legislation, although not always spelled out in so detailed a fashion.

9.30 Discretion if notice out of time. There is little authority upon the exercise by the justices of the discretion to allow the defence to be raised notwithstanding the failure to serve a notice at the required time. If there is no prejudice to the prosecution, it is unlikely that leave would be refused, and, indeed, refusal of leave would be difficult to justify in the light of the object of the provision. If the only prejudice suffered by the prosecution is loss of the opportunity to proceed against the third party, the position is more difficult. It is submitted that where the prosecutor is able to interview a third party and, if appropriate, call him as a witness in rebuttal or as part of the prosecution case, it is appropriate to grant leave, even though that third party could not be prosecuted because the time for commencement of the proceedings had expired. It is hard to see that the inability of the prosecutor to pursue a third party could be a justification for refusing to the defendant an opportunity fully to put his defence, at least in the absence of bad faith on the part of the defendant.

In *R. v. Redbridge Justices, ex p. London Borough of Redbridge* (1983) 2 T.L.R. 43 only five days notice was given although this was not commented upon by the Divisional Court. In *Coupe v. Bush* (unreported, CO 2915-96) a magistrates' court gave a defendant leave to raise a due diligence defence even after he had given evidence and been cross-examined. This procedure led the court into difficulties, however. The court refused the prosecutor leave to address the court on the due diligence defence raised (see paragraphs 10.83 to 10.87 below for the procedure in the magistrates' court), which decision was criticised by the Divisional Court, and led to the remission of the case for re-determination by another bench. The fact that no notice had been given, and, more importantly, the fact that the defence was not raised in evidence before the defendant left the witness box meant that the prosecution should have been given an opportunity to address the justices on the defence thus raised.

9.31 Adequacy of the notice. The adequacy of the notice has been the subject of judicial consideration. The defendant must give such information as he has, but he must properly have investigated. In *McGuire v. Sittingbourne Co-operative Society Ltd* (1976) 140 J.P. 306 the company pleaded that the offence was committed by one or more of the shop staff and named all the assistants involved. The Court found that there was insufficient investigation and that the defendant could not therefore establish the defence. In the *Redbridge Justices* case (above) the notice read "It is impossible for the defendant company to identify precisely the person concerned and . . . it was one or another of the persons named hereunder who were . . . employees at the defendant company's store". The Magistrates found that the defence was made out. In *Malcolm v. Cheek* [1947] 2 All E.R. 881 the name of a former employee was given although he could not be traced and was thought to be abroad. This was adequate.

9.32 Prosecuting the true defaulter. Where the prosecution decide to proceed against a person named in a defendant's notice as well as the person originally summoned, considerable complications can arise, particularly if the person whose act or default is said to have occasioned the offence, was to have been a witness for the original defendant. It is not uncommon in regulatory offences where an employer is blaming a member of his staff for an error, that the employee is invited to come to give evidence for the employer, admitting his mistake. This consideration has been known to have prompted the prosecutor to lay an information against the employees too, for the purpose of putting pressure on employers to abandon their defence. Commencing criminal proceedings against individuals for this purpose is, it is submitted, an abuse of process. There can, of course, be no objection to the commencement of proceedings against individuals where the prosecuting authority considers them to be to blame and the public interest justifies such approach. The prosecutor must be careful to reflect upon whether a decision to prosecute is justified. Failure to do so may result in an adverse costs order (see Chapter 13 below). Secondly, the prosecutor must be confident that he has sufficient evidence implicating the person named in the defendant's notice to persuade the court that there is a case to answer

Where the employee is also prosecuted, this may not only set up a conflict of interest between the employee and the employer, but where the trials of the employee and employer are then to be heard together, the employee will not be compellable as a witness on behalf of the employer. In addition, even if the trials are not joined, the employee will have a privilege against self-incrimination and need answer no questions which tend to incriminate him. Unlike the early form of third party proceedings where the person named was joined by the defendant (see paragraph 7.83 above for an example), the prosecutor must be able to prove his case against each new defendant. This will usually mean that the new defendant should have been interviewed under caution, although other direct evidence may be sufficient. Clearly, an interview under caution by another employee speaking on behalf of the company cannot be admissible against any new defendant unless the allegations contained in the interview are repeated by a witness or in an admissible document as direct evidence in the case (see paragraph 3.27 above).

Elements and ancillary requirements of the due diligence defence

9.33 As has been seen above (paragraph 9.14), the due diligence element of the defence may not stand alone, but may either specify or encompass other notions which should be satisfied. Clearly when the legislation specifies that the defendant must prove a particular aspect which might otherwise be treated as a part of the due diligence test, the defence cannot be proved unless the particular consideration is proved. Where the legislation merely refers to the general standard of due diligence, the test may in theory be satisfied even though the elements customarily part of the test are not. The particular elements are set out below.

Act or default of another person

9.34 Act or default. It is thought that where a person is to be prosecuted as a third party for his act or default, only a wrongful act or default would suffice (see paragraph 7.87 above). A wrongful act is one which involves the commission of an offence, but it is not clear whether a third party who would have a defence of due diligence can be regarded as an actor or defaulter for the purposes of the defence run by a primary offender. It is hard to see why the blame to be attached to another should be material. If a third party has innocently (say) supplied defective goods to a retailer, having perhaps unknowingly acquired it himself in a defective condition from his supplier, the retailer is not the more culpable by reason of the third party's innocence. In contrast it is not a defence merely because a third party is also at fault (*Padgett v. Coventry City Council* (1998) 106 I.T.S.A. 5 M.R. 24; *Tarleton v. Nattress* [1973] 1 W.L.R. 1261).

9.35   **Another person.**   "Another person" may be:

(i)   an unknown person (but see *McGuire v. Sittingbourne* [1976] 140 J.P. 306);

(ii) a supplier, importer, inspector, examiner, wholesaler or any other person in the chain of supply. Some considerations which apply to independent contractors may also apply to those with a direct contractual relationship;

(iii) an independent contractor: unlike an employee, an independent contractor is a person who may not be under the control of a defendant. Just as an employee may, by operational requirements and the contract of employment, be controlled, so may an independent contractor in some circumstances. The degree of control will depend upon the relationship, bargaining position, relative skills and other expertise of the parties to the contract. It follows from this that the due diligence requirements may be stringent even in relation to the acts of independent contractors.

(iv) an employee (*Tesco Supermarkets Ltd v. Nattrass* [1972] A.C. 153) other than a director, manager, secretary or similar officer who represents the directing mind and will of the company. If there is no system of supervision of the employee, a due diligence defence will not be made out (*R. C. Hammett Ltd v. London C.C.* (1933) 49 T.L.R. 209; *Alex Munro (Butchers) Ltd v. Carmichael* [1990] S.C.C.R. 275; contrast *Lewin v. Ratnersthorpe Road Garage Ltd* (1984) 148 J.P. 87 where adoption of a Code of Practice and instruction of salesmen in its operation together with regular meetings reinforcing the importance of its observance was sufficient).

It is important, however, correctly to identify the person with the responsibility for the act or default complained of. Where a third party has been an agent of another, it may be his principal that is the person responsible and to be named, rather than the agent (*Lester v. Balfour Williamson Merchant Shippers Ltd* [1953] 2 Q.B. 168).

Reliance on information supplied to him

9.36   **Reliance.**   A due diligence defence will not be proved merely by stating that there has been a reliance on another (*Naish v. Gore* [1971] 3 All E.R. 737 and cases cited in paragraphs 9.27 above). That said, a person who has relied on information furnished by another better equipped to give the information may reasonably have done so, and the more limited the resources of the defendant, the more reasonable the reliance on another. Also see *Coventry City Council v. Lazarus* [1996] C.C.L.R. 5 and paragraph 9.27(7) above.

Mistake

9.37   **Mistake.**   Where the statutory provisions make reference to a mistake, as, for instance, in Section 24(1)(c) of the Trade Descriptions Act 1968, the mistake envisaged is one of fact. A mistake as to the law cannot found a defence (*Stone v. Burn* [1911] 1 K.B. 927; *Allard v. Selfridge & Co. Ltd* [1925] 1 K.B. 129). A mistake is an act done unintentionally (*per* Viscount Caldicut L.J. in *Mercer v. Pyramid Sand and Gravel Co.* [1944] 109 J.P. 54). Unlike the "act or default of another" defence, it must be made by the person charged with the offence and not by someone under his control (*Walkling Ltd v. Robinson* [1929] All E.R. 658;

Hall v. Farmer [1970] 1 All E.R. 729). In *Birkenhead District Co-operative Society v. Roberts* [1970] 1 W.L.R. 1497, the company could not rely to establish the mistake made upon the act of an assistant who applied the wrong label.

Accident or some other cause beyond the defendant's control

9.38 Accident. The notion of accident as a defence is not re-enacted in contemporary legislation, although it lingers on the statute book, for example in the Trade Descriptions Act 1968 as well as other less frequently litigated provisions (such as Section 18 of the Agriculture and Horticulture Act 1964).

9.39 Cause beyond control. Considerations of control, on the other hand, always arise in due diligence defences, however expressed. Reference has already been made to the acts of persons who may be beyond the control of the defendant. In *R. v. Swaysland* [1987] B.T.L.C. 299 an advertiser was charged when an advertisement placed by him was muddled by the local newspaper so that the wrong headings related to the products promoted. The advertiser had had no opportunity to correct the copy, so that the matter was beyond his control and he was entitled to acquittal. An example of computer error could fall within this category too; see, for example, the defence in *Berkshire County Council v. Olympic Holidays* (1994) 158 J.P.N. 337, where it was said that the computer may have malfunctioned and no other explanation could be offered. Due diligence was established.

Retailer's defences

9.40 Special defences. Regulatory legislation frequently has in its sights a particular class of trader whose standards are to be maintained by the use of the sanctions afforded in the statute. Those whose conduct is to be governed, but who may not be in a position to achieve the outcome desired by legislators, may have the benefit of special defences, or may be permitted to prove the due diligence defence by establishing a lesser number of criteria. Subsection (3) and (4) of section 21 of the Food Safety Act 1990 (paragraph 9.16 above) are an example of this. The defence is intended to benefit, in particular but not exclusively, retailers of food. In the case of retailers who allege reliance on another or the act or default of another, what is to be proved and what need not be proved depends on whether the sale is to be under the name or mark of the defendant. If it is, the defendant needs to have carried out checks on the food or to prove that it is reasonable for him to rely on his suppliers' checks, and prove too that he did not know and had no reason to suspect that anything he did would occasion the offence. If the food is not sold under his name or mark the defendant needs to prove that he did not know and could not reasonably have been expected to know that he would occasion the offence. A similar provision exists under section 10 of the Consumer Protection Act 1987, where it is a defence to the sale of goods contravening the general safety requirement that the goods were supplied in the course of a retail business and the supplier neither knew nor had reason to believe that the goods did not comply.

9.41 Did not know and had no reason to believe. Notwithstanding that these provisions give rise to an apparently lesser test, retailers cannot be complacent. In *Old Barn Nurseries v. Oxer* (1994) (unreported) CO 1764–94, appellants who were found to have breached the general safety requirement under section 10 of the Consumer Protection Act 1987 contended that under the terms of the retailers defence they "did not know and had no reason to believe" that an offence was committed. They argued that the magistrates were not entitled to find that the retailers should have carried out testing of the goods. The Divisional Court did not accept that this was a consequence of the distinction between the statutory language of this provision and a due diligence defence. They held that retailers should test against obvious dangers. Had this been done, the retailers could have warned against the immediate risk which the goods (candleholders) posed.

Defence to publication offences

9.42 Special defence. Where goods or services are advertised and that advertisement may give rise to an offence, it is common for there to be a statutory defence for the protection of the publisher. A common form is in Section 25(3) of the Fair Trading Act 1973, also found in the Trade Descriptions Act 1968, s.25:

> "In proceedings for an offence . . . committed by the publication of an advertisement it shall be a defence for the person charged to prove that he is a person whose business it is to publish or arrange for the publication of advertisements and that he received the advertisement for publication in the ordinary course of business and did not know and had no reason to suspect that its publication would amount to an offence under . . . this Act".

See also Consumer Protection Act 1987, s.24; Food Safety Act 1990, s.22, etc.

Warranty defences

9.43 Although previously more common than under modern legislation, a warranty defence remains available in relation to offences under Part IV of the Weights and Measures Act 1985 concerning the quantity or pre-packing of goods. The defence under section 33 of the Act requires that a defendant proves:

(i) that he purchased goods from another as being of the quantity which the seller represented or purported to sell or which was marked on a container or document to which the proceedings relate, or as conforming with the statement marked on any container or with the legal requirements regarding pre-packing;

(ii) that he bought the goods with a written warranty of quantity or conformity;

(iii) which he (or, in the case of an employee, his employer) believed and he had no reason to believe was inaccurate;

(iv) if the person giving the warranty was outside Great Britain or any designated country that the person charged had taken reasonable steps to check the accuracy of the statement; and

(v) that the goods had remained unchanged as to quantity or state while in his possession.

Further provision is made that the defendant shall not be permitted to rely on the warranty unless not less than three days before the hearing he has given a copy of the warranty to the prosecutor with an indication that he intends to rely upon it, the name and address of the person who gave it and he has sent a like notice to that person. The person giving the warranty has a right to appear at the hearing and give evidence.

9.44   Warranty offences.   In tandem with the defence set out above, offences are created of wilfully attributing to any goods a warranty given in relation to others (section 33(5)) and of giving a false warranty in writing. There is a defence to the latter offence if all reasonable steps were taken when the warranty was given to ensure that the information contained in it was, and would for the relevant period continue to be, accurate (section 33(6)).

9.45   Although the warranty is of limited significance in the regulatory scheme, the associated thinking has formed the framework for the due diligence defence, and, in particular, the caution with which the court has approached the question of reliance on others.

Offences which contain statutory exceptions

9.46   Where a regulatory offence sets out a prohibition with an exception, the burden of proving the exception may fall on the defendant, although note that the decision in *Polychronakis v. Richards and Jerrom Ltd*, *The Times*, November 19, 1997 may make these cases the exception rather than the rule (see paragraphs 6.5 to 6.11 above). Characteristically, where the burden may lie on the prosecution, these elements are contained in the words "without reasonable excuse", "without reasonable cause to believe", "so far as is reasonably practicable".

CHAPTER 10

Proceedings in Court

CRIMINAL CASES

Procedure before determination of mode of trial

Defects in the information

10.1 Form of the allegation. On receipt of a summons, the allegation set out in the information should be clear to the defendant. The summons will specify the date and place for the first hearing and require the defendant to appear to answer the information. The summons should be in the following form or a form with no significant differences (see paragraph 8.31 above), although defects in the form of the summons, provided that section 123 of the Magistrates' Courts Act 1980 is applicable, will not be fatal to the prosecution (*R. v. Godstone Justices, ex p. Secretary of State for the Environment* [1974] Crim.L.R. 110):

THE MAGISTRATES' COURT SITTING AT WESTINGHAM

To the accused: ABC Stores Limited
ABC House,
South St.,
Westingham

You are hereby summoned to appear on Friday, November 13, 1998 at 10 am. before the Magistrates' Court sitting at the Victoria Law Courts, High Street, Westingham to answer the information of:

Westingham City Council by Joseph Bloggs (Environmental Services Department) who states that between February 28, 1995 and March 30, 1997 you as an employer under the Management of Health and Safety at Work regulations did at the in-store bakery at ABC Stores, Paradise St, Westingham, fail without reasonable excuse to discharge a duty to make a suitable and sufficient assessment of the risks to the health and safety of your employees to which they are exposed when at work, contrary to *Regulation 3(1) of the Management of Health and Safety at Work Regulations 1992* and *Section 33(1)(c) of the Health and Safety at Work, etc Act 1974*

Date of information April 5, 1998   Dated May 17, 1998

                                                                  Alan Makepeace
                                                                  Justice of the Peace,
                                                                  Westingham

All communications to be addressed to the clerk to the Justices, Victoria Law Courts, High St., Westingham.

IMPORTANT

Please read the notice on the back of this form before completing this portion

Name .... Date of Hearing ....

*I intend to enter a plea of GUILTY

*I intend to enter a plea of NOT GUILTY and intend to call witnesses .....

* The name of my solicitor is .... who will represent me at the hearing.

Delete as applicable

10.2   Amendment.   It is not the summons, but the information which forms the basis of the prosecution case against the defendant. The summons is no more than a means of achieving the attendance of a defendant at court to answer an appropriate information. If he takes no objection to appearing in answer to the summons, he will be taken to have waived any defect in the summons, no matter what it is. The same is not the case in relation to an information. It frequently arises that at court an application for a change to the allegations in the information is made. This could be by way of a mere alteration of the wording: it is not uncommon that efforts to follow the statutory language result in an information which is unintelligible or at least inaccurately expressed. It could also be by way of the substitution or addition of a new allegation.

10.3   Changing the wording.   Section 123 of the Magistrates' Courts Act 1980 specifies that no objection shall be allowed to any (*inter alia*) information because of a defect in form or substance or due to a variance between any evidence adduced at the hearing and the information. This provision has not been interpreted by the courts as permitting a case to proceed with a total discrepancy between the information and the allegations pursued by the prosecution. There are three types of error (*New Southgate Metals Ltd v. London Borough of Islington* [1996] Crim.L.R. 334). First, where the variance is only slight, there is no need to amend. Secondly, in other circumstances falling short of the third situation, namely an error which is so fundamental that the information cannot be rescued (such as the naming of the wrong defendant (see paragraph 7.5 above) or the failure to disclose any offence), an amendment must be made (*Garfield v. Maddocks* [1974] Q.B. 7 *per* Lord Widgery C.J. at page 12). The conviction of a defendant of an offence other than that stated in the information is improper and liable to be quashed by the Divisional Court (see *Hunter v. Coombs* [1962] 1 All E.R. 904). Often the question of amendment of an information arises as a matter of good housekeeping by the prosecution early in the hearing or sometimes at a preliminary hearing (see below).

10.4   When may an information be amended?   It is sometimes difficult to draw a distinction between those occasions when the defect is irremediable, and those when it is proper to allow an amendment. A number of situations have been discussed in the authorities.

  (i) *Offence identifiable.* An information is capable of amendment if it is good enough to allege an identifiable offence: it can properly be amended so long as the same offence appears (*Simpson v. Roberts The Times*, December 21, 1984). In *Fernandez v. Broad*, New Law, July 10, 1996, an oral information in respect of noise nuisance (under the Environmental Protection Act 1990, s.82) had been laid by the appellant and drawn up in the justices' clerks office in the form of a summons. The information made a number of serious errors – it described the respondent's premises as those of the Council and suggested that the Council had failed to abate the nuisance. The stipendiary magistrate dismissed the information as fundamentally flawed. The appellant appealed by way of case stated. The Divisional Court referred to the decision in the case of *Cole v. Wolkind* [1981] Crim.L.R. 252 and affirmed that the correct principle was that the magistrate should permit amendment unless an information was so flawed that no offence was disclosed or it did not give a defendant enough information to deal with the point. It appears, moreover, that a new summons may be issued to replace an original summons in improper form even after the time for commencing proceedings would prevent the laying of an information (*R. v. Fairford Justices, ex p. Brewster* [1976] Q.B. 600).

An example of a flawed information arose in *R. v. Birmingham Justices, ex p. Matthews* (1996) 104 I.T.S.A. 11 M.R. 24, where the Divisional Court held that informations alleging offences under section 14 of the Trade Descriptions Act 1968 were null because, in some cases, they did not indicate to whom a statement was alleged to have been made, and in other cases did not indicate why the statement was said to have been false (although contrast *Jevons v. Cosmoair plc* (unreported February 13, 1997 DC) in which the Divisional Court held that the circumstances of the case rendered the failure to identify the complainant unimportant.

(ii) *Wrong statutory references:* if the information sets out the statutory language, but then refers to the wrong section number or omits to refer to any statutory provision or refers to the wrong one, the magistrates may properly permit amendment (*Thornley v. Clegg* [1982] Crim.L.R. 405; *New Southgate Metals Ltd v. London Borough of Islington* [1996] Crim.L.R. 334). In the latter case, the Divisional Court held that a reference to the wrong statute was so trivial that the conviction could be upheld, notwithstanding that there was no amendment. The Divisional Court took into account that the full particulars of the offence were set out and the prosecution had not been put on notice of any defect by the defendant in the magistrates' court.

(iii) *Different offence:* it seems that even if a different offence is alleged, the information may be amended, provided that the defendant has had notice of the facts of the newly preferred offence and is not prejudiced. In *R. v. Newcastle upon Tyne Justices, ex p. John Bryce (Contractors) Limited* [1976] 2 All E.R. 611, the justices allowed an amendment of information to allege a new offence arising out of the same facts, even though a fresh information could not then have been laid because the time within with the proceedings could be commenced had expired (see paragraphs 8.15 to 8.24 above). "Prejudice" does not include the mere loss of the chance to rely on the limitation, but if the new offence were to raise a hitherto uninvestigated matter, that might constitute prejudice to the defendant. Guidelines were given on the amendment of an information out of time in *R. v. Scunthorpe Justices, ex p. M, The Times*, March 10, 1998. This case concerned section 127 of the Magistrates' Courts Act 1980 (see paragraph 8.16). The Divisional Court's reasoning was that the purpose of the limitation was to ensure that cases were charged and tried as soon as reasonably practicable after their commission, and that amendment after that time could occur if the information had been properly laid within the time period. But where the amendment was to allege a different offence, the new offence must allege the same misdoing – that is, must arise out of the same or substantially the same facts as the offence first charged, and the amendment must be in the interests of justice. In *R. v. Newcastle Upon Tyne Magistrates' Court, ex p. Poundstretcher Ltd* (New Law 498031901, March 3, 1998) the same court found that a slightly higher fine imposed under the substituted offence did not mean that the new charge was "significantly more serious" within the meaning of the test applied in *R. v. Pain, Jory, Hawkins* (1986) 82 Cr App. R. 141, and, applying the *Scunthorpe* guidelines, there was no reason why the amendment should not have been allowed.

(iv) *Wrong defendant named:* see paragraph 7.5 above.

If information which requires to be amended is not amended, not only might the conviction be quashed in the Divisional Court, but on appeal to the Crown Court by way of rehearing there is no power of amendment (*Kirklees Metropolitan Borough Council v. Haigh,* Current Law Week, Issue 13, 1996, *R. v. Swansea Crown Court, ex p. Stacey* (1990) 154 J.P. 185).

10.5   Addition or substitution of offences.   The difference between the addition of an allegation and the substitution of an allegation, is that substitution involves the withdrawal of a charge as well as the addition of another. The justices can grant an application to withdraw a charge without an adjudication as to the merits (*R. v. Redbridge Justices, ex p. Sainty* [1981] R.T.R. 13). It is the duty of the court to make inquiries into the position and assure itself that its procedure is not being abused (*R. v. Liverpool St. Magistrates, ex p. Ellison* [1989] Crim.L.R. 369).

10.6   Duplicity and other defects in the summons.   An information may not charge more than one offence (Magistrates' Courts Rules 1981, rule 12). If an information alleges facts constituting two different activities, there are two offences set out in the information. But merely because an information alleges more than one act, it does not follow that it is duplicitous, providing that all acts are descriptive of a single offence. So an allegation of felling 90 trees within 3 days was not duplicitous (*Cullen v. Jardine* [1985] Crim.L.R. 668) but an information under the Fodder Plant Seeds Regulations 1985 naming several different purchasers were bad for duplicity (*M.A.F.F. v. Nunns Corn & Coal (1987) Ltd* [1990] Crim.L.R. 268). It seems that the difficulties encountered in the latter case could have been overcome had the procedure followed in *DPP v. Shah* [1984] 1 W.L.R. 866 been adopted. In that instance informations under the Food Hygiene (General) Regulations 1970 were set out in one document in which the particulars common to all were set out together. It was held that this was valid under rule 12 of the Magistrates' Courts Rules 1981.

10.7   The consequence of duplicity.   Where an information is found to be duplicitous, the prosecutor must be put to his election as to the offence upon which he wishes to proceed. The other offences are struck out and the single offence retried, usually before a different bench of magistrates. See rule 12(3) of the Magistrates' Courts Rules 1981. If the prosecutor declines to make an election, the information will be dismissed (Rule 12(4)). The defendant may, in the event of amendment, wish to seek an adjournment, which the court must grant if it appears to the court that the defendant has been unfairly prejudiced (rule 12(5)).

If the defendant is convicted on the basis of a duplicitous information the Divisional Court may quash the conviction, although if the point was not taken in the magistrates' court that may be a relevant consideration for the higher court (see Chapter 12 below).

10.8   Taking the point on defective process.   The objection that the information is defective in some fashion may be taken, in theory, at any time. For instance, it can be taken in the closing speech of the defence advocate, particularly where the issue is one of the inadequate form of the information, rather than its duplicity. If the issue is one of duplicity and the point is only taken by the defendant at the closing of the hearing, the magistrates may, if they find that the complaint of duplicity is justified, order a new hearing but award costs against the defendant. Where the point is raised by a prosecutor, it could be made on a date fixed for hearing of preliminary issues (if any) (see paragraph 10.24 below), or on a remand date.

Representation of parties

10.9 Prosecution. The effect of the Prosecution of Offences Act 1985 has been that all criminal cases commenced by the police are conducted by the Crown Prosecution Service, although the right to bring a private prosecution remains, subject to the power given to the Crown Prosecution Service to intervene (Prosecution of Offences Act 1985, s.6(1)). This power to intervene, however, does not extend to prosecutions by local authorities, a nationalised industry or other body constituted for the public service. In particular, local authorities are entitled to prosecute in their own name (see Chapter 2 above). Representation in a magistrates' court is by a solicitor or barrister including a Crown Prosecutor (Prosecution of Offences Act 1985) except that an informant may prosecute his own case without a lawyer. This means not only that private citizens may represent themselves, but also that public bodies (such as the National Television Licence Office or the Federation Against Copyright Theft Ltd) may appoint informants who then prosecute. Moreover, local authorities may appear through their authorised officers (see paragraph 2.38 above).

10.10   Defendants.

(i) A defendant in person may have the reasonable assistance of a friend (sometimes referred to as a McKenzie man, following the decision in *McKenzie v. McKenzie* [1971] p. 33). He does not need the leave of the court to do so, but the court may withdraw the right if it is unreasonable in nature or degree, improper or not *bona fide*, or was provided in a way which impeded the proper administration of justice (*R. v. Leicester City Justices, ex p. Barrow* [1991] 3 W.L.R. 368). A defendant cannot be represented in his absence by a McKenzie friend (*R. v. Teeside Justices, ex p. Nilssou* [1991] C.O.D. 58.

(ii) A non-legal representative of a corporation may carry out a limited function on its behalf, namely, making a statement in answer to a charge in committal proceedings, consenting to summary trial and entering a plea of guilty or not guilty.

(iii) A limited company can appear through a director, solicitor or barrister.

The first hearing and subsequent adjournments

10.11   Guilty pleas. If there is to be a plea of guilty, the first hearing in the magistrates' court may result in the disposal of the matter, provided that the magistrates accept jurisdiction if required to determine the mode of trial (see paragraphs 10.14 to 10.17 below).

10.12   Adjournments (remands). In the magistrates' court, matters which are to be tried either way are said to be "remanded" when they are adjourned. The postponement of a summary trial is usually described as an adjournment. An adjournment can be of the first hearing or any subsequent hearing.

10.13 Adjournment of the first hearing. There will not, as a matter of practice, be a final disposal of the case on the first hearing where there is to be or has been a plea of not guilty. There can be no final disposal where the matter will be more suitable for trial in the Crown Court. Accordingly, the magistrates' court, as a matter of convenience and courtesy, may liaise with the prosecutor and the defendant in respect of dates for listing a first hearing and has a formal power to adjourn any case in the presence or absence of either party (Magistrates' Courts Act 1980, s.4(4) (as substituted by the Criminal Justice and Public Order Act 1994) and s.10)). The justices' clerk also has a power in certain circumstances to adjourn the hearing (Justices' Clerks Rules 1970, Sched. 1 as variously amended). The first hearing is often used for the purposes of ascertaining the parties' likely conduct of proceedings, setting a time-table and (if the offence charged is an either way offence and advance information has been served) the first hearing can be to determine whether the case is appropriate for summary trial or to be tried in the Crown Court. If the matter is to be tried summarily, a plea may be taken. Entry of a not guilty plea almost invariably results in adjournment for trial at a later date.

Mode of trial and committal

10.14 Determination of the mode of trial. Where the offence is triable either way, the matter must be committed to the Crown Court if the court decides that the offence is more suitable for trial on indictment or if the defendant has not agreed to be tried in the magistrates' court (Magistrates' Courts Act 1980, s.4(1). Additionally, a summary offence may be committed to the Crown Court for trial with an offence or offences triable either way if the summary offence is founded on the same facts or evidence as a count charging an indictable offence, or if it is part of a series of offences of the same character. This provision, introduced by section 40 of the Criminal Justice Act 1988 is intended to overcome the problems created by litigation of substantially similar issues in two different places before different tribunals of fact and law during the same period.

10.15 Factors relevant to choice of mode of trial. Regulatory offences are, in the main, tried summarily and magistrates rarely decline to hear cases of a quasi-criminal type. A notable regulatory exception is the case of "clocking" cars involving allegations of dishonesty prosecuted under section 1 of the Trade Descriptions Act 1968. Another example unauthorised use of trade marks whether prosecuted as an offence under The Trade Marks Act 1994 or The Trade Descriptions Act 1968. These are treated more seriously and are closer to the realm of true criminal cases. The issues which magistrates are principally required to address in deciding whether to commit for trial are set out in section 19 of the Magistrates' Courts Act 1980 and amplified in the National Mode of Trial Guidelines 1995 (although no express reference is made to any regulatory offence in the Guidelines). The following matters are relevant:

    (i) the nature of the case;

    (ii) whether its circumstances make it serious;

    (iii) whether the punishment which a magistrates' court would have power to inflict would be adequate.

In any case where justices have a doubt about the appropriate level of sentence for the offence before them, they should consult their clerk (*R. v. Flax Bourton*

Magistrates' Court, ex p. Commissioners of Customs & Excise, The Times, February 6, 1996).

In considering these matters, the magistrates' court will, under the Guidelines, assume that the prosecution version of the facts is correct. A specimen allegation, moreover, may turn an individual count into a matter serious enough to be committed to the Crown Court, as may any complex question of law or fact likely to arise. See on specimen counts *R. v. Bradshaw* [1997] 2 Cr. App. R. (S.) 128. Another instance which might lead to committal in the Crown Court, is where there is or may be an issue as to the obligation to disclose relevant material in which there is a public interest in non-disclosure (see paragraphs 10.56 to 10.66 below). In *R. v. Bromley Justices, ex p. Smith; R. v. Wells St Magistrates' Court, ex p. King* [1995] 1 W.L.R. 994, the Divisional Court commented that the magistrates would be well-advised to commit a case for trial should such an issue be likely to emerge. Most important to regulatory cases is the consideration under the Guidelines that, unless otherwise stated, either way offences should be tried summarily unless the court considers that its sentencing powers are insufficient.

An infrequent consideration (but which could, for instance, arise in connection with the Property Misdescriptions Act 1991 and some byelaws), is that justices should commit to the Crown Court for trial an "either way" case which involves the exercise of a bona fide claim or assertion of title to land (*Andrews v. Carlton* (1928) 93 J.P. 65).

10.16   Electing or rejecting jury trial.

Criminal Procedure and Investigations Act 1996.   Under Part I of the Criminal Investigations and Procedure Act 1996, one reason to seek to retain the case in the magistrates' court may be to avoid the mandatory disclosure by way of defence statement of the case for the defendant (see paragraph 10.73 below). (It is not wholly clear whether the provisions of section 1(1) of the 1996 Act do, in any event, cover corporate defendants faced with "either way" allegations, although they would appear to relate to individual defendants facing regulatory informations: the provisions, which refer to a "person" also describe him as variously under or over 18, which suggests that they are applicable to natural persons only).

Position prior to the operation of Part I of the 1996 Act.   The following reasons for the choice by defendants not to exercise their right to elect jury trial are frequently advanced:

(i)   *Avoiding the jury:* regulatory defendants often perceive that jury trial would offer a more unsympathetic forum in that the jury might identify more closely with the consumer or other complainant than with the business trying to evade liability.

(ii) *No prosecution closing speech:* the defendant is advantaged by the magistrates' court procedure, particularly where a due diligence defence is to be run, because the prosecutor is not permitted to address the justices as to the facts after the defence case except with the leave of the court (which is not usually forthcoming). Even if leave is given, the defendant is given a further right to address the justices. This gives a tactical advantage to the defendant.

(iii) *Expert evidence:* before April 1997, the defendant could reserve the element of surprise in relation to any expert evidence called in the magistrates' court. In the Crown Court, the Crown Court (Advance Notice of Expert Evidence) Rules 1987 (amended by the Crown Court (Advance Notice of Expert Evidence (Amendment) Rules 1997 in respect of investigations commenced after April 1, 1997) require disclosure of an expert report relied upon by the defence. Advance notice rules under section 20(3) and (4) of the Criminal Procedure and Investigations Act 1996 now require notice of expert evidence to be given in the magistrates' court (Magistrates' Court (Advance Notice of Expert Evidence) Rules 1997).

(iv) *Costs:* the expenditure on costs which may be ordered to be paid in the event of conviction is likely to be less in the magistrates' court. In *R. v. F. & M. Dobson Ltd, The Times,* March 8, 1995, the Court of Appeal (Criminal Division), reduced a fine following conviction in the Crown Court for absolute offences, but upheld a costs order of £7,834 because the defendants had brought it upon themselves by electing trial by jury. On the other hand, in *R. v. Sentonco* [1996] 1 Cr. App. R. (S.) 174, it was held to be wrong to order the defendant to pay more by way of costs because he had elected jury trial than would have been appropriate in the magistrates' court. This was not, however, a regulatory case.

(v) *Appeals:* in the event of conviction, there is a further tier of appeal to the Crown Court if trial takes place in the magistrates' court. Appeal to the Crown Court involves a complete rehearing of the facts, so that omissions in the evidence before the magistrates could, in principle, be remedied on appeal (see Chapter 12, below).

(vi) *Sentencing:* many regulatory offences carry no sentence of imprisonment in the magistrates' court and a limited fine (see Chapter 11, below) although the magistrates may commit the case to the Crown Court for sentence in the event that the case turns out to be more serious than anticipated so that greater punishment should be inflicted than the magistrates' court has power to impose. The power to commit the case to the Crown Court for sentence arises by section 38 of the Magistrates' Courts Act 1980. Section 20 of the Magistrates' Courts Act 1980 requires that if the defendant is offered summary trial, he must be warned that there is power to commit him for sentence to the Crown Court. As a matter of tactics there is a good chance that, jurisdiction having been once accepted, the matter will not be committed for sentence unless new facts emerge in the course of the trial. The defendant therefore may reasonably hope that penalties imposed in the event of conviction will be those lesser penalties which can be inflicted in the magistrates' court.

10.17 Summary trial: Change of activity. Section 25 of the Magistrates' Courts Act 1980 permits the magistrates at any stage in a summary trial to discontinue proceedings and proceed (whether following an adjournment or not) as examining magistrates. The court must begin to hear evidence in relation to the summary trial before the power to discontinue is exercised: it cannot be a mere change of heart (*R. v. St Helens Magistrates' Court, ex p. Critchley* [1988] Crim.L.R. 311) and it is not enough to hear material which is not directed at the issue of guilt or innocence of the accused. Trial must mean a proper and fair trial, not one which is commenced to fulfil the ancillary motive of committing the case to the Crown Court (*R. v. Birmingham Stipendiary Magistrate, ex p. Webb* (1992) 157 J.P. 89).

10.18   Dishonesty.   If the offence alleged involves dishonesty, the defendant may wish to choose a jury trial because he may anticipate that a jury will relate better to that "human" issue. Moreover, if the trial involves the interpretation of relatively complicated European regulations, and the defence involves an allegation of lack of understanding or exasperation with it, juries are often perceived (possibly wrongly) to be more sympathetic than magistrates.

10.19   Procedure for committal.   The committal procedure was to have been abolished and replaced with transfers from the magistrates' court to the Crown Court by provisions contained in the Criminal Justice and Public Order Act 1994. Following opposition from justices' clerks and trial programmes which were not wholly successful, the committal procedure has been retained and amended by the Criminal Procedure and Investigations Act 1996. The amendments to the provisions of the Magistrates' Courts Act 1980 governing committal proceedings appear in Schedule 1 of the 1996 Act and insert new sections 5A to 5F into the 1980 Act. The principal difference is that it is no longer possible to conduct a so-called "old-style" committal. The evidence, which may be put before the magistrates in a number of forms, is read by the magistrates and if it discloses any offence which may be tried on indictment (that is, not just the offence alleged in the information), the magistrates may commit the case to the Crown Court for trial. Where the defendant is legally represented, the defendant may consent to the committal without the need for the magistrates to read the documents, but all documents upon which the defendant is to be committed must be presented to the court. It is now permissible to submit copies of statements, depositions and other documents (Magistrates' Courts Act 1980, s.5F, as substituted).

10.20   No case on committal.   The defendant may submit that the committal papers disclose no case to answer. The court may dismiss the charge "where . . . the prosecution evidence, taken at its highest, is such that a jury properly directed could not properly convict on it" (*R. v. Galbraith* 73 Cr. App. R., CA). See also, *R. v. Shippey and others* [1988] Crim.L.R. 767, *Brooks v. DPP* [1994] 1 A.C. 568. Where no application to dismiss is made or it is not wholly successful, the court must commit the case to a convenient Crown Court. The magistrates' clerk will ask if the alibi warning is appropriate, and, where so, will give to the defendant a notice setting out that he must provide particulars of alibi within 7 days or he may be prevented from relying on an alibi in the Crown court.

10.21   Publicity of committal proceedings.   Reporting restrictions prevent publication of details in the press save for the identification of the defendants, the charges they face and the decision of the court whether to commit or not. A defendant may apply to lift reporting restrictions, which the magistrates may allow only if it is in the interests of justice to do so.

Trial of more than one allegation or more than one defendant

10.22   Several offences.   Where there are several offences, the court should decide on the first hearing or an adjourned hearing if the offences may properly be tried together. Clearly, this decision can only be taken where mode of trial (if appropriate) has been determined in favour of trial in the magistrates' court. If several offences are to be committed to the Crown Court, the question of whether the matters should be tried separately arises only at the Crown Court stage.

10.23   Several defendants.   Two or more defendants may, even if they are charged on separate informations, be tried together if the facts are connected. The test of whether the facts are connected is not whether the facts of each charge are similar or contemporaneous, but whether the charges have a common factual origin (*R. v. Barrell and Wilson* (1979) 69 Cr. App. R. 250). An example of where this may be particularly appropriate is if there is both a primary and secondary offence alleged in respect of the same incident (see paragraphs 6.20 to 6.89 above for secondary offences). In deciding whether different offences and defendants should be tried together, the justices should hear representations and decide whether it would be fair and just to the defendant(s) to allow a joint trial (*Chief Constable of Norfolk v. Clayton* [1983] 2 A.C. 473). The mere absence of the defendant's consent is not enough to prevent a joint trial, although the magistrates must not order a joint trial if it would not be just to the accused person. The justices' considerations should include questions as to whether similar fact evidence or evidence of system arising in each case can be admitted in the other case or cases. If separate trials are ordered, it is a matter of discretion for the justices whether each trial should be before a differently constituted group of magistrates. Magistrates must refuse to try the second case if there would be a real problem over approaching a second trial impartially (*R. v. Sandwich Justices, ex p. Berry* [1982] Crim.L.R. 1221)

Preliminary Points: General

10.24   Taking a preliminary point.   If a trial is to remain in the magistrates' court, it is permissible for magistrates to fix preliminary hearings to deal with certain matters, such as public interest immunity from disclosure (see paragraphs 10.56 to 10.66 below) or other preliminary issues, for example, whether there has been an abuse of process (see paragraphs 10.26 to 10.47 below). It is in some cases desirable that the same constitution of the bench of magistrates should hear both the preliminary issue and the main trial (*R. v. Bromley Magistrates' Court, ex p. Smith and Wilkins* [1995] 1 W.L.R. 994). Clearly, this cannot occur on every occasion. In *R. v. South Worcestershire Magistrates' Court, ex p. Lilley, The Times,* February 22, 1995, one item of evidence which was said to be too sensitive in the public interest to disclose, was read by the magistrates in the absence of the accused or his representative. It was held that a refusal in those circumstances to adjourn the matter to a differently constituted bench of magistrates would be so unreasonable that no reasonable magistrates could come to that conclusion (*i.e.* "*Wednesbury* unreasonable") – so that the refusal was susceptible to judicial review. The Divisional Court commented that not every *ex parte* application would entitle the defendant to a trial before a differently constituted bench.

10.25   Admissibility.   Care must be taken where the matter merely concerns admissibility. If the issue which arises is as to the exclusion of "unfair" evidence under section 78 of the Police and Criminal Evidence Act 1984 (paragraph 10.105 below), there is no entitlement to a preliminary hearing. The justices should usually deal with the application when it arises in the trial or leave the decision to the end of the trial with the object of ensuring that the trial is fair and just to both sides (*Vel v. Owen* [1987] Crim.L.R. 49). Although it is possible to hold a preliminary hearing, or some sort of *voir dire* to determine the admissibility of evidence, particularly if the issues are limited and will not involve evidence from the defendant, it is often better practice in the magistrates' court to hear the disputed evidence as part of the overall case and to defer the decision to the end of the evidence (*Halawa v. Federation against Copyright Theft* [1995] 1 Cr. App. R. 21). This is particularly the case where the matters which could arise in a *voir dire* as a consequence of evidence given by the defendant would also arise in the context of the other issues in the wider case.

Abuse of process

10.26 Application. Objection to proceedings on the ground that their continuation constitutes an abuse of the process of the court applies as much in regulatory cases as it does in more serious matters (*R. v. South Tyneside Justices, ex p. Mill Garages, The Times*, April 17, 1995).

The time for taking the objection

10.27 Divided views. In proceedings which may be committed to the Crown Court, a contention that proceedings are an abuse of the process of the court may be taken in the magistrates' court before committal, although the authorities are divided as to whether this is best practice. A number of authorities confirm that the power to stay proceedings on the grounds that to allow them to continue would be an abuse of the process of the court exists in both the magistrates and the Crown Court, including when the magistrates are sitting as examining justices (*Bennett* (above), *R. v. Telford Justices, ex p. Badhan* [1991] 2 All E.R. 854). It is, however, a power which is to be most sparingly exercised. One line of authority expresses the sentiment that questions of abuse should be raised at the earliest opportunity, whereas other authorities deprecate the practice of taking the point before the case is committed to the Crown Court, asserting that the issue can properly be taken in the Crown Court. If the applicant is unsuccessful and is convicted, the question of abuse can be raised in the Court of Appeal (Criminal Division) on appeal.

10.28 The first line – raising the abuse at the first opportunity. See paragraphs 8.25 to 8.28 for discussion as to circumstances when the court may consider whether there has been an abuse of the process of the court prior to issuing the summons. Where the summons has been issued, there is judicial support for the defence practice of raising the question of abuse at an early stage. For example, in *R. v. Badhan* [1991] 2 Q.B. 78, Mann L.J. at page 90 said "We think that a plea of abuse should be open to the accused subject at the earliest opportunity". In *R. v. Horseferry Road Magistrates' Court, ex p. Bennett* [1994] 1 A.C. 42, Lord Lowry said that "the convenience of staying the proceedings at an early stage is obvious, when that can properly be done". In *R. v. Horseferry Road Magistrates' Court, ex p. I.B.A.* [1986] 2 All E.R. 666, Lloyd L.J. thought that even if the existence of the offence was doubtful (as opposed to obviously non-existent) it should be investigated at the earliest stage before further expense is incurred. See also *R. v. Ashton* [1984] 1 A.C. 9 at 20.

Where trial is to be in the magistrates' court, the time for taking the objection is either at a special hearing before trial or at trial. If the point is taken at trial and then there is a conviction, the question whether proceeding was an abuse of the process of the court can be determined upon an appeal by way of case stated or, if other matters are also to be raised, in the Crown Court. (For appeals see Chapter 12 below). In *R. v. Aldershot Youth Court, ex p. A.* [1997] 3 *Archbold News* 2, DC the Divisional Court lent its support to the suggestion that the question of abuse should be raised as a preliminary point before plea.

10.29   Raising the abuse of process at the trial.   In *R. v. Croydon Justices, ex p. Dean* [1993] 3 All E.R. 129, Staughton L.J. expressed the view that it was appropriate to wait to raise an allegation of abuse at trial. He adverted to the *Attorney General's Reference (No. 1 of 1990)* [1992] 1 Q.B. 630, but nevertheless granted a prerogative order on an application for judicial review, having taken into account that an earlier prosecution application before a differently constituted Divisional Court to overturn the leave to apply for judicial review had been unsuccessful (for the procedure on judicial review see paragraphs 12.39 below).

The nature of abuse of process

10.30   "Wider and narrow range" abuse.   The jurisdiction of the Divisional Court to stop an abuse of power is now recognised to be a wide ranging and flexible one. It goes significantly beyond the powers enjoyed by the lower criminal courts, although the boundary between matters which may be raised in the lower courts ("narrow range" abuse relating to the process of the court) and those which must be reserved for the Divisional Court ("wider range" abuse relating to the abuse of power) is not always easy to find. In *R. v. Horseferry Road Magistrates' Court, ex p. Bennett* [1994] A.C. 42 Lord Griffiths commented in relation to the powers of the Divisional Court to control matters affecting criminal cases:

> "The great growth of administrative law during the latter half of this century has occurred because of the recognition by the judiciary and Parliament alike that it is the function of the High Court to ensure that executive action is exercised responsibly and as Parliament intended. So also should it be in the field of criminal law and if it comes to the attention of the court that there has been a serious abuse of power it should, in my view, express its disapproval by acting upon it".

The House of Lords ruled in that case that there had been a "wider range" abuse because the defendant had been unlawfully brought within the jurisdiction by the police to stand trial. It is likely that matters such as a challenge to the legality or implementation of a local authority's prosecution policy, or some issues which are associated with the decision to prosecute could only be challenged as an abuse of power – in the "wider range" category. Others, particularly those arising from the conduct of the prosecution may be justiciable within the narrow range class by the courts of trial.

10.31   The criminal courts' powers to stop abuse.   The magistrates' courts' and Crown Courts' powers are within a more narrow range than those of the Divisional Court, save that they have a power to allow an adjournment for application to the Divisional Court where a wider ranging allegation of abuse is raised (*Bennett* (above)). The description of the narrow powers possessed by the criminal courts were described by Sir Roger Ormrod in *R. v. Crown Court at Derby, ex p. Brooks* (1984) 80 Cr. App. R. 164 at 168-169:

> "The power to stop a prosecution arises only when it is an abuse of the process of the court. It may be an abuse of process if either (a) the prosecution have manipulated or misused the process of the court so as to deprive the defendant of a protection provided by the law or to take an unfair advantage of a technicality, or (b) on the balance of probability, the defendant has been, or will be, prejudiced in the preparation or conduct of his defence by delay on the

part of the prosecution which is unjustifiable . . . The ultimate objective of this discretionary power is to ensure that there should be a fair trial according to law, which involves fairness both to the defendant and to the prosecution."

10.32 Powers to be sparingly exercised. In the *Attorney General's Reference (No. 1 of 1990)* [1992] 1 Q.B. 630, (a case concerning delay) the Court of Appeal (Criminal Division) stated that a stay for delay or another reason:

(i) could be allowed only in the most exceptional circumstances; and

(ii) still more rarely where there was no fault on the prosecution or complainant; and

(iii) never where it was due to the complexity of the case or contribution by the defendant.

This approach has been applied in a regulatory case. In *R. v. South Tyneside Justices, ex p. Mill Garages, The Times* April 17, 1995, the defendant sought judicial review of the magistrates' refusal to stay informations under section 1 of the Trade Descriptions Act 1968. The prosecution had been commenced within the period laid down by section 19(1). The Divisional Court referred to the importance of investigation, regardless of whether the representations founding the charge were oral, written or by conduct and stressed that the same principles which govern the conduct of the court in serious cases where abuse is alleged also govern regulatory matters. It refused the defendant's application; referring to the importance of completion of the investigation before the commencement of proceedings.

10.33 Avoiding unfairness. It is important to note, on the other hand, that the existence of the power to stay for an abuse of process has been referred to by the Divisional Court as of potential comfort where certain findings of law could cause unfairness in other cases (see, for example *R. v. Shrewsbury Magistrates' Court, ex p. Simon Dudley Limited* [1997] I.T.S.A. 11 M.R. 30, Divisional Court) where the court held that knowledge of an offence in the possession of one Council official was not sufficient to cause time to run for the purposes of a limitation provision, because the officials charged with the duty to prosecute offences were unaware of the facts. But see as to this, paragraphs 8.23 and 8.24 above also).

10.34 Fair trial impossible. Although the magistrates have a discretion to stay proceedings in the event that unconscionable delay has caused prejudice, it is difficult to see that the discretion should ever be exercised in favour of allowing a prosecution to continue in the light of clear evidence that there could be no fair trial. Exercise of the discretion in this way would be "*Wednesbury* unreasonable". On the other hand, there may be no power to stop a prosecution where the defendant has indicated an intention to plead guilty, at least in a delay case (*R. v. Derby Crown Court, ex p. Brooks* (1984) 80 Cr. App. R. 164).

Depriving the defendant of a protection or taking unfair advantage of a technicality by manipulation or misuse of the process

10.35 Bad faith not necessary. It appears that it is not essential to establishing an abuse that the prosecution should have acted mala fide in manipulating or misusing the process of the court, although the presence of an intention to act unconscionably is a material factor in the exercise of the discretion and the absence of bad faith can be so. So, in the *Attorney General's Reference (No 1 of 1990),* (above) the court regarded the absence of fault by the prosecution as preventing a successful plea that there was an abuse of the process of the court, although the court appeared to be addressing its consideration principally to abuse by delay, rather than to other abuses. In contrast, in *R. v. Brentford Justices, ex p. Wong* [1981] 1 All E.R. 884 where the prosecution had issued proceedings before taking the decision to prosecute, the Divisional Court expressed a clear view that this was an abuse of the process of the court, even though there was no evidence of intention to abuse the court proceedings. The matter was remitted to the magistrates for inquiry. Donaldson L.J. said:

> "It is perhaps hard on the prosecutor to characterise that as an abuse of the process of the court. He thought that he could legitimately do this. For my part, I do not think that he can . . . it is open to the magistrates to say 'this is an abuse of process. We therefore decline jurisdiction and we dismiss the summonses'. It is a matter which has to be investigated by the magistrates."

There is authority for the proposition that where an abuse of process is addressed to an ancillary matter (in that case bail and custody time limits) the court cannot intervene in the absence of *mala fides* (*R. v. Wirral District Magistrates' Court, ex p. Meikle* [1991] C. O. D. 2).

10.36   Bad faith.   As a general principle, the court cannot intervene to stay proceedings merely because it disapproves of the legitimate motives of the prosecutor in proceeding against a defendant (*R. v. Ampthill Magistrates' Court, ex p. Neely, The Independent,* August 16, 1993). Where the prosecution is in bad faith, however, the position is different. Although bad faith is not a necessary component of conduct which is an abuse of the process of the court, where a prosecutor acts in bad faith or for an ulterior motive, that alone may be enough to cause the court to intervene to prevent the abuse. An example was *Sherwood & Hart v. Ross, Steward, Ross and Raey* [1989] Crim.L.R. 576 where private parties had been in dispute for some time and each side had instructed solicitors. Civil proceedings had been threatened but no mention was ever made of criminal proceedings. On the last day of the period permitted for prosecution, an information was laid. The defendant alleged an abuse of process. Even though there was no prejudice to the defendant by the conduct of the prosecutor, the court would not permit the prosecutor to pursue proceedings in bad faith. A similar instance was *R. v. Bury Justices, ex p. Anderton* [1987] Crim.L.R. 638 in which summonses were issued against the Chief Constable of Greater Manchester and others alleging a conspiracy to pervert the course of justice in relation to the issue of access orders and search warrants. The Divisional Court held that the real purpose of the proceedings was to get discovery of certain material that, two days later in the Chancery Division, was ordered unnecessary to be disclosed. The criminal prosecution was determined to be an abuse of the process of the court. Contrast, however, the cases of *R. v. Milton Keynes Magistrates' Court, ex p. Roberts* [1995] Crim.L.R. 224 and *R. v. Leominster Magistrates' Court, ex p. Aston Manor Brewery Company, The Times* January 8, 1997. In the former case, assistance and resources lent by a party injured by an offence was held not to be an abuse of process because the decision to prosecute had been taken independently by the Trading Standards Officer. The prosecution was not, therefore, tainted by the motivation of a person interested in the outcome. In the latter case, a bottled water company had sued a rival for passing off and breach of statutory duty. It also notified the council, who prosecuted and used the same Counsel as had been used by the plaintiff in the civil proceedings. The prosecuting Counsel had certain documents relating to the civil case which he declined to disclose on the basis that they were confidential and privilege had not been waived. Subsequently he withdrew from the prosecution. It was held that the Council was, nonetheless, unable to exercise its duty as a prosecutor independently, and so the Divisional Court stayed the proceedings as an abuse of the process of the court.

10.37 Prosecution misconduct not involving the process of the court. This category of case may not be an abuse of process at all. Where the defendant has been subjected to some illegality resulting in unfairness to him there may have been an abuse of power. Such a case may fall outside the jurisdiction of the magistrates' or Crown Court but within the wider powers of the Divisional Court (*Bennett* (above)) although in *R. v. Croydon Justices, ex p. Dean* [1993] 3 All E.R. 129, the Divisional Court considered that the Crown Court would have had power to intervene, notwithstanding that the abuse alleged was a promise by police officers not to prosecute the defendant upon which he had relied, presumably because the unfairness smacked of bad faith. In *Bennett* Lord Oliver specifically referred to *ex p. Dean* as an example of doubt cast on the bona fides of the prosecution in the context of the unfairness of a trial to an accused who has been invited to prejudice his own position on the faith of the undertaking. A similar issue was addressed in *R. v. Wyatt* [1997] 3 *Archbold News* 2, CA, where the prosecution indicated that in a certain eventuality, which occurred, they would offer no evidence. It was an abuse for the prosecution then to apply to add a lesser charge and prosecute for that. Also see *R. v. Bloomfield* [1997] 1 Cr. App. R. 153, CA, in which the prosecution were prevented from resiling from a promise to offer no evidence. But it is important to recall that prejudice is essential. In *Mokhra v. DPP*, December 10, 1996, the Divisional Court found that magistrates were correct to reject a submission that to continue proceedings would be an abuse after the police had written to the defendant stating that no action would be taken for driving with excess alcohol, and even though the defendant had, on receipt of the letter, thrown away his half of the specimen and could not therefore challenge the analysis. He had made no effort to challenge the prosecution analysis before receipt of the letter or have the sample analysed independently, and therefore the justices were entitled to find that there was no prejudice. In particular, the Divisional Court commented that, rather than complain of abuse, the defendant could have made an application to exclude the evidence of the analysis under section 78 of the Police and Criminal Evidence Act 1984. The Divisional Court added that an abuse of process could only be maintained in exceptional circumstances, and those circumstances would never arise where an application could be made under section 78.

10.38 Depriving the defendant of a protection. It is not an abuse of process merely to deprive the defendant of a protection if there is no manipulation or misuse of the process, so that to use the procedures of the court in a way which is disadvantageous to the defendant is not an abuse of process where the use made of them is not in bad faith. For instance, in *R. v. Rotherham City Council, ex p. Brough* [1991] Crim.L.R. 522 the prosecution arranged for a return date a while hence so that it was intended to and did fall after the accused's 17th birthday. The defendant was therefore not treated as a juvenile. That conduct was held not to be male fide, and so not an abuse, but it was an error of judgment. Moreover, the defendant had not been prejudiced. The Divisional Court declined to intervene.

10.39   Influencing the mode of trial.   It is permissible for the prosecution to put charges or substitute charges to ensure trial either in the Crown Court or in the magistrates' court. If charges are substituted to achieve this objective, however, they must be charges which are both appropriate and proper and which could have been brought against the defendant from the outset (*R. v. Redbridge Justices, ex p. Whitehouse* (1992) 94 Cr. App. R. 332; *R. v. Canterbury and St Augustine Justices, ex p. Klisiak* [1982] 1 Q.B. 398). Where, however, new charges were levelled at the defendant because the magistrates considered the matter suitable for summary trial, that was deemed to be an abuse of the process of the court (*R. v. Brooks (Christopher)* [1985] Crim.L.R. 385. The prosecuting solicitor had admitted that the new charges were brought because he was not satisfied with the justices' decision and he was not going to have it. The prosecution should not act as an informal court of appeal from justices decisions.

Specific issues: Multiple prosecutions

10.40   Multiple prosecutions.   There may come a point where commencing fresh prosecutions against a defendant who has already been convicted several times in respect of the same published material which gives rise to an offence whenever it is read (see *Wings v. Ellis* [1985] 1 A.C. 272) would be an abuse of the process of the court. The court in *R. v. Thomson Holidays Ltd* [1974] 1 Q.B. 592 addressed this consideration. The submission on behalf of the defendants that a second prosecution should be stayed and alternatively that the penalty in respect of the second prosecution should be nominal was rejected. The court accepted that multiple offences could lead to multiple prosecutions. Particular reference was made to the provisions of section 30 of the Trade Descriptions Act 1968 (now repealed and replaced by section 130 of the Fair Trading Act 1973: see above). The court asserted that the provision was to enable (then) the Department of Trade and Industry to collect information about intended prosecutions and give advice about them and, by so doing, prevent oppressive numbers of prosecutions based upon the same course of conduct. If that was the function then of the DTI it is now the function of the Director General of Fair Trading under section 130 of the Fair Trading Act 1973 Act. The court did accept, nonetheless, that there might come a time when to go on prosecuting would become oppressive so that proceedings should be stayed or penalties imposed nominal. That time had not come after one prosecution. In *Wings* (above) Lord Hailsham commented (at page 285) that the finding that the same conduct by the defendant could result in many offences did not mean that "a prosecution policy of excessive zeal involving repeated attempts to convict a firm in respect of each separate communication of an individual copy of a brochure ought to meet with anything but reprobation from the courts. That must depend on the circumstances." In practice, repeated prosecutions tend to emanate from different prosecuting authorities, although prosecuting authorities are generally aware, through their information network, of the progress of prosecutions in other areas of the country and are often content to await the outcome of an on-going prosecution elsewhere. It is notable, however, that in *R. v. Birmingham Justices, ex p. Matthews and others* (1996) 104 I.T.S.A. 11 M.R. 24 there were no less than 93 connected informations arising from the same published document. It is not clear whether an objection on the grounds of abuse of process by reason of oppressive prosecution would have succeeded: most of the informations failed because they failed sufficiently to identify the offence alleged.

Specific issues: Double jeopardy

10.41   Double jeopardy.   There are at least three circumstances where, after a first prosecution, a second prosecution on the same or similar charges has caused the court to intervene to stay the proceedings. The jurisdiction is quite independent of considerations of *autrefois convict* or *acquit* (*R. v. Beedie*, *The Times*, March 14, 1997). The considerations arising in such cases could have some limited application where related charges are brought against, say, an importer and retailer, or in some cases where multiple prosecutions (see above) have arisen from multiple offences.

10.42 Fresh proceedings. In *R. v. Horsham Justices, ex p. Reeves* (1982) 75 Cr. App. R. 236, committal proceedings lasting 3 days had taken place in the magistrates' court and the justices had found no case to answer. The prosecution served further charges based on the original charges, although shortened and simplified. This was held to be an abuse of process even though a finding that there is no case to answer is not equivalent to an acquittal. *R. v. Manchester City Stipendiary Magistrate, ex p. Snelson* [1977] 1 W.L.R. 911, in which there had been no hearing prior to the dismissal of the proceedings by magistrates, was distinguished. The Divisional Court held that the prosecution was not entitled to treat the first committal as a dummy run. The second proceedings were vexatious, and to allow a second bite at the cherry would encourage poor preparation. Also, the decision in *R. v. Haringey Magistrates' Court, ex p. Cragg*, *The Times*, November 8, 1996, is illuminating, and draws something in its reasoning from the principles described in this paragraph and in the subsequent two paragraphs: section 1(2) of the Dangerous Dogs Act 1991 makes it an offence (*inter alia*) to allow a pit bull terrier of which he is the owner or in charge to be unmuzzled in a public place. Section 5 allows the destruction of a pit bull terrier in the absence of a prosecution of any person. One person (not the owner) was prosecuted under section 1(2) of the Act and acquitted. On return of the dog to the owner following failure of the prosecution, police commenced proceedings for a destruction order. It was held that the second set of proceedings against the owner (which, it was conceded, would have been impossible had the owner been the defendant in the prosecution under section 1(2)) was an abuse of the process of the court. Also see *R. v. Bradford Stipendiary Magistrate* [1997] New Law, June 6; *R. v. Liverpool Magistrates' Court, ex p. Slade* [1997] New Law June 6, *R. v. South East Hampshire Magristrates, ex p. CPS* [1998] 4 Archbold News 4, *Environment Agency v. Campbell*, *The Times*, May 18, 1998.

10.43 Issue re-litigated as part of second trial. Where a clearly identifiable issue in the previous trial has been resolved, the court must consider in a subsequent trial whether the allegation forms such an essential part of the subsequent charge as to make it oppressive or prejudicial to invite the court to take a different view (*Connelly v. DPP* [1964] A.C. 1254, *R. v. Moxon-Tritsh* [1988] Crim.L.R. 46). So where a defendant was charged both with causing death by reckless driving and with driving with excess alcohol, the Divisional Court held that the more serious charge should be heard first. The defendant alleged that he had had a drink after the accident and was not driving with excess alcohol. The only evidence of recklessness was excess alcohol. The offence of driving with excess alcohol was of strict liability, in respect of which the burden of proving a defence lay on the defendant. Trial of the strict liability offence first would have been to take unfair advantage of the procedure of the court and to deprive the defendant of the protection offered to defendants, in particular, that the prosecution must bear the burden of proof (*R. v. Forest of Dean Justices, ex p. Farley* [1990] R.T.R. 228). Moreover, to attempt to prosecute offences arising out of the same facts on an ascending order of gravity is particularly objectionable. (see Lord Devlin in *Connelly v. DPP* (above) and *R. v. Elrington* (1861) 1 B. & S. 688). A departure from this rule should only occur if there are special circumstances, so that in *R. v. Beedie* [1998] QB. 356, the Court of Appeal allowed an appeal on the ground that to prosecute a defendant for manslaughter where he had already been convicted of an offence in the same facts under the Health and Safety at Work etc. Act 1974 was an abuse of process.

10.44 Related defendant acquitted. Where a case against another defendant has resulted in acquittal, some Crown Court decisions have suggested that it may be an abuse of process to proceed against a second defendant with a view to re-litigating the same issue. This could have particular significance in regulatory cases where a wholesaler, manufacturer or importer is prosecuted in respect of the same matter as is a retailer; say, relating to the unsafety of a toy or the unfitness of certain food. It could also be of relevance where a trader is prosecuted in respect of the same facts by more than one local authority. In *R. v. Intervision Limited and Norris* [1984] Crim.L.R. 351, a company, A Ltd, had been assigned all distribution rights by I Ltd. A Ltd was charged with the possession of obscene publications for gain and was acquitted. I Ltd alleged that proceedings against it were an abuse of process as the question of the obscenity of the items in question, affecting the same market, had already been determined. The court referred to the duty of the prosecutor (the DPP in that case) said to arise under sections 1 and 2 of the Magistrates' Courts Act 1980 to ensure that all relevant prosecutions were brought together. This decision was followed in *R. v. Noe* [1985] Crim.L.R. 98 where a husband and wife ran two shops a mile apart from each other and were charged with possession of (*inter alia*) the same three video tapes. The husband was acquitted and the wife subsequently alleged that it was an abuse of process for her to be prosecuted. It was decided that the matter affecting her should have been tried at the same time as the matters affecting her husband. On the other hand, in *R. v. John Smith* [1986] Crim.L.R. 46 a retailer who was prosecuted for possession of obscene videos relied on the acquittal of the distributor to allege an abuse of the process of the court. The acquittal of the distributor had involved a finding by the jury that the videos were not obscene. The judge took the view that both *Intervision and Noe* could be distinguished on the facts and, in any event, were probably wrong. Moreover, there was no evidence in the later case as to the evidence which had been before the jury in the case concerning the distributor, so it could not be said that the same issues were being re-litigated. These decisions are first instance, Crown Court decisions but may be some guide to the factors to be taken into account when raising any similar argument.

Delay

10.45 Time when occuring. Delay is relevant whether it occurs before the laying of the information (*R. v. Derby Crown Court, ex p. Brooks* (1984) 80 Cr. App. R. 164, *Daventry District Council v. Olins* [1990] C.O.D. 244, DC) or between the laying of the information and the issue or service of the summons (*R. v. Fairford Justices, ex p. Brewster* [1975] 2 All E.R. 757; *R. v. Watford Justices, ex p Outrim* [1983] R.T.R. 26). Presumably it would be relevant too where the conduct of the trial by the prosecution proceeded so lingeringly that prejudice ensued. It was commonly said that where there had been a substantial delay there was no abuse unless that delay was attributable to prosecution misconduct (see, for example, *R. v. West London Stipendiary Magistrate, ex p. Anderson* [1984] Crim. L.R., *R. v. Grays Magistrates' Court, ex p. Graham* [1982] 1 Q.B. 1239). Since the decision of the Divisional Court in *R. v. Telford Justices, ex p. Badhan*

[1991] 2 All E.R. 854, that appears to be no longer the position although in *Attorney General's Reference (No. 1 of 1990)* [1992] 1 Q.B. 630, the Court of Appeal made it clear that a stay for delay would be granted only even more rarely than in the most exceptional circumstances where there was no fault on either the prosecution or any complainant and never where the delay was due to the complexity of the case or the contribution of the defendant.

10.46 Prejudice. Mere delay is insufficient, however, to stop the trial. The defendant must show on the balance of probabilities that he has suffered serious prejudice to the extent that no fair trial could be held, bearing in mind the powers of the court to admit or exclude evidence under the Police and Criminal Evidence Act 1984 and at common law (*Attorney General's Reference (No. 1 of 1990)* [1992] 1 Q.B. 630). It is a relevant factor that an offence is a regulatory one because the consequences of delay are often more likely to be an inability to investigate the offence (*Daventry District Council v. Olins* [1990] C.O.D. 244, DC). This is evidence of prejudice, although in *R. v. South Tyneside Garages, ex p. Mill Garages, The Times*, April 17, 1995 the court stressed that there was no different principle to be applied in a regulatory case from any other.

In trials on indictment, some of the adverse consequences of delay can be mitigated by directions to the jury (*R. v. B.* [1996] Crim.L.R. 406; *R. v. King* [1997] Crim.L.R. 298, but contrast *R. v. J.* [1997] Crim.L.R. 297).

10.47 Procedure. In the case of delay, the proper procedure has now been determined to be to make complaint about the alleged abuse in the court of trial or before the examining justices (*Badhan* above) and thereafter to appeal from any conviction which may follow on the basis that there was an abuse of process rather than to take proceedings in the Divisional Court and further hold up the trial (see paragraphs 10.27 to 10.29 above).

Disclosure of material known to the prosecution: Advance information

10.48 In the magistrates' court before mode of trial. The Magistrates' Courts (Advance Information) Rules 1985 provide that in the case of proceedings for an offence triable either way a defendant is entitled before the hearing in which the mode of trial (summarily or on indictment) is determined, to advance information as to the prosecution case. If requested (and the prosecutor is obliged to serve a notice informing the defendant of his rights to advance information as soon as possible after the service of a summons or after charge) the prosecution must provide either a summary of the evidence or a copy of the statements on which the prosecution intends to rely. Any document referred to in the summary or statement upon which reliance is to be placed must also be served (rule 4). An express reservation is made for a case where a prosecutor is of the opinion that a witness might be intimidated or the course of justice might be perverted (rule 5). At the hearing to determine the mode of trial, the court is obliged to satisfy itself that the defendant is aware of his right to advance information before proceeding with the hearing (rule 6). If a request for advance information is made and not complied with, the court has power to adjourn the case until it is satisfied that the defendant's case will not be substantially prejudiced by the non-compliance (rule 7). There is no power for the justices to order disclosure (*R. v. Dunmow Justices, ex p. Nash* (1993) 157 J.P. 1153) and it is not an abuse of process to fail to give advance information (*King v. Kucharz* [1989] C.O.D. 469, DC) although continual default, which is more serious than mere ineptitude, might constitute an abuse of process

(*R. v. Willesden Magistrates' Court, ex p. Clemmings* (1988) 152 J.P. 286). If the court declines to adjourn following a failure to give advance disclosure, a record of the reasons for finding that the defendant was not substantially prejudiced must be recorded in the register of adjudications kept by the clerk under rule 66 of the Magistrates' Courts Rules 1981 (Magistrates' Courts (Advance Information) Rules 1985).

10.49   Summary trials.   In the case of offences which are triable only summarily there is no statutory obligation of disclosure of the prosecution witness statements. The trial will not be unfair if statements are not disclosed, but nevertheless it is good prosecution practice (*R. v. Kingston-Upon-Hull Justices, ex p. McCann* (1991) 155 J.P. 569).

10.50   Complainant identity.   The identity of a complainant, or at least the facts surrounding his complaint, should be made known to a defendant at an early stage in a regulatory case, before advance disclosure, to prevent prejudice to the defendant such that he cannot properly prepare his case (*Daventry District Council v. Olins* [1990] C.O.D. 244, DC).

10.51   Committals.   In a matter which is in due course transferred to the Crown Court, the statements of prosecution evidence must become available before committal (see paragraphs 10.19 above), and further evidence to be relied upon in the Crown Court is served by way of notice of additional evidence.

Disclosure of unused material:

Prior to the implementation of Part I of the Criminal Procedure and Investigations Act 1996: The Common Law

10.52   In the Crown Court.   In a case to be tried on indictment, the investigation of which began before April 1997, "unused material", (which includes statements of witnesses not relied upon, unedited statements and other statements of witnesses who are to be relied upon and documents referred to in those statements, as well as other material) must, if it has or might have some bearing on the case or the circumstances of the offence, be disclosed (Attorney General's Guidelines: Disclosure of Information to the Defence in cases to be tried on Indictment, (1981) 74 Cr. App. R. 302; *R. v. Saunders & others* unreported, September 29, 1990, CCC (transcript no. T881630)). The obligation on the prosecution to make disclosure of unused material does not arise before committal in cases which are to be tried on indictment (*R. v. Crown Prosecution Service, ex p. Warby* (1994) 158 J.P. 190).

10.53   Exceptions.   The requirement to disclose set out in the Attorney's Guidelines was subject to certain common exceptions, which include:

(i)   where a statement which is believed to be true might be used to cross-examine a witness likely to give a false statement to the defence;

(ii)   where a statement is believed to be false but is from a close relative or friend of the defendant who might give evidence for the defendant;

(iii)   where the statement is neutral but it is thought that false evidence might subsequently be given in favour of the defendant;

(iv) where disclosure is thought likely to lead to intimidation or subornment of a witness;

(v) where it is not in the public interest.

The continued relevance of these considerations (apart from that of public interest disclosure, for which see below) has been defended in *R. v. Winston Brown* [1997] 3 W.L.R. 447, although attention was drawn to the fact that the Attorney's guidelines were rules of practice not of law.

10.54 Common law duties include the magistrates' court. Recent decisions of the Court of Appeal (Criminal Division) in the cases of *Ward* [1993] 2 All E.R. 577, *Davis* [1993] 2 All E.R. 643 and *Keane* (1994) 99 Cr. App. R. 1, have clarified the independent common law duties on the prosecution to make disclosure of material which might assist the defence. These cases, which all concerned trials on indictment for serious offences, have underlined the common law duty of the prosecution to disclose all relevant material to the defence unless there are good reasons (such as the public interest) for not doing so and have outlined the procedures to be followed. The duty extends to less serious cases and to the magistrates' court (see paragraph 10.59 below). The duty continues throughout the pre-trial and trial period and extends to all varieties of matter. The obligation of disclosure will in some circumstances exist even where there is to be a guilty plea, because the defendant may have made his decision to plead guilty on the basis of false evidence, so that any conviction might be manifestly unfair (*R. v. Bolton Magistrates' Court, ex p. Scally* [1991] 1 Q.B. 537).

10.55 Examples of material for disclosure in regulatory cases. In the case of regulatory offences, particular matters which may be of relevance to the defendant, are:

(i) reports of experts (whether they uphold the line taken by the prosecution, or more importantly still, if they reject it). This will include any letters sent by the expert to the prosecutor about the subject matter or about his report, and any working notes;

(ii) records of experiments and tests undertaken in respect of any matter in issue, or potentially in issue in the case;

(iii) knowledge in the possession of the prosecutor of expert tests and experiments (even if not recorded in a document) which may assist the defendant;

(iv) previous convictions of, and disciplinary action against prosecution witnesses, or other facts which may impugn the credibility of a prosecution witness (*R. v. Knightsbridge Crown Court, ex p. Goonatilleke* [1986] 1 Q.B. 1, *R. v. McCarthy* (1994) 158 J.P. 283);

(v) previous inconsistent statements by prosecution witnesses (*R. v. Liverpool Crown Court, ex p. Roberts* [1986] Crim.L.R. 622, *R. v. Dye and others* [1992] Crim.L.R. 449, *R. v. Halton Justices, ex p. Hughes* (1991) 155 J.P. 837);

(vi) statements of potential witnesses not relied upon by the prosecution (although see the limitations on this requirement permitted under the

Attorney General's Guidelines (see paragraph 10.52 above) and also the decision in *R. v. Mills* [1997] 3 W.L.R. 458);

(vii) where the prosecutor is a local authority, records of inspections by T.S.O.s or E.H.O.s or other officers charged with prosecution on a previous occasion to that upon which it is alleged an offence was committed, evidenced or investigated;

(viii) details of connected investigations – which might mean details relating to potential co-defendants or others who have not been prosecuted;

(ix) pocket notebook entries;

(x) internal reports of facts from investigating officers to those with the responsibility for the decision to prosecute (but not including requests or instructions to lawyers for advice or representation): it may be that a claim for public interest immunity could be made out for such documents, however. By analogy, reports sent by the police to the CPS are immune from production because of the need to protect the freedom of communication between investigating officers and their advisers (*Evans v. Chief Constable of Surrey* [1988] Q.B. 588);

(xi) a copy of the record of the decision to prosecute;

(xii) in the case of a local authority prosecutor, letters written to or telephone attendances with the Home Authority;

(xiii) Where there is a written prosecution policy (see paragraphs 2.11 to 2.14 above), such a policy is (arguably) disclosable to the defendant;

(xiv) the scope of disclosure is not generally thought by local authorities to extend to material appearing in relation to certain types of prosecution and certain defendants on the computer network utilised by local authority prosecutors, although it is arguable that such information should be disclosed. On the other hand, issues of public interest immunity almost certainly arise.

Where information is given to a prosecuting authority orally, that does not make it exempt from disclosure, although of course, to make disclosure the information may need to be written down by the prosecuting authority.

10.56 **Immunity.** At common law, if material is not disclosed, it is for the court, not for the prosecution to decide so. There are three levels of sensitivity which justify three different procedural approaches. The basic rule is that if the prosecution wishes to rely upon sensitivity or public interest immunity, then wherever possible (*i.e.* in most cases):

(i) notice that an application for a ruling is to be made is to be given to the defence;

(ii) at least the category of material held is to be indicated;

(iii) the defence is to be given the opportunity to make representations.

10.57 **"Category sensitive" immunity from disclosure.** If the revelation of even the category of material held is contrary to the public interest, application should to be made by the prosecution *ex parte* for an order permitting the material to be withheld and the court may order whether the defence should be allowed to participate or whether the material should not be revealed. The fact that an application was to be made is to be revealed to the defence except in highly exceptional and rare cases where even knowledge of the fact of an *ex parte* application would be contrary to the public interest.

10.58   "Application sensitive" immunity from disclosure.   An *ex parte* application in such cases could then be made secretly. In such exceptional cases the judge is required to decide what procedure should then be followed. There is no obligation to give disclosure of unused material prior to committal so that examining magistrates should be spared considerations of public interest immunity from disclosure (see paragraph 10.15 above).

10.59   Summary trial.   As with Crown court cases, the rules governing disclosure have been radically altered by the 1996 Act in relation to cases the investigation of which commenced after the beginning of April 1997. In respect of cases where the investigation began before that date, the common law rules apply, as do the considerations of public interest immunity. (Also see paragraph 10.63, below.) In *R. v. Bromley Magistrates' Court, ex p. Smith and Wilkins* [1995] 1 W.L.R. 994, it was held that magistrates did have power, following the above decisions, to rule upon disputed issues in summary trials. This case involved an allegation that the defendants were unlawfully in possession of a pit bull terrier. The defence sought disclosure from the prosecution of (*inter alia*) all previous cases in which the prosecution expert had given evidence. The magistrates decided that they had no power to order so. The Divisional Court disagreed that there was no power to order disclosure in the magistrates' court, but also held that the material in question was not of a disclosable category, particularly in the light of the way in which the application was made.

10.60   CPS practice in summary trials.   The Attorney General's Guidelines do not apply to summary trial but the CPS practice on summary trials was disclosed by counsel for the Crown on instructions in the *Smith and Wilkins* case (above). There is a written code as to the circumstances in which disclosure was to be given in summary cases, and the Divisional Court deprecated its non-revelation, although in the light of the matters which counsel put forward did not insist that the document was brought before the court. The code provides that except in the case of non-imprisonable traffic cases (to which the same principles are applied informally) disclosure was effected by providing the material itself or by provision of a list ("the C Schedule") inviting access to all documents. The test, upheld as an appropriate test in *R. v. Winston Brown* (above) namely that those documents which can be seen on a sensible appraisal:

   (i)   to be relevant or possibly relevant;

  (ii)   to raise or possibly raise a new issue whose existence is not apparent from the material the prosecution intends to use;

 (iii)   to hold a real prospect of providing a lead on evidence which goes to (i) or should be disclosed. This includes all witness statements, unedited statements, records of interview and records of defendants not charged and other records. The CPS mark the schedule as to whether the documents are to be disclosed or not.

10.61   Other prosecutors.   In the light of the above it appears that prosecutors other than the CPS should adopt a similar procedure and some local authorities do.

10.62   Procedure in the Magistrates' court.   For a consideration of the consequences of public interest immunity issues in the Magistrates' Courts, see paragraph 10.54 above.

Part I of The Criminal Procedure and Investigations Act 1996

10.63   Application.   This Part of the Act governs the conduct of police and other persons who have a duty to conduct a criminal investigation with a view to a decision in due course whether a person should be prosecuted for and/or is guilty of an offence (section 1). It therefore applies in respect of investigations beginning after April 1, 1997, to Environmental Health and Trading Standards Officers as well as to other investigators charged with a duty to investigate. It applies to summary trials as well as to trials which are to be heard in the Crown Court, and the procedure is governed by the Magistrates' Courts (Criminal Procedure and Investigations Act 1996) (Disclosure) Rules 1997 (S.I. 1997 No. 703). There is some doubt whether under the 1996 Act:

   (i) in the case of offences which are capable of being tried on indictment, the provisions extend to a corporate defendant who agrees to be tried summarily. See section 1(1) and note that the references to an accused's age suggest that only a natural person is contemplated, and

   (ii) in the case of matters where a plea of guilty has been entered, the provisions apply.

If the provisions do not apply, presumably the common law provisions above will continue to do so.

10.64   Primary disclosure.   Where the new Act applies, and whether the matter is to be tried summarily or on indictment, the prosecutor must conduct the investigation in accordance with the provisions of the Code of Practice (No. 2) Order 1997, (S.I. 1997 No. 1033), and must either disclose to the accused material:

   (a) in the possession of the prosecution which has been acquired in the course of investigating the accused; and

   (b) which has been inspected pursuant to a Code of Practice for the conduct of the investigation under Part II of the Act,

and which might, in the prosecutor's opinion, undermine the prosecution case; or:
give to the accused a written statement to the effect that there is no such material of that description (section 3).

There is no duty to furnish to the defendant material which reinforces the prosecution case but which the prosecution has, for some reason, decided not to rely upon, unless it is derived from an investigation under the Code.

10.65   Secondary disclosure.   Whether the prosecution will become liable to make secondary disclosure depends upon whether the defendant is required or chooses to submit a defence statement of his case. If the case is committed to the Crown Court, the defendant will be required under section 5 of the Act to disclose his defence. He must provide to the court and to the prosecutor a statement setting out the nature of his defence, indicating matters upon which he takes issue with the prosecution, and set out in relation to each such issue identified the reason why he takes issue. Notice must be given within the relevant period prescribed by regulations under section 12 of the Act. In summary trials, the defence statement is voluntary. The secondary duties of the prosecutor arise following receipt of the defence statement. The prosecutor must disclose material not previously disclosed which might reasonably be expected to assist the accused's defence, or, if there is none, to make a written statement to that effect. The duty of disclosure is a continuing one and is not limited to documents in the prosecution's possession. It also extends to information.

10.66   Abuse of process and non-disclosure.   Failure by the prosecution to comply with the time periods laid down in the regulations under section 12 will not, of itself, be an abuse of the process of the court. If there is such delay that the defendant is denied a fair trial, section 10 envisages that prosecutions will be stayed as an abuse of process (see paragraph 10.45 above).

Procedure for summary trials

PTR

Pre-trial matters

10.67   Pre-trial review.   It has become increasingly common for a pre-trial review to be conducted prior to a summary hearing in the magistrates' court in regulatory cases. This is often conducted by the justices' clerk who has the power to ask the defendant whether he will plead guilty or not guilty and to fix a date, time and place for trial (Justices Clerks Rules 1970, Sched. 1 para. 4B, as inserted). It is a vehicle for other informal directions, too. It is, for instance, not unusual for a direction to be given that the parties must disclose a list of authorities prior to the hearing. Defendants' legal representatives should, however, approach such directions with caution. In criminal proceedings in the Magistrates' Court the defence is in general not required to disclose its case prior to the hearing and legal representatives who agree, say, to the disclosure of a list of authorities to the prosecution may prejudice their client. While surprise may not be an instrument of fairness, its tactical advantage has been seen on many occasions.

Save for the fixing of a date, the Magistrates' Clerk has no formal authority to compel compliance, but the machinery of litigation is lubricated by co-operation. There is no reason, for example, why the magistrates' court should not be told in advance of the cases which will be required in court so that the clerk can read them at his leisure before the hearing, provided that he is also requested not to disclose the same to the prosecution.

The plea

10.68   The plea.   The plea is frequently taken at a hearing prior to the commencement of the trial. It is not part of the trial itself in the magistrates' court (*R. v. Horseferry Road Magistrates' Court, ex p. K, The Times,* February 22, 1996).

    (i)   *Individual defendants:* where a defendant is an individual or a partner in a
        firm, a plea of guilty can only be taken from him personally (*R. v.*

Wakefield Justices, ex p. Butterworth (1969) 114 Sol.Jo. 30) unless the provisions as to pleading guilty by post apply (see below), although, notably the Editors of Stone's Justices Manual (129th ed.) consider that counsel or solicitor representing absent accused may enter a not guilty plea on his behalf (Stone's Manual 1–461 and note).

(ii) *Corporate Defendants:* where the defendant is a company, a director, secretary, or other representative may appear in court and enter a plea on behalf of the corporation (Magistrates' Courts Act 1980, s.12 and Sched. 3).

10.69 Plea of guilty by post. Section 12 and 12A of the Magistrates' Courts Act 1980 (as amended) provide for a plea of guilty by post. Section 12 applies to a summary only offence which does not carry more than three months imprisonment. A proportion of regulatory offences – such as a food labelling offence – can be disposed of in this fashion. The procedural requirements are that the defendant shall have been served with:

(i) a notice explaining the effect of section 12;

(ii) a statement of the facts relating to the charges and which may claim costs (*R. v. Coventry City Justices, ex p. D.P.P.* [1991] 1 W.L.R. 1153). This statement will be placed before the court in the event of a guilty plea;

(iii) a notice containing information about the accused, such as previous convictions, if it is intended that the court should receive that information.

The statement of facts is read out to the court by the clerk together with any mitigation which the defendant may have sent. This procedure does not permit the administration of justice in secret (see *R. v. Oldham Justices, ex p. Morrissey* [1959] 1 W.L.R. 58). The court may proceed to sentence immediately or may adjourn for the attendance of the defendant. Section 12A permits the court to apply the above procedure to other matters if the clerk of the court has received notice from the prosecutor that the above documents have accompanied the summons and:

(i) the clerk has received notice in writing from the defendant or his legal representative that he wishes to plead guilty without an appearance; or

(ii) the clerk has not received such notification and the accused appears before the court at the time and place appointed for the trial.

Where the defendant in fact appears, he has an opportunity to put forward his mitigation orally. The benefit of this provision to the defendant may be that the full facts are not put before the court but only "a concise statement of facts": on the other hand, where the facts contain substantial mitigation which has been omitted, this procedure could work to the disadvantage of the defendant. The court must give credit for a guilty plea under section 12A when sentencing in respect of a plea of guilty by post by reason of section 48 of the Criminal Justice and Public Order Act 1994.

10.70 Change of plea. Where a plea of not guilty has been entered and the defendant wishes to change his plea, the justices should not investigate the defendant's motivation for the change (*R. v. Eccles Justices, ex p. Fitzpatrick* (1989) 89 Cr. App. R. 324). Where a defendant has indicated by post an intention to plead guilty, but wishes to withdraw the notification, the court must proceed as though no notification had been given (Magistrates' Courts Act 1980, s.12). Where there has been a plea of guilty in person and the defendant wishes to change it to not guilty, the court may consider his application at any point up to conviction. The discretion to permit change of plea is a matter of judicial discretion which should only be exercised in clear cases and very sparingly (*S. v. Manchester City Recorder* [1971] A.C. 481). If the offence alleged is triable either way, the inevitable consequence of allowing a change of plea from guilty to not guilty is that mode of trial proceedings must be commenced afresh (*R. v. Bow St. Magistrates' Court, ex p. Welcombe* (1992) 156 J.P. 609). The previous plea of guilty may be treated as evidence of a confession of fact, but the court should weigh its probative value against its prejudicial value and should not generally admit it to evidence (*R. v. Rimmer* [1972] 1 W.L.R. 268).

10.71 Equivocal pleas. An equivocal plea is a plea of guilty entered in the context of an assertion which is inconsistent with guilt. It is an issue which should not arise where the defendant is legally represented but it sometimes occurs that a plea is entered following a lawyer's mistaken view of the law. Justices may allow a change of plea, but are entitled to investigate the facts, for example, whether the defendant was solely influenced by his lawyer's misapprehension (*P. Foster (Haulage) Ltd v. Roberts* [1978] 2 All E.R. 751). Equivocal pleas can arise where a defendant is not represented, particularly if he is motivated by a desire to "get the matter over with" but does not truly acknowledge guilt. If the defendant says something which casts doubt on the correctness of the plea and he is unrepresented, the magistrates must enter a plea of not guilty on his behalf and try the case (*R. v. Blandford Justices, ex p. G* [1967] 1 Q.B. 82).

It is only in rare instances that an appeal on an equivocal plea will be allowed (if there is a conviction on an equivocal plea, appeal is the only remedy because the magistrates are *functus officio*). The Crown Court must be satisfied on hearing from the appellant that the plea was equivocal, and will then seek affidavit evidence from the clerk to the justices or the chairman of the Bench as to the event in the magistrates' court. Only then will the Crown court enter an equivocal plea.

10.72 Special pleas: autrefois acquit and convict. Strictly, these pleas can only be raised in the Crown Court, although it is now clear that the same principles must be applied in the magistrates' court (*DPP v. Porterhouse* (1989) 89 Cr. App. R. 21). The issue is whether the defendant has been acquitted or convicted previously by a court of competent jurisdiction of the same or substantially the same offence as that currently before the court. The plea cannot be raised in a case where the defendant was never in jeopardy of conviction, so it does not arise where a case is summarily dismissed to allow substitution of a new allegation (*Broadbent v. High* [1985] R.T.R. 359), or where previous proceedings were irregular (*R. v. Marsham* (1912) 76 J.P. 284), but it can be relied upon where a court has dismissed information because the prosecution have no witnesses at court and an adjournment has been refused (*R. v. Swansea Justices, ex p. Purvis* (1981) 145 J.P. 252, although see *R. v. Pressick* [1978] Crim.L.R. 377). It is not a valid objection that a defendant has been convicted of a previous summons which alleged an offence of imparting false or misleading information to a different complainant (*Wings Ltd. v. Ellis* [1985] 1 A.C. 272).

Defence statements

10.73 Defence statements. The disclosure of the defence case remains, in the magistrates' court, a voluntary matter, subject to the need to serve expert evidence in advance: see paragraphs 1 to 16 above). Under the provisions to be brought into force in the Criminal Procedure and Investigations Act 1996, there is no requirement for a defence statement setting out the defence in the magistrates' court. If a defence statement is served, however, the defendant may subject himself to adverse comment by the court and enable adverse inferences to be drawn if:

(i) there is delay in making the statement; or

(ii) if the defendant conducts different defences at trial from those disclosed in a defence statement.

In these circumstances, it must be questionable whether it is of benefit to surrender the traditional advantage of surprise that the defendant has been accustomed to enjoy prior to this Act.

The hearing

10.74 The venue and tribunal. If the matter is to remain in the Magistrates' Court, the trial will be before justices of the peace or a stipendiary magistrate. Where lay magistrates hear the case, they will usually sit as a bench of three, but sometimes only two justices comprise the bench. In the latter instance, if the bench is unable to agree whether to acquit or convict, there must be an adjournment to a different bench for a re-trial (*R. v. Redbridge Justices, ex p. Ram* [1992] 1 Q.B. 384). In many courts "enforcement offences" days are set aside for the hearing of regulatory matters or a court is specially allocated to the case, but in some magistrates' courts, the case forms part of the ordinary list. (Where the court is aware that there will be a plea of guilty, it is likely that the matter will be listed in the ordinary list.)

10.75 "Bias". The need for the actual and apparent impartiality of the court applies as much to the justices' clerk as to the justices themselves (*R. v. Richmond and Gilling West Magistrates, ex p. Steel* [1993] Crim.L.R. 711). The test is whether in the eyes of the reasonable man there is a real danger (and not just a reasonable suspicion) of bias (*R. v. Gough* [1993] 2 W.L.R. 883). There are statutory prohibitions on justices from sitting in certain types of case with which they might be concerned; a member of a local authority must not sit in proceedings brought by or against the authority of which he is a member, for instance (Justices of the Peace Act 1997, s.66) although he may hear proceedings bought by police officers or rating, council tax or Community Charge matters (Justices of the Peace Act 1997, ss.66(5), 67) and may also hear control of pollution matters even though he may be a councillor or employee of the prosecutor (Control of Pollution Act 1974, s.106). Any direct pecuniary interest, no matter how small, will amount to bias, although an indirect pecuniary interest in the outcome may not do so. Contrast, for example, *R. v. Hammond* (1863) 27 J.P. 793 where it was held that a justice holding shares in a company should disqualify himself or *R. v. Altrincham Justices, ex p. Pennington* [1975] Q.B. 549 where a co-opted member of an education authority and school governor should have made known her connection with the proceedings in a case where the victim of a weights and measures offence was a school, and *R. v. Mulvihill* [1990] 1 W.L.R. 438 where a judge was not disqualified from trying a case of robbery of a company in which he held shares. Whereas a direct pecuniary interest in or connection with the subject matter or persons involved in the proceedings will of necessity disqualify a magistrate, a mere interest should be declared so that the parties may choose whether to make representations as to bias.

10.76 Knowledge of the defendant's bad character. It infrequently occurs that magistrates learn of the defendant's previous convictions. In itself, this does not lead to bias, and it is as a matter of practice rather than jurisdiction that a defendant should be tried before a magistrate who has not dealt with him previously (*R. v. Metropolitan Stipendiary Magistrate, ex p. Gallagher* (1972) 136 J.P.N. 80). On the other hand, where a justice learns of a defendant's previous convictions during a trial, this will normally mean that the justice will become disqualified (*R. v. Birmingham Justices, ex p. Robinson* (1986) 150 J.P. 1). The clerk should try to avoid justices seeing unrelated charges in the list, but this is a matter of good practice not of law.

10.77 Disqualification on the grounds of behaviour. This may apply both where justices make a mistake in procedure which is consistent with reaching a premature conclusion (*R. v. Midhurst Justices, ex p. Thompson* [1974] Q.B. 137; *R. v. Marylebone Justices, ex p. Yasmin Farrag* [1981] Crim.L.R. 182, *R. v. Liverpool Justices, ex p. Topping* [1983] 1 W.L.R. 119, *R. v. Marylebone Magistrates, ex p. Perry* (1992) 156 J.P. 696; *R. v. Ely Justices, ex p. Burgess* (1993) 157 J.P. 484; *R. v. Marylebone Magistrates, ex p. Joseph, The Times*, May 7, 1993) but also where the justices have been paying inadequate attention, such as where the chairman appeared to be asleep (*R. v. Weston-super Mare Justices, ex p. Taylor* [1981] Crim.L.R. 179). In *R. v. Romsey Magistrates' Court, ex p. Gale and Green* [1992] 156 J.P. 567, one of the magistrates typed out what he would say if the defendant were to be convicted and read it out. This gave the impression of bias and the conviction was quashed. If an allegation of bias is justifiably capable of being levelled in the course of proceedings, the proper procedure is for the justices to disqualify themselves so that there can be a fresh trial before a different bench – unless the matter can be cured (such as where one person was asleep) by the withdrawal of that individual.

10.78 Publicity. This is frequently a matter of concern to the regulatory defendant, anxious that infringements should not adversely affect his market. A Magistrates' Court is required to sit in public, subject to any enactment to the contrary (Magistrates' Courts Act 1980, s.121(4)). There is an inherent jurisdiction to control the conduct of the proceedings, and it may depart from the general rule to the extent necessary to serve the interests of justice, where its application would frustrate or render impracticable the administration of justice (*Attorney General v. Leveller Magazine Ltd* [1979] A.C. 440). Moreover, a court may hear mitigation "*in camera*" if there are compelling reasons to do so. Compelling reasons will not include the adverse effect on trading that public knowledge of the offence might engender: the public generally has a right to be informed of the commission of offences against its interest. Where, however, there are compelling reasons (such as where the mitigation might reveal details of a secret process or other sensitive material) the court should sit *in camera* to consider the application (unless the application is plainly misconceived) and announce the decision in open court (*R. v. Ealing Justices, ex p. Weafer* (1982) 74 Cr. App. R. 204). If the decision is in favour of a private hearing, the court should thereafter re-convene *in camera*.

An alternative procedure is to agree a statement of facts relevant to the mitigation and to hand the statement to the justices in open court, but without revealing the contents (*R. v. Reigate Justices, ex p. Argus Newspapers* (1983) 147 J.P. 385).

10.79   Newspaper reports.   The Contempt of Court Act 1981 permits both the postponement and prohibition of the reporting of proceedings but only in the most limited circumstances. Postponement of news reports is permitted only where it appears necessary to avoid a substantial risk of prejudice in the proceedings or other pending or imminent proceedings (section 4(2)). The court may prohibit the publication of a name or other matter which has been withheld from the public (section 11). In *R. v. Dover Justices, ex p. Dover District and Wells* [1992] Crim.L.R. 371, the court considered the question of the damage that court proceedings may do to the business of a defendant, and said:

(i) that it would be very rare for an order prohibiting publicity to be made simply because the defendant had been acquitted; and

(ii) that even if severe economic damage would be done to the accused and his business before trial, that was not a sufficient reason to depart from the general rule that nothing should be done to discourage the proper and fair reporting of proceedings (*Attorney General v. Leveller Magazine Ltd* [1979] A.C. 440).

10.80   Applications for adjournments of a summary trial and trial in the absence of the accused.   Quite different from a hearing at which it is not anticipated that the trial will commence, and is so adjourned to a subsequent date, is a hearing at which a trial could occur but an application is made for an adjournment by a party. This is often because a witness is absent or expected evidence has not become available (such as a late expert's report) but could also be for any number of other reasons.

There is a balance to be drawn: on the one hand justices must pay attention to the need for expedition in criminal cases (*R. v. Aberdare Justices, ex p. D.P.P.* (1991) 155 J.P. 324). On the other hand, if, in all the circumstances there is a risk of unfairness to the accused if an adjournment is refused, it must be granted (*R. v. Kingston-upon-Hull Justices, ex p. McCann* (1991) 155 J.P. 569). The factors which may be relevant include:

(i) whether either side would be prejudiced by an adjournment;

(ii) whether either side would be prejudiced by the refusal of an adjournment; this and the former consideration can be investigated by inquiry about the nature of the evidence in question by the magistrates or, on their behalf, the clerk. Where the defence seek an adjournment and allege prejudice, the position is complicated by the duty which the defence representative may owe to his client not to disclose the defence. There is no obligation on the defendant to disclose the nature of his defence nor to say what witnesses he will call. Clearly, if a defence statement has been served, this problem will have disappeared. However, the proper procedure currently is that the clerk should ask the defendant to specify what prejudice would be occasioned if the adjournment were refused, and advise the justices (*R. v. Bracknell Justices, ex p. Hughes* (1990) 154 J.P.N. 46);

(iii) whether an adjournment would cause the case to become stale or defeat the public interest in speedy justice;

(iv) whether there have been previous adjournments and, if so, at whose request; where there have been a number of adjournments, justices will sometimes express the view that the case must go ahead on the next occasion. If there is an application for an adjournment on the next occasion, that view is a factor which can be taken into account, but the justices must exercise their discretion afresh: the opinion of the previous bench cannot fetter the discretion of the subsequent bench (*R. v. Aberdare Justices, ex p. D.P.P.* (1991) 155 J.P. 569; also see *R. v. Crawley Justices, ex p. D.P.P.* (1991) 155 J.P. 841);

(v) whether the party seeking the adjournment is to blame for the problem at the root of the application.

10.81 Dismissing an information. If the court is not minded to allow an adjournment, the prosecution and defence must be allowed to call what evidence they have. The magistrates' court has power to dismiss an information only after "hearing the evidence of the parties" (Magistrates' Courts Act 1980, s.9(2)). It is therefore improper merely to dismiss the application because, say, the prosecutor says he does not wish to proceed that day. If the adjournment is refused, he should be offered the opportunity to call evidence. If he calls no evidence, the case may then be dismissed (*Harrington v. Roots* (1984) 149 J.P. 211).

10.82 Trial in the absence of the accused. Section 11 of the Magistrates' Courts Act 1980 permits trial in the absence of the accused if either it is proved that the summons was served on him a reasonable time beforehand or if he has appeared on a previous occasion and had notice of the time and place of the adjourned hearing. Obviously, if there is cogent evidence that the accused is too ill to attend but would wish to do so, the court should adjourn to enable him to be present. The provision is particularly to deal with minor cases and so is particularly appropriate to regulatory offences where no allegation of dishonesty is made. It is undesirable to deal with more serious cases where the defendant risks a custodial sentence in his absence.

Absence does not include where the defendant in person is not there but his representative is: in these circumstances the defendant is deemed to be present (Magistrates' Courts Act 1980, section 122).

The case is heard by oral evidence or section 9 statements with any interview being summarised or read. Where the interview shows a potential defence to a matter the burden of proving which lies on the prosecution, the court should not declare that there is a reasonable doubt and dismiss the information, but rather adjourn the case for a proper hearing so that the defendant can be present for cross-examination (*DPP v. Gokceli* (1989) 153 J.P. 109).

If the court proceeds under section 11 to hear a case in the absence of the defendant and he is convicted, the court may subsequently re-open the issue if it is in the interests of justice so to do, by directing that the defendant be tried before a different bench (section 142(2) of the Magistrates' Courts Act 1980). This provision does not apply where there has been a guilty plea nor where the defendant has sent a notification under section 12 that he wishes to plead guilty without an appearance (*R. v. Epping and Ongar Justices, ex p. Shippam Limited* (1986) 150 J.P. 425).

Order of events in a summary trial

10.83 Prosecution opening. Before calling any evidence, the prosecutor may address the court (Magistrates' Courts Rules 1981, rule 13). Where there is a likelihood of a due diligence defence, the prosecutor is likely to address the potential issues which he can foresee, at least in outline, at this stage. This is usually the only opportunity that the prosecutor has to address the facts upon which a due diligence defence may rest, without the leave of the magistrates. Consequently, the more remote in time the opening becomes, the more easily it will lose its persuasive impact. This is a problem, not only in a lengthy case, but more particularly where the case takes longer than expected and adjournments may cause lengthy delays due to unavailability of court space and the same bench of magistrates. A lengthy delay between the start and conclusion of the evidence may be a good reason to invite the magistrates to hear afresh from the prosecutor at a later stage (see paragraph 10.86 below). (But if it becomes clear that a case will be held over a number of days spread over a long period so that justice cannot be done, it is also not improper to discontinue the hearing and start again with a new bench sitting on consecutive days: *R. v. Ripon Liberty Justices, ex p. Bugg* (1991) 155 J.P. 213).

10.84 Evidence. The prosecution calls its evidence first, which could be in the form of oral testimony or documentary evidence, formal admissions, photographs, etc. Each witness, if his evidence is not read, will be examined in chief and cross-examined, and, if necessary, re-examined to clear up any ambiguities arising out of cross-examination. Provided that the evidence gives rise to a case to answer both as to fact and law, the defendant then has an opportunity to call evidence in support of his defence. Sometimes evidence in rebuttal is called, but this may only be when an issue arises unexpectedly in the trial. Evidence in rebuttal cannot be called if the need for it should have been foreseen (*R. v. Day* [1940] 1 All E.R. 402) but if the issue is a technical oversight by the prosecution, such as formally to prove a statutory rule or order, the court may allow further evidence after the prosecution has closed its case and, indeed, after the defence evidence (*Price v. Humphries* [1958] 2 Q.B. 353). In *Derbyshire County Council v. Kwik Save Group* [1997] C.O.D. 19, the Divisional Court held that an application made by the Crown to re-open its case on a prosecution under the Fire Precautions Act 1971 should have been allowed to establish the number of persons at work at the relevant premises, so as to establish liability. A due diligence defence had been indicated by the defence and all prosecution evidence admitted under section 9 of the Criminal Justice Act 1967.

In the context of due diligence defences, the nature of which may not have been foreseen by the prosecution, the arguments in favour of evidence in rebuttal or re-opening the prosecution case may be stronger than in other cases where the nature of the defence may be easier to foresee. For instance, if a defendant were to give evidence that he could not have anticipated the events that led to the offence, the prosecution may wish to call rebutting evidence of a prior warning or previous offence – evidence which would not have been admissible unless that defence was raised. For further considerations as to the calling of evidence, see paragraphs 10.82 to 10.100 below.

10.85 Submission of no case to answer. Rule 13 of the Magistrates' Courts Rules does not make provision for the making of a submission of no case to answer because such a submission is not a speech. A submission of no case may be made without prejudice to the Defendant's right to call evidence subsequently and make closing submissions. The test is, by analogy, that in *R. v. Galbraith* [1981] 1 W.L.R. 1039: if there is no evidence upon which a reasonable bench of magistrates directing themselves properly, could convict the defendant, there is no case to answer. The submission is one of law, and the magistrates may raise it of their own motion provided that the prosecution is given an opportunity to answer their concerns.

10.86 Order of speeches. It is open to a defendant to make an opening rather than a closing speech, but if he does so he forgoes his right to make a closing speech. The court may grant leave to make a second speech – and if granted, leave should be given to the other party. If both parties address the court for a second time, the defendant must be allowed to have the final word (Magistrates' Courts Rules 1981, r.13).

10.87 The decision. The magistrates will give their decision after hearing submissions. Their obligation is to convict or to dismiss the allegations (Magistrates' Courts Act 1980, s.9). They are not obliged to give contemporaneous reasons for reaching their finding, or, indeed, any reasons unless there is an application to them to state a case. There is, however, an increasing tendency for magistrates to give brief oral reasons for their findings, at least in regulatory cases. This is particularly helpful, especially where their findings as to a due diligence system might be expected to influence future conduct by the defendant.

EVIDENCE

Witnesses of fact

10.88 Interviewing witnesses before trial. As a rule, a party may interview and prepare proofs of evidence from and call such witnesses as he likes. A defendant is not required to disclose proofs of witnesses of fact at any stage. Accordingly, when defence witnesses give evidence, the prosecution may be largely unprepared for what they will say unless a defence statement has been served (paragraph 10.73 above) or unless the interview under caution has dealt adequately with the issues raised (paragraphs 3.26 to 3.36 above). On the other hand, the prosecution will have been under a duty to disclose proofs of evidence in certain circumstances (see paragraphs 10.48 to 10.50) and must have given advance disclosure of evidence which it proposes to call in the case of offences which are capable of being tried on indictment.

Sometimes, in the course of preparing for trial, a defendant would wish to interview a prosecution witness prior to that witness giving evidence in court. There is no property in a witness, so there is no reason why this should not occur, although the address of a witness is not now normally disclosed (Magistrates' Court (Witnesses Addresses) Rules 1990). Where a defendant to a trial in the magistrates' court wishes to interview a witness to be called by the prosecution, he may do so pursuant to the above rules, although rules of professional conduct require that an opportunity be given to an appropriate person, such as a trading standards officer, to be present at the interview. A witness is never obliged to participate in an interview, but as a matter of practice an adverse inference could, in some circumstances, be drawn from his refusal. An interview such as that envisaged by the rules may either provide good material for cross-examination of the witness by the defence, or may alert the prosecution to the areas of weakness in its' or the defence case.

10.89 Order of witnesses. The prosecutor has a discretion as to the order in which he will call oral evidence, although it is customary for evidence to be called chronologically or in order of importance where possible. Witnesses of fact should remain outside court until they are called in to give evidence, although this is a matter of practice not a rule of law (*R. v. Bexley Justices, ex. p. King* [1980] R.T.R. 49). In regulatory cases this practice is sometimes relaxed by agreement. Moreover, where the principal prosecution witness is an employee of the prosecutor (which will be the case with an E.H.O. or T.S.O.) he may also be the only person available to represent the authority and instruct the legal representative. In those circumstances, he is usually permitted by agreement to remain in court for the opening and any earlier witness. After he has given evidence, there is no reason why he should not remain, even if he has been released by the court. Expert witnesses may remain in court throughout.

10.90 Order of witnesses: defence. If the defendant is to give evidence, he must give his evidence before any other witness of fact, unless the court directs otherwise in the exercise of its discretion (Police and Criminal Evidence Act 1984, s.79). No express provision is made for the situation where there is a corporate defendant, but it is practice for the witness most close to the events occasioning the alleged offence to give evidence first, even though that witness may not be part of the directing mind and will of the company (see paragraphs 7.33 to 7.42 above) and may, indeed, not be the witness who has given an interview under caution (if any) on behalf of the company. As with prosecution witnesses, the principle that witnesses of fact should remain outside until they are called is often abrogated in regulatory cases by agreement. Where the defendant is a corporate defendant, it is not always easy to determine who is to be regarded as a witness and who is to be regarded as a representative of the company and therefore a client who is entitled to be in court throughout.

10.91 Witness statements as memory refreshing documents. It was formerly the position that a witness statement could never be used in the witness box as a means of refreshment of the witnesses memory, but could be looked at outside the court before the witness gave evidence. Only contemporaneous documents could be used to refresh a witnesses' memory. Since the decision in *R. v. Da Silva* [1990] 1 W.L.R. 31, it has been clear that a witness may, while giving evidence, look at a statement he made earlier if the court accepts:

(i) that the witness cannot recall the details of events because of lapse of time;

(ii) that he made a statement nearer the time when he could remember the events described;

(iii) that he had not read the statement before coming into the witness box;

(iv) that the witness wishes to look at the statement before he continues to give evidence.

In *R. v. South Ribble Magistrates, ex p. Cochrane* [1996] 2 Cr. App. R. 544, a witness was permitted to look at his earlier statement even though he had been given a hurried opportunity to re-read his statement prior to giving his evidence.

10.92 Editing evidence. It is sometimes necessary or desirable to edit witness statements to exclude irrelevant or prejudicial material or to make a single statement out of several statements by the same witness. It is common to edit statements at the request of the defendant, particularly where the editing of the statement will enable it to be read and avoid the calling of a witness. The Practice Direction given by the Lord Chief Justice, which applies equally to the Crown Court as to the Magistrates' Court, provides that editing may be undertaken by a legal representative of the prosecutor. Where a composite statement is to be made, it must be prepared in compliance with the terms of the statutory provisions (section 102 of the Magistrates' Courts Act 1980 or section 9 of the Criminal Justice Act 1967) and must be signed by the witness. Deletion of passages in a single statement may be undertaken by alteration of a copy – the prosecutor marking in red ink those passages upon which he will not rely. The direction makes further reference to the greater need in summary proceedings for fresh statements (Practice Direction (Crime: Evidence by Written Statements) [1986] 1 W.L.R. 805).

In committal proceedings, exhibits should not be edited, the matter being left to the determination of the trial judge. In summary proceedings, however, it is sometimes necessary to edit exhibits as well as witness statements. The extent to which this is permissible will depend on the nature of the document and the perceived prejudice to the defendant. Where the exhibit is an interview, the same principles as apply to a witness statement are applied by paragraph 2(e) of the Practice Direction (Crime: Tape Recording of Police Interviews: Preparation for Proceedings in the Crown Court), 89 Cr. App. R. 132.

Expert evidence

10.93 Nature of expert evidence. Either side to civil or criminal litigation may call expert evidence where the subject is one upon which competency to form an opinion can only be acquired by a course of special study or experience. This can include mere repeated contact with the topic in the course of work without formal training (*R. v. Oakley* [1979] R.T.R. 417). Trading Standards Officers and Environmental Health Officers are frequently invited to give opinion evidence, whether intentionally or otherwise, and that evidence is, when given, treated as expert evidence. Were that not so, their opinion evidence would be inadmissible. Objection to the opinions of an E.H.O. or T.S.O. should be taken before the evidence is given and the question whether the testimony is of an expert nature is a matter for the court to determine (*R. v. Silverlock* [1894] 2 Q.B. 766). In *R. v. Koon Cheung Tang* [1995] Crim.L.R. 813, the Court of Appeal (Criminal Division) considered the evidence of an E.H.O. who had expressed her view as to the risks of contamination from her observations in a kitchen, but who had no particular qualification for quantifying such risks. The Court reflected that the evidence was before the jury, that it was a normal case and there was no need to quantify the chance of harm. The Court did not allow the appeal against conviction.

10.94 Evaluation of expert evidence. That expert witnesses may also be giving evidence of fact does not preclude them from putting forward expert evidence where appropriate, although where the proposed expert is a T.S.O. or E.H.O. (if such a person is an expert: see above) and so also an employee of the prosecution, his expert evidence will, in practice, be rendered less persuasive. The purpose of expert evidence is to furnish the tribunal of fact with "the necessary scientific criteria for testing the accuracy of their conclusions, so as to enable the judge or jury to form their own independent judgment by the application of these criteria to the facts proved in evidence" (*per* Lord President Cooper in *Davie v. Edinburgh Magistrates* 1953 S.C. 34 at page 40). It follows that the fact that expert evidence is given on one side only does not mean that the Court is required to follow that evidence. The Court can accept or reject that opinion, provided that there is other evidence upon which it is possible to reach a contrary view (*R. v. Bailey* (1977) 66 Cr. App. R. 31n; *Anderson v. R* [1972] A.C. 100 (P.C.)).

10.95   A recent case which demonstrates the way in which mixed expert and factual evidence can be utilised is *P & M Supplies (Essex) v. Walsall Metropolitan Borough Council* [1994] Crim.L.R. 580 in which magistrates prevented a defendant prosecuted under section 10 of the Consumer Protection Act 1987 from:

   (i) cross-examining a Trading Standards Officer as to his experience of similar deficiencies in similar toys in other cases;

  (ii) calling evidence from the British Standards Committee as to its opinion as to the risks involved in the type of toy in question;

(iii) calling evidence from the trade to show that the risks in question were normal.

The Divisional Court allowed an appeal because the decision "reasonably safe" required considerations of matters such as the standards of the trade and the experience of a body such as the British Standards Committee as part of the relevant evidence.

10.96   Need for expert evidence.   Although expert evidence may be of assistance in determining matters of reasonableness, quality and other nebulous concepts, it cannot replace the need for evidence of fact and for argument. In *Goldup v. John Manson Ltd* [1982] Q.B. 161, the Divisional Court held that the bare evidence of an expert as to the standard of meat could not prove what was "the standard demanded by the purchaser" within the meaning of the Food and Drugs Act 1955. The standard demanded by a purchaser was a matter which could be proved by evidence of the contract of sale or by inferences from the surrounding negotiations or circumstances.

On the other hand, in some instances, expert evidence is essential to the success or otherwise of a case. Where a due diligence defence is dependent upon the taking of samples, it seems that the defendant is unlikely to succeed in the absence of expert evidence as to the adequacy of the sample (*P&M Supplies (Essex) Ltd and Devon County Council* (1991) 156 J.P. 328, and see paragraph 9.18 above).

10.97   Expert's duty to the court.   Expert witnesses have a special duty to the Court. In civil cases (and there is no reason for an expert to take a different stance in criminal cases) detailed consideration has been given to the standards to be expected of an expert. In *The Ikarian Reefer* [1993] 2 Lloyds Rep. Cresswell J., set out some rules for experts which are likely to be regarded as of general application. These are:–

   (i) expert evidence should be, and should be seen to be, the independent product of the expert, uninfluenced by the exigencies of the litigation in which he is involved (*Whitehouse v. Jordan* [1981] 1 W.L.R. 246 *per* Lord Wilberforce at page 256);

  (ii) the expert should provide independent assistance to the Court in an unbiased way. He should never act as an advocate for the party who has called him (*Pollvitte Ltd. v. Commercial Union Assurance Co. Plc* [1987] 1 Lloyds Rep.379; *Re. J.* [1991] F.C.R. 193).

(iii) An expert should state the facts or assumptions upon which his opinion is based. He should consider material facts which would detract from his concluded opinion (*Re. J.* above);

(iv) An expert should make clear when a matter falls outside his expertise;

(v) If an expert's opinion is not properly researched because of an insufficiency of data or other reason he must say so. If he could not state that his report is unqualifiably true, he must alert the Court to the qualification (*Derby & Co. Ltd v. Weldon & Others, The Times,* November 9, 1990).

It is no doubt considerations of this sort which prompted Glidewell L.J. to assert in *R. v. Ward* [1993] 2 All E.R. 577 that "an expert witness who has carried out or knows of experiments or tests which tend to cast doubt on the opinion he is expressing is in our view under a clear obligation to bring the records of such experiments and tests to the attention of the solicitor instructing him so that it may be disclosed to the other party. No doubt this process can often be simplified by the expert for one party (usually the prosecution) supplying his results, and any necessary working papers to the expert advising the other party (the defence) directly". A requirement that the defence should alert the prosecution to possible weaknesses in its expert evidence seems startling.

10.98 Opinion as to "the ultimate issue". It had for a long time been in doubt whether an expert is entitled to give his opinion as to the very matter that the court is required to find, or whether he must stop short of that. In *R. v. Stockwell* (1993) 97 Cr. App. R. 260, Lord Taylor C.J., giving the judgment of the Court of Appeal made clear that the mere fact that the expert expresses a view on the matter which the jury has to find is not more significant than an expression of opinion so close to the ultimate issue that his opinion on the matter to be determined was obvious. But, the "ultimate issue" must be within the scope of his expertise before he can express a view on it. What is less clear is the status of remarks by experts which express the value judgment which it is incumbent upon the magistrates to find, but that issue is only a related one to the scope of the expert's expertise. A common example, notwithstanding the *Manson* case (above) is where the analyst comments that certain food is "not of the quality reasonably demanded by a purchaser". Whereas an analyst may be an expert as to the composition of the food, he is not an expert as to that which is reasonably to be demanded by a purchaser. It is submitted that this falls outside the area of the expert's expertise and is not admissible at all, let alone not conclusive of the issue.

10.99 Short cuts for the prosecutor to prove expert matters. It is sometimes the case that the prosecution evidence will include evidence from a public analyst or other expert examiner of a sample that has been taken. Where statutory provision is made for the circumstances of sampling or examination, it is common that provision is made that, in the absence of a request that the analyst or examiner attend as a witness, the expert's certificate (possibly in statutory form) shall be sufficient evidence of the matters appearing in it. See, for example, section 30(8) of the Food Safety Act 1990. (The public analyst is appointed under section 27 of the Act by the food authority.) This may suggest that the justices must accept the content of the certificate in the absence of a challenge to its content, so displacing the rule applicable to expert evidence generally (see paragraph 10.94 above). Although the statutory provision frequently makes reference to the "facts" appearing in the certificate, this has been interpreted in the context of the Food and Drugs Act 1938 as including matters of opinion (that is, matters of expertise) (*McCulloch v. Hannam* [1951] 1 All E.R. 402). Where the analyst's certificate contains matter falling outside his expertise, the statutory provision may have the effect of rendering sufficient what would otherwise be inadmissible. Accordingly, the analyst must be requested to give his evidence orally if the prosecution will not agree to edit the certificate to delete the disputed words. The defence can then make submissions to the justices in respect of the expertise of the analyst and/or cross-examine him accordingly.

10.100 Expert reports. In addition to statutory provisions such as that referred to above, section 30 of the Criminal Justice Act 1988 permits, with the leave of the court, an expert report to be admitted in evidence without oral evidence. In granting or refusing leave the court must have regard to the contents of the report, the reasons why it is proposed that the expert will not give oral evidence, the risk of unfairness to the accused (including the risk of his inability to contravert any statements in the report) and other relevant circumstances.

Documentary evidence

10.101 Nature. Documentary evidence forms many types. Commonly in regulatory trials, an interview under caution is produced in written form as an exhibit by the trading standards or other investigating officer. Other documents may comprise computer print outs, till receipts, invoices, booklets, newspaper advertisements, staff instructions, etc. A statement in a business document may be admitted as evidence of the facts shown on its face under section 24 of the Criminal Justice Act 1988 if:

(i) the document was created or received by a person in the course of his business, or as a paid or unpaid office holder; and

(ii) the information in the document was supplied by a person (whether or not the maker of the statement) who had or may reasonably be expected to have had personal knowledge of the matters dealt with. Where the information in the document was supplied only indirectly, each person through whom the information was supplied must have received the information in the course of his business or as an office holder.

The court has power to exclude the document under section 25 if the interests of justice so require, and the court must look at, among other matters, the nature and source of the document, the extent to which the document furnishes evidence which would not otherwise be available, its relevance and the extent to which the defendant may be prejudiced by the lack of an opportunity to cross-examine. More stringent requirements exist in respect of statements produced for the purposes of the criminal investigation (sections 25 and 26).

10.102 Computer records. Particular care needs to be taken with computer records, which are frequently relied upon as evidence by the prosecution, even though the prosecution witnesses are unable to bring any evidence to bear on the functioning of the computer itself. This issue has been highlighted in a case concerning misleading price indications under section 20 of the Consumer Protection Act 1987, where the prosecution sought to rely upon a computer print out (till receipt) as evidence of the price at which goods would be available to the consumer (*Dudley Metropolitan Borough Counncil v. Debenhams plc* (1994) 159 J.P. 18). In fact, the issue did not need to be determined because the prosecution's failure to comply with Code B, meant that the defendant succeeded in any event. Section 69 of the Police and Criminal Evidence Act 1984 requires that there be evidence that:

(i) there are no reasonable grounds for believing that the statement was inaccurate through improper use of the computer;

(ii) that at all material times the computer was operating properly, or that, if not, any deficiency would not affect the accuracy of the computer-generated document.

This evidence can be provided by a certificate in the form envisaged in schedule 3 Part II of the Act, but without any evidence as to the operation of the computer, and where the issue is critical to the success or failure of any charge, the prosecution case may fall on a submission of no case to answer by the defendant. Defendants must similarly recall that the evidence must be given where any version of events is dependent upon an interpretation of a computer record.

Excluding evidence

10.103 Admissibility of evidence. The admissibility of evidence is a matter which magistrates are frequently called upon to decide. The general rules for determining whether evidence is admissible or not are outside the scope of this work, although applications to exclude certain classes of document or oral evidence arise not infrequently. The most common of these are discussed below. In the magistrates' court, the magistrates are both the tribunal of fact and arbiters of the law. This has the consequence that where there is prejudicial material about which a ruling as to admissibility must be reached, the magistrates may become aware wholly or in part of the prejudicial matters. In *Halawa v. Federation Against Copyright Theft* (1995) 159 J.P. 816 the Divisional Court held, applying *Vel v. Chief Constable of North Wales* [1987] Crim.L.R. 498, that the justices must either deal with the question of admissibility when it arises or leave a decision to the end of the trial. Where it would be unjust for the evidence to be heard and a decision taken at the end of the trial, there should be a *voir dire* at the request of the defendant.

10.104 Fairness. Where an allegation is made that evidence has been unfairly obtained as a consequence of the manner of the investigation, objection may be taken. The most common routes to exclude evidence are under sections 76 and 78 of the Police and Criminal Evidence Act 1984. Section 76 deals with the admissibility of confessions which can be excluded if obtained by oppression or if there was anything said or done which might render the confessions unreliable. In the context of regulatory cases, the most likely situation in which this section may be relied upon is where investigating officers have failed to observe the requirements of Code C (see paragraphs 3.26 onwards). This must be dealt with in a trial within a trial, rather than at submissions at the end of the trial (*R. v. Sat-*

Bhambra (1988) 152 J.P. 365; *R. v. Liverpool Juvenile Court ex p. R* [1988] Q.B. 1). For further consideration of the admissibility of interviews under caution see paragraph 3.34, above.

10.105   Section 78 of the Police and Criminal Evidence Act 1984.   This provides:

"(1) In any proceedings the court may refuse to allow evidence on which the prosecution proposes to rely to be given if it appears to the court that, having regard to all the circumstances, including the circumstances in which the evidence was obtained, the admission of the evidence would have such an adverse effect on the fairness of the proceedings that the court ought not to admit it.

(2) Nothing in this section shall prejudice any rule of law requiring a court to exclude evidence."

This, again, has particular relevance in regulatory cases where there has been a failure to follow the guidance of the Codes of Practice identified under the Police and Criminal Evidence Act 1984. An instance of another situation arose in *London Borough of Ealing Trading Standards v. Woolworths plc* [1995] Crim.L.R. 58, in which it was averred that evidence obtained when a trading standards officer sent his 11 year old son to make a purchase of an "18" rated video was unfair. The magistrates excluded the evidence under section 78 on the basis that this amounted to an entrapment. The Divisional Court reiterated the views expressed in *R. v. Sang* [1980] A.C. 402 and *Director of Public Prosecutions v. Marshall* [1988] 3 All E.R. 683 that entrapment was not a defence and allowed the prosecution appeal. Another example where section 78 may be relied upon is if investigating officers have exceeded their powers, for instance, to make a test purchase (see paragraph 3.10 above).

Trial in the Crown Court

10.106   Generally.   Many of the matters which have arisen for discussion in relation to the magistrates' court also apply in relation to the Crown Court. Moreover, a detailed work, such as Archbold Criminal Pleading Evidence and Practice, 1998 edition is more appropriate for consideration of the procedures and evidence available in the Crown Court, than is a book which is intended to highlight matters of particular interest in regulatory cases. Comment is only made, therefore, where there is a point of particular departure from the Magistrates' Court procedures described above, the most obvious of which is that trial in the Crown Court will involve trial before a jury, although the judge must rule upon any dispute of law and direct the jury accordingly. Where there is a dispute of law which the judge must determine (for example, as to the interpretation of a statute), that point must be argued, usually in the absence of the jury, at the latest before final speeches by Counsel (*R. v. Day, The Times* October 3, 1991; *R. v. Miles* [1992] Crim.L.R. 657).

10.107   Defence Statements.   Compulsory disclosure in cases committed to the Crown Court is now mandatory in the Crown Court. Part I of the Criminal Procedure and Investigations Act ties in the notions of extensive disclosure of documents by the prosecutor (for which see paragraphs 10.56 to 10.66 above) with the disclosure (mandatory in the Crown Court) of the defence case. The obligation arises:

   (i) after committal; and

   (ii) after receipt of a notice of material which might in the opinion of the prosecution, undermine the case against the defendant, or a notice that there is no such material (section 5).

The defendant is required to set out in writing:

   (i) the nature of his defence in general terms;

   (ii) the matters on which he takes issue with the prosecution;

   (iii) the reason why he takes issue with the prosecution.

He must also give details of any alibi on which he proposes to rely. This statement triggers the obligation of secondary disclosure (see paragraph 10.65 above).

10.108 Plea and directions. There are now three types of preliminary hearing in the Crown court in cases other than serious or complex frauds. There may be a preparatory hearing where the accused is committed for trial after April 15, 1997 if the judge determines that the indictment reveals that the case will be one of such complexity or of such a length that it is thought that such a hearing should be used. The procedural model is then taken from the provisions relating to serious or complex frauds and it is unlikely that regulatory offences will be greeted with this procedure except on the rarest of occasions (Criminal Proceedure and Investigations Act 1996). Pre-trial hearings under the Act may be held after committal but before the defendant is put in the charge of the jury or a plea of guilty is accepted. At these hearings, the judge may rule as to admissibility of any evidence or on a question of law. The third type arises in Crown Court Centres which have adopted the practice direction (Practice Direction (Crown Court: Plea and Directions Hearings)[1995] 1 W.L.R. 1318). This enables key issues to be identified and the plea to be taken. The case will then be adjourned for trial.

10.109 Representation. The right to conduct a trial in the Crown Court is limited to Counsel and Solicitors who have obtained a qualification as an advocate. Only in rare cases will a private prosecutor be permitted to prosecute (*R. v. Crown Court at Southwark, ex p. Tawfick (Crown Prosecution Service Intervening), The Times*, December 1, 1994).

10.110 The jury. At the commencement of the trial and usually after arraignment and plea, twelve jurors are selected at random by the clerk of the court from the jury panel who have been summoned to attend the Crown Court. The prosecution may ask for a juror to stand by or challenge any juror for cause. The defendant may challenge a juror for cause after the juror has been called but before he takes the oath to try the case. In some regulatory cases it is common for the judge to ask of the jury whether they are, for example, employed by a local authority which is prosecuting, or employed by a defendant where the defendant is a large company.

10.111 The order of events. The prosecutor will open the case to the jury, setting out the facts and avoiding the use of emotive language, before calling evidence. After the prosecution evidence, the defence have a right to make a submission that there is insufficient evidence for there to be a case to answer. The test is the same as that in the magistrates' court (paragraph 10.85 above), although the submission is one of law made to the judge. As in the magistrates' court, the judge has a limited discretion to allow merely formal matters to be proved, even though the prosecution's case has been closed (see *R. v. Francis* 91 Cr. App. R. 271, CA, *R. v. McKenna* 40 Cr. App. R. 65 but contrast *R. v. Central Criminal Court, ex p. Garnier* [1988] R.T.R. 42 where the prosecution had advance notice that the point would be taken and yet closed its case without calling the disputed evidence). To avoid the risk of a successful application by the prosecution to re-open its case and call the omitted evidence, the defence may frequently be well-advised not to draw attention to a factual oversight by the prosecution until the speech to the jury, when the point can be made. If a submission of no case is not made or fails, a defendant is entitled to have his representative make an opening speech (or, if he is not represented, to do so himself) if at least one witness of fact other than the defendant is to be called. Counsel for the prosecution always makes his speech to the jury before defending counsel or solicitor or the defendant himself if he is acting in person.

Civil Cases

10.112 Generally. Some issues affecting regulatory offences in the magistrates' courts fall to be dealt with by way of civil, rather than criminal proceedings. The most common example of this is an appeal against an executive notice (see paragraph 4.30 above).

10.113 Complaint. Civil proceedings involving an appeal under a statute are started by a complaint laid by the complainant (Magistrates' Courts Rules 1981, rule 34). There is a prescribed form (Magistrates' Courts (Forms) Rules 1981, Form 98), but, as with information, a complaint may also be laid orally. In the case of an appeal against an enforcement notice, it is the person upon whom the notice has been served that will be the complainant, and the time for making the complaint is laid down by the legislation giving rise to the complaint. Once the complaint is laid, the justices' clerk must apply his mind judicially to the complaint to determine whether a summons should be issued (for the comparable procedure relating to informations, see paragraphs 8.8 onwards above). As with the issue of a summons following information, the primary considerations will be the time within which the information is laid, the territorial jurisdiction of the justices (described in the Magistrates' Courts Act 1980, s.52) and whether a cause of complaint is shown. The summons will be in Form 99 (Magistrates' Courts (Forms) Rules 1981. Unlike information, a complaint will not be defective if it raises more than one cause of action (*Tyrrell v. Tyrrell* (1928) 92 J.P. 45).

10.114 Absence of the parties. Absence of the complainant on the hearing day may result in the dismissal of the complaint unless evidence from the complainant has been given on a previous occasion, in which case the court can continue to hear the defendant. If the court does not dismiss the complaint and no evidence has previously been heard, the case must be adjourned. If the defendant does not attend, the magistrates may proceed to hear the case or to adjourn. If they proceed to hear the case, they must have been satisfied by hearing evidence on oath or by certificate that the summons or notice of an adjourned hearing served a sufficient time before the hearing date (Magistrates' Courts Act 1981, ss.54 to 57, Magistrates' Courts Rules 1981, r.67).

10.115 Hearing. In civil cases the rules of disclosure (paragraphs 10.52 and 10.66 above) which are applicable to criminal cases do not apply, although the duties upon expert witnesses to assist the court are the same in both civil and criminal cases (see paragraph 10.97 above). Unlike the county court or High Court, there are no rules for the discovery of documents although the parties to a hearing of a complaint may clearly make informal requests of the other side and cross-examine if those requests are not complied with.

10.116 Order of events. If there are no preliminary points, the complainant may address the court by opening his case before calling his evidence. In the case of an appeal against a notice, this means that his case must address the facts which have occurred, the nature of the notice and the reasons why the notice is inappropriate. The defendant may then make an opening speech and call his evidence, or may call his evidence before making a closing speech. If he opens, he may not also close without the leave of the court. As with criminal proceedings, the complainant may call evidence in rebuttal. If the complainant has opened his case before calling evidence, he is not entitled to a further speech without the leave of the court – and the defendant is then also entitled to a second speech. Where leave is given for second speeches, the complainant is to be heard last (Magistrates' Courts Rules 1981, r.14). The magistrates will then reach their decision.

10.117 Evidence. Not all rules as to the admissibility of evidence are the same in civil proceedings. For example, sections 76 and 78 of the Police and Criminal Evidence Act 1984 do not apply, nor are business documents to be admitted in the same way. (Contrast paragraphs 10.103 to 10.105 above.) An appeal under a statute to the magistrates' court is by way of a rehearing, so that even before the coming into force of the Civil Evidence Act 1995, magistrates could admit hearsay evidence on the hearing of an appeal because the court was allowed to examine the material that would have been available to the previous decision-maker, namely the local authority (*Westminster City Council v. Zestfair Ltd* (1989) 153 J.P. 613). Additionally, the court could look at matters arising since the service of the notice founding the appeal (*Rushmoor Borough Council v. Richards* (1996) 160 L.G.R. 460).

10.118 Civil Evidence Act 1995. This Act provides that hearsay evidence from a competent source shall not be excluded on the ground that it is hearsay although certain safeguards as to the treatment of hearsay are provided for in sections 2 to 6 of the Act. The safeguards and supplementary provisions do not apply where the evidence would be admissible anyway (section 1(4)), for example because hearsay evidence was before the body from whom appeal is made. Some common law provisions formerly admitting hearsay are preserved in the 1995 Act (as they were in the 1968 Act) except that relating to an admission adverse to a party, which is now governed by the 1995 Act. The supplementary safeguards include provision that:

(i) a party intending to call hearsay evidence must give such notice of his intention and particulars relating to that evidence on request as is reasonable and practicable in the circumstances, unless the parties agree otherwise. A failure to comply with this requirement may be taken into account in considering the course of proceedings and as a matter which adversely affects the weight of evidence given.

(ii) a court must have regard in assessing the weight of evidence in particular to:

(a) whether it would have been reasonable and practicable to have called that person as a witness;

(b) whether the original statement was made contemporaneously with the occurrence or existence of events;

(c) whether it involves multiple hearsay;

(d) whether the person involved had a motive to conceal or misrepresent matters;

(e) whether the original statement was edited or made in conjunction with another or for a particular purpose;

(f) whether the circumstances of its introduction suggest an attempt to prevent proper evaluation of its weight.

10.119 Documents.   A statement contained in a document must be proved by the document or a copy authenticated in a manner which the court may approve (section 8). Documents which constitute the records of a business or public authority may be produced without further proof, and an officer of a business or authority may produce a certificate that certain documents are part of the records of a business. An absence of a record may be proved by affidavit from an officer of the company or public authority (section 9). The court may disapply these provisions to any particular document or class of document (section 9(5)), presumably, where it is disputed on reasonable grounds.

CHAPTER 11

Mitigation and Penalties

SENTENCING

Jurisdiction of the Magistrates' Court

11.1 Committal for sentence. Where a magistrates' court has accepted jurisdiction in a case which can be tried either on indictment or summarily, it does not follow that sentencing in the magistrates' court will follow, although that is the usual practice. Section 38 of the Magistrates' Courts Act 1980, as amended by the Criminal Justice Act 1991 and Criminal Justice and Public Order Act 1994 provides:

"(1) This section applies where on the summary trial of an offence triable either way . . . a person who is not less than 18 years old is convicted of the offence.

(2) If the court is of opinion—

(a) that the offence or the combination of the offence and one or more offences associated with it was so serious that greater punishment should be inflicted for the offence than the court has power to impose; or

(b) . . . the court may, in accordance with section 56 of the Criminal Justice Act 1967, commit the offender in custody or on bail to the Crown court for sentence in accordance with the provisions of section 42 of the Powers of the Criminal Court Act 1973 . . .

(3) The preceding provisions of the section shall apply in relation to a corporation as if—

(a) the corporation were an individual who is not less than 18 years old; and

(b) in subsection (2) above, paragraph (b) and the words "in custody or on bail" were omitted.""

For some time following the amendment in 1991 there was doubt whether, once the magistrates had accepted jurisdiction (see paragraphs 10.15 and 10.16 above), the matter could be committed to the Crown Court for sentence. In *R. v. Manchester Magistrates' Court, ex p. Kaymanesh* (1994) 15 Cr. App. R. (S.) 838 it was held that it was ordinarily wrong, once the defendant had given up his right to jury trial, to commit the matter for sentence in the Crown Court where the powers of sentencing were increased. This was particularly the case where magistrates had accepted jurisdiction for a matter which did not carry a sentence of imprisonment on summary trial. In *R. v. North Sefton Magistrates' Court, ex p. Marsh* [1994] Crim.L.R. 865 the Divisional Court reviewed the above case and other, inconsistent, authorities and concluded that there was power to commit the matter for sentence notwithstanding that jurisdiction had been accepted and notwithstanding that no new matters had come to light which rendered the case more serious. The Divisional Court accepted with approval the observation in *R. v. Dover Magistrates' Court, ex p. Pamment* [1994] 15 Cr. App. R. (S.) 778 that a magistrates' court should exercise its discretion to accept jurisdiction with care, because a defendant should be able to conclude that once jurisdiction had been accepted he would not on the same facts be sent to the Crown Court for the imposition of a more serious penalty than that which could be imposed in the magistrates' court.

11.2   Absolute offences.   It is particularly the case with absolute offences that the court will rarely commit for sentence. However, it is open to the court, on hearing the facts, to realise that the conduct of the defendant and his intention make the case more serious than it seemed at first, such that committal to the Crown court might be appropriate. If the principle in *R. v. Sandhu* [1997] Crim.L.R. 288 (in which the Court of Appeal held that on a trial of a strict liability offence evidence should not be admitted at trial beyond proof of the elements required for that offence: evidence beyond that, which might tend to show a particular state of mind is not an optional extra) were to be followed strictly it might be thought that a strict liability offence would never be committed for sentence. In fact, evidence as to a defendant's mental state does become relevant whenever any due diligence defence is run, and, indeed, can in practice emerge in a way which is indistinguishable from the evidence necessary to prove the offence. If the prosecutor has not, the matter having reached the sentencing stage, opened and led evidence as to any matters which might show a particular state of mind in relation to the commission of the offence, the court is as a matter of practice likely to sentence on the basis of the facts as they have been invited to find them in the course of the trial. If, however, there is material relevant to sentencing which might suggest intention to commit an offence (such as previous identical convictions), this can be introduced following conviction and the court would be obliged to consider this in the context of the seriousness of even an absolute offence.

11.3   Sentencing powers of the magistrates' courts.   In regulatory cases, the penalty which may be applied by the magistrates' court is usually laid down, so far as any sentence of imprisonment or fine is concerned, by the statute giving rise to the offence, rather than by the general law. If the offence which the defendant must meet is inchoate, such as aiding and abetting or conspiracy, the maximum penalties are those provided for the substantive offence, except that it appears that the liability for an inchoate offence may be capped by legislation which limits sentencing powers in the absence of contrary express provision. Unless legislation expressly excludes the provisions of section 31 of the Magistrates' Courts Act 1980, the powers of magistrates to impose a period of imprisonment are limited to 6 months for each offence – even if the governing legislation would permit a longer period. Two sentences of 6 months imprisonment can be made to run consecutively (section 133 of the 1980 Act). The maximum fine which can be imposed for offences which could be tried either way, in the absence of express provision, is "the prescribed sum" (currently, £5,000) (Magistrates' Courts Act 1980, s.32). It is common for higher penalties to be expressly provided for in regulatory cases. For example, an offence under section 8 of the Food Safety Act 1990 attracts a maximum fine of £20,000. In such a case, it is thought likely that an inchoate offence might fall to be governed by the powers in the Magistrates' Court Act, rather than by the higher penalties which apply to the substantive offence.

In the Crown Court

11.4 Sentencing in the Crown Court. In the Crown Court the maximum powers which the court has, whether following committal for sentence or after a plea of guilty or trial, are those which the statute giving rise to the offence or the general law provides. The Crown Court has no inherent sentencing limitations. Only if the Crown Court is sitting in an appellate capacity from the magistrates will its powers be limited to those which pertained in the court below (see paragraph 12.12 below).

Assessing the Offence

11.5 Seriousness. Seriousness is the principal governing factor which will enable the court to assess the starting point for sentencing. This notion is at the root of many sections of the Criminal Justice Act 1991 including those dealing with imprisonment (section 1), fine (section 18) and community sentences (section 6). The seriousness of the offence is determined by its nature, any aggravating or mitigating factors relating to the offence itself, its prevalence, and any previous convictions of the defendant. The assessment of seriousness in regulatory offences frequently requires a weather eye to be kept upon the maximum statutory penalties. The court should engage in an approximation of the point in the scale of seriousness where the offence might lie relative to the maximum penalty, recalling that it is inappropriate for the maximum penalty to be imposed except for the most serious of cases of that type. For an example of the way in which the court may approach the question of whether a maximum penalty should be imposed, see *R. v. Foster* [1997] 1 Cr. App. R. (S.) 394.

The nature of the offence and its seriousness

11.6 Regulatory offence. The starting point for consideration of any regulatory offence is a mental reminder that it is a regulatory offence (or, in the case of conspiracy or aiding and abetting, based on a regulatory offence). Accordingly, it is quasi-criminal and intended to promote standards of good behaviour for the benefit of the public by deterrence:

> "Consumer protection, which is the purpose of statutes of this kind, is achieved only if the occurrence of the prohibited acts or omissions is prevented. It is the deterrent effect of penal provisions which protects the

consumer from the loss he would sustain if the offence were committed. If it is committed he does not receive the amount of any fine. As a tax-payer he will bear part of the expense of maintaining a convicted offender in prison"

per Lord Diplock in *Tesco Supermarkets Ltd v. Nattrass* [1972] A.C. 153 at 194B-E.

Deterrence is at the heart of the strict liability offence and is entwined with the notion that liability is to be imposed on a person responsible even where the offence occurred without his knowledge or intent so as to prompt him to take such steps as will be necessary to avoid the offence. It might be thought that therefore there is no retributive element in regulatory sentencing, but not only does that not coincide with the dicta of the sentencing court in many instances, also the deterrent element is often difficult in practice to distinguish from retribution. Moreover, a distinction must be drawn between those offences which have in fact been committed in circumstances of moral turpitude (where retribution might be thought more appropriate) and those which have not (where deterrence should be overwhelmingly the predominant element of the sentencing decision). An example of the court expressing a deterrent approach in the case of deliberate illegality with a view to gain is *R. v. Hammerton Cars* [1976] 3 All E.R. 758, a "clocking" case, in which Lawton L.J. said:

". . . In plain English they took a chance the mileage readings were genuine. Traders in second hand cars should not take such chances and if they do and are prosecuted to conviction the Courts should discourage them by taking all the profit out of the transaction and a good deal more."

Also see *R. v. Curr* (1980) 2 Cr. App. R. (S.) 153 (offences of carrying on a consumer credit business without a licence) where the "good deal more" referred to above was said to be by way of "punishment".

11.7 Retribution and deterrence. In *R. v. F. and M. Dobson Ltd* (1995) 16 Cr. App. R. (S.) 957, in a case where a chocolate manufacturer had sold a bar of chocolate containing the blade of a Stanley knife, Lord Taylor C.J. commented on the sentencing process in a case of public risk and appeared to accept that the elements of retribution and deterrence both applied in regulatory cases but emphasised the importance of deterrence. He said:

"We accept that clearly culpability must be an important factor in deciding what is the appropriate penalty to impose. But we also consider that deterrence is a major factor for the court to consider. Where a manufacturer is producing foodstuffs or confectionery likely to be put in the consumer's mouth without close inspection and with confidence that what is being consumed is wholesome, there is a high duty on the company to do all that it can to see that no foreign bodies, and particularly foreign bodies as dangerous as a Stanley knife, get into their product. In the present case the company had taken many steps, but they had not taken the step which the learned judge referred to and which they instantly took after the complaint was made.

It is important that when the court does have to consider a case of this kind the message should not go out that any company, providing it has a good record hitherto, can regard one bite of a Stanley knife or other unwholesome object, as something the court will overlook on the first occasion. It is important that manufacturers should be kept on their toes as to the need to take all precautions to prevent incidents of this kind. Accordingly, a fine of some substance must be imposed . . .".

Notwithstanding those words, the Court of Appeal reduced the fine from £25,000 to £7,000 in respect of a chocolate covered Stanley-knife blade thought to have been a bar of chocolate.

11.8 Alternative more serious offence. In addition to the above considerations, in some instances, more serious offences might have been committed, and the court should not ignore the seriousness of the facts merely because a lesser allegation has been levelled (*R. v. Nottingham Crown Court, ex p. DPP* (1996) 160 J.P. 78). A sentence for the lesser offence may properly involve the element of retribution which might be regarded as unexceptionable in relation to the greater offence, although taking the facts into account does not mean that there will inevitably be parity between the sentence which might have been imposed had there been a conviction on a more serious charge. An example where this overlap between a lesser and greater offence commonly arises is where the same conduct could give rise to the regulatory offence of applying a false trade description to goods or the offence of obtaining goods by deception.

11.9 In practice, many regulatory prosecutions are brought on grounds which appear to engage a desire for retribution (that is, many enforcement policies make it an express consideration of importance that a complaint has been made by a consumer which must be perceived by the public to be acted upon. The complaint may then be enforced by prosecution even though the defendant is otherwise reliable and willing to be cautioned or modify his practices or otherwise avert the risk of recurrence. In these instances, it is hard to conclude that the motive for enforcement by way of prosecution is other than of that retribution). The likelihood that a consumer will not be at risk again will not in practice usually result in a nominal penalty or absolute discharge unless the court can be satisfied that prosecution was not in the public interest.

11.10 Prosecution not in the public interest. A prosecution which is not in the public interest is likely to be (but may not always be) equated with a prosecution which is not serious. Certainly, in the context of the sentiments expressed by Viscount Dilhorne in *Smedleys Ltd v. Breed* [1974] A.C. 839, the two notions could be interchanged. In a prosecution concerning the discovery of a caterpillar in a tin of peas, he commented that the prosecutor had not criticised the process (there was no due diligence defence under the Food and Drugs Act 1955) and that the risk of it happening was remote. He then said:

"In these circumstances, what useful purpose was served by the prosecution? Why, despite the full disclosure made by the appellants, was one instituted? . . . in cases where it is apparent that a prosecution does not serve the general interests of consumers, the justices may think fit, if they find that the Act has been contravened, to grant an absolute discharge."

11.11 Risk to the consumer. In cases which involve no dishonesty, the factor which appears of paramount importance in assessing the seriousness of regulatory cases is the degree of risk of injury to the consumer by the conduct of the defendant, taken together with the steps taken to eliminate that risk. Thus it was, for instance, that Alain Baxter was sentenced to four months imprisonment for contravening the provisions of section 8 of the Food Safety Act 1990. He was a chef who had worked unpaid to provide a feast for 300, including seafood, roast turkey, rib of beef, chicken and mayonnaise made with fresh eggs, for the wedding of his childhood friend. The food had been left to stand in a marquee for up to four hours – during which time the temperature reached 85 degrees Fahrenheit. A short time after the reception, three quarters of the guests became ill and six were admitted to hospital with salmonella poisoning. One guest suffered a miscarriage ("Chef must serve time after wedding treat turns sour" *The Times* May 29, 1997). The same concern about exposing the consumer to risks to her safety was expressed in *R. v. Gold* (1995) 16 Cr. App. R. (S.) 442 in which a Fiat car was described as "a lovely car", when it was in fact dangerously corroded and "potentially lethal". A sentence of four months imprisonment was imposed, although an earlier offence was also treated as an aggravating factor.

11.12   Deliberate misconduct.   In the same vein, deliberate misconduct which seeks to take advantage of the consumer is likely to be regarded as serious. Thus in *R. v. Curr* (1980) 2 Cr. App. R. (S.) 153, the appellant had pleaded guilty to six offences of carrying on a consumer credit business without a licence, contrary to the Consumer Credit Act 1974. Balcombe J. said:

> "Laws of this kind are passed to protect the weak from the depredations of persons such as the appellant. The view of this court is that the appropriate punishment for offences of this nature is a heavy fine of such an amount as will not merely deprive of their profit those who carry on such businesses in defiance of the law but will also impose an additional amount by way of punishment. A sentence of imprisonment may also be appropriate in cases such as this where the appellant made it clear that he intended to defy the law; but it would not ordinarily be appropriate unless there were some circumstance of that nature."

In this case, not only had the defendant charged rates of interest at about 800 per cent per annum, he had said to police that he had no time to carry on his business in a lawful way. Persistent offending similarly adds to the seriousness of the offence (*R. v. Booth* [1997] 1 Cr. App. R. (S.) 103).

11.13   Dishonesty.   In the same way, offences of "clocking" cars, which involve allegations of dishonesty (as in *R. v. Gold* (above) are serious. See, for example, *R. v. Starr* (1983) 75 Cr. App. R. (S.) 315. In *R. v. Gupta* (1985) 7 Cr. App. R. (S.) 172 Lawton L.J. said:

> "This appellant . . . expected to get a substantial fine. Dishonest secondhand motor-car dealers who "clock" vehicles should expect not to get a substantial fine but a sentence imposing immediate loss of liberty *plus* a substantial fine. It is very important in these cases that not only should dishonest secondhand car dealers be punished, in the sense of losing their liberty, but the very large profits which they make from this kind of behaviour should be taken away from them by substantial fines."

The defendant's immediate custodial sentence of 12 months was suspended as to 6 months in the light of the defendant's previous good character and plea of guilty. In *R. v. Booth* [1997] 1 Cr. App. R. (S.) 103, the Court of Appeal laid down brief guidelines in a case concerning four specimen counts of supplying goods to which a false trade description had been applied. The same false trade description (a description in an advertisement as "skeleton keys" of what were only "slim jims" – flat pieces of metal which used to be of value for opening cars some time ago, but which are virtually useless for the modern car, coupled with subsequent refusal to refund the purchase price to dissatisfied customers) had been applied for two and a half years and about £54,000 had been received by him in consequence. The Court said that the first sentencing principle is that custodial sentences are appropriate where "this kind" of fraud on the public is committed. The level of sentence is then related to the gravity of what is done, its scale and its persistence. A sentence of nine months following a plea of guilty was upheld.

11.14 Exploitation. A further consideration which the courts will treat seriously is an exploitation of the vulnerabilities of potential consumers. In *R. v. Foster* [1997] 1 Cr. App. R. (S.) 394, the Court of Appeal reduced to 18 months from 2 years a term of imprisonment for conspiracy to supply goods to which a false trade description had been attached. The goods related to a slimming diet in respect of which false claims had been made. *R. v. Gold* (above) exemplifies the court's approach where the consumer is in no real position to test or check the false assertions of the person making a false statement: a point also referred to in assessing the seriousness of the conduct of the defendant in *R. v. Burridge* (1985) 7 Cr. App. R. (S.) 125, where repairs were dishonestly said to have been carried out to washing machines:

> "This type of offence when repairs are said to be done to machinery, and it is a matter of practical impossibility for the customer to determine whether they have been done or not, are easy to commit and very difficult to detect. It is important that dishonest tradesmen of this sort should be actively and sharply discouraged from taking advantage of the public who cannot check the work for themselves"

per Lord Lane C.J. A sentence of three months imprisonment was upheld.

11.15 Proof. It is important that the court considers carefully what matters are proven in relation to the intention of the defendant. An example of how problems occur arose in *R. v. Lester* (1975) 63 Cr. App. R. 144 in which the defendant pleaded guilty to five counts of applying a false trade description contrary to section 1 of the Trade Descriptions Act 1968. He asked for seven similar offences to be taken into account. He was a motor salesman of cars which had been "clocked", that is, the odometers had been altered to reduce the number of miles that the car appeared to have travelled. He was sentenced to 6 months imprisonment notwithstanding that it was said in mitigation for him that he did not know of the falsity of the odometers. On appeal, a fine of £280 was substituted. The Court of Appeal (Crim. Div.) said that the explanation for the sentence may have been, in the absence of any direct evidence of knowledge, that the judge took the view that the Defendant had shut his eyes to the obvious. However, if the judge was minded to draw an inference adverse to the defendant, he ought to have indicated what was provisionally in his mind and offered the defence the opportunity to call evidence. It was wrong in principle to have passed an immediate custodial sentence on a defendant who had been in the trade for several years and had a clean record.

11.16 Specimen counts.   Where the prosecution allege a number of offences, it is common for charges to be taken as "sample" or "specimen" allegations. Although in the case of *R. v. Clark* [1996] 2 Cr. App. R. 282 it appeared that the practice of sentencing on specimen charges, had not survived the provisions of section 31 of the Criminal Justice Act 1991, this case was subsequently disapproved (*R. v. Barry* 1997 (unreported) and distinguished (*R. v. Bradshaw* [1997] 2 Cr. App. R. (S.) 128) but the reasoning upheld in *R. v. Kidd* [1998] 1 W.L.R. 604. It must now be very unlikely that specimen counts can be used in any circumstances where the defendant does not admit informations or charges levelled against him. If it is possible still to sentence, by agreement, on a specimen basis, this is likely to arise where a compromise has been reached between prosecutor and defendant as to the number of allegations on which sentencing may occur. The fact that the allegations are a sample will increase the seriousness of the individual offences, but sentence on each individual count cannot exceed the maximum for that allegation. Prosecutors therefore need to take care to select a sample which will not tie the hands of the sentencing court.

PREVIOUS CONVICTIONS AND CAUTIONS

11.17 Relevance.   Previous convictions and cautions for similar or associated offences are of relevance in every regulatory case which concerns an individual and are often of relevance, too, in the case of a corporate defendant. The significance of citing previous convictions is, as with the wider criminal law, that it may constitute a guide for the sentencing court as to the seriousness of the offence and the efficacy of the sentence (see Criminal Justice Act 1991, s.29). Repeated convictions of a company for similar offences may rebut a notion advanced in mitigation that the company could not have been expected to have foreseen the events in question, or that there were merely unfortunate mistakes due to staff errors. For the above reasons on summary conviction previous offences are, where relevant, cited by the prosecutor.

11.18 Proving previous convictions.   Where the defendant attends court, there is rarely any problem in proving previous convictions, because the record is usually admitted. If the defendant has not attended, or if the record is denied, it can be proved by a certified copy of the court record of conviction together with proof of identity. Where the offence of which a person is convicted is summary, the usual method of proving any previous summary convictions is by reliance on a notice to cite previous convictions in the form prescribed in Form 29 and 30 of the schedule to the Magistrates' Courts (Forms) Rules 1981. The court may take account of convictions cited on that form if it is proved that the notice has been served on the defendant at least seven days before the hearing.

11.19 Cautions.   Previous cautions may be cited. If necessary, the signed record can be produced in respect of the earlier offence to prove the caution. LACOTS asks local authorities responsible for cautioning to assist in the recording of cautions by completing a pro-forma notification for forwarding to the Office of Fair Trading for entry on the Central Register of Convictions (LACOTS advice paper CO 11 94 5). Where the caution has been administered by the police on a previous occasion, there may be a separate record kept in accordance with Home Office circular No. 18 1994.

11.20 "Spent" convictions and cautions. Section 5 of the Rehabilitation of Offenders Act 1974 provides the period before a conviction becomes "spent" so that it should not generally be referred to in criminal proceedings. Although criminal proceedings are an exception to the prohibition on referring to spent convictions, little notice is generally taken of spent convictions for sentencing purposes. The record of conviction should show those which are spent, and they should not be read out by the prosecutor or antecedents officer. Applicable periods of rehabilitation for an adult charged with a regulatory offence are:

(a) where the sentence has exceeded six months imprisonment – 10 years (unless the sentence is more than 30 months, in which case there is no rehabilitation);

(b) where the sentence does not exceed six months – seven years;

(c) where there has been a fine – five years.

If further offences are committed within the rehabilitation period, the end of the rehabilitation period is extended to the end of the last period unless the subsequent offences are summary only (Rehabilitation of Offenders Act 1974, ss.5 and 6).

Where previous offences were made the subject of a caution, a formal caution should not normally be cited in court more than three years after the offence for which it was issued. This advice, previously given in Home Office circulars on the use of cautions, has been adopted by LACOTS.

Prevalence

11.21 The prevalence of a crime may be a justification for taking a more serious view of it, although section 2(2)(a) of the Criminal Justice Act 1991 prevents a defendant from being made the subject of a special example. In *R. v. Starr* (1983) 5 Cr. App. R. (S.) 315, as well as *R. v. Gupta* (above) and *R. v. Hewitt* (1992) 13 Cr. App. R. (S.) 131, the Court of Appeal made reference to the prevalence of the offence of "clocking" as a reason which justified the imposition of a custodial sentence. For some regulatory offences, courts may have regard to informal "mental starting point" lists designed to assist magistrates in achieving consistency of approach. Such documents do need to be treated with caution because they could operate as a fetter on the sentencing decision.

SENTENCING OPTIONS

11.22 Sentencing process. Before the sentence can be imposed, the court is obliged to take into account both the matters relating to the circumstances of the offence and the mitigation (Criminal Justice Act 1991, s.3(3)). (For matters arising on, and the approach to mitigation see paragraph 11.42 onwards below.) It is quite often the case that after the assessment of the matters relating to the offence, the court will have in mind a provisional sentence, which provisional view may then be mitigated on hearing about the circumstances of the offender and other relevant matters. This part of Chapter 11 sets out a number of sentencing options of particular relevance to regulatory cases. It is not an exhaustive list of the powers of the courts, many of which are only of marginal relevance in regulatory cases.

Imprisonment

11.23 Imprisonment is not normally an appropriate penalty for a regulatory offence unless the offence which has been committed is in reality one of fraud or has subjected the public to actual and serious harm. In any event, it cannot be a penalty where a corporate defendant is before the court, nor where the defendant is a partnership, although an individual defendant who happened to be a partner of a business would clearly be eligible for imprisonment in an appropriate case, and a third party could be convicted. For example, in *R. v. Burridge* (1985) 7 Cr. App. R. (S.) 125 a director of a small company which repaired washing machines was sentenced to 3 months under section 20 of the Trade Descriptions Act 1968 (offence due to an act or neglect of director) where false statements as to the nature of services provided by his company were made. Generally, imprisonment is not an appropriate remedy in trade descriptions cases unless there has been dishonesty (*R. v. Haesler* [1973] Crim.L.R. 586). Where there is dishonesty, however, imprisonment may follow *(R. v. Booth* [1997] 1 Cr. App. R. 103). In "clocking" cases, it is not unusual. For further comment on seriousness in regulatory cases, see paragraphs 11.5 to 11.16 above.

11.24 Court's powers. In any regulatory case, the court shall not pass a custodial sentence on the offender unless it is of the opinion that the offence or the combination of the offence and others associated with it is so serious that only a sentence of imprisonment can be justified (Criminal Justice Act 1991, s.1). The court must, moreover, explain to the offender in ordinary language and in open court why a custodial sentence is being passed. This involves giving a reason for reaching the view that only a sentence of imprisonment is justified. In the magistrates' court, that reason must also be recorded in the warrant of commitment to prison and in the register of conviction. In the Crown Court, sentencing remarks will have been recorded and transcribed.

11.25 Pre-sentence report. Before reaching the conclusion that only a custodial sentence is appropriate, the court must obtain and consider a pre-sentence report unless it is of the opinion that it is unnecessary (Criminal Justice Act 1991, s.3). No sentence is invalidated by the failure to obtain a pre-sentence report (section 3(4)).

11.26 Consecutive and concurrent sentences. Two important principles run side by side. The first is that consecutive sentences should normally be imposed where the two offences arise out of the same incident. Where there is a continuing pattern of conduct which gives rise to the same offence committed on two separate occasions, it will be a matter of fact and degree whether they are to be treated as arising out of the same incident or whether they are separate offences. If they are separate offences, the sentences should run consecutively unless they offend against the "totality" principle – a principle of sentencing practice now given the force of law by section 28(2)(b) of the Criminal Justice Act 1991 (see paragraph 11.45 below).

Fines

11.27 General. In the case of an individual, a fine may properly be imposed with a sentence of imprisonment where that is appropriate, particularly if it is clear that the offender has profited from the offence (see paragraphs 11.6 to 11.13 above). Where it is clear that the offender has not profited, imposing a custodial sentence together with a fine would be an inappropriate course. It is also inappropriate to impose a heavy fine to avoid imprisonment.

11.28 There is no general limit to the fine which may be imposed in the Crown Court (see Powers of the Criminal Courts Act 1973, s.30), although statutes may, in some cases, provide a ceiling on the fine. The position is different in the magistrates' court where a maximum limit applies, either by virtue of the provisions of the Magistrates' Courts Act 1980 or by virtue of the legislation which has been infringed (see paragraph 11.3 above).

Offences triable either way

11.29 The statutory maximum: Meaning. During the last two decades the provisions of legislation imposing fines following conviction for offences in the magistrates' court were brought into a single framework, with fines limited to a statutory maximum or referable to a point on a standard scale. By virtue of section 31(2) of the Magistrates' Courts Act 1980, conviction of an offence triable either way in the magistrates' court or in the Crown Court may be visited in the magistrates' court with a fine not exceeding "the prescribed sum" (at present equivalent in value to "the statutory maximum": see the Interpretation Act 1978, Sched. 1) unless the statute provides for a higher penalty. Where the statute provides for one penalty on first conviction and a different penalty on subsequent convictions, the statutory maximum applies to each offence (section 32(3)). The statutory maximum does not apply, however, where the penalty is a continuing one for each day after conviction where a state of affairs is not remedied. An example of this type of provision appears in section 80(5) of the Environmental Protection Act 1990:

> ". . . shall be liable on summary conviction to a fine not exceeding level 5 on the standard scale together with a further fine of an amount equal to one tenth of that level for each day on which the offence continues after the conviction".

Level 5 of the standard scale is the equivalent of the statutory maximum (Criminal Justice Act 1982, s.37). For a fuller explanation of the meaning of the standard scale see paragraph 11.29 below.

11.30 Statutory maximum: subordinate legislation. Section 51 of the Criminal Justice Act 1988 provides that where an offence triable either way is created by subordinate legislation prior to the coming into force of that section, the maximum fine shall be the statutory maximum unless a higher fine was specified. Similar provisions to those referred to in relation to offences under primary legislation apply in relation to subordinate legislation providing for differential fines on subsequent convictions and for continuing penalties after conviction.

Summary offences

11.31   The standard scale.   Recently created summary offences make reference to a point on the standard scale if a higher fine is not specifically provided for. The standard scales (under section 37(2) of the Criminal Justice Act 1982, as amended by the Criminal Justice Act 1992) are:

level	amount of fine
1	£200
2	£500
3	£1,000
4	£2,500
5	£5,000

Offences which make reference to a particular fine which corresponded with a figure in the standard scale at 1982 values, has had substituted that point on the scale by section 46 of the Criminal Justice Act 1982. That provision applies to offences the maximum penalty for which may already have increased under Part III of the Act as well as to penalties not so increased.

Where an enactment has no express power to fine but allows for imprisonment, the maximum sum which can be imposed is level 3 on the standard scale, except that the fine in fact imposed must not have a longer period of imprisonment in default of payment (under Schedule 4 of the Magistrates' Courts Act 1980) than the period of imprisonment specified in the legislation. Similar provisions apply in respect of subordinate legislation (Criminal Justice Act 1982, s.52). Moreover, Part III of the Criminal Justice Act 1982 makes the framework of sentencing for summary offences comparable to that for offences triable either way which are tried summarily. Sections 35 and 36 abolish enhanced penalties under primary and subordinate legislation and sections 38 and 40 increase fines under legislation made prior to 1977 which were not increased by or after the Criminal Law Act 1977.

Imposing a fine

11.32   Fixing the amount of fines.   Before fixing a fine the court must inquire into the financial circumstances of an individual offender and must fix the amount of the fine in so far as the financial circumstances are known or appear (Criminal Justice Act 1991, s.18). Section 20 of the Criminal Justice Act 1991 enables a financial circumstances order to be made requiring him to give to the court information about his means; it is an offence to give information which the offender knows to be false and it is also an offence to make a statement recklessly or knowingly to fail to disclose information. The Act further envisages the making of an official request for information to which similar offences relate on false disclosure or non-disclosure (section 20A). Where an offender has not furnished information, or has been convicted in his absence following non-appearance, the court must make such determination of his means as seems fit. Section 21 provides for remission of fines in circumstances where the court is later satisfied that had it had the results of a means inquiry when sentencing, it would have imposed a lesser penalty.

No similar provision relates to corporate offenders for whom enquiry is not generally made. If there is a particular matter relating to the financial situation of a limited company the offender itself must take steps to bring the matter to the court's attention, and, if relevant, the court must take account of the matter. In *R.*

v. Mayfield Garage (Halifax) Ltd (1987) 9 Cr. App. R. (S.) 438 the court accepted that the total penalty imposed on the defendant company for failure to comply with the conditions of a petroleum spirit licence was nearly half the annual pre-tax profits, and took that factor into account in reducing the fines.

11.33 Enforcement of fines. Magistrates will usually grant time to pay, whether for a matter of weeks or by way of instalments (Magistrates' Courts Act 1980, s.75). Non-payment may result in a warrant of distress, a warrant of commitment, or attachment of earnings. If a person upon whom a fine is imposed wilfully defaults in payment, he may have to serve a sentence of imprisonment in default. This period may be set at the time of sentencing only if it appears that the defendant has sufficient means to pay, or that he is unlikely to remain at his place of residence for long enough for the fine to be enforced by the usual means, or if a custodial sentence is also imposed at the same time. In the magistrates' courts, maximum periods of imprisonment in default are prescribed by Schedule 4 of the Magistrates' Courts Act 1980, and in the Crown Court by section 31 of the Powers of the Criminal Courts Act 1973 as amended in each case. Where a fine is imposed on a company which fails to pay, the magistrates' court clerk may, if a warrant of distress does not raise sufficient to meet the fine, apply for the winding up of the company (Magistrates' Courts Act 1980, s.87A).

Absolute and conditional discharge

11.34 Where the sentencing court considers that it is inexpedient to inflict a punishment on the offender, having regard to the circumstances including the nature of the offence and the character of the offender, the court may order him to be discharged absolutely or subject to a condition that he commits no further offence within a period not exceeding three years (Powers of the Criminal Courts Act 1973, s.1A). If a conditional discharge is ordered and the offender commits a further offence within the specified period, he may be sentenced for the first offence afresh in any way in which he could have been dealt with if he had just been convicted of the offence.

The courts have imposed an absolute discharge in cases where they consider the case to have been trivial, or, if not trivial, one which should not have been brought. An example of this was *Smedleys Ltd v. Breed* [1974] A.C. 839 (see paragraph 11.4 above). A further instance occurred in *Mulvenna v. Snape* (1995) 159 J.P. 717 in which the court was critical of the prosecution of a "lowly" employee for obedience to the instructions of her employer, so incurring a liability for obstruction of a trading standards officer.

Community sentences

11.35 An individual convicted of a regulatory offence may be required to undertake a community sentence, but it is an appropriate sentence only where the offence is or offences are sufficiently serious to warrant such a sentence but not so serious that only a custodial sentence can be justified (Criminal Justice Act 1991, s.6). A community order (curfew, supervision or attendance centre order are not discussed here) includes any of the following orders:

— probation order

— community service order

— combination order (combination of the above save that the number of hours of community service required must be not less than 40 nor more than 100).

The court needs to address the following issues which arise under section 6 of the 1991 Act:

(i) is the offence serious enough to warrant a community sentence?

(ii) what order or orders are the most suitable for the offender? This involves taking into account the offender's circumstances and obtaining a pre-sentence report unless the court considers that it is unnecessary so to do (section 7);

(iii) what restrictions on the offender's liberty are commensurate with the seriousness of the offence? This, again, involves consideration of the circumstances of the offence including any aggravating or mitigating factors.

Compensation orders

11.36 Nature of order. A compensation order is not a form of sentence. It is a summary means of redressing a civil wrong which is being dealt with in the criminal courts because it is also an offence (*Attorney General's Reference (No. 10) of 1992* (1993) 15 Cr. App. Rep. (S.) 1) although it is not only a wrong which is actionable as a tort which may be the subject of compensation. Compensation may be ordered by virtue of section 35 of the Powers of the Criminal Courts Act 1973 where personal injury, loss or damage results from an offence or any other offence formally taken into consideration, and it is ancillary to another form of sentence. In the case of compensation for death and bereavement, section 35(3A) to (3D) limits the amount recoverable. In *R. v. Gateway Foodmarkets Ltd* [1997] 2 Cr.App. R. 40, the maximum amount recoverable under the civil law had been paid to the deceased's estate by way of *ex gratia* payment. The judge ordered a further £5,000 to be paid by way of compensation. Although section 35(3D) of the Act limits the amount of compensation payable to that recoverable under the Fatal Accidents Act 1976, the civil courts would have taken into account the ex gratia payment. The Court of Appeal set the compensation order aside, and also commented that they would have been prepared to have decided that the powers of the criminal court to order compensation was limited to that sum which would have been recoverable in civil proceedings.

In the magistrates' court, the maximum sum which may be awarded is £5,000, although the amount is unlimited in the Crown Court. If the court does not make a compensation order in circumstances when it is empowered to do so, it must give reasons, and, in the magistrates' court, these must be recorded in the register of convictions (Powers of the Criminal Courts Act 1991, s.35 and Magistrates' Courts Rules 1981, r.66(10A)).

Compensation may relate not only to a single incident but to a continuing wrong, such as where a landlord had failed to abate a statutory nuisance in respect of which a notice under section 82(6) of the Environment Protection Act 1990 had been served (*R. v. Crown Court at Liverpool, ex p. Cooke* [1996] 4 All E.R. 589).

11.37 Complicated cases. In *R. v. Lester* (1975) 63 Cr. App. R. 144 (a trade descriptions case concerning "clocked" cars) the court considered whether it was appropriate to make a compensation order. Bridge L.J. said:

> "The Court has considered . . . whether it would be appropriate . . . to make compensation orders in favour of the purchasers of some or all of the cars in relation to which the offences were committed, pursuant to section 35 of the Powers of the Criminal Courts Act 1973. There is some doubt in our minds as to whether in such cases as the present, where it is at least arguable whether any civil liability arises from the commission of an offence under the Act of 1968, there is "any loss or damage resulting from the offence" within the meaning of those words in section 35(1) of the Act of 1973. But without expressing any considered view on the matter, we have unhesitatingly reached the conclusion that this is not the kind of straightforward case where it would be appropriate for the criminal courts to order compensation. If in law compensation could properly be ordered, there must be considerable difficulty in quantifying the appropriate figure. That is not a suitable order for the exercise of the power of a criminal court, which will normally only make orders dealing with civil liability where no complexity arises".

In *R. v. Canning* (1993) 15 Cr. App. Rep. (S.) 371, in contrast, the court made a compensation order in the sum of £990 in a "clocking" case concerning three counts of applying a false trade description and one of supplying goods to which a false trade description had been applied, as well as imposing a period of 6 months imprisonment. (Note that in general compensation should only be ordered as well as imprisonment if there is little chance that the offender will re-offend after his release in order to pay the compensation *(R. v. Wilkinson* [1980] 1 W.L.R. 396)).

11.38 Specimen charges. Where a plea of guilty to specimen charges is entered and the defendants admit other similar offences which do not appear on the information or indictment charged the court cannot award compensation in respect of the other matters unless they are formally taken into consideration *(R. v. Crutchley and Tonks* (1993) 15 Cr. App. Rep. (S.) 627). This contrasts with the power of the court to take other admitted offences which are represented by a sample into account for the purposes of calculating sentence. See paragraph 11.16 above.

11.39 The means of the defendant. In cases where the means of the defendant may be a relevant issue his legal representatives must ensure that (as with the imposition of a fine) his limited means are fully before the court. In *R. v. Ellis* (1993) 158 J.P. 386, the Court of Appeal stressed that a compensation order should only be made on the basis of the defendant's existing financial circumstances and not on the basis of optimistic speculation for the future.

Deprivation orders

11.40 Nature. In regulatory cases, a deprivation order sometimes falls to be made – particularly if the regulatory offence is a counterfeiting offence. A deprivation order may be made, ancillary to other sentences and to be taken into account before a fine is imposed, under section 43 of the Powers of the Criminal Courts Act 1973, as amended. The power exists to deprive the offender of property if it has been used or was intended for the purpose of committing or facilitating the commission of an offence or if the offence itself consists of his being lawfully in possession of the property in question.

Confiscation and forfeiture orders

11.41 Description. Where a person is convicted of an offence described in Schedule 4 of the Criminal Justice Act 1988, or such an offence is taken into consideration, and the offence was committed after January 1, 1996, a magistrates' court may confiscate any property by which he has benefited or pecuniary advantage obtained, if that benefit is £10,000 or more. The offences are:

(a) offences relating to sex establishments under the Local Government (Miscellaneous Provisions) Act 1982;

(b) supplying or possessing video recordings of unclassified work under the Video Recordings Act 1984

(c) use of unlicensed premises under the Cinemas Act 1985;

(d) offences relating to the making, dealing in or using unlawful recordings or dealing with infringing articles under the Copyright, Designs and Patents Act 1988;

(e) offences concerning goods where there has been an unlawful use of a trade mark.

In the Crown Court, the court's powers apply to any indictable offence (except drug trafficking) committed after November 1, 1995. The procedure is usually commenced by a notice from the prosecution, although the court may consider that the confiscation process should be undergone in the absence of such a notice. The court must address:

(a) whether there has been a benefit;

(b) either the amount of the benefit or the amount that might be realised by order, whichever is the less.

The making of the order is mandatory where the court has decided to proceed under section 71 of the 1988 Act, although the requirement is relaxed to a mere power if the court is satisfied that the victim has commenced or is likely to commence civil proceedings. For further information on forfeiture see paragraphs 4.41 onwards.

MITIGATION

11.42 Varied considerations. In regulatory cases as with other offences, mitigation can be put forward on many bases. Section 28 of the Criminal Justice Act 1991 provides that nothing in Part I of the Act shall prevent the court from taking into account in mitigation "any such matters, as, in the opinion of the court, are relevant in mitigation of sentence". Express reference is made in section 28(2) to mitigation as a result of taking into account any other penalty included in the sentence (as for instance where a fine is imposed as well as imprisonment). Mitigating material has an impact in two ways:

(i) where it relates to the offence, it may reduce the seriousness of the offence and so take the offence out of a particular bracket into which it might otherwise belong;

(ii) even though it does not reduce the seriousness of the offence, it may make the sentence which might otherwise be imposed, inappropriate.

The plea

11.43   Stage at which plea entered.   Where a plea of guilty has been entered, rather than a conviction following a trial, the plea of guilty is itself a mitigating factor. Section 48 of the Criminal Justice and Public Order Act 1994 has underlined the importance of a guilty plea in mitigation of the penalty by requiring the court to take into account the stage in the proceedings at which the plea was entered. Moreover, if, as a result of taking such information into account, the court imposes a less severe penalty than would otherwise have been imposed, the court is required to say so. In the Crown Court, in other sorts of cases, it has been practice for a long time to take into account an early plea of guilty and give a "discount" from a sentence of imprisonment for it. In *R. v. Hollington and Emmens* (1985) 7 Cr. App. R. (S.) 364, the Court of Appeal commented in relation to the entry of pleas:

"This court has long said that discounts on sentences are appropriate, but everything depends on the circumstances of each case. If a man is arrested and at once tells the police that he is guilty and co-operates with them in the recovery of property and the identification of others concerned in the offence, he can expect to get a substantial discount. But if a man is arrested in circumstances in which he cannot hope to put forward a defence of not guilty, he cannot expect much by way of a discount. In between comes this kind of case, where the court has been put to considerable trouble as a result of a tactical plea. The sooner it is appreciated that defendants are not going to get full discount for pleas of guilty in these sort of circumstances, the better it will be for the administration of justice".

The 1994 Act has applied the practice of rewarding some guilty pleas to all courts and to all types of sentence. The stage at which the plea has been entered may therefore be relevant even to a regulatory offence, as may the fact that the defendant has co-operated with the enforcement authority. This will now be so even where the court would only be minded to, or be able to, impose a financial penalty. That said, in the magistrates' court and in the majority of regulatory cases, the true impact of a plea of guilty is hard to assess. Indeed, some regulatory practitioners consider that where the choice for the defendant is between attempting a due diligence defence and pleading guilty, a trial of the issues in a magistrates' court can be a better way to present the defence mitigation than is the cold delivery of an explanation of a failure of a system. Such practitioners would argue in support of that contention that magistrates can be more sympathetic to the human failings of witnesses with whom they have been invited to identify, than to a defendant who blames third parties who are his subordinates as an explanation of his guilt.

11.44   Factors which may reduce the discount.   Some matters which are recognised to affect the discount for a guilty plea are:

(i) *Tactical plea:* a tactical plea is generally recognised as one entered for an ulterior purpose, such as to avoid conviction before Christmas or in the hope of an adjourned date being fixed before a bench which it is thought may be more favourable. It is not a tactical plea if there is a genuine reason for a not guilty plea being entered and then changed. An example of the latter situation might be where the court requires pleas to be entered before the defendant has had an opportunity to conduct a full investigation of matters of which he had no personal knowledge. In those circumstances, however, it is more desirable to postpone the entry of pleas to the charge to an adjourned date.

(ii) *Overwhelming evidence:* just as a defendant who surrenders to the police and admits a crime which, in the absence of this, could not have been proved against him, is entitled to more than the usual discount (*R. v. Hoult* 12 Cr. App. R. (S.) 180), so a defendant who could have no plausible defence is not entitled to a discount as substantial as it might have been were there less evidence against him (*R. v. Davis* 2 Cr. App. R. (S.) 168).

(iii) *"Newton" hearing:* if the defendant pleads guilty to a count in the indictment, but puts forward a view of the facts which is substantially different from that put forward by the prosecution, the court may hold a hearing to determine the issue (*R. v. Newton* (1983) 77 Cr. App. R. 13). If the defendant's version is not accepted by the court, the discount may be reduced, although it does not follow that he will lose all credit for his plea (*R. v. Stevens* 8 Cr. App. R. (S.) 297 and *R. v. Jauncey* (1986) 8 Cr. App. R. (S) 401). Although hearings of this type are very rare in magistrates' courts and more so where a regulatory offence is involved, it could be appropriate, say, where the prosecution alleges dishonesty in a "clocking" case (see paragraph 11.13 above) which the defendant denies. In *R. v. Hewitt* (1991) 13 Cr. App. R. (S.) 131, a "clocking" case, the court bore in mind that the mitigating effect of a guilty plea was diminished by the fact of a Newton trial of issues which went against the defendant, and upheld a custodial sentence together with the imposition of a fine of £500 on each of eight counts.

(iv) *Specimen charges:* where the charge to which a guilty plea was made was a sample count drawn from a larger number of offences which are admitted by the defendant, it may be appropriate to withhold the discount or reduce it (*R. v. Costen* (1989) 11 Cr. App. R. (S.) 182). See paragraph 11.16 above.

Totality

11.45 Offences arising out of the same transaction. Sometimes a single action or omission of the defendant gives rise to a number of offences. Whether the defendant then appears before the court for one offence or for more than one offence arising out of the same facts, is a matter of the prosecution's discretion. For example, a vendor selling food to which no "best before" label was attached because the food was so old that it predated the requirement to place the label on the food might commit an offence under the Food Labelling Regulations 1996 and might also commit an offence of selling food not of a quality demanded by the purchaser (or other more serious charge) under the Food Safety Act 1990. If both matters are charged, a prudent defence solicitor may seek to persuade the prosecutor to accept a plea to one charge (preferably the less serious) and let the other lie on the file or (better, from the defendant's point of view) to offer no evidence in respect of it, resulting in an acquittal. The concern is that the court may be tempted to punish twice the same guilty conduct. Where a custodial sentence is under consideration, concurrent sentences should be given for offences arising from the same facts, unless there are exceptional circumstances (such as *R. v. Wheatley* 5 Cr. App. R. (S.) 417 where an additional penalty to driving while disqualified was added because the defendant had also driven with excess alcohol). Where the court is concerned with financial penalties only, the same reasoning also applies, and there may be occasions where the court may award no separate penalty in respect of the offences which lie behind the first.

11.46 "The totality principle". Where the court is required to sentence for several offences, even though they are not connected, sentences will run consecutively unless "the totality principle" requires that they be concurrent or that there should be no separate penalty. The principle is that the court must look at all the offences before it can decide what is an appropriate penalty for them overall, rather than carrying out an arithmetical, cumulative exercise. In *R v. Chelmsford Crown Court, ex p. Birchall* (1989) 11 Cr. App. R. (S.) 510, a haulage contractor had pleaded guilty to 10 offences of using an overweight goods vehicle. The justices applied a formula to each offence, starting with a £400 fine and adding £20 for each percentage that each lorry was overweight. This produced a total fine of £7,600. The Divisional Court quashed the sentence as an error of law. A fine of £1,300 was substituted.

Knowledge and participation

11.47 Culpability. As has been seen above, culpability is a factor in sentencing for crime, even quasi-crime. Arguably, where the fact that a person has taken deliberate steps to cause the offence aggravates its seriousness, it feeds the retributive elements of sentencing rather than merely the deterrent elements (see above), and in mitigation an absence of or explanation for culpability may reduce both aspects. In strict liability offences, dishonesty is an aggravating factor (see above); but equally, where a principal is liable for an act of his employee, that is a mitigating factor, particularly if he has taken some measures to foresee and avert the crime. Even if there has been no dishonesty or imprisonment is not a likelihood, the ultimate disposal, whether the amount of the fine or the granting of an absolute or conditional discharge, may significantly be affected by an assertion of "moral innocence" on the part of the defendant.

11.48 Measure of responsibility. Where individuals are prosecuted, those having different roles will fall to be considered differently. In the main, employees who act honestly and on instructions but commit an offence fall to be treated less harshly than their employers (*Mulvenna v. Snape* (1995) 159 J.P. 717), although this rule may diminish as the employee acquires a personal gain and where he acts knowingly. In *R. v. Parkinson and others* (1984) 6 Cr. App. R. (S.) 423 employees charged with tachograph offences alleged that they had acted under pressure from their employer to make false entries. Stocker J. commented:

". . . the Court wishes to reiterate that in future on trial on indictment where there is evidence that drivers have persistently disregarded the regulations at least in part for their own gain it would no doubt be appropriate, in our view, to impose custodial sentences . . .".

Employers who deliberately flout regulations affecting public safety cannot expect leniency: indeed, being an employer in a case of deliberate breach is likely to be an aggravating factor:

". . . this man was the managing director, in charge of a company, with evidently a number of vehicles. An offence by him was a more serious one than by one of his employees and demanded a severe sentence to discourage others in his position. These offences are serious in their nature and cause danger to the public. The very fact that employees, or drivers, may regard them simply as bureaucratic interference with their livelihood is itself a reason for imposing significant sentences because the conduct is very much worse than it is regarded if that is right"

per Staughton L.J. in *R. v. McCabe* (1989) 11 Cr. App. R. (S.) 154, a tachograph case.

11.49   Steps to avoid commission of the offence.   In the case of strict liability offences, the steps taken to avoid an offence are highly relevant, even where those steps are insufficient to establish due diligence (where due diligence is a defence). It will not be sufficient to claim mitigation on the basis that instructions have been given to another to avoid the commission of the offence if the implementation of those instructions has not been overseen. So in *R. v. Lightwater Valley Ltd* (1990) 12 Cr. App. R. (S.) 328, where the defendants pleaded guilty to two counts under the Health and Safety at Work, etc. Act 1974 of failure to take such steps as were reasonably practicable for the safety of the staff and visitors, accidents had occurred. In both cases, the cause of the accidents was said to be a failure adequately to supervise employees. £3,000 fines were imposed on each count and the defendants appealed. Ian Kennedy J., upholding the sentences, said:

"The duty of the appellants is to take those steps which are reasonably practicable for the safety of their staff and their visitors. They are a commercial undertaking. They choose – perhaps they are forced – to employ young people who are insufficiently mature and insufficiently responsible to give the close attention that is required. In that case it is their duty to employ more responsible supervisory staff. It is wholly insufficient for the management to recognise that the staff disobey orders when their backs are turned, however much they may genuinely regret that, if they do not implement a better level of supervision to ensure that orders are obeyed . . ."

11.50   Offence provoked by action of the prosecution.   Where there is evidence that the offence would not have been committed at all but for the activities of a prosecution investigator, the court may mitigate the penalty if it thinks it right to do so (*R. v. Sang* (1979) 68 Cr. App. R. 240). An instance of where a supply which would not have been made, were it not for the actions of the prosecution, but which resulted in the commission of an offence occurred in *Datta v. Phillips* Due Diligence Reporter, May 1996. Following a visit from a T.S.O. the defendant had withdrawn from sale pyjamas infringing safety requirements. Later the T.S.O. made a test purchase of the goods under his powers in section 28 of the Consumer Protection Act 1987, which the defendant had to comply with. The defendant argued that the test sale was not a supply within the meaning of the Act. Rejecting that argument, the Divisional Court expressed the view that the defendant should have relied upon a due diligence defence under section 39(1) to avoid liability.

Individual characteristics

11.51 Previous good character. That good character is a mitigating factor in the general principles of sentencing is undeniable (*R. v. Sykes* (1980) 2 Cr. App. R. (S.) 173). Good character is relevant, too, at least in regulatory offences which are committed deliberately (*R. v. Waring and Canning* (1994) 15 Cr. App. R. (S.) 371), and probably not to be disregarded where the commission of the offence has been unintentional, because in the latter instance, good character may demonstrate care in conducting business affairs.

11.52 Co-operation with investigators. In *R. v. Waring and Canning* (above) the court recognised as important mitigation, too, the considerable co-operation by the defendants in the investigation of three counts of applying a false trade description to goods and one of supplying goods to which a false trade description has been attached, counts with which the defendants were subsequently charged. An allied consideration is that a defendant who assists investigators to identify others who are operating illegally may hope to have a discounted sentence. The extent of the discount is a matter for the sentencing court, rather than a matter of tariff (*R. v. Lowe* (1977) 66 Cr. App. R. 122). The mitigating characteristic is, in the main, a matter of public policy or expedience, rather than to be regarded as an attribute of the defendant (*R. v. Sinfield* (1981) 3 Cr. App. R. 258), although if the defendant suffers as a result of the assistance that he has given, for example, because he has been assaulted, this should be acknowledged in sentence (*R. v. Thomas* (1985) 7 Cr. App. R. (S.) 95). This principle, derived from the approach to sentencing "true" crime, is likely to have significance where both the defendant is charged with a offence with a "true crime" element and where the information concerns the commission by others of offences with a "true" crime element, for example, because dishonesty is involved or where the defendant can give information about passing off or counterfeiting of other manufacturers' goods. It is submitted that the value of this sentencing principle in mitigating offences which involve no dishonesty or deliberateness, or where the defendant reports matters which do not involve a significant proportion of the same or are not serious, is likely to be small. It must be a matter of degree, however. Credit might be given for the reporting of environmental offences which would otherwise be difficult to detect, but it is hard to see how credit could ever be given for information about, say, food labelling offences committed by others.

11.53 Personal financial difficulties which led to the commission of the offence. In *R. v. Waring and Canning* (above), the court acknowledged as a mitigating factor that financial difficulties had led to the commission of the offence.

11.54 Financial difficulties to which regard must be had in fixing a financial penalty. It is one matter to impose a deterrent penalty, and another to impose so great a penalty that it cannot reasonably be met by the defendant. The court must bear in mind the position of the defendant's business (if appropriate) in meeting any financial penalty (*R. v. Mayfield Garage (Halifax) Ltd* (1987) 9 Cr. App. R. (S.) 438).

11.55 Efforts to make good the wrong. Frequently, the efforts to make compensation to the complainant are relied upon in mitigation. As a general rule, this may be regarded as good mitigation where the efforts to make compensation are considerable. So the efforts by the defendants to make amends were of mitigating value in *R. v. Waring and Canning* (above), but in *R. v. Crosby and Hayes* (1974) 60 Cr. App. R. 234, the Court of Appeal drew attention to the fact that merely because the defendant has resources to make compensation this does not, of itself, justify a reduction in sentence, and, in particular, a defendant should not be treated differently from one who has funds available for the reason that he is not in a position to make compensation.

11.56 Delay between the offence and sentence. In *R. v. Foster* [1997] 1 Cr. App. R. (S.) 394, the court took into account that seven years had passed between the commission of the offences and sentencing, seven years which had considerably changed the defendant. This period was not sufficient to avert a custodial sentence.

11.57 Other losses resulting from the offence. Where the defendant's business perishes as a consequence of the prosecution, that is a factor in mitigation (*R. v. Foster, R. v. Waring and Canning* above).

11.58 Factors arising out of the conduct of the proceedings against the defendant. It is recognised that certain factors relating to the conduct of the proceedings against the defendant can justify mitigation of the penalty. An example of this is where the court concludes that the prosecution should not have been brought: that is, the decision to prosecute is thought to be flawed (*Smedley Ltd v. Breed* [1974] A.C. 839).

11.59 Difficulties which any sentence might cause to third parties. This consideration usually relates to the families of defendants, such that it may be a mitigating factor if exceptional hardship will be caused by the penalties imposed. Where the defendant is a businessman, and his business may founder, it is a factor that employees and creditors may similarly be caused significant hardship.

CHAPTER 12

Appeals and Reviews

THE APPELLATE STRUCTURE

Summary

12.1 General. This chapter considers the appellate system as it affects regulatory offences. Consideration is also given to the means of appealing from orders made by the magistrates' and Crown Courts in civil proceedings associated with regulatory offences – such as appeals against enforcement orders. Matters such as bail and legal aid are not discussed, nor are rights which might lie in the event of an infringement of the European Convention on Human Rights, (of which Articles 6 [fair administration of justice] and 7 [prohibition on retroactivity in the criminal law]) are most likely to have impact on regulatory offences. Clearly, when these rights are incorporated into domestic law as is proposed, they may gain added importance in relation to regulatory matters. This chapter does pay attention to applications for judicial review which are commonly brought as an alternative to appeal in regulatory cases. Each avenue of appeal or review is set out in turn below.

In addition to its role in supplementing the powers of an appellate court, judicial review can be a means of determining matters associated with prosecutions. Albeit that in some cases it may be a remedy which is an alternative to appeal, it is also an available check on administrative action where there is no on-going prosecution, but a prosecution is a likely outcome of the course adopted by the prosecuting authority. An example of this might be where judicial review is sought of the decision to prosecute, or where a challenge is made to byelaws, or to the decision to serve an enforcement notice before any prosecution is commenced (see, for instance, *R. v. Wicks Ltd* [1997] 2 All E.R. 801).

12.2 Outline of appeals. In outline, the availability of appeals, subject to meeting the requisite criteria, can be set out as follows:

From the magistrates' court: criminal cases

12.3 From the magistrates' court to:

    (i) the Crown Court (Magistrates' Courts Act 1980, s.108);

    (ii) the Divisional Court by way of case stated (Magistrates' Courts Act 1980, s.111);

(iii) the Divisional Court by way of an application for judicial review (Supreme Court Act 1981, s.31 Ord. 53 of the Rules of the Supreme Court, r.1). Although this is not strictly an 'appeal', this chapter treats the procedure analagously.

12.4 If there is an appeal to the Crown Court, appeal thereafter lies to:

(i) the Divisional Court by way of case stated;

(ii) the Divisional Court by way of an application for judicial review (where appropriate).

12.5 Appeal lies from the Divisional Court directly to the House of Lords, if permitted (see paragraph 12.42 below).

12.6 In addition to the above, the magistrates' court has limited power to reconsider its own decisions:

— to rectify mistakes etc. under section 142 of the Magistrates' Courts Act 1980, and

— to remit penalties, for example under the Remission of Penalties Act 1859, section 1; Magistrates' Courts Act 1980; Powers of the Criminal Courts Act 1973, section 37.

From the magistrates' court: Civil cases

12.7 In civil cases (such as an appeal against an executive notice), the avenue of appeal may be laid down by statute – for example, section 38 of the Food Safety Act 1990 which provides for an appeal from the magistrates to the Crown Court, or may be dependent upon section 111 of the Magistrates' Courts Act 1980 which allows an appeal by way of case stated to the Divisional Court by any person who was a party to any proceeding before a magistrates' court. This includes civil proceedings. The Divisional Court in its capacity to review the actions of inferior courts may make prerogative orders (see paragraphs 12.43 to 12.46 below) to control the conduct of civil proceedings in the magistrates' court.

Appeals from the crown court as the court of trial

12.8 Appeal lies:

(i) to the Court of Appeal in every matter relating a trial on indictment;

(ii) to the Divisional Court by way of case stated only where the matter does not relate to trial on indictment (Supreme Court Act 1981, s.28);

(iii) to the Divisional Court by way of Judicial Review only where the matter does not relate to trial on indictment (Supreme Court Act 1981 s.29).

12.9 Appeal lies in a permitted case, from both the Divisional Court and the Court of Appeal, to the House of Lords.

APPEALS FROM THE MAGISTRATES' COURT:

Criminal cases

General

12.10 Outline. An appeal, as such, from the magistrates' court lies, for the defendant, in two directions: the Crown Court or the Divisional Court. For a complete rehearing on the facts, together with an opportunity to present the evidence again, or to bring new evidence, appeal to the Crown Court is appropriate. Indeed, the Divisional Court, even when sitting in its capacity to review the decisions of a lower court, has no power to investigate facts which have emerged since conviction *(R. v. Huyton J.J.s, ex. p. Roberts* [1988] C.O.D. 43 – although contrast *R. v. Wolverhampton Crown Court, ex p. Crofts*, 76 Cr. App. R. 8 where the Divisional Court used certiorari to quash the decision of a Crown Court to allow an appeal against conviction because the Crown Court had reached its decision on the basis of perjured evidence: also *R. v. Knightsbridge Crown Court, ex p. Goonatilleke* [1986] Q.B. 1 where the failure to disclose the bad character of a prosecution witness amounted to a denial of natural justice). The fresh hearing is before a Judge of the Crown Court sitting with at least one and usually two magistrates. Appeal may be made against conviction or sentence or both. The court hearing the appeal has the same powers of sentence following conviction as did the magistrates. See paragraph 12.15 below for expansion of these matters.

For the prosecution, an appeal against a refusal to convict lies only by way of case stated to the Divisional Court on point of law or jurisdiction. The defendant's right of appeal to this court against conviction or sentence is also on a point of law or jurisdiction. A point of law includes irregularities in the trial and behaviour and decision-making which is "*Wednesbury* unreasonable" as well as matters such as the application of a wrong legal principle. The hearing is conducted by reference to the case stated by the magistrates and other documents which were in evidence before the magistrates, but the Divisional Court will not, except in the most exceptional circumstances, concern itself with the evidence given in the case except in so far as it appears in the case stated by the magistrates. The Divisional Court has power to impose sanctions itself and it has a discretion to remit the case to the magistrates' court for further consideration. See paragraphs 12.18 to 12.29 below.

In addition to these two avenues of appeal, there is also a discretion to seek judicial review of certain decisions of the magistrates' court in a proper case. It is not to be regarded as a means of circumventing the avenues of appeal which are already available to the Defendant, however: indeed the reverse is, broadly speaking, the case. Detailed consideration of the circumstances when judicial review is available and the remedies it may give are set out at paragraphs 12.47 to 12.51 below.

Appeal from a magistrates' court to the Crown Court

12.11 When appeal lies. An appeal lies against both conviction and sentence (which does not include an order for costs: Magistrates' Courts Act 1980, s.108). The right to appeal is halted, however, if the appellant also makes an application to the Divisional Court by way of case stated (Magistrates' Courts Act 1980 s.111(4)). If the appellant concurrently makes an application for leave to apply for judicial review, this will not have the consequence of determining the right of appeal to the Crown Court but may make it unlikely that the Divisional Court will entertain the application before it, on the principle that a defendant is not entitled both to a fair trial and a fair appeal (*R. v. Peterborough Justices, ex p. Dowler* [1996] 2 Cr. App. R. 561). Where both avenues of redress are pursued, the applicant for judicial review must inform the Divisional Court of the existence of the proceedings in the Crown Court at the outset of any hearing before the higher court (*R. v. Mid-Worcester J.J.s, ex p. Hart* [1989] C.O.D. 397).

12.12 Powers. The Crown Court has at any stage a power to correct any error or mistake made in the order or judgment of the court below, and, at the end of the hearing of the appeal, may confirm, reverse or vary any part of the decision appealed against, including any determination not to impose a separate penalty, and may impose a different punishment, whether more or less severe, provided that the court may not impose a punishment which could not have been imposed by the lower court (Supreme Court Act 1981, s.48). Where an appeal is made against sentence in respect of one of several convictions, the court has power to vary the sentence imposed for all the convictions. It does not follow from the above, however, that the powers of the appellate court are identical to the powers which existed below. For example, whereas the magistrates' court may have power to correct a defective information, the Crown Court has no such jurisdiction (*R. v. Swansea Crown Court, ex p. Stacey* [1990] R.T.R. 183). It appears, however, that where a magistrates' court could have ignored a defect by reliance on the provisions of section 123 of the Magistrates' Courts Act 1980 (see paragraph 10.3 above), the Crown Court can proceed likewise.

12.13 Notice of appeal. The procedure is laid down in the Crown Court Rules 1982 (as amended). Notice of appeal is given in writing to the clerk of the magistrates' court not later than 21 days after the day on which the decision appealed against is given. If the trial of the appellant has been adjourned (but not deferred under section 1(1) of the Powers of the Criminal Courts Act 1973) after conviction, the period of 21 days runs from the date of sentence. This period can be extended by the Crown Court before or after the 21 days has expired, on an application in writing setting out the grounds for extension. The decision to extend time is a discretionary one for which the court is not obliged to allow time for an oral hearing nor is the court required to give reasons for a refusal (*R. v. Croyden Crown Court, ex p. Smith* (1984) 77 Cr. App. R. 277). If granted, notice of extension must be given by the appellant to the parties affected. The notice of appeal must set out whether the appeal is against conviction or sentence and the grounds of appeal. The Crown Court notifies the other parties of the hearing time and date.

12.14 The hearing of the appeal. Although the appeal is by way of a rehearing, amendments to the information made during the course of the trial below will not be reviewed. Where such a decision is capable of appeal, the appropriate route will be by way of application to the Divisional Court (*Fairgrieve v. Newman* (1985) 82 Cr. App. R. 60). In other respects, however, if a party wishes to rely upon evidence given below, he must call it again unless it can be agreed between the parties. An appellant who is represented need not attend in person, provided that his representative is present. An appellant who is not represented may conduct the appeal himself, give evidence and make a speech. If the appellant does not attend at all, the Court may hear the appeal in his absence, and if neither party attends, the Court may dismiss the appeal (*R. v. Guildford Crown Court, ex p. Brewer* (1988) 87 Cr. App. R. 265).

12.15   Appeals against sentence.   The Crown Court when hearing an appeal against sentence by way of a rehearing should repeat the reasoning underlying the sentencing process, and should compare the sentence arrived at with that imposed by the magistrates. If there is only an insignificant difference, the sentence imposed below should be upheld. Otherwise, the appeal should be allowed to the extent of the difference *(R. v. Knutsford Crown Court, ex p. Jones)* 7 Cr. App. R. (S.) 448). This process must take into account the steps taken by the magistrates to arrive at a sentence, however. For example, if the magistrates have deferred sentence, the Crown Court must take account of the defendant's expectation arising out of the deferral *(R. v. Isleworth Crown Court, ex p. Irvin, The Times,* December 5, 1991). Where there is an issue as to the facts upon which sentence must be imposed, the Crown Court must determine this according to the facts found by the magistrates as the court of trial *(Munroe v. DPP* [1988] Crim.L.R. 823) unless the question has arisen for the first time in the Crown Court or unless the Crown Court has heard an appeal against conviction as well as against sentence. The court may either determine the facts itself or remit the matter to the justices for determination if the factual basis for sentencing is unclear. It is quite proper for there to be a "Newton" hearing to determine the factual basis for sentencing (*i.e.* for the Crown Court to hear contested evidence) if there is a substantial contest between the prosecution and defence version of events. In other cases, the court may apply its common sense to the versions put before it, but, in relation to conflicting matters must as far as possible accept the defendant's account of events *(R. v. Smith* (1986) 8 Cr. App. R. (S.) 169).

12.16   Reasons.   The Crown court must give brief reasons for its decision *(R. v. Harrow Crown Court, ex p. Dave* [1994] 99 Cr. App. R. 114). The justices must make decisions as to fact but, as with a jury, must take the law from the judge.

12.17   Appeal from the Crown Court to the Divisional Court.   Appeal from the decision of the Crown Court in its appellate function lies to the Divisional Court by way of case stated or judicial review. Rule 26 of the Crown Court Rules governs the procedure to be followed where an application is made to the Crown Court to state a case. The procedure is very similar to that which applies where an application is made to the magistrates' court for a case to be stated, save that the decision whether to state a case is made by the judge who presided over the appeal and, if he considers that the application is not frivolous, he will draw up the case. The other parties to the proceedings have the opportunity to put forward an alternative case and to decide whether they will participate in the appeal. An application for leave to apply for judicial review of a decision of the Crown Court in its appellate capacity is very similar to the procedure applicable in respect of an application concerning a decision of the magistrates' court. It is important, when deciding whether to seek judicial review or invite the Crown Court to state a case to recall that if the defendant wishes to challenge the dismissal of an appeal against conviction, the Divisional Court sitting in its capacity to review rather than in its appellate jurisdiction will have no power to remit the matter to the Crown Court for redetermination. If the defendant is successful in the Divisional Court, the conviction will still stand. The defendant must then have the appeal relisted in the Crown Court, and a differently constituted Crown court must determine the appeal against conviction *de novo (R. v. Leeds Crown Court, ex p. Barlow* [1989] R.T.R. 246). Also see paragraph 12.20 below as to the choice between judicial review and appeal by way of case stated.

Appeal from magistrates to the Divisional Court by way of case stated

12.18   Appropriateness of case stated.   An appeal to the Divisional Court by way of case stated may be made following conviction where the magistrates have erred in law or have exceeded their jurisdiction (section 111 of the Magistrates' Courts Act 1980). It may be applied for by the prosecutor or the defendant. A point of law may be taken by either party in a criminal case even though the matter was not raised in the magistrates' court (*Whitehead v. Haines* [1965] 1 Q.B. 200), although the position is more difficult if, had the point been taken below, evidence would or might have been addressed to that issue. In those circumstances, the Divisional Court will decline to allow the new point to be argued (*Ross v. Moss* [1965] Q.B. 396. Also see *Braham v. DPP* (1994) 159 J.P. 527 where the Divisional Court would not review the exercise by the magistrates of a discretion to exclude evidence under section 78 of the Police and Criminal Evidence Act 1984). For the defendant, appeal by way of case stated involves an abandonment of the right to appeal to the Crown Court (section 111(4)) even if the case stated is subsequently not proceeded with (*R. v. Crown Court at Winchester, ex p. Lewington* [1982] 1 W.L.R. 1277).

Questions of fact and discretion cannot be redetermined in the Divisional Court unless they are so serious as to qualify as matters of law, namely if:

(i)   there was no evidence on which the facts found could have been based;

(ii)   the exercise of the discretion was so unreasonable that no reasonable bench of magistrates could have come to it (*i.e. Wednesbury* unreasonable, after the decision in *Associated Provincial Picture Houses v. Wednesbury Corporation* [1948] 1 K.B. 223).

Questions of sentence, similarly, do not arise for consideration in an appeal by way of case stated unless the sentence was so outside the normal discretionary limits as to imply an error of law (*Universal Salvage Ltd and Robinson v. Boothby* [1984] R.T.R. 289).

12.19   Powers of the Divisional Court.   The powers of disposal of the High Court are set out in section 28A of the Supreme Court Act 1981. It must decide the stated questions and:

(a)   reverse, affirm or amend the determination of the justices; or

(b)   remit the matter to the justices with its opinion;

and make such ancillary order as it thinks fit. Usually this is limited to an order as to costs.

12.20   Judicial review contrasted.   Care needs to be taken to ensure that the correct form of application to the Divisional Court is pursued. Some complaints, for example, a complaint which involves a denial of natural justice, is better brought by way of judicial review for certiorari (*R. v. Wandsworth Justices, ex p. Read* [1942] 1 K.B. 281; *Rigby v. Woodward* [1957] 1 W.L.R. 250 and see paragraphs 12.31 to 12.46 below). In particular, where complaint is made of an interlocutory decision (such as a refusal to allow an adjournment), case stated is not available and an application for judicial review might be the only method by which the concern could be ventilated prior to the conclusion of the proceedings in the court below. In such an instance, of course, it would be highly unusual for it to be appropriate to seek leave to apply for judicial review at an interlocutory stage at all (see paragraph 12.36 below). On the other hand, an appeal by way of case stated is appropriate where the identification of the facts found is, or may be, critical to the resolution of the issue *(R v. Morpeth J.J.s, ex p. Ward* (1992) 95 Cr. App. R. 215).

12.21 Procedure. As magistrates do not usually give reasons for their decisions in the ordinary course of determining the issues before them, the prospective appellant may be unaware or the grounds upon which he has lost. (Increasingly, magistrates are showing a willingness to give brief reasons in regulatory cases; a practice which assists the defendant or prosecutor to know whether there is mileage in requesting the statement of a case).

The first step is to invite the magistrates to state a case on the question of law or jurisdiction involved. This must be in writing and done within 21 days after the day on which the decision was given. The application for the case to be stated must be signed by or on behalf of the applicant. The application must specify the question or questions of law or jurisdiction upon which a request is required (section 111 (2), (3) of the Magistrates' Courts Act 1980 and rule 76 of the Magistrates' Courts Rules 1981). Failure to identify the question or questions may be fatal to the application. The requirement to specify the question or questions is mandatory rather than directory *(R. v. Croydon Justices, ex p. Lefore Holdings Ltd* [1980] 1 W.L.R. 1465). It follows that the consequences of a failure to identify the question will depend upon the degree of compliance with the requirement *(R. v. Croydon Justices* (above); *Robinson v. Whittle* [1980] 1 W.L.R. 1476; *R. v. Bromley Magistrates' Courts, ex p. Waitrose Ltd* [1980] 3 All E.R. 464).

12.22 Calculation of time. Time for requesting the case to be stated begins to run on the day after the day when the final decision was made (section 111(3)) and, if the application is posted, ends on the date when it is posted *if* it would in the ordinary course of post have been received by the magistrates' court within the 21 day period, notwithstanding that in fact the 21 day period expires before the court receives the application *(P & M Supplies (Essex) Limited v. Hackney London Borough Council* (1990) 154 J.P. 814). The High Court has no power to extend the period *(Michael v. Gowland* [1977] 2 All E.R. 328; *Bristol and West Building Society v. Hickmott* (1980) 144 J.P. 443).

12.23 Recognisance. The magistrates may require as a pre-condition to appeal a recognisance to prosecute the appeal without delay and to submit to the judgment of the High Court (section 114). The effect of a recognisance is not that money is immediately paid, but that the surety must promise in prescribed form (Form 121) that, in the event that he does not prosecute the appeal, etc., he will deliver the payment. It is therefore akin to a performance bond: a fact which magistrates are entitled to recall when setting the amount of the recognisance which they require. The recognisance may be entered at any time before the case is stated *(Stanhope v. Thorsby* (1866) L.R. 1 C.P. 423). Where the appellant is a company, the recognisance should be entered by a director *(Southern Counties Deposit Bank v. Boaler* (1895) 59 J.P. 536). The amount of the recognisance is not fixed and the court is required to take into account the means of the prospective appellant *(R. v. Newcastle-upon-Tyne Justices, ex p. Skinner* [1987] 1 W.L.R. 312). It is common for magistrates' courts to fix the sum of £50 as a recognisance in a regulatory matter.

12.24   Drafting the case. It is usual for the magistrates' clerk to draft the case to be stated for the justices, although it is increasingly common practice for the applicant to submit a draft for approval and amendment by the magistrates. (There has been no expression of approval for this practice by the Divisional Court, who are unlikely, in most cases, to know that this has been done). The editors of *Stone's Justices' Manual* (Butterworths) recommend the following practice which has been approved in *Tesco Stores Ltd v. Seabridge* [1988] Crim.L.R. 517:

(i)   on receipt of a proper application, the justices' clerk should prepare a draft case unless the justices are likely to refuse to state a case. (The magistrates may refuse to state a case if the application is frivolous (section 111). For an example of a frivolous application, see *R. v. Mildenhall Magistrates' Court, ex p. Forest Heath District Council, The Times,* May 16, 1997, where the complaint amounted in truth to no more than that the magistrates preferred one version of events to another);

(ii)   for the purposes of preparing the draft, the justices clerk should consult the justices and may discuss the matter informally with either or both parties;

(iii)   the first draft should be sent to the justices and to the parties within 21 days from the date of receipt of the application;

(iv)   when the draft is sent to the parties they must be informed that they have 21 days within which to make representations;

(v)   the justices' clerk may discuss the case informally prior to the making of representations;

(vi)   immediately after the expiry of the date by which representations should be made, the justices' clerk should advise the justices of any representations and agree with them the final form of the case;

(vii)   the case must be signed by at least two of the justices or the justices' clerk within 21 days of the last date for making representations and the final signed form is sent to the applicant or his solicitors.

If any of the time limits are not complied with, the parties and the Divisional Court should be advised as to the reasons (rule 79). Non-compliance with the time limits may be fatal to the appeal: in *Parsons v. F.W. Woolworth & Co. Ltd* [1980] 1 W.L.R. 1472, the Divisional Court refused to decide on the case because the applicant had asked the justices' clerk to delay issuing the case to the parties while he obtained permission from the local authority to enter into the recognisance. He had caused or been responsible for a breach of the directory provisions of the Magistrates' Courts Rules 1968, and therefore the court dismissed the appeal without a hearing on the merits, notwithstanding that it accepted that it had jurisdiction.

12.25   Content of the case. The form of the case stated is prescribed in Form 155; also see the Practice Direction ([1972] 1 W.L.R. 4). It must include the facts found by the court but not the evidence on which this was based, either as part of the case or separately (*Cotgreave and Cotgreave v. Cheshire County Council* (1992) 157 J.P. 85) except that where one of the issues for the Divisional Court is that there was no evidence to support a particular finding of fact, the evidence upon which that fact might have been founded must be set out; the contentions of the parties; the decision of the justices and the questions upon which the opinion of the Divisional Court is sought.

12.26 Draft case. The form of the case when drafted will follow a comparable form to that set out below by way of illustration:

IN THE HIGH COURT OF JUSTICE
QUEENS BENCH DIVISION
B E T W E E N :

ABC STORES LIMITED   Appellant

and

WESTINGHAM CITY COUNCIL   Respondent

Case stated by Justices for the City of Westingham in respect of their adjudication as a
Magistrates' Court sitting at Victoria Law Courts, High Street, Westingham.

CASE

1. On the 5th April 1997, an information was preferred by the Respondent against
    the Appellant that the Appellant between 28th February 1995 and 30th March
    1997 at its in-store bakery without reasonable excuse did fail to make a suitable
    and sufficient assessment of risks to the health and safety of its employees,
    contrary to regulation 3(1) of the Management of Health and Safety at Work
    Regulations 1992 and section 33(1)(c) of the Health and Safety at Work Act
    1984.

2. We heard the said information on the 17th May 1997 and found as follows:
    ......
    [where there is an allegation that there was no evidence upon which a certain
    conclusion could have been based, the relevant evidence should be briefly
    summarised. Except in this circumstance, evidence should not be set out, but facts
    found referred to] thus
    The following is a short statement of the evidence as to
    ......

3. It was contended by the appellant that:

4. It was contended by the Respondent that

5. We were referred to the following authorities . . .

6. the Court found . . .

    And accordingly, the company's defence failed and we found the company guilty
    and fined it £2,000 with £2,500 contribution to prosecution costs: 14 days to pay.

QUESTIONS

7. The questions for the opinion of the High Court are:

(i) Was the decision that . . . . . . a decision to which a reasonable bench of
     magistrates could properly come?

(ii) Was there evidence upon which the said decision could properly be founded?

    Signed

12.27 Where the magistrates refuse to state a case. The only ground upon which the magistrates may lawfully refuse to state a case is where they find that the application is frivolous, although if a request is made by the Attorney General, under no circumstances may it be refused (Magistrates' Courts Act 1980, section 111(5)). If the applicant requires it, the magistrates are required to furnish to the applicant a certificate stating that the application has been refused; and, in fact this is usually done where there is a refusal, notwithstanding that no request has been made. The test for what is frivolous is whether the application is "futile, misconceived, hopeless or academic" – conclusions to which the justices would not often or lightly come (*Regina v. Mildenhall Magistrates' Court, ex p. Forest Heath District Council, The Times* May 16, 1997).

The applicant may challenge a refusal to state a case by seeking an order for mandamus. Mandamus lies to compel magistrates to perform their duties (Supreme Court Act 1981, s.29(4)). An example of an instance where the court was critical of the defendant for seeking mandamus to compel the statement of a case, rather than at once challenging the final adjudication, arose in *R. v. Southwark Crown Court, ex p. Brooke* [1997] C.O.D. 81, where the applicant complained that no reasons had been given for a Crown Court decision and had asked for a case to be stated. When the Crown Court refused, he sought an order of mandamus. The court indicated that it would have been more appropriate for him to have sought judicial review of the adjudication, rather than set two separate procedures in motion.

Where the magistrates do state a case, but do so inadequately, section 28A of the Magistrates' Courts Act 1980 (introduced by the Statute Law (Repeals) Act 1993) permits the case to be sent back for amendment. This obviates the need to apply for mandamus where the complaint is about the content of the case: instead, application is made on notice to the other parties, supported by affidavit.

12.28 Lodging the case. After the case has been received, it is for the applicant to lodge it within 10 days with the High Court. Notice of entry of appearance is then sent to the Respondent within four days.

12.29 Parties to an appeal by way of case stated. It is usual for the parties to an appeal by way of case stated to be the defendant and the prosecutor. The justices themselves are rarely joined: only if there is an allegation of impropriety might it be appropriate. When accused of misconduct, they may be heard through counsel in the appeal, but, where the magistrates merely perceive the need to explain an event in the conduct of the case below, they may submit an affidavit for the consideration of the High Court (Review of Justices' Decisions Act 1872, s.2). The affidavit should be made by one or more of the magistrates (*R. v. Sperling* (1873) 37 J.P.Jo. 87). It is only in the most exceptional circumstances that cross-examination on the affidavit might be permitted (*R. v. Kent Justices, ex P. Smith* [1928] W.N. 137; *R. v. Stokesley (Yorks.) Justices, ex p. Bartram* [1956] 1 W.L.R. 254). The Divisional Court must take the affidavit into consideration before reaching a conclusion other than affirming the justices decision (Review of Justices' Decisions Act 1872, s.3).

Where the appeal concerns an issue of sentencing, or some other reason makes it appropriate (for example, where the case concerns the exercise of executive functions or is of particular political sensitivity or of legal difficulty) the Divisional Court may appoint an *amicus curiae*.

Where justices take part in the appeal, they may be made liable in costs (*R. v. Llanidloes Licensing Justices, ex p. Davies* [1957] 1 W.L.R. 809n.; *R. v. Newcastle under Lyme Justices, ex p. Massey* [1994] 1 W.L.R. 1684).

12.30   Appeal from the Divisional Court to the House of Lords. As with an appeal from the Divisional Court hearing an application for judicial review, appeal lies to the House of Lords only if the Divisional Court certifies that there is a point of law of general public importance and if leave to appeal is given either by the Divisional Court or by the House of Lords (see paragraph 12.42 below).

"Appeal" from the magistrates to the divisional court by way of judicial review

12.31   Appellants. Either the prosecutor or the defendant may apply for judicial review of an action or decision of the magistrates which is unlawful or irregular. Judicial review is a discretionary remedy: the mere fact that an error or irregularity can be established will not, as of right, entitle the applicant to relief.

12.32   What jurisdiction? Judicial Review or case stated? Judicial review may not always be sought as an alternative to an appeal by way of case stated, even though an appeal by way of case stated may in fact rely upon the same complaint of "irrationality, illegality and procedural impropriety" which is the bedrock of an application for judicial review, (*per* Lord Diplock in *Council of Civil Service Unions v. Minister for the Civil Service* [1985] A.C. 374). In general, appeal by way of case stated is the preferred route for persons aggrieved by a final decision of the magistrates to take to the Divisional Court for the following two reasons:

  (i) judicial review is intended to be a remedy of last resort, after all other avenues of appeal have been exhausted. That is not to say that the defendant must have exercised every other avenue of appeal, but as a general rule, the defendant is expected to adopt an alternative appeal where it is at least an appropriate procedure. This may mean in some circumstances that where an appellant alleges a procedural unfairness in the magistrates' court which can be cured by a rehearing in the Crown Court, he will be expected to adopt the course of appealing to the Crown Court in preference (*R. v Peterborough Magistrates' Court, ex p. Dowler* [1996] 2 Cr. App. R. 561). This will almost always be the expectation if complaint is made as to sentence. The Crown Court would have the time and material upon which the correct sentence could be assessed (*R. v. Ealing Justices, ex p. Scrafield* [1994] R.T.R. 195). This principle is not to be applied with great strictness, however. In *R. v. Hereford Magistrates' Court, ex p. Rowlands, The Times,* February 17, 1997, the Divisional Court was anxious to stress that the right to appeal to the Crown Court, particularly if unexercised, should not ordinarily weigh against the leave to move for or the grant of judicial review.

  (ii) the procedures of an appeal by way of case stated enable the Divisional Court to know what the magistrates have found as facts (*R. v. Crown Court at Ipswich, ex p. Baldwin* [1981] 1 All E.R. 596).

On the other hand, judicial review may offer a wider range of remedies than those offered on an appeal by way of case stated (see paragraph 12.38 below). Also, as with *R. v. Southwark Crown Court, ex p. Brooke* [1997] C.O.D. 81, taking proceedings by way of judicial review may obviate the need for more than one application.

12.33 Natural justice. Judicial review of decisions of the magistrates' courts are concerned with a denial of natural justice. Where the court has simply reached the wrong decision as a matter of law, an appeal by way of case stated is an adequate procedure to ventilate the issue in the High Court. Judicial review proceedings are appropriate where it is the manner of reaching the decision which is the subject of scrutiny, not the decision itself (*Chief Constable of the North Wales Police v. Evans* [1982] 1 W.L.R. 115). Examples of flawed procedures in the magistrates' court are:

(i) where the magistrate has appeared to be biased (*R. v. Altrincham Justices, ex p. Pennington* [1975] Q.B. 549) or not paying attention (*R. v. South Worcestershire Justices, ex p. Daniels* (1996) 161 J.P. 121);

(ii) where the defendant has not been given a proper opportunity to prepare his case (*R. v. Thames Magistrates' Court, ex p. Polemis* [1974] 1 W.L.R. 1371);

(iii) where material information in the possession of the prosecutor has not been disclosed to the defendant (*R. v. Leyland Magistrates, ex p. Hawthorn* [1979] Q.B. 283; *R. v. Halton Justices, ex p. Hughes* (1991) 155 J.P. 837);

(iv) where the clerk appears to have participated in the decision-making process (*R. v. Barry (Glamorgan) Justices, ex p. Kashim* [1953] 1 W.L.R. 1320, *R. v. Eccles Justices, ex p. Farrelly, The Times,* June 17, 1992).

12.34 Errors of the prosecution. The jurisdiction may arise where there has been an error on the part of the court itself, but also where there has been an error on the part of the prosecutor which is analogous to fraud or is fraudulent (*R. v. Burton on Trent Justices, ex p. Woolley* [1996] Crim.L.R. 340). This can be classified as "procedural unfairness" (see *R. v. Leyland Justices, ex p. Hawthorn* [1979] Q.B. 283) or *sui generis* (*R. v. Dolgellau Justices, ex p. Cartledge* [1996] Crim.L.R. 336). There does not need to be actual fraud or dishonesty on the part of the prosecutor, but a "*suppressio veri*" which can be a "*suggestio falsi*" – such as the suppression of details of witness statements or other evidence which might assist the defence – may occasion a judicial review (*R. v. Liverpool Justices, ex p. Roberts* [1986] Crim.L.R. 622, *R. v. Bolton Justices, ex p. Scally* [1991] 1 Q.B. 537, *ex p. Cartledge* (above)). There can never be a judicial review on the grounds of a breach of natural justice where the reason for the unfairness was due to the conduct of the defendant or his legal representative (*R. v. Home Secretaary, ex p. Mehdawi* [1990] 1 A.C. 876 H.L., *ex p. Cartledge* (above)).

12.35 Relevance of the plea. The jurisdiction lies following a conviction after a plea of not guilty and, sometimes, at an interlocutory stage against an interlocutory decision, if the means of reaching the decision was flawed. Judicial review can also be permitted in some limited cases even where there has been a guilty plea if the prosecutor has behaved in such a way that the defendant has been deprived of a fair opportunity to decide the nature of his plea (*R. v. Bolton Justices, ex p. Scally* [1991] Q.B. 537; *ex p. Cartledge* (above)).

12.36 Interlocutory applications. There is no power in the justices to state a case until they have reached a final determination on the matter in full (*Streames v. Copping* (1985) Q.B. 920). This means that if an objection is to be raised in the

Divisional Court before the determination of a summons, it must be by way of an application for judicial review. That is not to say that the Divisional Court encourages applications before the case is concluded, but there are circumstances which arise to make this desirable. An instance was in *R. v. Greater Manchester Justices, ex p. Aldi GmbH & Co. KG* (1995) 159 J.P. 717, where the court had granted an adjournment to enable another party to be brought before it. The other party challenged the decision of the magistrates. Lord Justice Butler-Sloss said:

". . . the underlying purpose of *Streames v. Copping* is one with which I would respectfully agree, which is one cannot have justices stating cases on interlocutory points from time to time when what ought to happen in that sort of case is a determination of the summonses and the whole matter to be dealt with by the Divisional Court. But in this particular case, rather unusually, the issues have arisen because of the adjournment. It is right and proper that the court should deal with it at this stage . . . the undesirability of the use of . . . judicial review in interlocutory matters [is] because . . . we do not want to use the valuable weapon of moving for judicial review on various points that might come up for hearing before the magistrates. But in this case it appears to be the only avenue by which this court can deal with the question as to whether the magistrates were wrong to amend the summons".

12.37 Appeals against sentence. As with appeals by way of case stated, applications for judicial review of the sentencing decision will rarely arise. In most cases, the matter should be dealt with by way of appeal to the Crown Court for a re-hearing (see *R. v Peterborough Magistrates' Court, ex p. Dowler* [1996] 2 Cr. App. R. 561). As sentencing is a discretionary matter, the Divisional Court will not review the decision unless there has been an error of law or jurisdiction. If the sentence imposed is within the band of available sentences, the Divisional Court will not interfere unless the sentence is so severe that it was by any acceptable standard "truly astonishing" (*R. v. Crown Court at Acton, ex p. Bewley* (1988) 152 J.P. 327) or, put another way, so very much outside the range of sentences normally passed as to be wrong in law (*R. v. Crown Court at St. Albans, ex p. Cinnamond* [1981] Q.B. 480).

12.38 Remedies if judicial review is granted. Since the amendment of Order 53 in 1977, the precise remedy which is sought in the circumstances of any case has become less significant than it was historically, where applying for the wrong remedy could be fatal to the success of otherwise meritorious proceedings. Nevertheless, each remedy has a distinct and sometimes complementary function.

(i) *Certiorari: certiorari* lies to quash a decision of the magistrates' court where there has been an error of law on the face of the record or where there has been some procedural error. If the decision is quashed, section 31(5) of the Supreme Court Act 1981 provides that the matter may be remitted to the magistrates' court with a direction for reconsideration in accordance with the findings of the High Court. If the case concerns a sentence which could not properly have been imposed by the magistrates, the court may, instead of quashing the decision and remitting the matter, substitute any sentence which the court below would have had power to impose (Supreme Court Act 1981, s.43).

(ii) *Mandamus:* if the Divisional Court makes an order of mandamus, it is to compel the person named in the order (usually, the justices) to carry out an act in accordance with their duties. Mandamus is also the appropriate order to compel reluctant magistrates to state a case (Magistrates' Courts Act 1980, s.111(6) and see paragraph 12.27 above). Mandamus cannot be used, however, to control the exercise of a discretion by the magistrates nor to govern the way in which proceedings are to be conducted below (*R. v. Wells Street Stipendiary Magistrate, ex p. Seillon* [1978] 3 All E.R. 257; *R. v. Rochford Justices, ex p. Buck* [1978] Crim.L.R. 492).

(iii) *Prohibition:* this order prevents the continuation of the proceedings in an unlawful manner, so it may be used, for example to prevent a biased tribunal from sitting, or to prevent a departure from its declared adjudication, or where to allow the proceedings to continue would be an abuse of the process of the court.

12.39 Other remedies. The other administrative remedies, such as injunction or declaration have little impact on the work and decisions of the magistrates' court and are rarely applied for. These remedies provide greater scope where the Divisional Court is considering executive, rather than judicial, conduct. Where damages are sought, the court may award damages if it is satisfied that, had the action been begum by writ, the applicant would have been awarded damages (Supreme Court Act 1981, s.31(4)). The court, moreover, has power to allow the damages claim to proceed as if begun by writ in all cases where the award of damages appears to be the principal objective. See *R. v. Blandford J.J.s, ex p. Pamment* [1990] 1 W.L.R. 1490.

12.40 Procedure.

(i) *Application for leave to move:* the first stage of judicial review proceedings is by way of an application to the Divisional Court of the Queens Bench Division of the High Court for leave to move for judicial review using Form 86A and a supporting affidavit. This application must be made as soon as possible and, in any event, within three months from the decision complained of unless the court considers that there is good reason for extending the period (Rules of the Supreme Court, O. 53, r.4). Where the remedy sought is certiorari in respect of a conviction or other decision, the date of the decision is the date when grounds for applying first arose (r.2(2)). The leave application will normally be dealt with by a single judge of the Crown Office. A copy of his order is sent to the applicant. Whether leave is granted or refused, it is common for the judge to comment briefly on the application and any matters which he believes need to be further considered. If leave is not granted on the written application, it may either be refused, or the matter may be listed for an *ex parte* oral hearing (usually 20 minutes). At the oral hearing, the prospective Respondent may attend but will not be heard. If leave is refused, the applicant may renew his application orally before the Divisional Court (this procedure is a distinction from civil cases, where there is no right to renew an application before the full court). The substantive application for judicial review may not be made on any ground without leave in respect of that ground (*R. v. Advertising Standards Authority, ex p. City Trading Ltd* [1997] C.O.D. 202).

Where there is an application for certiorari or prohibition, the High Court in granting leave may also direct a stay in the magistrates' court (RSC, O.53, r.3(10)(a)).

(ii) *Discharge of leave:* where leave has been granted following an *ex parte* hearing or by a decision on the papers, the respondent is permitted to apply for a discharge of the leave. This should only be in an obvious case, and use of this procedure is generally discouraged.

(iii) *The substantive application:* the applicant must serve within 14 days of the grant of leave the originating motion, together with a copy of the statement lodged with the leave application on "all persons affected". This will usually include the clerk to the magistrates and must include him where the applicant seeks relief against the court or an officer of the court (RSC, O.53, r.5(3)).

The Respondent should file its evidence as soon as practicable, and, unless the court otherwise directs, within 56 days of the service of the documents on him (R.S.C. O.53 r.6).

Additionally, there is power to make application for interlocutory orders including discovery, interrogatories, etc.

(iv) *The hearing:* the hearing is oral, before the Divisional Court. Any person who appears to be a proper opponent to the application may be heard, even if he has not hitherto been served with notice of the proceedings (RSC, O.53, r.9).

12.41   The justices.   The justices do not appear on an application for judicial review unless their bona fides or other matter as to their character or credit is in issue, or unless the Master of the Crown Office has conveyed a request from the Divisional Court to the Magistrates' Clerk that they appear and be represented. They may file an affidavit if they wish to make any observations in relation to the matters alleged, even where it may be inappropriate to appear (see the Review of Justices' Decisions Act 1872 and paragraph 12.29 above).

12.42   Appeal to the House of Lords.   Appeal lies from a decision of the Divisional Court on a substantive application for judicial review to the House of Lords, but only

(i) with leave granted either by the Divisional Court or the House of Lords, and

(ii) if the Divisional Court has certified in accordance with section 1 of the Administration of Justice Act 1960 that the point involves a question of law of general public importance.

There is no appeal from a decision of the Divisional Court on a renewed application which refuses leave to move for judicial review.

Civil cases in the Magistrates' Court

12.43   General.   Where proceedings are begun by complaint in the magistrates' court, for example, where there is an appeal against an executive notice, the proceedings are likely to have a civil character even if the statutory provision does not expressly say so, notwithstanding that they may be ancillary to a regime which is enforced under the criminal law. The avenues of challenge to the decisions and orders of the magistrates sitting in this capacity are primarily determined by the statute which confers to the right to proceed before the magistrates. So, for example, section 38 of the Food Safety Act 1990 confers a right of appeal on a person dissatisfied by the magistrates' decision to uphold an improvement notice (and certain other matters justiciable in the court) to the Crown Court. This right would not exist in the absence of express provision, and the avenues of appeal would be limited to those to the Divisional Court of the High Court. As with a challenge to a decision in criminal proceedings, the disgruntled litigant may request the justices to state a case under the powers conferred in section 111 of the Magistrates' Courts Act 1980, or may apply for judicial review of the processes at work before the justices.

12.44   Application to state a case.   It seems that in civil proceedings, unlike criminal proceedings, the magistrates may have a discretion to state a case before a final determination of the proceedings before them, but it is a power which should be exercised sparingly *(R. v. Chesterfield Justices, ex p. Kovacs and Fawbert* [1990] C.O.D. 367). The procedure for stating a case is identical to that pertaining to a criminal case, save that the hearing in the Divisional Court may be conducted by a single Judge of that court.

12.45   Judicial review.   As with a criminal case, a person dissatisfied with the procedures adopted in the magistrates' court may seek leave to appply for judicial review. In a civil case, if leave is refused after an oral hearing, there is no further right to renew that application before the full court (RSC, Ord. 53, r.3).

12.46   Appeals from the Crown Court as an Appellate Court.   If there is a right of appeal to the Crown court, there exist corresponding routes by way of case stated and judicial review to the Divisional Court to those applying in the magistrates' court.

APPEALS AFTER A TRIAL BY JURY

Appeals from the Crown court (following trial on indictment) to the Court of Appeal

12.47   Jurisdiction.   In the absence of express statutory provision, the Court of Appeal (Criminal Division) has no power to hear interlocutory appeals in relation to trial on indictment. Therefore, any appeal by a defendant on an interlocutory matter where there is a trial on indictment must await conviction. Appeal is not as of right. An appeal against conviction only lies with the leave of the Court of Appeal or if the judge of the court of conviction certifies that the case is fit for trial (Criminal Appeal Act 1968, s.1). The judge at the trial should not grant a certificate unless he considers that the chance of successful appeal is substantial (Practice Direction (Crown Court: bail pending appeal) [1983] 1 W.L.R. 1292). Conviction includes a plea of guilty *(D.P.P. v. Shannon* [1975] A.C. 717) although the occasions when appeal against conviction is allowed following a plea of guilty are usually limited to those where the defendant has not intended to admit the nature of the charge or where his will has been subverted. An appeal against sentence lies only with the leave of the Court of Appeal.

12.48   Appeal against conviction. The sole consideration upon which the Court of Appeal may now act is whether the conviction is "unsafe", following amendment of section 2 of the Criminal Appeal Act 1968 by the Criminal Appeal Act 1995. If the conviction is not unsafe, the Court of Appeal must dismiss the appeal. If the conviction is unsafe, the Court of Appeal must allow it. It seems that this consideration may include a number of elements, drawn from the cases decided prior to the amendment of the 1968 Act. Issues which give rise to an appeal include:

  (i)   a misdirection to the jury in the summing up, such as a misdirection on the law, a misdirection as to the proper approach that the jury should adopt, a failure to refer to the defence case, etc.;

  (ii) fresh evidence;

  (iii) inconsistent verdicts;

  (iv) wrongful admission or exclusion of evidence;

  (v)   defects in the indictment

  (vi) matters arising during the conduct of the trial, such as inappropriate judicial interventions, inappropriate press reporting, etc.

When these factors are considered together, the court may be able either to form a reasoned view that there has been a miscarriage of justice or may have an impression that there may not have been a fair trial – referred to as the "lurking doubt" test. This test can be applied where the Court of Appeal, having weighed up the issues, is left with a "lurking doubt" that there might have been a miscarriage of justice. It is a "reaction which may not be based strictly on the evidence as such: it is a reaction which can be produced by the general feel of the case as the court experiences it" (*per* Widgery L.J. in *R. v. Cooper* [1969 1 Q.B. 267 at 271). It is clear, however, that the Court of Appeal will not have regard to inadmissible evidence in order to give rise to the doubt – the doubt must be left after the admissible evidence has been considered (*R. v Wallace and Short* (1978) 67 Cr.App.R. 291).

12.49   Appeal against sentence.   Appeal against sentence will be allowed only where the court below has erred in some way. The court will not merely substitute its own view for that of the trial judge. Thus the Court of Appeal may adjust the sentence where:

  (i)   the sentencing judge has gone wrong in law;

  (ii) the sentencing judge has relied upon inaccurate facts;

  (iii) the sentencing judge has failed to take a matter into account or has taken an improper matter into account;

  (iv) the sentence is wrong in principle or manifestly excessive.

12.50   Procedure. The procedure is governed by the provisions of the Criminal Appeal Act 1968 and the Criminal Appeal Rules 1968. Appeals against conviction or sentence must be initiated within 28 days of the conviction or sentence appealed against, unless an extension of time has been permitted. Unless leave has been given by the trial judge, the application will be made initially in writing or, sometimes, orally before a single judge of the Court of Appeal for leave to appeal. This decision will be taken on the basis of draft grounds of appeal, which, if leave is granted, may subsequently be perfected. If leave is refused an application may be renewed to the full Court. In some instances, the question of leave to appeal and the appeal itself are heard together. Leave is only given if the appeal succeeds.

Appeals from the Crown court (as the court of first trial) to the Divisional court

12.51   Divisional court by way of Judicial Review.   The jurisdiction of the Divisional Court to hear applications from parties dissatisfied with a decision of the Crown Court is yet more limited than in applications for judicial review of decisions made in the magistrates' court. Section 29(3) of the Supreme Court Act 1981 provides that

> "In relation to the jurisdiction of the Crown Court, other than in its jurisdiction in matters relating to trial on indictment, the High Court shall have jurisdiction to make such orders of mandamus, prohibition and certiorari as the High Court possesses in relation to the jurisdiction of an inferior court".

Accordingly, although there is a power to hear applications from the Crown court, it is excluded for matters relating to trial on indictment. In fact, this means, in most instances, although some examples of orders made before or after a trial can be found which fall the other side of the line and are therefore capable of review. The expression "matters relating to trials on indictment" has been the subject of consideration in a number of cases: for example, *R. v. Crown Court at Chelmsford, ex p. Chief Constable of Essex* [1994] 1 W.L.R. 359; *R. v. Manchester Crown Court, ex p. D.P.P.* [1993] 1 W.L.R. 1524; *Re Ashton* [1994] 1 A.C. 9.

CHAPTER 13

Costs

CRIMINAL CASES IN THE MAGISTRATES' COURT

13.1 General principles. The usual practice in the Magistrates' Court is that the successful party will apply for an order for provision to be made for his costs. The statutory provision for the award of costs is made in the Prosecution of Offences Act 1985, as amended, together with the Costs in Criminal Cases (General) Regulations 1986 and the Costs in Criminal Cases (General) (Amendment) Regulations 1991. There is no inherent jurisdiction in the magistrates' court by which these powers can be extended. Additionally, the Lord Chief Justice has handed down a Practice Direction which gives advice as to how the Amended Regulations should be applied (Practice Direction (Costs in Criminal Proceedings) (1991) 93 Cr. App. R. 89. No consideration is given in this Chapter to the position of a legally-aided defendant, to whom different considerations may apply.

Prosecution success

13.2 *Inter partes* costs order. Where the prosecution succeeds, the prosecutor may request an order for his costs against the unsuccessful defendant. The Court has power to order the defendant to pay such prosecution costs as it considers "just and reasonable". The amount of the costs has to be specified in the order (Prosecution of Offences Act 1985, Section 18). If, following the conviction, however, the court has ordered a financial penalty (fine, compensation, forfeiture, etc.) and the sum ordered to be paid is less than £5, the court shall not order the payment of any costs under the section unless in the particular circumstances, it considers it right to do so (section 18(4)). Before an order for costs can be made, the Court must consider whether the defendant has the means and ability to pay the costs. As a rule, the assessment as to the offender's means to pay is comparable to the assessment which is carried out in relation to a fine. As with a fine, the Court may order that the costs be paid on an instalment basis (see the Magistrates' Courts Act 1980, s.75) and it is a general rule that the instalment should not take more than a year to discharge. This is, however, not an invariable practice and in some cases it is appropriate for payment to be discharged over a longer period provided that it is not an undue burden (*R. v. Olliver and Olliver* (1989) 11 Cr. App. R. (S.) 10 where payment of the total of fines, compensation orders and costs would take two and a half years).

13.3 Proportionality. If the order for costs followed a plea of guilty, the Court may take that into account in assessing the amount of costs (*R. v. Matthews* (1979) 1 Cr. App. R. (S.) 346; *R. v. Maher* [1983] Q.B. 784). The relevance of the plea of guilty is that the Court must consider the proportionality of the costs order and the facts, and the weight given to any plea of guilty will depend on the nature of the case and the stage at which the plea is offered. In *Maher* (above), the court emphasised that it was not to be regarded as only in an exceptional case that costs would be awarded against someone who had pleaded guilty. If an arithmetical calculation of the amount of costs incurred by the prosecution produces an amount which is out of proportion to the gravity of the offence, the Court should not make an order for the arithmetical basis (*R. v. Tottenham Justices, ex p. Joshi* [1982] 1 W.L.R. 631). This same principle is applied in a different way where the court imposes a small fine. Although the authorities are not entirely consistent (see, for example, *R. v. Bushell* (1980) 2 Cr. App. R. (S.) 77; *R. v. Boyle* (1995) 16 Cr. App. R. (S.) 927), it is a recognised principle that the sentencing court should not impose a small fine and a substantial order for costs (*R. v. Jones* (1988) 10 Cr. App. R. (S.) 95). Moreover, the costs must not become a disguised penalty so that the costs order is an additional punishment (*R. v. Highgate Justices, ex p. Petrou* [1954] 1 W.L.R. 485). The court must also have regard to the totality of the financial burden (*R. v. Glenister*, unreported, November 28, 1975). It is, appropriate, however, that a costs order should be made, and, correspondingly, an increased level of compensation to the prosecution be allowed, where a defendant has unnecessarily prolonged the trial of a case in which he has no real prospect of acquittal (*R. v. Yoxall* (1972) 57 Cr. App. R. 263; *R. v. Malkiat Singh* (1982) 4 Cr. App. R. (S.) 38).

13.4 Local authority prosecution. Where the prosecution is by a local authority or other body charged with the duty of prosecuting offences, the relevant body is entitled to claim costs in respect of time spent for the purposes of preparing the prosecution, notwithstanding that the persons carrying out the investigation were employees of the enforcement body carrying out their employment (*Neville v. Gardner Merchant Ltd* (1984) 148 J.P. 23). In the above case Kerr L.J. made it clear that the fact that the person in question is salaried and only doing his job, is of no significance to the question of costs, and he further indicated that if the facts revealed that the whole of the costs of the investigation were the result of a specific complaint and not a routine inspection, it would be right to award the whole sum. This suggests that it might be inappropriate to award the whole sum if some of the costs were incurred in routine activities, such as the official time spent in carrying out a routine visit or routine testing which unearths a contravention.

13.5 Calculation of costs. The same principles as to the amount of the sentence apply where a local authority is the prosecutor as apply where the CPS have commenced proceedings, so that in either instance the prosecutor may expect his estimate of costs to be reduced where there is a plea of guilty, the offence is not serious or the offender has insufficient means to pay. Also, the award may be reduced where the court takes the view that costs have been improperly incurred. It is nevertheless possible for prosecutors to create a schedule of calculation of estimated prosecution costs for presentation at the end of the trial, or earlier (see below). In the case of a regulatory offence this is likely to include the following items:

Staff costs
Number of personnel at x hours at £y [rate of pay] per hour

Disbursements
e.g. photographs
company or other searches
experts fees
sample fee

Institution of proceedings,
e.g. obtaining committee authority, providing advance disclosure, drafting
summonses
Solicitor (and Counsel where applicable) attending at court

Solicitors costs of preparation
Brief fee
Witness expenses

13.6 Details of costs before the hearing. The *Gardner Merchant* decision has recently been upheld in *R. v. Associated Octel Co. Ltd (Costs), The Times,* November 15, 1996 in which the Divisional Court observed that the appropriate procedure was that the prosecution should serve upon the defendant full details of the costs at the earliest possible opportunity so as to enable the defence to consider the costs and make representations as to quantum. Moreover the defendant should make clear to the prosecution the objections that he wishes to raise, or at least make it plain to the court exactly what the nature of the objections would be. In a number of other cases the court has stressed the responsibility of representatives to have available at court material upon which the court can make a decision as to costs whether that be the prosecution's estimate or the defendant's means to pay (*R. v. West London Magistrates' Court, ex p. Kyprianou; R. v. Wright* unreported, November 12, 1996; *R. v. Maher* (above)).

13.7 Private prosecutions. If the prosecution is not a public authority (that is, not the CPS, or a police force, a local authority, a government department or body receiving money provided by parliament or a nationalised industry) then the prosecutor may be able to claim costs from central funds in respect of indictable offences, but not in respect of offences which are summary only. In this case the procedure is either (a) for an amount to be agreed by the prosecutor and the Court and specified in the order or (b) for an amount to be taxed by the Clerk to the Justices unless the Court considers that it is inappropriate for the prosecutor to recover the full costs. If it is inappropriate for the full costs to be recovered, the Court may assess a just and reasonable amount unspecified in the order. These rules are set out in section 17 of the Prosecution of Offences Act 1985. The Practice Direction (above) indicates that an order for the payment of a private prosecutor's costs from central funds should be made unless there is good reason for not doing so, for instance where proceedings have been instituted or continued without good cause.

There is no power to order an award of prosecution costs from central funds in respect of an offence triable only summarily unless the order is made in the Divisional Court or the House of Lords (section 17(1)(b) of the 1985 Act).

13.8 Collection of costs. Costs are enforceable in the magistrates' court in the same fashion as a fine.

13.9 Appeal against costs orders. There is no right of appeal from the magistrates' court to the Crown Court under section 108(3)(b), although an appeal may be made to the Divisional Court if the magistrates have made an error of law, including acting upon an improper principle, having taking into account something which should not have been taken into account, or failing to take into account something that should have been taken into account (*R. v. Tottenham Justices, ex p. Joshi* [1982] 1 W.L.R. 631).

Defendant successful

13.10 Defence costs. An order for costs out of central funds in favour of the accused is called "a defendant's costs order". This may be made where on a summary trial information is dismissed or where information is not proceeded with or examining justices do not commit for trial (Prosecution of Offences Act 1985, section 16(1)). Failure to proceed with information includes the situation where the prosecution cannot proceed because their summonses were laid out of time (*Patel v. Blakey* (1987) 151 J.P. 532) or where the prosecution is withdrawn (*R. v. Bolton Justices, ex p. Wildish* (1983) 147 J.P. 309) or if it is discontinued (*DPP v. Denning and Pearce* [1991] 2 Q.B. 532). In the *Wildish* (above) case, the court held that an application for costs could be made either on the date that the information was withdrawn or on a subsequent date.

13.11 Defendant's costs order normally made. The Practice Direction makes clear that a defendant's costs order should normally be made unless there are positive reasons for not doing so. Examples of such reasons are that:

(i) the defendant's own conduct has brought suspicion on himself and misled the prosecution into thinking that the case against him is stronger than it is;

(ii) there is ample evidence to support a conviction that the defendant is acquitted on a technicality which has no merit;

(iii) the defendant is convicted on some charges but acquitted on others.

The Court may order that only part of the costs incurred by the defendant be paid and, as with an order for prosecution costs from central funds, may direct that the authority responsible for taxation (in the magistrates' court that is the justices' clerk) investigate any particular item or items of expenditure as part of the process of taxation of the costs.

13.12 Defendant's own conduct. The exceptions to the general rule that a defendant's costs order should be made if the proceedings end otherwise than in conviction, have been considered in *Melville v. The Crown Court at Southwark* (1995) *The Independent*, November 13, QBD, October 25, 1995, CO 3391/95). The Crown Court had (on appeal) upheld a finding that there was no case to answer on charges of using premises as a sex establishment, although the court also found that they would have been prepared to convict of permitting the premises to be used in that capacity. They declined an application for a defendant's costs order on the basis that:

(i) on a date other than that for which he was prosecuted, the defendant was working in the premises and appeared to be in charge;

(ii) he was generally unco-operative with council investigating officers;

(iii) there was evidence on which he might have been convicted of permitting the unauthorised use of the premises.

The Divisional Court analysed these three points and concluded that the defendant's presence on another day was not evidence in relation to the offences of which he was in fact charged; that lack of co-operation could not have been evidence against the defendant and could not, therefore, have been relevant to the decision to prosecute; and that the fact that he might have been guilty of an associated offence could be put no higher than that the Council had charged him with an offence of which he was *not* guilty and failed to charge him with offences of which he *was* guilty. Moreover, as he had not been charged with the alternative offence, the defendant had not been given an opportunity to refute it, so that it was inappropriate to deny him a costs order on that ground. The defendant was granted a defendant's costs order in respect of the magistrate's court, Crown court and Divisional Court hearings. On the other hand, in *Mulvenna v. Aldi Stores GmbH* (1995) 159 J.P. 717, the Divisional Court, while finding that a summons could not be amended to name a different company, declined to award costs to the successful defendant, on the basis that the company had contributed to the prosecution confusion by using the wrong stationery and not identifying themselves correctly. Similarly, in *R. v. Spens, The Independent* March 18, 1992, Henry J. refused a defendant's costs order where a defendant had acknowledged in interview that there were two schools of thought as to the propriety of practices which had formed the basis of the prosecution, even though the indictment was subsequently ordered to lie on the file. McCullough J. refused a defendant's costs order when John Fashanu was acquitted of conspiracy, the refusal being based on the fact that he "declined to utter a word to defend himself against a conspiracy charge throughout a two-year investigation and two trials", *The Times* August 9, 1997, "Players must pay huge bill for their costs". Another example arose in *Berkshire County Council v. Olympic Holidays Ltd* [1994] 158 J.P. 421, where the respondents had failed to honour the custom in the trade of offering the lower price when a question of misleading price indications arose. Although the respondents were successful in the Divisional Court, the court refused to allow the respondents their costs before the justices because they had attracted the prosecution by their behaviour.

13.13 Technicality. It is not a technicality that the accused is found not guilty on an excess alcohol charge because the police have failed to follow a statutory procedure (*Wareing v. DPP* (1990) 154 J.P. 443).

13.14 Divisional Court. in the *Melville* case (above) the Divisional Court substituted the orders for costs because it was clear that a defendant's costs order should have been made. On the other hand, if the Court, in the exercise of its discretion, does not pay proper regard to the Practice Direction (currently Practice Direction (Crime: Costs) [1991] 1 W.L.R. 498) on costs, the Divisional Court has power to remit a decision back to the Court with a direction to reconsider an award of costs in the light of the guidelines (*R. v. Horseferry Road Justices, ex p. Underwoods (Cash Chemists) Limited* (1985) 81 Cr. App. R. 334).

13.15 Quantum of defendant's costs order. Section 16(6) of the 1973 Act provides that the order shall be such a sum as the court considers reasonably sufficient to compensate the defendant for the costs incurred by him. That may include costs paid by a third party provided that the defendant also remains liable for those costs (*R. v. Miller & Glennie* [1983] 1 W.L.R. 1056). This can be of particular significance where an employee is prosecuted and the employer meets the solicitor's bill for the defence. Only if it could be shown that there was an express or implied agreement binding on the solicitors that the employee would not have to pay the costs in any circumstances, could the presumption of personal liability which arises when the defendant is the client of the solicitor be rebutted. As for those matters which are regarded as reasonably incurred, these are determined by the Costs in Criminal Cases (General) Regulations 1986. The appropriate question to determine whether any item falls within regulation 7 is whether the defendant acted reasonably in incurring the costs, not whether he could have taken another step which would have avoided them. So, in *R. v. Dudley Magistrates' Court, ex p. Power City Stores Ltd* (1990) 154 J.P. 654, the question asked on taxation whether the case could have been conducted by junior counsel or solicitor was inappropriate, the correct question was whether the defendant acted reasonably in instructing leading counsel. There is no provision for the payment of interest on costs (*Westminster City Council v. Wingrove and another* [1991] 1 Q.B. 652).

Improperly incurred costs

13.16 Costs incurred by improper conduct. Under Section 19(1) of the Prosecution of Offences Act 1985 and the 1986 Regulations it is provided that if at any time during criminal proceedings the Court is satisfied that costs have been incurred by one party as a result of an unnecessary or improper act or omission by or on behalf of another party to the proceedings, the Court may, after hearing the parties, order that all or part of the costs so incurred be paid by the other party. In *Suffolk County Council v. Rexmore Wholesale Services Ltd* (1994) 14 Tr.L. 5, the defendant in a regulatory case succeeded on a defence of due diligence. The magistrates ordered that the prosecutor pay the costs of the defendant on the basis that an obvious and serious question was raised in the defence. The Divisional Court held that this approach was not appropriate. Instances where an *inter partes* costs order might be obtained are if the prosecution has been brought by a body in contravention of its own prosecution policy.

13.17 Wasted costs order. Additionally the Court has power to make a wasted costs order if it considers that a legal or other representative of either party has incurred costs as a result of any improper, unreasonable or negligent act or omission which the Court considers it unreasonable to expect that party to pay, taking into account the subsequent events (Prosecution of Offences Act 1985, section 19A). "Improper" relates to conduct which amounts to any significant breach of a substantial duty imposed by a relevant code of professional conduct, including conduct regarded by the consensus of professional opinion (*Ridehalgh v. Horsefield* [1994] 3 All E.R. 848). "Unreasonable" describes vexatious conduct which is intended to harass the other side rather than aid resolution of the case. "Negligent" denotes a failure to act with the competence reasonably to be expected of ordinary members of the profession (*Ridehalgh* above). In *Re A Barrister (Wasted Costs Order) (No. 1 of 1991)* [1992] 3 W.L.R. 662, the court set out five steps:

(i) the court should formulate the complaint clearly and precisely;

(ii) where relevant, a transcript of the relevant part should be obtained;

(iii) if the matter arises at an interlocutory stage, the defendant and prosecution may need to be present;

(iv) a three stage test should be applied:

(a) had there been an improper, unreasonable or negligent act?

(b) had any costs been incurred in consequence?

(c) should the court exercise its discretion, and, if so, in what specific sum?

(v) to reach a conclusion, the court should, after formulating the complaint, hear from the representative and give a formal ruling;

(vi) the precise sum referred to should be specified. If this was not possible, then the procedure set out in the Practice Direction should be followed; see Practice Direction (Crime: Costs) [1991] 1 W.L.R. 498.

CIVIL CASES IN THE MAGISTRATES' COURT

13.18   In a civil case on a complaint the general rule is that the unsuccessful party pays to the successful party such costs as are just and reasonable (Magistrates' Courts Act 1980, s.64). Unlike the position in criminal cases, the officials of the court cannot tax the defence costs, so that in a civil case, the defendant must be fully armed at the end of the hearing with full particulars of the costs, and the justices must decide what figure is just and reasonable.

COSTS AGAINST THE JUSTICES

13.19   Costs awarded against the justices.   In some limited circumstances, it is possible following an appeal to obtain an order for costs against magistrates who act perversely or in flagrant breach of elementary principles (*R. v. York City Justices, ex p. Farmery* (1988) 153 J.P. 257). For consideration of this see paragraph 12.29 above.

CRIMINAL CASES IN THE CROWN COURT

13.20   Powers.   The powers exercised in the Crown Court to award costs are comparable to those that apply in the magistrates' court, save that the Crown Court enjoys the power of the Supreme Court to exercise its inherent jurisdiction over the conduct of solicitors, so that the court may order a solicitor to pay costs thrown away personally, without making a wasted costs order. The Practice Direction makes clear that this should be exercised only in exceptional circumstances where the statutory power does not apply and the solicitor must be given an opportunity to make representations. As with the wasted costs order procedure, this hearing will usually be in chambers.

13.21   Role of the judge.   In the Crown Court, the judge is required to be diligent in considering the incidence of costs, particularly in relation to interlocutory orders and applications. The Guide to the Award of Costs, published by the Royal Courts of Justice in 1991 comments:

"[The judge] should keep the question of costs at the forefront of his mind at every stage of the case and ought to take the initiative himself without any prompting from the parties. The judge should consider the costs when giving or refusing to give directions and when deciding applications, including applications for adjournments. He should, without using hindsight . . . condemn inefficiency or incompetency on the part of the prosecuting authority, solicitors or counsel appearing for any party and, conversely, commend good and expeditious work. To this end he should see that specific comments are recorded in the court log for the benefit of the taxing officer, but only after following the proper procedure set out in the practice direction."

Prosecution costs

13.22 *Inter partes* orders. The same considerations apply in the Crown Court to the award of costs in favour of the prosecution as apply in the magistrates' court. Although the choice of trial by jury is not reason for making an order for costs where none would otherwise be made (unless the defence was hopeless: see paragraph 13.11 above), in assessing the amount of the costs which it is just and reasonable to expect an offender to pay it may be appropriate for the Crown Court to take into account an election for trial in a trivial case. For example, in *R. v. F. & M. Dobson Ltd, The Times,* March 8, 1995, the Court of Appeal reduced fines awarded in the Crown Court against an offender but declined to reduce a costs order of more than £7,000 expressly because the defendants had brought the extent of the costs on themselves by electing trial by jury. Also see *R. v. Bushell* (1980) 2 Cr. App. R. (S.) 77 (a case of obtaining a pecuniary advantage by deception where the defendant left a restaurant without paying about £21 of the bill) where Lawton L.J., having denounced the perception that the chances of acquittal in dishonesty cases are improved in the Crown Court above the magistrates' court said:

"We wish to state as clearly as we can that in this class of case if defendants elect trial by jury they should appreciate that they are exposing themselves to a much higher rate of costs, if costs are awarded against them, than if they elect to be dealt with before magistrates. It is to be hoped that those advising defendants will point this out to them, because it is our opinion that when the kind of situation which has arisen in this case comes about, costs on the Crown Court scale should be awarded if the defendant has the means to pay . . ."

13.23 Collection of costs. Payment of costs is enforceable as though on summary conviction (Administration of Justice Act 1970, Sched. 9). See paragraph 13.8 above.

Defendant's costs

13.24 Crown court powers. The Crown court may make a defendant's costs order (*inter alia*) where a person is not tried for an offence for which he has been indicted or committed for trial, or where a person is tried on indictment and acquitted.

13.25   Indictment ordered to lie on the file.   In *R. v. Spens, The Independent* March 18, 1992, Henry J. found that he had power to make a defendant's costs order under section 16(2)(a) where the court ordered that the indictment should "lie on the file" marked "not to be proceeded with without the leave of this court or the Court of Appeal". This procedure is not inevitably a final determination of the criminal proceedings, because circumstances might arise in which leave to resurrect the indictment would be given, but it does amount to a decision for the present not to try a person for an offence for which he was indicted.

13.26   Discretion to make the order.   The considerations set out in the Practice Direction apply equally to the Crown Court as to the magistrates' court (see paragraphs 13.11 to 13.13).

13.27   Scope of the order.   Section 21 defines proceedings so as to include the proceedings in the court below. This has the consequence that where the order is silent as to the court below, those costs will be included. Where for any reason the Crown court does not wish the scope of its order to extend to the conduct of the proceedings in the magistrates' court, express exclusion should be made.

Improperly incurred costs

13.28   Wasted costs and sums disallowed.   In the Crown Court, the principles governing the exercise of these discretionary decisions is the same as in the magistrates' court.

APPEALS

13.29   On appeal, the Divisional Court, Court of Appeal and House of Lords have power to make Defendant's costs orders (section 16(4A) of the Prosecution of Offences Act 1985) and orders for the payment of prosecution costs from central funds (section 17(1) of the Act) as well as *inter partes* orders.

Index